Derivatives Regulation

Derivatives Regulation

Rules and Reasoning from Lehman to Covid

David Murphy

OXFORD
UNIVERSITY PRESS

OXFORD
UNIVERSITY PRESS

Great Clarendon Street, Oxford, OX2 6DP,
United Kingdom

Oxford University Press is a department of the University of Oxford.
It furthers the University's objective of excellence in research, scholarship,
and education by publishing worldwide. Oxford is a registered trade mark of
Oxford University Press in the UK and in certain other countries

First Edition published in 2022
Impression: 2

Published in the United States of America by Oxford University Press
198 Madison Avenue, New York, NY 10016, United States of America

British Library Cataloguing in Publication Data
Data available

Library of Congress Control Number: 2021948617

ISBN 978-0-19-284657-0

DOI: 10.1093/law/9780192846570.001.0001

Printed and bound by
CPI Group (UK) Ltd, Croydon, CR0 4YY

This book was designed by the author in Lato, a family of modern sans serif typefaces designed by Łukasz Dziedzic, and Minion Pro, a family of serifed typefaces inspired by the fonts of the late Renaissance, designed by Robert Slimbach.

Preface

Financial crises have been a feature of my working life. Two years into it, in 1997, the Asian financial crisis hit. In those days, OTC derivatives documentation came on paper, and I vividly remember the frighteningly tall stack of all the derivatives transactions with Lehman Brothers that a colleague had to review after worries started to circulate about the health of that firm. Lehman made it through 1997, but the following year saw the Russian crisis of 1998 and the failure of the hedge fund Long Term Capital Management. There was another episode of stress in 2000–2001, when a bubble in internet stocks burst. The global financial crisis of 2008 was the big one. This time, the rumours about Lehman failing turned out to be true, and the fallout from its failure was a global crisis that affected billions of people's livelihoods.

With this history, it is natural for me to be interested in why episodes of financial stress are so common. The problem is not weak regulation. Bank and market regulators have very substantial legal authority and powers of suasion. They can change the financial system on a whim, and, as we shall see, they have. Financial regulation is enormously costly both in terms of the burden of complying with it, and the requirements it places on capital, liquidity, management, and reporting. This makes financial services more expensive for everyone.

It has been my privilege to work with many financial regulators, and among their number are some of the cleverest, most public-spirited people I have ever met. They are typically unstinting in their efforts to pursue the mandate of their organizations. So incompetent regulators are not the root cause of financial instability.

Many of these good people will disagree with much of this book, and I apologize to them and anyone else who is offended by what I write. However, the financial system is too important to let the possibility of offence be a barrier to trying to understand and improve the lamentable performance of financial regulation. In short, if it worked as well as it claims to, and as well as it would have to for its costs to be justified, financial stress would not be so prevalent. Nor would we have intervene to improve market quality—but we do. In March 2020, after the onset of the Covid pandemic, aggressive authority action was required to enable systemically important markets to function. All is not well with the finance system if it cannot do its job in stress.

Derivatives are an excellent case study for opening up questions of financial regulation because so much new policy has been made regarding them since 2008. If the current rule making system is capable of doing a good job, it has had ample opportunities to do so with derivatives.

Two projects convinced me that an investigation into what was going on deserved a book-length treatment. The first was the Financial Stability Board's Derivatives Assessment Team, which Sayee Srinivasan and I co-chaired from 2017 to 2018, and which reported at the end of that year. This—spoilers—revealed that the end users of derivatives had been badly served by the post-crisis reforms. Then the UK Prudential Regulatory Authority's Proprietary Trading Review, which I wrote in 2020, demonstrated that making banks safer has come at the expense of market quality. The wonderful opportunity to join the Department of Law at LSE as a Visiting Professor in Practice gave me the time, space, and a conducive environment to support an exploration of these issues.

In such an investigation, I believe that it is important to look at incentives, mandates, and culture. Something as complex as financial regulation, and as deeply embedded in governing, does not take its character from a single person or a small cadre's wishes. It arises through a continuing dialogue within a transnational network of individuals, each situated in a particular institutional structure. In order to understand why someone advocates for a given policy, it might be helpful to ask what their employer's mandates, culture, and norms are, what the legal, social, and political context is, how their advocacy affects their professional status and relationships, and what the power relations are in the dialogue this statement is a part of. This, I suggest, is an efficacious stance for improving our understanding of regulation.

The attitude I have adopted in this book is one of hope. I think that financial regulation is a necessary endeavour and that it can be carried out legitimately, effectively, efficiently, and for the benefit of society. The fact that it currently has substantial flaws should be a spur to debate how to shape new institutional arrangements for financial regulation which would serve us all better.

Acknowledgements

I am profoundly grateful to my colleagues in LSE Law for their support in writing this book. Jo Braithwaite first suggested that what was then a 40-page working paper was in fact a badly camouflaged book proposal, and encouraged me to rip off the disguise. She and Sarah Paterson were enormously helpful in encouraging and supporting the project. The School has been a deeply nurturing environment, and my particular thanks (in alphabetical order) are due to Julia Black for her deep insights into financial regulation, Ross Cranston for his thorough and thoughtful analysis of the development of English commercial law in the nineteenth and twentieth centuries, Veerle Heyvaert for her insights into regulatory theory, David Kershaw for his hugely supportive leadership, Kai Möller for his account of the doctrine of proportionality, Niamh Moloney for bringing me into the fold and giving me the space to let the book grow, and Emmanuel Voyiakis for his discernment on questions of legitimacy and administrative law.

The perspectives in this book were informed by discussions with many other people, including Paul Bedford, Paul Brione, Christina Brinkmann, Richard Haynes, Barry King, Edwin Schooling Latter, John McPartland, Aniruddha Rajan, Vicky Saporta, Alison Scott, Robert Steigerwald, and Michael Wood. My coauthors deserve particular thanks for the collaboration, their insights and their tolerance: Jo Braithwaite, Edwin Budding, Fernando Cerezetti, Rod Garratt, Pedro Gurrola Perez, Henry Holden, Melanie Houllier, Jorge Cruz Lopez, David MacDonald, Mark Manning, Paul Nahai Williamson, Travis Nesmith, Michalis Vasios, Nick Vause, and Haoxiang Zhu have all borne this burden with good humour. Sayee Srinivasan is similarly delightful to work with, thoughtful, and a touchstone of good sense. Many thanks should go to him and the other members of the Derivatives Assessment Team, its academic experts, and its secretariat for their considerable efforts and insights, and to Anita Dhuru and Amy Jiang for their support on the Proprietary Trading Review.

A number of people generously helped me in particular areas. Harry Begg and Elsa Massoc gave me highly salient suggestions on the international political economy literature; Gary Gensler was enormously frank and open about the origins of the clearing mandate; Nigel Hall kindly shared some difficult-to-find archival material as well as his acumen on the history of the Liverpool cotton trade; and Catherine Turner helped me with a question on Derrida: my thanks are due to them all.

A particular acknowledgement must go to the late Robert Cox: his insights and kindness are very much missed. Rebecca Lewis was gracious enough to read the manuscript and give many helpful and thoughtful comments on it—but all the errors, omissions, and mis-judgements that remain are, of course, my own.

Contents

II. Regulations

III. Perspectives on Rules and Rule Making

Figures

Abbreviations

ABS	Asset-backed security
APC	Anti-procyclicality
ARM	Adjustable rate mortgage
BCBS	Basel Committee on Banking Supervision
BIS	Bank of International Settlements
CBA	Cost-benefit analysis
CCAR	Comprehensive Capital Analysis and Review
CCP	Central counterparty
CCR	Counterparty credit risk
CDO	Collateralized debt obligation
CDS	Credit default swap
CE	Current exposure
CFTC	Commodity Futures Trading Commission
CGFS	Committee on the Global Financial System
CM	Clearing member
CME	Chicago Mercantile Exchange
CPMI	Committee on Payments and Market Infrastructures
CRR	Capital Requirements Regulation
CSA	Credit Support Annex
CVA	Credit valuation adjustment
DAT	Derivatives Assessment Team
DF	Default fund
EAD	Exposure at default
ECB	European Central Bank
EE	Expected exposure
EL	Expected loss
EMIR	European Market Infrastructure Regulation
EPE	Expected positive exposure
ESMA	European Securities and Markets Authority
ETD	Exchange-traded derivative
FCM	Futures commission merchant
FDIC	Federal Deposit Insurance Corporation
FED	Federal Reserve
FICO	Fair Isaac Corporation
FMI	Financial market infrastructure
FRA	Forward rate agreement
FRTB	Fundamental review of the trading book
FSB	Financial Stability Board
FX	Foreign exchange
GBP	British pound
GSE	Government-sponsored enterprise
HKEX	Hong Kong Futures Exchange (now Hong Kong Exchanges and Clearing)
IASB	International Accounting Standards Board
ICE	Intercontinental Exchange
IFRS	International Financial Reporting Standards
IM	Initial margin
IMF	International Monetary Fund
IOSCO	International Organization of Securities Commissions
IRB	Internal ratings based method
IRS	Interest rate swap
ISDA	International Swaps and Derivatives Association

JPY	Japanese yen
KRX	Korea Exchange
LBCA	Liverpool Cotton Brokers Association
LCH	London Clearing House
LGD	Loss given default
LREM	Leverage ratio exposure measure
LSOC	Legally segregated but operationally commingled
LTV	Loan-to-value Ratio
MAGD	Macroeconomic Assessment Group for Derivatives
MBS	Mortgage-backed security
MIFID	Markets in Financial Instruments Directive
MPOR	Margin period of risk
OTC	Over-the-counter
NYMEX	New York Mercantile Exchange
NZFOE	New Zealand Futures and Options Exchange
PD	Probability of default
PFE	Potential future exposure
PFMI	Principles for Financial Market Infrastructures
PRA	Prudential Regulatory Authority
QIS	Quantitative impact study
RCAP	Regulatory consistency assessment programme
RTS	Regulatory technical standards
RWA	Risk-weighted assets
SA	Standardised approach
SEC	Securities and Exchange Commission
SEF	Swaps execution facility
SGEI	Service of general economic interest
SIMM	Standard initial margin model
SOFR	Secured Overnight Financing Rate
SONIA	Sterling Overnight Index Average
UL	Unexpected loss
USD	US dollar
VAR	Value at risk
VIX	Volatility Index
VM	Variation margin
VMGH	Variation margin gains haircutting
WTI	West Texas Intermediate

Introduction

A simple plan for writing a book about modern derivatives regulation is to begin with the financial crisis of 2008. The text would continue by showing how the causes of this crisis motivated regulatory reform, and describe the resulting rules. The market stress associated with the onset of Covid in early 2020 would then provide a good test of the performance of these policies, nicely bracketing the period that began with the failure of Lehman.

This plan does not work. The events of the crisis do not motivate many of the rules that were made. Moreover, some of the causes of the crisis remain at best partially addressed, while others have been tackled several times in different ways.

Matters become even more complex when we consider the fact that losses from interest rate, equity, FX, and commodity derivatives were minimal in the 2008 crisis. Even the most implicated asset class, credit derivatives, had at most a supporting role. The 2008 crisis was created by real estate exposures. The primary cause of losses was residential mortgage lending. Yet the immediate international regulatory response to the crisis was to transform OTC derivatives markets while leaving the regulatory treatment of residential mortgages untouched.[1]

The Puzzle of Post-Crisis Derivatives Regulation

This leaves us with a puzzle. Why did regulators enact so many rules about derivatives when they did not cause the crisis? In order to solve this puzzle, we have to understand not just what regulators did, but the forces that shaped their actions. On the way, we will learn much about post-crisis financial regulation and the quality of its rules more broadly.

The 'what regulators did' part is not trivial: describing post-crisis derivatives regulation, even in overview, is a substantial task. We will have to deal with risk-

[1] The subsequent bank regulatory response did eventually address the capital requirements for residential mortgages, but this was not until December 2017, more than ten years after the first major turmoil in the residential mortgage backed securities market. Even then, the changes did not represent a significant increase in regulators' estimates of the risk of residential mortgage lending. (The December 2009 modifications to the Basel Accord imposing a 10% Loss Given Default ('LGD') floor for claims secured by residential mortgages do not count because they did not have a substantial capital impact and because they were the continuation of pre-crisis policy making, not a response to the crisis.)

based bank capital regulation and the leverage ratio; with the clearing mandate and the uncleared margin rules; with market regulation and with central counterparty policy. The aim is not to give a comprehensive account of any particular jurisdiction's rules, but rather to survey the key policies finalized between September 2008 and May 2020, illustrating them with standards set at the global level or in the EU, UK, or US as best suits the narrative. Some policies have achieved their intended effects at reasonable cost, while others have not, or have had unintended side effects, so the major impacts will be surveyed too. The post-2008 reforms are now nearly complete, so now is a good time to undertake this.

Uncovering the mechanisms involved in shaping derivatives regulation, and hence gaining insight into why it is as it is, will entail the use of a variety of tools from different areas, and a substantial broadening of scope, compared to the simple plan above. We will see that regulation is fundamentally about constructing and using knowledge. This leads us to enquire about the nature of this rationality, and what it would mean for it to be accurate and useful. We will also need to look at how regulatory knowledge is constructed and the forces that shape this process.

All of this means that our approach has to be broad and cross-disciplinary. It will be helpful to interrogate the legitimacy of financial regulation, the communities within which it is made, its relationship with the law, the role that regulatory arrangements play in wider strategies of government, what it would mean for regulatory rules to capture their object accurately, and how regulators talk to each other, the executive that empowers them, and those they regulate. En route, there will be encounters with Australian cyclists, Cleopatra's nose, Dutch flood plain engineers, a model of the Khedive's palace, the *Mona Lisa*, and the penny post.

The payoff of this approach is not just a better understanding of post-crisis derivatives regulation, but also of financial regulation more broadly. It is also a vital precursor to regulatory reform. Simply tweaking the least well-conceived rules would help, but it is not nearly enough. The institutional arrangements of financial regulators are seriously questionable too. We suggest that reform here is necessary in order to make large and lasting improvements to the efficiency and effectiveness of financial regulation.

The Revised Plan

Our approach to post-crisis derivatives regulation, given the issues discussed above, requires three parts. Part I, comprising Chapters 1–3, sets out the background to post-2008 derivatives regulation and the motivations for it. Chapter 1 provides background, introducing derivatives, their risks, and the fundamental ideas behind their treatment in prudential regulation. Derivatives create or transform a variety of risks, so quantitative models of risk will be important in this chapter.

The initiating event of global regulatory reform—the financial crisis of 2008—is considered in Chapter 2. The causes of the crisis are considered, as are the lessons regulators took from it. Moving to the other end of our time period, Chapter 3 considers the market events around the onset of Covid in 2020, illustrating some of the successes and failures of post-crisis rule making.

Part II, comprising Chapters 4–7, discusses the major elements of derivatives regulatory reform: this forms our account of what regulators did after 2008. We will see that regulation seeks to control the risks created by derivatives. It does this in two main ways: by constraining derivatives contracts; and by requiring that parties entering into them have minimum levels of various kinds of resources, such as capital, which can help if things go wrong.

The most important derivatives market intermediaries are banks, so we begin with the principal bank capital rules affecting derivatives. The leverage ratio is discussed in Chapter 4. Consideration of this rule makes it clear that regulation proceeds not just by making rules, but also by promulgating a narrative about them. Alertness to these stories, how they are constructed, and the alternatives to them, reveals much about the underlying and often unchallenged assumptions of the regulators. Chapter 5 then turns to risk-based capital regulation, and the various capital requirements for market and counterparty credit risk. These are essentially models of various derivatives risks, and they have differing approaches, drawbacks, and levels of prudence.

The changes to derivatives market structure are considered in Chapter 6. This chapter discusses post-crisis regulatory requirements to use a particular form of market infrastructure: central counterparties. It also discusses requirements for how derivatives are executed, and policy around the collateralization of bilateral, or uncleared derivatives.

Clearing requirements made central counterparties more systemically important than they used to be, so regulators also intervened to enhance standards for their robustness. Chapter 7 discusses the risks of these entities, the regulatory principles for them defined in transnational standards, and the implementation of these principles in various national rules.

Part III turns to the complicated and multifaceted question of why the authorities enacted these reforms, how the rules were made, and what it might mean for them to be good. A number of different areas of scholarship will be used as searchlights to illuminate different aspects of these questions.

Rule making typically involves action by a public body, so administrative law will be relevant. Chapter 8 therefore discusses the policy making process and its relationship with and review by the law.

Regulation has costs, benefits, and side effects which vary over time, and shape the system they seek to control, so perspectives from economics can be valuable. Chapter 9 considers this, setting out the general principles of the quantitative analysis of financial regulation, and applying these principles in two case studies of the post-2008 derivatives reforms. The first examines the authorities' justification of their policies; the second adopts a more exploratory approach to an analysis of the policy regarding the variability of central counterparty margin.

Chapter 10 turns to regulation *of* modelling and regulation *as* modelling. It first discusses how regulators treat banks' use of quantitative models, highlighting the requirements for addressing the limited applicability of models, assessing their ongoing performance, and ensuring that their users remain alert to the risks of their use. Regulators' own models are seen to be prone to the same issues, motivating the need for similar precautions.

The sociology and political economy of financial regulation is discussed in Chapter 11. Like any profession, regulation has its own professional myths and rituals of belonging. One of the most prominent myths is that of technocracy—of the value of independent expertise. This claim is probed, revealing some of the features of the boundary conflict between politics and financial regulation and, in the process, situating financial regulation within the regulatory state.

Chapter 12 summarizes our insights into post-crisis derivatives regulation and considers their implications for the scholarship of regulation. It presents some suggestions for alternative approaches to particular public policy issues in derivatives, to the policy making process, and to the institutional arrangements of financial regulation, which might serve society better.

A bibliography of work referred to is provided, and the relevant rules, laws, and standards finalized at the cut-off date of May 2020 are listed separately following the bibliography. All websites referred to were accessed in July 2021.

In Short

This book has been motivated by several key ideas. One is that the financial system, its regulators, and government are embroiled in a relationship of mutual support and dependency, and that the consequences of this arrangement have not always served us well. In particular, in the years leading up to 2008, it allowed the preconditions for a crisis to develop.

After one duly hit, there was a short, intense period of debate about what should replace the prior regulatory ideology. Derivatives were vulnerable. It was convenient for them to be blamed, so, despite the lack of evidence that they were responsible for the crisis, a massive programme of derivatives regulation was initiated.

We suggest that the resulting regulatory framework is inefficient, partially ineffective, and sometimes counterproductive. It lacks legitimacy, and has disguised essentially political questions as technocratic ones, allowing these questions to be answered by regulators. An uncoerced debate about how the financial system can serve society best, then an evidence-based exploration of how to reform regulation in furtherance of this is proposed.

The role of regulatory knowledge will be central in our account. We suggest that much of regulation is a modelling exercise. Like most models, prudential regulation involves cramming a messy reality into fixed categories, and making inferences from these categories. Good practice in this situation is to be honest about the situated, contingent nature of the model, transparent about the data, mechanisms, and norms used in its construction, and alert to when it might fail. These features are not prominent in regulatory practice, and framing the rule making process around them would be a substantial and necessary improvement.

Part I

Context and Motivations

1

Core Ideas in Derivatives

Introduction

1.1 Derivatives markets are vital venues for risk transfer. They are very large,[1] diverse,[2] global,[3] and, in many cases, highly liquid.[4] The benefits of derivatives to society have been recognized for centuries.[5] They allow parties with risk that they do not want to bear to transfer it, and they facilitate parties who are willing to take on risk to do so, usually in exchange for a fee. A range of intermediaries facilitate this trading. The activities of these parties together allow financial risks to be borne by the parties best (or, at least, better) able to manage them.

1.2 As noted in the Introduction, there has been an enormous amount of policy making affecting these markets since 2008.[6] Their structure has been changed by regulatory fiat. Many market participants have been required to hold much higher levels of resources to support their derivatives activity. As a result, it has become more costly to transfer risk. Before we can discuss this, though, some scene-setting and background is needed so that the regulators' interventions can be properly explained and contextualized.

---

1 Bank of International Settlement ('BIS') statistics for the first half of 2019 report an outstanding notional of OTC derivatives globally of over \$640 trillion, while the derivatives trade association ISDA reports that as of 2019, over \$480 billion of margin had been pledged against the risk of these transactions. See https://stats.bis.org/statx/srs/table/d5.1 and https://www.isda.org/2020/04/14/isda-margin-survey-year-end-2019/respectively.

2 The BIS, ibid., reports multi-trillion dollar notionals in interest rate, foreign exchange, equity, credit, and commodity derivatives, with 55 countries listed as having meaningful turnover.

3 The gross positive fair value, for instance, of US derivatives held by foreigners is over \$2 trillion: see https://home.treasury.gov/data/treasury-international-capital-tic-system-home-page/using-tic/us-derivatives-contracts-with-foreigners-holdings-and-cash-settlements.

4 Daily turnover in single currency interest rate derivatives alone, according to the BIS, averaged \$6.5 trillion in April 2019: see https://www.bis.org/statistics/rpfx19_ir.pdf.

5 As Stulz (2014) describes, these benefits include effective, convenient risk transfer; price discovery; and making primary (non-derivative) markets more efficient.

6 See Arias-Barrera (2018), Helleiner et al. (2018), and, for the official sector view, FSB (2020).

Derivatives Contracts and Risks

1.3 We begin with the key ideas used to construct prudential policy for derivatives. Regulation constrains how parties enter into derivatives and places resource requirements on market participants based on regulators' estimates of the risks involved in their derivatives activity. Therefore, the types of contractual arrangements typically available and the methods for estimating the risks of derivatives will be important. The nature of these contractual arrangements affects the risks involved, so this dependence will be reviewed. Most readers will have some familiarity with derivatives, so the aim is to fix terminology and to sketch some of the ideas which will be important later: aficionados of derivatives and their treatment in regulation may wish to skip straight to Chapter 2.

Transacting derivatives and the obligations this entails

1.4 A derivative is a contract between two parties. Each party makes a commitment to do something, either now or later. For instance, one might pay the other a sum of money now in exchange for the right to buy an asset at a fixed price in the future; or both parties might promise to make a series of payments to the other on fixed future dates, with the size of one series of payments fixed and the other dependent on some market rate. Derivatives transfer risk because their value changes as market variables move.

1.5 Contracts involve the future: parties to them make promises about what they will do. This means that there is a risk, known as counterparty credit risk, that a party might not keep their promise, and that this will lead to a loss for their counterparty. Counterparty credit risk is one of the main risks in derivatives, and its mitigation is one of the key issues in derivatives regulation.

1.6 Derivatives can be categorized based on how they are transacted:

- over-the-counter (or 'OTC') derivatives are transacted bilaterally, directly between two parties;[7] whereas
- exchange-traded derivatives are traded on an organized platform or at an established venue. Typically the exchange, or a closely related party, acts as counterparty to these transactions.

1.7 Parties are often obliged to make various payments as a result of their derivatives activity. This gives rise to funding liquidity risk: the risk that a party does not have enough cash to make a required payment, or can only obtain it at

[7] In the past, this was often a purely private relationship: one party might telephone the other, or exchange emails with them. Now it is common for trading to happen via an electronic platform: one party might request a quote for a given derivative, various competing counterparties would answer the request, and one would be selected to consummate the trade.

unexpectedly high cost. Funding liquidity risk can create counterparty credit risk by threatening the viability of the party suffering funding stress.[8]

Options and counterparty credit risk

1.8 Different derivatives create different amounts of counterparty credit risk. For instance, if an option is sold, the seller receives the option premium from the buyer, often at or near the start of the transaction. The option buyer has no further obligations once they have paid for their derivative. On the other hand, if the buyer exercises the option, their counterparty has committed to sell the option underlying at the strike price. Thus, all other things being equal, buyers have counterparty credit risk to options sellers, but not vice versa.[9]

1.9 Consider an option that can only be exercised at maturity. The value of this instrument before this point can be estimated using standard techniques, such as the Black-Scholes formula. If the option seller fails after receiving the premium but before maturity, the buyer will suffer a loss of this amount. This possibility means that the value of the option written by a counterparty who might fail to perform is lower than that of one written by a risk-free counterparty. The adjustment to derivatives value due to the potential for counterparty non-performance is known as a 'credit valuation adjustment' (or 'CVA').

Replacing a transaction

1.10 If a derivatives counterparty fails to perform, they might need to be replaced. Suppose that a party, *A*, enters into a derivatives transaction with *B*, but *B* then defaults. In order to restore its risk position, *A* must replace its contract with *B*. The cost of doing this depends on the value of the derivative being replaced *at the point of replacement*. If a new counterparty can be found soon after the default, and the market is both liquid and has not moved very much, then it is likely that the replacement transaction will be worth roughly the same amount as the one with *B*.[10] But if the market moves—something that becomes more likely the longer it takes to replace the trade—then the risk of loss is greater.[11]

1.11 Figure 1.1 illustrates the potential variability of the value of a derivative by plotting the price of a fixed strike and maturity S&P 500 call option through the period of market stress associated with the onset of the Covid-19 virus in 2020.

[8] The risk cuts both ways: if one party owes the other a large amount, paying it might cause the debtor to fail if it then runs out of liquidity, while not receiving it might have consequences for the creditor.

[9] Strictly, this applies to a limited range of options including standard, European or American style calls and puts.

[10] As well as market effects, may also be a value difference due to CVA.

[11] This risk may not crystallize: counterparty failure does not always lead to a loss.

The price of the option is shown on the left-hand scale and that of the index on the right. On the first day of June, the option we have chosen was worth \$66. Buying that same option one, two, three and four business days later would have cost \$85, \$123, \$113, and \$193 respectively.[12] This demonstrates that *B*'s loss can vary substantially depending on when *A* defaults and when the contract is replaced.

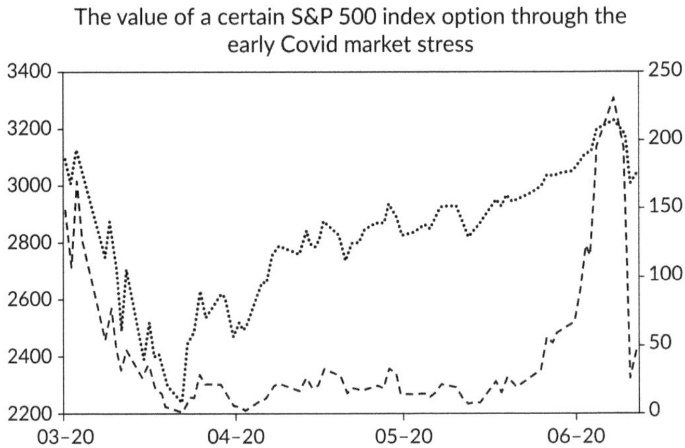

Figure 1.1- The level of the S&P 500 index (in lighter grey) and the value of an option on it (in darker grey) during the early Covid market stress

1.12 The 'current exposure' or 'CE' of a derivatives counterparty at a given point in time is defined as the present value of their portfolio if it is positive, and zero if it is negative. This is their current liability to us on the portfolio.[13]

Interest rate swaps

1.13 Interest rate swaps are one of the most common forms of OTC derivatives. Here, both parties undertake to make a series of payments. For instance, one might promise to pay a fixed amount every three months, while the other commits to pay an amount that depends on a floating rate.

1.14 Interest rate swaps are often quoted as a fixed rate which gives the swap a mid-market value of zero. That means the value of each stream of payments—those from *A* to *B* and those from *B* to *A*—is the same when the swap is transacted. Over time, interest rates move, and the values of the two legs tend to diverge.

1.15 The most common floating rates for swaps used to be ones based on a suite of floating rates known as Libor.[14] However, after scandals relating to how

[12] This substantial variation is due to the large movements not just in the S&P 500 index level but also in implied volatility.

[13] There is no exposure to us if we owe someone money.

[14] This is an abbreviation for the 'London Inter-Bank Offered Rate'. The Libor rate for a given currency and maturity was intended to represent the average interest rate at which a selection of

Libor was set, the market is now transitioning to a new set of reference rates, and increasingly interest rate swaps are being quoted as fixed versus these new floating rates. Examples of these new rates include the Secured Overnight Financing Rate, or SOFR, in US dollars, the Sterling Overnight Index Average, or SONIA, in British pounds and the Tokyo Overnight Average Rate, or TONAR, in Japanese yen.[15]

1.16 The valuation of interest rate swaps is a complex matter which depends on the two streams of payments and other arrangements between the parties, such as collateral posted. A high-level summary of the process follows.[16]

- Fixed legs involves a series of fixed payments at various points in the future. Their current value is therefore determined by discounting the value of those future payments into today's dollars.
- Future floating rates are estimated using the market prices of derivatives which depend on them, taking into account their contractual features. For instance, the price of an interest rate future on the compounded overnight SOFR, might be used to provide a market estimate of the expected future level of this rate. A process known as bootstrapping calculates market estimates of future interest rates.
- The value of the floating leg is then given by discounting payments calculated from estimates of the future value of the rate back to today.[17]

1.17 Suppose *A* and *B* transact a four year fixed for floating US dollar interest rate swap based on SOFR. Fixed for floating means that one party makes a series of fixed payments, while the other makes a series of payments based on a floating rate, in this case SOFR. We will assume for this swap that *A* and *B* each make a payment every year—these are known as the coupons on the swap—and that *A* pays annual compounded SOFR. It will be further assumed that the swap has an initial value of zero and that the market expectation of SOFR in the future is above the current rate, so that the SOFR forward curve points up. This means that *A*'s payments are expected to increase over time.

---

banks on the London money market would be prepared to lend to one another without collateral for the given maturity in the stated currency.

15 For a discussion of the origins of and motivations for the Libor replacement, see Hou & Skeie (2014). R. FSB (2020a) gives an account of the progress towards Libor replacements at the time of writing: references to official sector laws, rules, and standards are prefixed by an R and appear in a separate index.

16 See Brigo et al. (2013) for a more detailed discussion, including the effect of counterparty credit risk and funding, of what is a complex and technical area.

17 Depending on the situation, different curves might be needed for determining forward rates and discounting payments back to today.

1.18 For the swap value to be zero, the present value of the floating rate payments must equal the present value of the fixed rate payments. The only way this can be true, given that the floating rate payments go up during the life of the swap, is for the early floating payments to be below the fixed rate and the late ones, above it. Thus, early in the life of the swap, there will be net payments from *B* to *A*. Later on, this reverses, with *A* making net payments to *B*.

1.19 The structure of this flow of payments illustrates the credit risk embedded in this swap, given the shape of the SOFR curve we have assumed. The fixed rate payer has credit exposure to the floating rate payer which, assuming rates behave as predicted, reduces during the life of the swap.

1.20 A concrete example of the situation is shown in Figure 1.2. Here a four year fixed for floating swap where the notional—the amount the rates are applied to in determining the payments on each leg—is $20M. The swap has been valued at each coupon date from the perspective of the fixed rate payer (i.e. *B* in our example) assuming that the forward curve perfectly predicts future floating rates. *A*'s debt to *B* is reflected in the positive value of the swap for *B*.

Month	12	24	36	48
Swap Value	$30K	$65K	$32K	-

Figure 1.2- The expected value of a particular four year fixed for floating swap after each coupon payment

1.21 Interest rate swaps payments are usually made net: instead of each party exchanging gross payments, the parties calculate the difference between their obligations. The net debtor pays the net creditor on each coupon date. The value of the swap for *B* peaks roughly halfway through its life, so if *A* were to fail, *B*'s loss—the value of the future net coupons it will not now receive—would be greatest at this point.

1.22 Thus far, we have supposed that the forward curve accurately predicts future floating rates. Next it is necessary to consider what happens if the curve moves, that is if the expected level of future floating rates changes.

Adding volatility

1.23 Future floating rates are not known, but information about how much a given rate has moved in the past is available. We might estimate, for instance, that the annual volatility of the four year swap rate is 27%, based either on the prices of swaptions or on historical data.[18] From this, it is possible to construct a

[18] The value of an option to enter into a swap, or swaption, depends on how much the value of the swap might move before the option expires, and hence on market expectations of the volatility of

set of paths for future interest rates which are jointly consistent with our estimate of the future distribution of rates. If it was believed that interest rate returns were normally distributed, for instance, the paths would be selected so as to approximate an evolution of uncertainty based on the normal distribution.

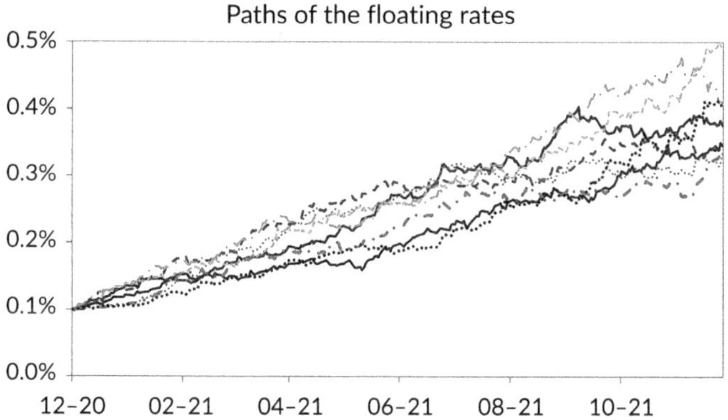

Figure 1.3- Eight scenarios for the three month floating rate for one year

1.24 For a swap, there would be scenarios for the evolution of the relevant floating rate: Figure 1.3 illustrates the idea.[19] The swap would be valued by assuming that each of these paths is followed: each possible value of the floating rate gives a possible swap value. If we pick a point in time and examine the swap value on each path at this point, this gives us distribution of its potential future values.

1.25 Figure 1.4 gives a schematic of the process.[20] It can be extended from a single derivative to a portfolio of derivatives: the underlying risk factors are jointly simulated until the longest maturity of any instrument in the portfolio, the whole portfolio is valued on each path, and the distribution of portfolio values through time is determined.[21] This distribution is useful because it gives a sense of how much the counterparty might owe in various states of the world, and how probable those states are.

1.26 Two terms are commonly used in the measurement of the distribution of potential future values of a portfolio of derivatives with a counterparty: the 'expected exposure' (or 'EE') is the average credit exposure at a point in time; while the 'potential future exposure' (or 'PFE') is a measure of the amount owed at some

floating rates. The utility of this kind of 'market consistent' measure of volatility versus backward-looking or 'historical' measures will be discussed further below. A volatility implied from swaption prices is a market consistent measure; one estimated from historical levels is a 'real-world' one.

19 In practice there would be thousands of simulated paths rather than the eight illustrated.

20 This figure is based on one originally published in Murphy (2013): my thanks are due to Springer Nature for permission to base this figure, Figure 1.9, Figure 1.12, and Figure 1.13 on that work.

21 A delicate modelling issue in this situation is selecting the model of risk factor comovement.

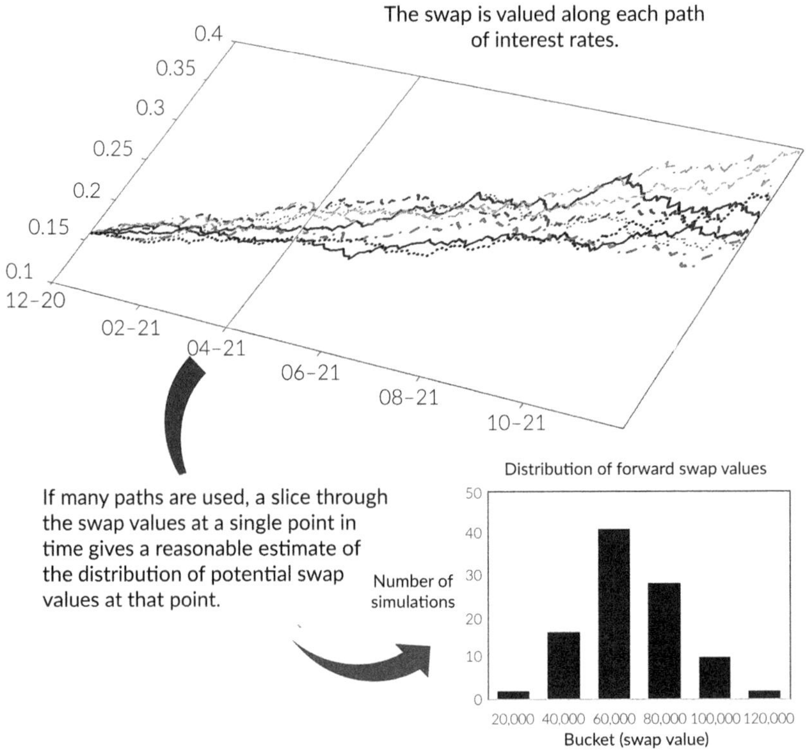

Figure 1.4– Schematic of the calculation of potential future swap values

level of confidence. It might be decided to measure PFEs at 99%: in this case, the loss should only exceed this amount in 1% of future states.

1.27 These concepts are illustrated in Figure 1.5. The distribution of portfolio values for a point in time is estimated. The credit exposure is the positive part of that distribution, and the expected exposure is the average credit exposure. The PFE is the chosen percentile of the distribution of credit exposures. This illustrates a key difference between CE and PFE: the CE is a known amount, whereas the PFE is estimated based on how much exposure might change between now and when the portfolio can be closed out. It depends on how long close-out takes and how confident we want to be that our measure of potential future exposure will not be exceeded.

The risks of derivatives and their users

1.28 The main risks of derivatives, and hence the main issues that derivatives regulation needs to address, are evident from the discussion above. Derivatives involve risk transfer, and can change in value as market factors move. Counterparties to derivatives can fail to perform. The portfolio of transactions with

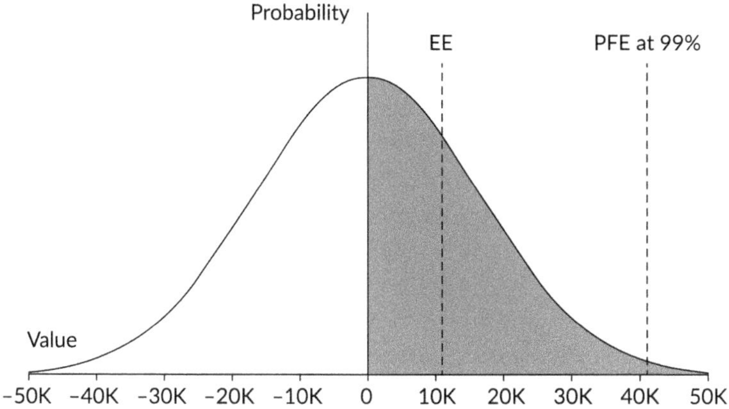

Figure 1.5– An illustration of expected exposure and potential future exposure for a distribution of portfolio values. The credit exposure is shown in grey

a counterparty represents risk transfer that the party wishes to have, so if their counterparty fails, they replace the portfolio. The cost of the failure is the cost of doing this. Derivatives trading usually involves obligations to make payments, so funding liquidity risk is involved. Thus, some of the key risks in derivatives are:[22]

- *Market risk.* Derivatives are risk transfer instruments: (nearly all) derivatives transactions change both counterparties' risk positions.[23]
- *Counterparty credit risk.* As discussed above, this has two elements: the current exposure and the potential future exposure. These elements are inextricably linked with market risk: the exposure only changes because the value of the portfolio changes, i.e. because of market risk factors.
- *Settlement risk.* Consider a British pound ('GBP') vs US dollar ('USD') foreign exchange ('FX') forward where *A* agrees to pay *B* \$1.34M, and *B* agrees to pay *A* £1M. If the forward GBP/USD rate changes to 1.3, then *A* poses current exposure to *B*, equal to the difference in value between the 1.34 strike forward and the now expected exchange rate of 1.3. However, absent other arrangements, once settlement on the forward is due, *B* might honour its side of the bargain, while *A* does not. This would entail a much bigger loss for *B*, as it receives nothing, despite paying £1M. Clearly, here, the gross amount is at risk. Because gross payments can be large, most markets have arrangements to mitigate settlement risk in derivatives.[24]

[22] See also paragraphs 1.63 and 1.45 for discussions of legal risk.

[23] Derivatives are sometimes transacted for other reasons, such as tax, regulation, or accounting.

[24] One common approach is to use a trusted third party to whom all payments are sent, and who only releases one payment when all the others related to the same commitment have been received. For a longer description, see PRC (2007).

- *Funding liquidity risk.* There are two different issues that are referred to as 'liquidity risk'. One is the risk that a demand for cash cannot be met when it is due, or can only be met at unexpectedly high cost. This is called funding liquidity risk because mitigating it depends on having adequate funding.
- *Market liquidity risk.* In contrast, market liquidity risk is the risk that when a position comes to be sold (or bought back, in the case of a short position), the price at which this is possible is unexpectedly far from market prices. This can happen either because the position is large, or because market quality is challenging and there are few counterparties who are willing to engage in new transactions of the size and type required. Market liquidity risk is important because changing risk profiles (including changes needed as a result of a default of a counterparty) involves trading, and hence the availability of market liquidity.

1.29 Market participants' motivations for trading risks vary. Some want to transfer risk, for instance because they are hedging risks that they already have; some aim to stay roughly risk flat while acting as market intermediaries and taking a fee for providing liquidity; and some are willing to take a variety of risks provided that the returns are high enough. These can be roughly characterized as end-users, dealers, and investors, although the categories are not disjoint. Dealers typically have relatively low net risk positions; their mission is to take a fee for intermediating transactions or providing customized solutions, not to take risk. The other two classes of market participant may have significant market risk positions in derivatives: these are often offset by positions in other instruments[25] or by sensitivities in the entities' earnings.[26]

Netting Derivatives Portfolios

1.30 It is common to have a portfolio of multiple trades with a given counterparty. In derivatives, the basic unit of analysis is often the portfolio rather than the

[25] An end-user might, for instance, be short a commodity future because they are a producer of that commodity: the offsetting position might quite literally still be in the ground. Or they might enter into an FX swap because they have issued a bond in one currency but the cashflows to service it are in another.

[26] This is a situation where an entity can reasonably predict that its earnings will depend on some market variable. As an example, consider a bank funding fixed rate mortgages that they have extended with floating rate deposits. The bank's net interest income will depend on the difference between what they pay on the deposits compared to what they earn on the mortgages. The former might be based on a short-term interest rate, so floating rates rising would reduce the bank's earnings. Paying fixed and receiving that floating rate on an interest rate swap would therefore hedge the risk to their earnings caused by the potential for floating rates to increase.

trade. Portfolios should typically be thought of being defined by the net properties of their components, with the derivatives used to construct them simply being one of the many ways of achieving the desired risk profile.[27]

1.31 The importance of taking a net perspective becomes bigger as portfolios grow. Consider a dealer conducting hundreds of swap trades a day. Their portfolio will typically start the day reasonably well hedged and hence low risk. The first few trades of the day will therefore tend to add risk. But as time goes on, it becomes more and more likely that a new trade will hedge existing ones—or at least diversify them. Thus, the market risk rises more slowly than the total notional in the portfolio does. The net payment obligations on the portfolio rise more slowly too, as a cashflow from one trade is likely to be partially offset by a cashflow in the opposite direction from another.

1.32 Various forms of netting need to work in order to achieve these efficiency benefits. These, and the means by which they are achieved, are examined in this section.

Payment netting

1.33 Payment netting is the substitution of a single net payment for two or more obligations between parties. If *A* owns *B* £150,000 and *B* owes *A* £40,000, then their joint obligations can be satisfied by a net payment of £110,000 from *A* to *B*.

1.34 There are various degrees of payment netting that parties can apply: netting is typically restricted to payments due on a single day and in one currency. (Many institutions, including nearly all banks, manage their liquidity in different currencies separately, so cross-currency netting[28] is uncommon.) It may also be restricted to payments within an asset class.[29]

1.35 It is also important to note that derivatives, as with other financial instruments, are traded between legal entities. Thus, the payment is owed from one particular legal entity to another. Many firms have multiple legal entities in the same groups: for banks, there can be thousands of separate firms. It is uncommon

---

[27] Benjamin (2010) at 800 suggests that the central role of net positions is one of the key narratives in financial markets.

[28] The global nature of the derivatives markets and the low liquidity of the money markets in some currencies outside their time zone means that it sometimes makes sense to make a payment in a different currency. If *A* owes *B* 400 million Swedish krona at 4pm in the New York trading day, when it is 10pm in Stockholm, both parties might prefer to make the payment in US dollars: *A* might have difficulty sourcing krona at that time and *B* might have difficulty investing them overnight.

[29] That is, two parties might net all payments in a given currency on equity derivatives and separately net all payments in a given currency on interest rate derivatives, but not conduct the final step of netting across asset classes.

(and often legally problematic) to net payments due from different legal entities, so there are often multiple payments between different banking groups originating from or heading to various legal entities within them.[30]

The enforceability of netting

1.36 Payment netting is one of the chief mechanisms for mitigating settlement risk in derivatives. Its efficacy, as with other forms of netting, relies on the nature of the obligation. Two parties could agree to payment netting as a matter of operational convenience, but settlement risk would only be reduced if the debt owed upon the failure of one of them was the net amount. Technically, this can be done in two ways: 'netting' refers to the situation where only a single debt of the net amount exists in law, while 'set-off' refers to the right to offset a debit with a credit and only pay the net amount.

1.37 The law surrounding netting and set-off is complex. It relates to an old question, that of 'calculating the true measure of damages' in bankruptcy.[31] In summary, the right to make a single payment in settlement of a portfolio of transactions after one of the counterparties to them defaults depends on the precise contract between the parties, the governing laws of both the transactions and the bankruptcy (which may of course be different), and the nature of the transactions. Netting is an important mechanism for reducing counterparty credit risk in derivatives because the gross claim can be much larger than the net claim.[32]

Close-out and netting

1.38 After a party to a portfolio of derivatives stops performing, its counterparty will want to terminate the transactions and, as discussed above, replace them. It needs to know under what circumstances it can terminate. Often, failure to make a contractual payment, if not cured (and perhaps if sufficiently material) is an event of default, so this would be one of the circumstances under which termination is possible. There will often be others, too, usually including default on other debt obligations, bankruptcy, and misrepresentation.

1.39 After an event of default, a notice of default must typically be served, the transactions with the defaulter valued, and a net claim presented to the defaulter's

[30] For a longer discussion, see, for instance, Giovanoli (1997).

[31] See Derham (2010).

[32] In most major derivatives jurisdictions, the right of a non-defaulting party to terminate transactions and net their termination values, under suitable contractual arrangements, is (again to simplify a complex issue) enforceable. But there are exceptions: one may occur when the defaulter is a Mainland China counterparty subject to bankruptcy proceedings. Another is when the counterparty is an organization which does not 'go bankrupt' in the ordinary sense, such as a multilateral treaty organization: here the analysis is more subtle.

estate. At the same time, new transactions will be entered into to replace what has been lost due to the default.[33] The right to do this is known as close-out netting. Derivatives counterparties view it as important to have:

- the right to terminate quickly, so that the value of the portfolio with the defaulter does not drift further;
- the right to net all the transactions in the portfolio to come to a single 'close-out' value, so that there is a single net obligation; and
- the right to determine that amount.

1.40 If the close-out value from the non-defaulter's perspective is positive, then they have a claim against the defaulter. If it is negative, then the non-defaulter is a debtor to the defaulter's estate. Netting therefore ensures that the counterparty credit risk is as small as possible, given the risk transfer in the portfolio. Without it, non-defaulters would be exposed either to unnecessary market risk, or to unnecessary counterparty credit risk, or both. Due to its benefits, nearly all major jurisdictions support close-out netting.[34]

Master agreements

1.41 The contractual technology for achieving close-out netting is often a master agreement. This is a umbrella document which sets the contractual terms of all of the transactions between two counterparties under its terms. It typically incorporates a definition of events of default and how they are handled, including the right to close-out, and how the portfolio is valued after an event of default. Together with supportive legislation, it provides for close-out netting, signalling that the two parties to it intend to treat all of the transactions under it as parts of a single whole, and for the non-defaulting party to close-out the portfolio on a net basis in the event of the other party's default. One way to think of this situation is that when a new transaction under a master agreement is agreed, it records the parties' intent to vary the underlying risk transfer between them by whatever difference the new trade makes to the net cashflows.

[33] 'What has been lost' is typically the net risk of the portfolio, so the replacement transactions will often be chosen to have the same risk profile as the portfolio with the defaulter, not to have the same trades as it.

[34] One group of scholars, partly motivated by analogies to other areas of bankruptcy law, notably in the United States, argues against close-out netting and/or the derivatives safe harbour discussed below. See, for instance, Roe (2011) or Schwarcz (2015). These arguments typically do not focus on the purpose of derivatives, namely transferring risk. The trades in a portfolio are just one way of recording the desired net risk transfer at a given point in time. If they did not net, then market participants would simply invent a different way of documenting transactions which did reflect their (net) intent.

1.42 A master agreement is only useful if its provisions will be respected in bankruptcy. There is now considerable case law around this situation which throws light upon when netting works, the pitfalls in the close-out process (notably in the valuation of the portfolio), and the time frames involved. To summarize a highly complex position, netting in most jurisdictions under a suitable master agreement works, but care is needed to document the parties' intentions and to conduct the close-out process reasonably and in accordance with the contractual arrangements.[35]

Arrangements for OTC derivatives

1.43 OTC derivatives and exchange-traded derivatives took different paths in their pursuit of an efficient market structure without too much unnecessary risk. The former arose as bilateral, private contractual arrangements. Netting in this context involves reducing the counterparty credit risk (including settlement risk) between pairs of counterparties as much as possible, while preserving the bilateral nature of contractual arrangements. Figure 1.6 illustrates this for four dealers.

1.44 There were substantial collective benefits to standardizing the form of these contracts. If most market participants use the same documentation, then its behaviour can be predictable, widely known, and reflective of a broad consensus about what is desirable. Analysis of enforceability can be thorough, performed once per jurisdiction, and its costs shared. It also allows market conventions for dealing with extraordinary events such as market disruption to be developed.[36] Finally, when a significant event happens, such as the transition away from Libor-based swaps to new reference rates, this can be done using a protocol developed and used industry-wide.[37]

1.45 The need for standard OTC derivatives contracts that supported close-out and netting stimulated the creation of a trade association known as 'ISDA' or the International Swaps and Derivatives Association.[38] One of the missions of ISDA is to develop contractual documentation globally for OTC derivatives.

---

35 See Braithwaite (2020) for a comprehensive account.

36 This is easier in some markets than in others. Most observers take the view that the market conventions for OTC interest rate derivatives have proven relatively robust, for instance. In contrast, one could give a reasonable account of the history of credit derivatives structured around the theme of 'Event *X* was not contemplated in the documentation of the time, and proved undesirable, so …'

37 See Bailey (2017) for a further discussion of the Libor transition.

38 ISDA's original name was the International Swap *Dealers* Association, reflecting a focus on the swap dealing banks who were most active in the early years of the OTC markets, and echoing the 'intermediaries tend to build infrastructure to suit intermediaries' theme in Chapter 7. ISDA was renamed as its attention extended to the OTC derivatives market beyond swaps and to more market participants.

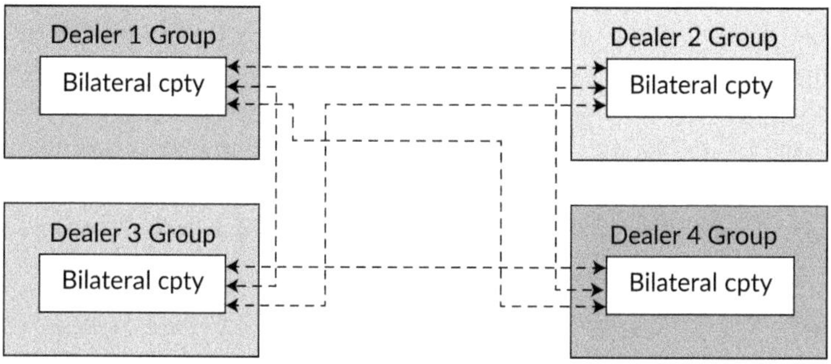

Figure 1.6– An illustration of bilateral OTC derivatives connections between four dealers

ISDA's documents include standard Definitions used in documenting transactions, Master Agreements which facilitate close-out netting, and Credit Support Agreements, which set out margin and other credit mitigation arrangements.[39] It also provides members with opinions on the enforceability of its documentation in various jurisdictions. Transactions with a notional value of over a quadrillion dollars have been traded in the global OTC derivatives market,[40] so this form of legal technology has been a notable success.

Arrangements for exchange-traded derivatives

1.46 Exchange-traded derivatives markets developed earlier than bilateral OTC markets and approached the issues of standardization, netting, and close-out in a different way. Here market participants were already meeting to trade at the exchange. This body naturally took the role of developer of standard transaction documentation. There was less danger of market fragmentation, as everyone trading at the same exchange used the same conventions: instead, there was competition between exchanges.

1.47 Market participants in exchange-traded derivatives were more numerous, diverse, and of lower average credit quality than OTC derivatives dealers, and they traded with each other more often but typically in smaller amounts. This meant that there was greater benefit in centralizing the monitoring and management of counterparty risk. The exchange, given its role as a trading venue, was the

[39] There are two major editions of the ISDA Master Agreement, published in 1992 and 2002; the overwhelming majority of OTC derivatives are documented under one of these Master Agreements or a document derived from them. For more details, see Harding (2002).

[40] The London Clearing House ('LCH') announced in January 2020 that they had cleared over $1.2 quadrillion of interest rate swaps: see their press release *LCH delivers record clearing volumes in 2019* available at https://www.lch.com/resources/news/lch-delivers-record-clearing-volumes-2019. Since interest rate swaps cleared at LCH are only a part of the total OTC derivatives market, the whole market is larger than this.

natural party to take this on. Thus, rather than contracting directly with each other, market participants soon agreed to use a central body associated with the exchange as an intermediary. This go-between is known as the central counterparty or 'CCP'. The 'clearing' of exchange-traded derivatives meant that after agreeing the trade, both parties would assign or 'novate' the trade to the CCP, so that it stood between them and insulated each from the risk of the other's failure.

1.48 Central clearing has the advantage that, rather than each party having to do due diligence on potential counterparties, the CCP can set standards for membership: in this sense, it is like a club. The terms of all cleared trades are set by the exchange, facilitating standardization. CCPs define how trades are cleared and settled: this is set out in a rule book for members. CCPs also specify requirements for margin and other resources which are required for trading, so a party cannot clear if it is inadequately resourced.

1.49 Exchange-traded derivatives therefore usually involve not just trading on an exchange, but also clearing through a central counterparty following its rules.[41] This facilitates netting: instead of the participants facing each other as they would in the bilateral market illustrated in Figure 1.6, everyone faces the CCP, and everyone can net all of their risk from trades on the exchange, no matter who they had traded with. This is known as multilateral netting. Because the CCP is counterparty to all cleared trades, it is responsible for default management. To support this, CCP rule books contain provisions which achieve the same effect as the close-out provisions in an ISDA Master Agreement.

1.50 Different CCPs developed different requirements for the parties that directly face them, their 'clearing members'. Over time, these standards converged somewhat, but at a given CCP they remained grounded in the practices of the associated exchange.[42]

1.51 The variability of the standards for clearing members meant that it was sometimes inconvenient for dealers to use the same entity as their clearing member for different exchanges. Figure 1.7 illustrates the topology of the market that developed, with central clearing of trades conducted at two different exchanges cleared at two different CCPs, and with different entities in each dealer's group facing each CCP.

1.52 The different characteristics of the exchange-traded and OTC derivatives markets led to different market structures, illustrated in Figures 1.6 and 1.7. Before 2008, the OTC derivatives market was based on bilateral contracts, often

[41] The development of exchange-traded derivatives infrastructure is discussed further in Chapter 7. See also Russo et al. (2002).

[42] The two different client clearing models, principal-to-principal and agency, discussed below, are an example of this.

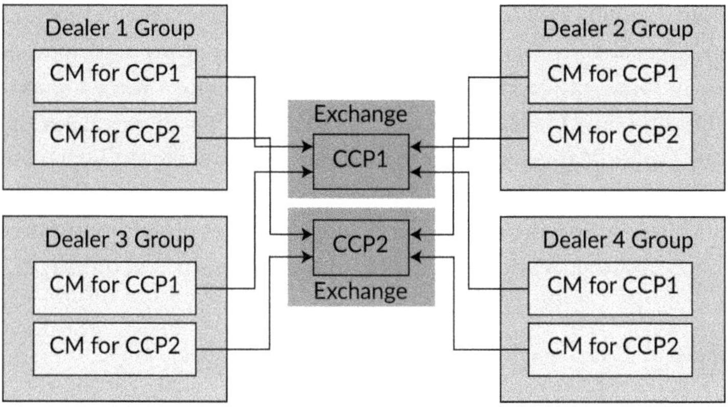

Figure 1.7– An illustration of the connections between four dealers created by exchange-traded derivatives

cross-border, creating a network of risk transfer and counterparty credit risk. Dealers, who were usually large financial institutions, competed with each other in a global market characterized by private law arrangements. In contrast, exchanges and their associated CCPs developed within national boundaries. They are club-like arrangements, mainly organized for the benefit of their clearing members, and with all trades conducted on a given exchange flowing through the associated CCP. Different exchanges competed as risk transfer venues, often with the same global financial institutions as their leading members, so a given dealer might face a number of different CCPs.

When can close-out occur?

1.53 Bankruptcy law often has the notion of a stay on claims, under which the creditors of an entity in bankruptcy or reorganization are prevented from enforcing contractual claims without authorization from the court. The idea is to give a troubled entity time to stabilize its affairs and reorganize without having to support the outflows of liquidity or the loss of assets pledged as security that would accompany the enforcement of claims.

1.54 Many countries' bankruptcy laws, including those of England and the United States, grant a 'safe harbour', allowing certain financial claims, typically including derivatives and secured financing arrangements such as repo, to be enforced. This means that portfolios protected by the safe harbour can be closed out quickly after a default: they are not stayed.[43]

[43] For conflicting views on the benefits, risks, and boundary of the derivatives safe harbour from a US perspective, see Sherrill (2015) and Schwarcz & Sharon (2015).

1.55 After the 2008 crisis discussed in the next chapter, the authorities introduced an alternative to bankruptcy for large banks known as resolution, with the aim of mitigating the risks of their disorderly failure. Since the exercise of close-out rights could make it more difficult to resolve a bank, regulators urged affected banks to adopt modifications to their derivatives contracts which limit their counterparties' termination rights should they enter resolution. Thus, for many large banks, resolution provides a form of reorganization without a derivatives safe harbour, and thus without the ability for counterparties to quickly close-out.

Collateral Against Derivatives Exposures

1.56 Netting is an effective risk reduction mechanism, but it seldom reduces risk to zero. A different approach, which can work either with or without legally enforceable netting, is the use of collateral. Here one party posts an asset to their counterparty which can be used to offset any loss should they default. The posting may be one-way or two-way, and the asset is typically either cash or a portfolio of securities. The terminology we will use is that 'margin' is the requirement for credit support, and 'collateral' is the asset posted. Thus, a CCP might issue a margin call, which is met by a clearing member posting eligible collateral.

1.57 Credit support obligations such as margin posting for derivatives portfolios are defined by the contractual documentation. For bilateral portfolios, this is typically the Credit Support Annex (or 'CSA') to the relevant ISDA Master Agreement, while for exchange traded derivatives, they are contained in the CCP's rule book. These documents specify:

- how the amount of collateral required is determined and by whom;
- when a margin call can be made and how long after that the poster has to meet it;
- how collateral must be posted and under what terms;
- what assets can be posted and if any discount, or 'haircut', is applied to their value;
- for cash collateral, how any interest paid back to the poster is determined;
- when the collateral can be taken and sold.

1.58 This section discusses the properties of collateralized derivatives portfolios.

Collateral, default, and exposure

1.59 Credit support requirements interact with events of default: failure to post collateral contractually due is often an event of default, and, after any event of default, it is usually agreed that the collateral can be taken, sold, and used to offset any loss as part of the close-out process. Any collateral which is not required to satisfy the defaulter's obligation is returned to them.

1.60 Collateral posting can sometimes introduce, as well as mitigate, counterparty credit risk. There are two common forms of posting: title transfer and security interest. In a title transfer collateral agreement, as the name suggests, the poster transfers title of the collateral asset to the recipient, and receives the conditional right to receive it[44] back if it is not required to mitigate the secured claim. This conditional right is usually unsecured.

1.61 Suppose *A* title transfers \$3M to *B* to offset the counterparty credit risk it poses to *B*, and *B* posts nothing. If *B* fails, and *A* closes out the portfolio at a value of \$2M, then *B* owes *A* the \$1M excess. However, *A*'s claim against *B*'s estate is unsecured. In contrast, in a security interest collateral agreement, *A* grants *B* an interest over assets, typically held by a third party and segregated by them. This often only grants the recipient—*B* here—the right to take sufficient collateral to meet the debt after an event of default. In this case, excess collateral posted by *A* does not create additional credit risk from the failure of *B*.

1.62 One significant difference among different credit support arrangements is the list of acceptable collateral. This ranges from very narrow, such as cash in the currency of the exposure only, to quite broad, with a wide range of bonds, and possible even equities, being accepted.

Estimates of counterparty credit risk after collateral

1.63 Collateralization is a process: the right amount has to be transferred when called for; it has to be put in the right kind of account; and the documentation must be robust in all the relevant jurisdictions. If properly conducted and legally robust, collateralization reduces the exposure on derivatives portfolios.[45] This means that expected exposure and potential future exposure measures introduced above need to be modified in its presence.

1.64 The calculation would proceed as before, simulating suitable paths of market risk factors and obtaining a distribution of portfolio values. Whatever collateral should be available under the terms of the credit support agreement is then applied. Figure 1.8 illustrates the process of determining the distribution of credit exposure after the effect of collateral: EE and PFE estimates are updated based on this new distribution.

44 Or, often, equivalent assets.

45 Thus, both the enforceability of collateral agreements in all the relevant jurisdictions, and the operational efficiency with which collateral is transferred, are important. When, as is often the case, collateral is an intermediated security, this process can involve numerous parties and governing laws. See Gullifer (2012) for further discussion of the legal risks in this process.

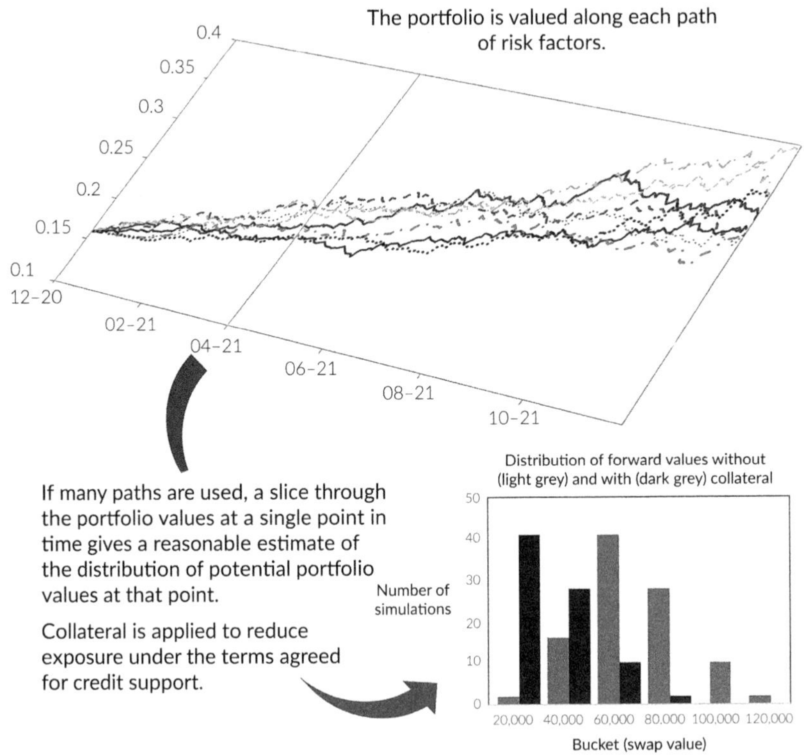

Figure 1.8– Overview of the process for estimating the distribution of credit exposure

Funding liquidity risk and collateral

1.65 There is a trade-off between counterparty credit risk reduction and funding liquidity risk creation. Counterparty credit risk for a party is lowest when the credit support arrangements agreed with its counterparties oblige them to post cash each day in the currency of the exposure, and require them to post within a short period of a collateral call. However, this arrangement requires the counterparties to obtain that cash every day. In stress, the amounts required could be large, and this is just the situation when liquidity is most difficult to find.

Margin requirements

1.66 There are two common forms of margin requirement: 'initial margin' (or 'IM') and 'variation margin' (or 'VM'). VM is collateral taken against the current exposure of a portfolio, while IM requirements provide protection against the change in value of a portfolio of derivatives between the last successful variation margin call and close-out, i.e. against the PFE.

1.67 Hedged parties have opposing variation margin requirements: if *A* does a trade with *B* which it hedges with *C*, and both trades are under credit support arrangements with daily VM, then any variation margin call from *B* will be offset by an inflow from *C*. It is convenient for whatever *C* posts to *A* to be eligible for posting on to *B*. Therefore, *A* will be reluctant to agree to collateral support arrangements where this is not true. Since the only collateral asset acceptable to everyone is cash, VM is often cash-only.

1.68 Initial margin can, depending on the agreement between the parties, be paid in cash or securities. If securities are used, a discount or 'haircut' is typically applied to their value, reflecting how much it might change during the close-out period.

1.69 Prior to the 2008 crisis, it was unusual for one dealer to agree to post IM to another: efforts were concentrated on ensuring that VM was exchanged, and that the mark-to-market of the joint portfolio it was based on was accurate as possible. More recently, regulations which require two-way posting of IM have been enacted: these are discussed in Chapter 6.

The margin period of risk

1.70 Consider a derivatives portfolio with a counterparty under a master agreement with daily variation margin. Suppose that it is the close of a trading day, and VM was posted this morning equal to the current exposure at yesterday's close. We now need to value the portfolio and the collateral using today's closing prices and call for extra collateral if required under the credit support arrangements, or pay it out, or both.[46] Any VM payments owed will be due tomorrow morning.

1.71 If the counterparty does not pay us, then there may be some grace period specified in the credit support documentation to cure the default: perhaps a few hours; perhaps days. At some point, if the default has not been cured, it will be possible to put the counterparty into default. Then the portfolio has to be closed out. If there is a loss, collateral has to be perfected[47] and sold.

1.72 The period estimated to be necessary between the last successful VM call and complete liquidation of the portfolio is known as the 'margin period of risk' or 'MPOR'. It might be reasonable to assume that it is a few days for a small or liquid derivatives portfolio; it could be significantly longer for illiquid portfolios or those that have many risk factors. It is always at least the period between variation margin calls plus any grace period for curing a failure to pay.

46 'Both' could happen because there are flows in multiple currencies: a party could be receiving cash in one currency, while paying it in another.

47 To 'perfect' collateral is to take the steps necessary to make it the unencumbered property of the party it has been posted to. This primarily refers to collateral posted under a security interest, where the collateral is typically held in an account for the benefit of the poster.

1.73 Initial margin should be sized to cover the estimated MPOR. One might therefore see a statement like 'IM is calculated at 99% for a five day MPOR', meaning that initial margin is sufficient to cover 99% of all possible moves in portfolio value over five days, and this period is estimated to be long enough to close-out the portfolio and apply available collateral against any loss. Figure 1.9 illustrates how initial margin is sized to cover the PFE over the MPOR.

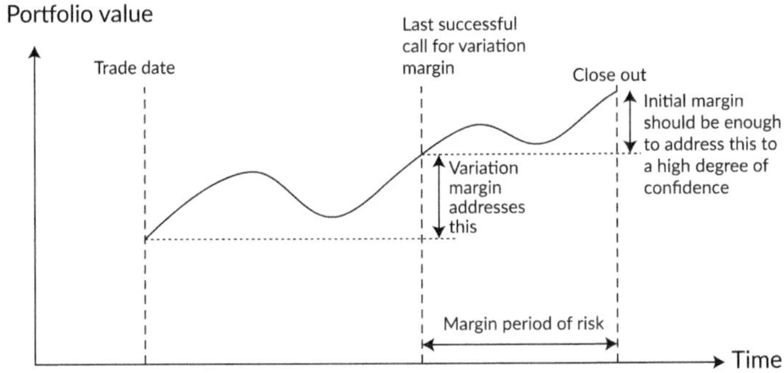

Figure 1.9– The uses of initial and variation margin

Novation

1.74 If one party to a bilateral OTC transaction wishes to terminate it before the trade's contractual maturity, then they can approach the other party. An early termination would have to be negotiated, unless it is provided for in the original documentation. The other party's terms may not be generous. Therefore it is helpful to have a mechanism for transferring a trade to a third party. This replacement of one counterparty by another is called novation.[48]

1.75 Novations can be performed on individual trades or on whole portfolios. Once a trade has been novated, it falls under the credit support arrangements with the new counterparty. Thus, the new counterparty will be bound by the terms of its ISDA Master Agreement and CSA, and both they and the party novating will have to abide by whatever collateral agreement is in place there. Meanwhile, any collateral that the novating party has posted to the old counterparty which is now not required can be returned. Novation can therefore substantially alter the collateral required both in total and fo each netting set.

1.76 Novation typically cannot take place without the consent of the remaining counterparty, partly because the entering party might be of significantly lower credit quality than the exiting one and/or have a materially less favourable CSA.

48 The process is similar to the assignment of a cleared trade to a CCP, hence the same name.

However, it is common for documents to specify that consent for a novation cannot be unreasonably withheld.

1.77 These issues do not arise in a cleared market. Here, because all clearing members face the CCP and use the credit support arrangements required by it, transactions can be assigned from one clearing member to another easily.

Credit Support and Credit Valuation Adjustments

1.78 One of the core ideas in derivatives valuation is to consider what the future cashflows might be in various states of the world. The value of a derivative is then the probability-weighted average of the present values of those cashflows.

1.79 Credit support arrangements complicate this picture because they introduce new cashflows. If cash collateral has to be posted, then this has to be funded. It may earn some interest, but at a rate that is often below where the poster funds, so the obligation to post cash collateral can introduce extra costs. In general, then, it is important to take account of credit support arrangements in derivatives valuation. A detailed account of this is beyond the scope of this book,[49] but some of the key effects of credit support arrangements on valuation and risk issues will be relevant.

Replicating portfolios and collateral

1.80 The idea of 'no arbitrage', at its simplest, says that there are no free lunches. In particular, if two trading strategies generate the same cashflows in all conditions, then they must have the same value. Thus, if a strategy can be constructed which has the same cashflows as a particular derivative in all (modelled) states of the world, then the cost of the derivative is the cost of conducting the strategy. This is a 'no free lunch' argument because if the costs differed, then profit without risk would be available by carrying out the cheaper of the two strategies and doing the opposite of the more expensive one.[50]

1.81 The well-known Black-Scholes formula for pricing options without collateral can be derived using this approach. A strategy for replicating the cashflows of the option is constructed. This involves transacting in the underlying and investing or borrowing cash as necessary at the risk-free rate.

1.82 This 'replicating portfolio' is based on the idea of continuous hedging. If the option loses \$500K for a 1% move in the price of the underlying, then the hedge position should gain the same amount for the same move. The size of the hedge

[49] For a longer discussion, see Andersen et al. (2018).

[50] This argument makes a number of unrealistic assumptions, including being able to borrow or lend at the same rate and being able to short securities without cost.

is readjusted continuously to ensure that every move in the derivative's value is matched by an equal and opposite move in the hedge's value. If this strategy is followed conscientiously, then the portfolio comprising the option and its hedges is never exposed to risk. By the 'no free lunch' principle, it must therefore grow at the risk-free rate.[51] The value of the uncollateralized option is therefore the cost of perfectly hedging it.

1.83 Once margin is present, a different hedging strategy may be needed to account for the funding of margin and the return on it. This illustrates the general point that the valuation of a derivative depends on the credit support arrangements it is subject to.

Credit valuation adjustments

1.84 A CVA is an adjustment to the value of a derivative or a portfolio which reflects the potential impact of counterparty non-performance, given the credit support arrangements that are in place. It can be thought of as the value of the counterparty credit risk.[52] This is low when there are credit support arrangements with daily cash variation margin, as the current exposure is only ever one day ahead of the collateral available. Initial margin posted by the counterparty would reduce this further, while IM posted to them, unless held so that it was remote from their bankruptcy, might increase it. The CVA therefore depends on the credit support arrangements, and the highest adjustment typically arises when there is no CSA in place.

1.85 The CVA is an input into the price dealers charge end-users for a derivative: a client wanting to trade without a CSA typically pays more for their derivatives than one who is willing to agree to daily variation margin. How much more depends on the credit-worthiness of the counterparty,[53] a notion that is often captured using a default probability.

1.86 Default probabilities are estimates of the likelihood of an unknown future.[54] There are two major approaches here, each leading to a different way of thinking about financial markets in general and CVA in particular.

---

[51] There are some conditions here, such as an absence of jumps in the value of the underlying. Also, *continuous* hedging is not possible: fortunately, discrete but regular hedging often closely matches the desired behaviour.

[52] For more details, see, for instance, Gregory (2020).

[53] See DAT (2018) for a discussion of these effects.

[54] One issue is that most credit risk modelling concentrates on estimating the probability of default of senior debt. However, this may not be the same as the probability of an event of default under an ISDA Master Agreement or a CCP rule book, as these typically have a wide range of triggers.

Types of default estimate

1.87 The first approach to estimating probabilities of default is to use classification and history. The counterparty is put into a class of similar companies, for instance using an industry sector and a credit rating. The historical likelihood of default of companies in the same class is determined. The assumption is that the counterparty at hand will behave as others in the same class have.[55]

1.88 One issue here is the extent to which historical estimates vary through the economic cycle. Companies tend to default at a greater rate in recessions, and this is especially so for lower credit quality companies. Thus, an average default rate across the economic cycle, known as a 'through the cycle probability of default', underestimates default rates in stress and overestimates them in placid conditions. On the other hand, it is more difficult to make estimates of probabilities of default contingent on current economic conditions, as there is less historical data to average over. Therefore, while so-called point in time estimates of probabilities of default take into account the current position in an economic cycle, they are more difficult to estimate reliably. They may also over- or undershoot if current estimates of future conditions are wrong.

1.89 Figure 1.10 illustrates the typical variation of long-term average historical probabilities of default by credit rating. These kinds of default probability are sometimes termed 'real-world'. A probability of default like this might be suitable for estimating expected credit loss provisions.[56]

1.90 There were significant CVA losses on some derivatives portfolios during and after the 2008 crisis, discussed in more detail in the next chapter. This brought the materiality of some banks' CVA risk to the fore. Around this time, there was a debate about the nature of CVA. Some market participants, mostly commercial banks, took the view that credit extension was their business, and that CVA is just an expected credit risk loss provision. Therefore they advocated calculating it using real-world probabilities of default.

---

55 More details on the validation of such estimates can be found in BCBS (2005a).

56 A 'provision' is a reduction in the value of an asset or increase in the value of a liability. An 'expected loss provision' is a reduction reflecting an estimate of future credit losses. Accounting standards require that these estimates of credit losses should be 'reasonable and supportable'. There are two slightly different approaches. In the United States, parties recognize a provision for their estimate of *lifetime* expected credit losses. In contrast, entities using International Financial Reporting Standards ('IFRS') provision for *one year* expected credit losses if the creditor has not experienced a significant increase in credit risk, and lifetime expected credit losses if it has. In both cases, current economic conditions are clearly relevant for the expectation of future losses, so point in time estimates of default probabilities will tend to be favoured over through the cycles ones for provisioning. See Cohen & Edwards (2017) for more details.

Credit Rating	Probability of Default
AAA	0.002%
AA	0.01%
A	0.04%
BBB	0.3%
BB	1.4%
B	7%
CCC	25%

Figure 1.10– Estimates of real-world one year probabilities of corporate default associated with a given credit rating

1.91 This approach was intellectually coherent, but it did not win out. Instead, an approach based on market estimates of default probabilities rose to prominence. Here, instead of asking:

How often might we expect a counterparty to default, given history?

as we would in calculating real-world probabilities of default, we instead ask:

How much would it cost to buy protection against losses caused by the default of a counterparty?

1.92 The key input in answering this second question is the counterparty's credit default swap ('CDS') spread, as buying CDS protection referencing a counterparty allows us to hedge the risk of their default. It is straightforward to infer a probability of default from a CDS spread by assuming that the whole of the spread is compensation for default risk. By fixing a recovery value, we can use the market compensation given default to calculate the default probability. The resulting probability is often larger than would be inferred using a historical approach. Amato & Remolona (2003) at 51 explain the phenomenon like this:

Spreads on corporate bonds tend to be many times wider than what would be implied by expected default losses alone ... In 1997–2003, for example, the average spread on BBB-rated corporate bonds ... was more than eight times the expected loss from default.

1.93 The reason for this is that credit spreads are compensation for taking more risks than just default risk. These additional non-default risks include credit spread volatility and market liquidity risk. A probability backed out from credit spreads is sometimes called a 'risk-neutral probability'.

1.94 Suppose that CVA is calculated using risk-neutral probabilities, and consider a counterparty with a portfolio and CSA that generates a material CVA. As noted above, this counterparty will typically have been charged for the CVA when each trade was put on, based on its CDS spread at that point. If this spread widens, the CVA would increase, and there would be a loss. In order to hedge this, a CDS referencing the counterparty can sometimes be purchased.

1.95 In general, the CVA is something whose value depends on a variety of market factors—the parameters which drive the value of the portfolio—and on the counterparty's credit spread. Thus, CVA hedging involves taking positions in all of these risks factors to eliminate the CVA's sensitivity to changes in them. If CVA hedging is successful, then any losses caused by increasing CVA will be offset by gains on the hedges. In this setting CVA can be thought of as a (complicated) derivative which should be marked to market along with its hedges.

1.96 This illustrates that there are two fundamentally different views of CVA: as a risk that is taken, like the credit risk in a loan; and as a risk that is hedged, like a market risk position. Each business model suggests a different kind of probability of default: real-world for the 'take the risk' model, and risk-neutral for hedging. Unfortunately, this diversity is not fully respected in accounting standards. These are often interpreted as disallowing the use of real-world probabilities, so most banks now mark CVA to market using risk-neutral probabilities.[57]

Regulating Counterparty Credit Risk

1.97 Thus far, derivatives contracts have been introduced and their risks discussed. The key technology of netting has been introduced, and collateral has been discussed. Close-out netting and collateralization are vital to mitigating the counterparty credit risk of derivatives. In this section, the key ideas used in the prudential treatment of counterparty credit risk by bank regulators are introduced.[58] These are based on the calculation of the exposure distribution through time for a derivatives portfolio illustrated in Figure 1.8.

1.98 Prudential requirements for a given risk typically define a measure, then use that measure to define a resources requirement. Capital requirements are a well-known example: bank regulators set a requirement for the amount of capital banks are required to have to support a given risk, based on some measure of potential losses. The earliest examples were capital requirements for credit risk, as credit risk is the most important risk in the banking system.

57 The general principle in IFRS is that the valuation of a derivative should be to a price which is the best estimate of where it could be transferred, capturing 'market participants' expectations about the liquidity, uncertainty and other associated factors'. So this does not actually require that CVA is marked to market; just that it should be marked where a buyer of the risk would mark it. See IFRS 13, *Fair Value Measurement*, 2013.

58 Broadly, this account relates to the internal models method for counterparty credit risk introduced in Basel 2. See Chapter 5 for a longer account of capital requirements for various derivatives risks.

1.99 The rules for counterparty credit risk are designed to feed into these credit risk rules: they 'preprocess' a derivatives portfolio to create a loan-equivalent, which can then be treated alongside all the other loans in a bank's banking book.

1.100 The credit risk rules are based on three properties of the riskiness of an obligation. The probability of default of a creditor has already been introduced above. The other two properties are the fraction of the amount owed which will be irrecoverable on default, the loss given default or 'LGD'; and the exposure at default, or 'EAD'. The LGD is a property of the counterparty and the seniority of the debt, so derivatives do not introduce substantial extra complexity into this measure. The main question is determining EAD: how should the exposure at default on a derivatives portfolio be estimated, given that it varies through time and as markets move? This is considered next.

Effective measures

1.101 One starting point is the expected exposure or EE. As discussed above, this is the average credit exposure at a point in time, i.e. the average of the positive part of the distribution of portfolio values. Regulators want to ensure that the EAD for a derivatives portfolio is a conservative estimate of the exposure. Suppose that EE is calculated for each business day in the next year,[59] giving a sequence of values EE(1), EE(2), ...EE(250). The 'effective EE' on a day is the maximum of the current expected exposure and the previous day's effective EE:

$$\text{effective EE}(1) = \text{EE}(1)$$
$$\text{effective EE}(n) = \max\left(\text{EE}(n-1), \text{effective EE}(n-1)\right)$$

1.102 The 'expected positive exposure' or 'EPE' is the average of the effective EEs. This is a kind of average of the credit exposure over the time period considered. Finally, the 'effective EPE' is the average over one year (or the maturity of the netting set, if shorter) of the effective EEs.

From effective EPE to EAD

1.103 The effective EPE is a reasonable candidate for the EAD over one year[60] on a derivatives portfolio, but regulators were concerned that this measure was not sufficiently conservative. Therefore it was decided to take the EAD as a multiple of the effective EPE by setting EAD = $\alpha \times$ effective EPE. The multiplier, α was set in international standards at 1.4.[61]

59 The bank prudential framework for credit risk is based on the next year's exposure, so this is used in the counterparty credit risk rules too.

60 The Basel 2 credit risk calculation is based on a one year horizon.

61 See Canabarro et al. (2003) for a discussion of the reason for the α parameter and an estimation of its value.

Portfolio credit risk models

1.104 The structure of the calculation of the capital requirement for credit risk is:

- for each asset, gather the relevant properties such as probability of default, exposure at default and loss given default;
- calculate the capital requirement for each asset based on those properties;
- add up the capital requirements to obtain a total.

1.105 This calculation needs to model how many creditors default in the same year. To see the problem, consider two situations. In the first, there is a portfolio of loans which is large and diversified across industries, countries, and types of firm. In the second, there is a portfolio of the same size, but all the loans are to High Street clothing retailers in the same country. Clearly in a situation which affects these retailers badly, such as Covid, the latter portfolio will be riskier than the former because many of the loans could become distressed together. This can be roughly thought of as a correlation: if many of the loans are correlated to a single factor, then a large loss on the portfolio is more likely than if they are not.

1.106 A model of portfolio credit risk needs to capture the relationship between defaults. It turns out that correlation is too simplistic a measure to capture all the situations of interest, so the term 'default comovement' is used to refer to the various ways in which the defaults of different obligors can be associated.[62]

1.107 Models of default comovement tend to share the following structure:

- The model postulates some relationship between defaults.[63]
- This model has some free parameters which must be calibrated.
- Some data—typically either the prices of traded securities or historical credit information—is used to calibrate the model.
- The model then makes predictions about the likelihood of various patterns of defaults.

1.108 One problem is that the relationship between the default of different counterparties depends not just on the shared characteristics of the counterparties—whether they are in the same industry, for instance—but also on the broader economy. When the global economy is growing, defaults tend to reflect idiosyncratic issues with individual firms or, at most, industry sectors or countries; but when the economy is in recession, many firms can fail in a short period of time.[64]

---

[62] This is often captured mathematically by the notion of copula: see for instance Fischer (2015) or Ackerer (2017).

[63] Or between related quantities such as the asset values of obligators.

[64] As we will see in Chapter 2, characteristics which are shared between different obligors can also increase the tendency for defaults to be correlated in some conditions.

Capital and unexpected loss

1.109 A risk measure usually quantifies how much might be lost were a situation to unfold badly. As we saw for credit exposure on derivatives, risk estimation often proceeds by first estimating the distribution of returns for some portfolio as risk factors move at a fixed time horizon, then taking some high percentile of it as the risk measure. This risk estimate is used to set the minimum level of loss-absorbing resources—capital—required for the portfolio.

1.110 For some portfolios, such as ones involving credit risk, it is conventional to separate positive income from the portfolio from losses and consider just the loss distribution.[65] The terms 'expected loss' and 'unexpected loss' are used here: the expected loss, or 'EL' on the portfolio is the average of the loss distribution, while the unexpected loss or 'UL' is estimated as some high percentile (99.9% perhaps) of it. Regulators and accounting standards setters require that banks provision for expected loss,[66] and the capital required for a portfolio of credit risk is UL minus EL. Figure 1.11 illustrates the ideas: the analogy with EE and PFE should be clear.

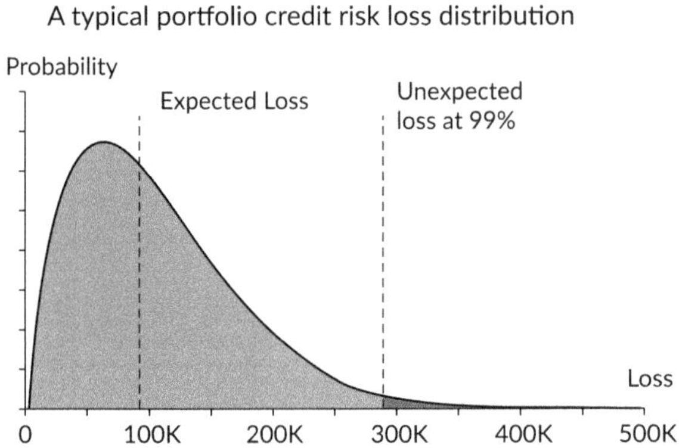

Figure 1.11- Expected and unexpected loss at 99% confidence for a typical shape of portfolio credit risk loss distribution. The area in darker grey is 1% of that of the whole distribution

1.111 A model of default comovement allows a number of individual exposures to different parties to be combined and properties of the resulting portfolio loss distribution, such as EL and UL, estimated.

[65] This is partly due to the accounting: in the amortized cost accounting used in the loan book, net interest income is recognized as it is earned, while provisions for expected loan losses are re-estimated each quarter over the life of the loan. When new provisions are taken, they reduce earnings. The risk being capitalized is therefore a loss to earnings caused by an increase in either expected loss or incurred loss provisions.

[66] Albeit in slightly different ways.

1.112 Regulators use a particular default comovement model known as the internal ratings based ('IRB') model. This uses a single systematic risk factor, to be thought of as the state of the global economy; different exposures are related through their correlation with this single risk factor.[67] In this setting, the step in the capital calculation 'Calculate the capital requirement for each asset' should be thought of as 'Calculate the incremental capital required for this asset, assuming a given correlation with the single risk factor'.

1.113 The choice of whether to use real-world or risk-neutral probabilities also occurs in default comovement models. Using real-world probabilities would be appropriate for modelling portfolios of loans, where, broadly, credit risk is run rather than hedged.[68] Risk-neutral probabilities would be appropriate for portfolios that are being hedged or marked to market.

Central Clearing of OTC Derivatives

1.114 One approach to mitigating the counterparty credit risk of derivatives is to ensure that there are resources available to absorb any losses that arise, either in the form of collateral or capital or both. Another is to change the structure of the market so that there is less direct counterparty credit risk, and to have a party with a lot of resources taking that risk: a central counterparty.

1.115 CCPs have already been introduced as entities which sit between two parties in a contract, so that neither is directly exposed to the counterparty risk of the other. Exchange-traded derivatives markets are typically entirely centrally cleared by a CCP affiliated with the exchange, and central clearing is common in securities markets, too. Latterly, central clearing was adopted by OTC derivatives markets: the arrangement illustrated in Figure 1.7 does not require that the derivatives were originally traded on an exchange. Regulators then mandated its use in many cases: this is discussed in Chapter 6.

1.116 The late adoption of OTC derivatives clearing partly reflects the fact that these transactions often involve much longer term exposures than securities settlement or exchange-traded derivatives, and trade sizes are often larger, so OTC derivatives CCPs need a lot of resources to be robust. Setting up a CCP for OTC derivatives is a substantial task.

---

67 Default comovement models which use this approach are known as single risk factor models. The regulatory choice uses an approximation to the loss distribution which approaches the real one when portfolios are large and well diversified, known as an asymptotic single risk factor model. For a further discussion, see BCBS (2005b).

68 Banks often hedge some credit risk in the loan book, but typically they do not seek to fully eliminate their exposure to it. In contrast, CVA desks often do seek to fully hedge credit spread risk.

1.117 The multilateral netting available through central clearing has already been discussed. This is so important that it is worth repeating: rather than having separate exposures to different market participants, a party facing a CCP only has a single net exposure to it. Multilateral netting often substantially reduces counterparty credit risk, and it is one of the principal benefits of central clearing.

1.118 It is a commonplace of explanations of derivatives central clearing to present a diagram which compares bilateral with centrally cleared markets, and to illustrate the latter with a single CCP at the centre, like a spider, with all trades going through it. This is an idealization, as many trades are not clearable and there are often multiple CCPs clearing various markets. Moreover, within banking groups, there are usually multiple entities trading derivatives, and different entities may be used for bilateral trades and to access different CCPs. Based on this, a somewhat more realistic picture of a small group of banks interacting with CCPs and each other using derivatives is given in Figure 1.12.

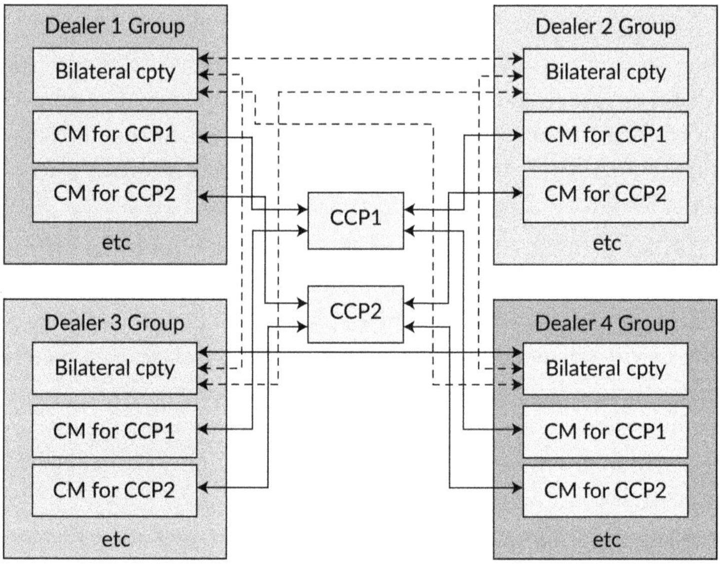

Figure 1.12– Conceptual schematic showing four financial institutions trading derivatives some of which are bilateral, some cleared at one CCP, and some at another. Cleared trades are shown using solid lines; bilateral as dashed ones

Participating in clearing

1.119 CCPs impose minimum standards on the parties they will accept as clearing members. These relate to both the standing and expertise of the party and performance at the CCP. Minimum levels of capital and/or credit quality, and the demonstration of sufficient systems and expertise to manage the products cleared, are typically specified. In addition, the performance requirements include posting initial and variation margin to the CCP on at least a daily basis. Many CCP rule books also give the CCP the right to issue not just initial and variation margin calls at the end of each trading day, but also to issue 'intraday' VM calls, perhaps if the market has moved significantly. Clearing members are required to meet these calls in cash within a period as short as two hours.

1.120 CCPs usually have a layer of mutualized resources which clearing members are required to provide, known as the 'default fund'. These resources are available to absorb potential losses caused by the close-out of a defaulting clearing member's portfolio, should that member's margin prove insufficient. (CCPs' management of defaults and the resources available for this are discussed further below and in Chapter 7.)

1.121 There are also other clearing member performance requirements, such as requirements to participate in CCP default auctions. These are discussed further in Chapter 7. Many derivatives participants either cannot meet the all of the requirements to be a clearing member or do not want to meet them, perhaps because they do not want to contribute towards the default fund. These 'clients' access clearing through a clearing member.

1.122 There are two main approaches to client clearing:

- Outside the United States, the client typically faces the clearing member as principal and the clearing member (or 'CM') in turn faces the CCP as principal. This is known as the 'principal-to-principal' model. The client to CM trade is governed by whatever arrangements these two parties have negotiated, as documented in a clearing agreement; the CM to CCP trade is governed by the CCP's rule book. If the client defaults, the responsibility for closing out falls on the CM, so the CM has counterparty credit risk just as it would have in a bilateral trade with the same client.
- US CCPs use a different paradigm known as the 'agency model'. Here the CM acts as agent for the client, introducing them to the CCP.[69] The CM also guarantees the client's performance to the CCP, so the CM is exposed to the credit of the client just as it is in the principal-to-principal model.

1.123 Adding clients into the picture complicates Figure 1.12 further, especially as clients may have bilateral trades with the group their clearing member is in as well as portfolios cleared at various CCPs. Figure 1.13 illustrates one possibility, with each group having clients using each CCP under principal-to-principal clearing.

[69] The term 'agency model' is ubiquitous, but OTC derivatives clearing is not a pure agency model in that the customer has few direct contractual remedies against the CCP, and the clearing member both guarantees the client's performance and enforces the CCPs' rules upon them.

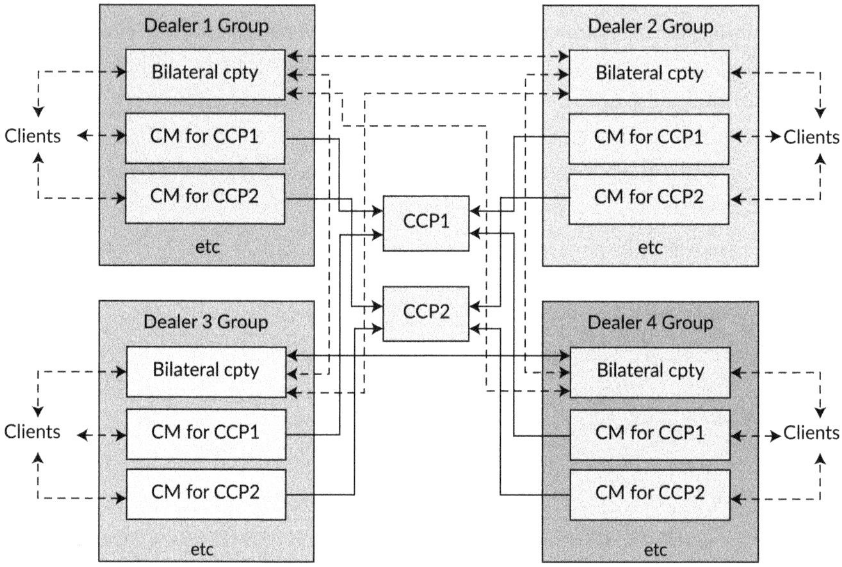

Figure 1.13– Conceptual schematic showing four dealers trading derivatives with each other and with clients

1.124 A clearing member's portfolio of its own cleared trades is known as its 'house' account at the CCP. These are kept separate from client trades, which may be held in a single account, with trades from different clients commingled; or into multiple accounts. The choice of how to handle client trades is known as the segregation model.[70] It affects the degree of 'fellow client' risk: if clients are commingled, and the clearing member fails, then a simultaneous default by one client could lead to losses for another.

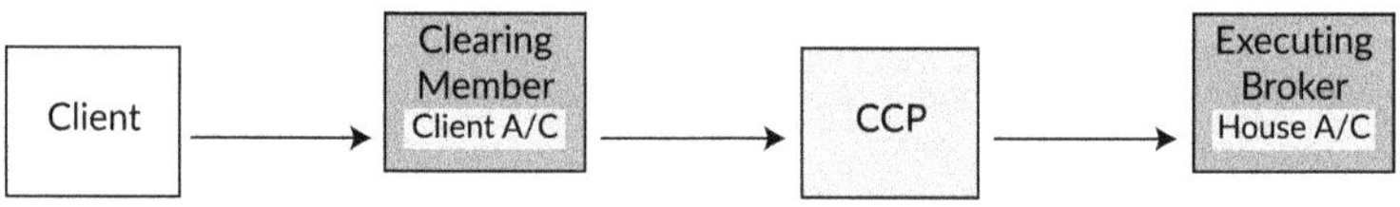

Figure 1.14– The accounts involved in clearing a client trade

1.125 A client trades a cleared derivative by finding a party to transact with who clears at the same CCP—or one of the same CCPs—as the client's clearing member. This party, known as the executing broker, might or might not be in the same group as the clearing member. The trade and the choice of CCP are agreed. The trade is cleared through the client's clearing member across the CCP, as illustrated Figure 1.14. The client and their clearing member have counterparty credit risk to each other, mitigated by whatever collateral support has been agreed

[70] This choice may be constrained by regulation.

between them. The client's clearing member is protected from counterparty credit exposure to the executing broker by the CCP, and from risk to the client by whatever credit support arrangements they have agreed with them.

Porting and standardization

1.126 One of the key features of clearing is that CCPs set standard terms for all the trades they clear. This means that clearing members share a common language, and any cleared portfolio should be readily analysable by all the CCP's clearing members.[71] Therefore it should be possible to move or 'port' a client cleared portfolio from one clearing member to another relatively easily, provided that there is sufficient margin in place.

1.127 CCPs have knowledge of the entire portfolio of each clearing member. This makes it easy for them to provide ancillary services. An important example here is the elimination of redundant trades. These arise if, for instance, *A* has a cleared trade with *B* and an exactly hedging trade cleared at the same CCP with *C*. From *A*'s perspective, these trades with the CCP offset each other perfectly. A process of optimization known as trade 'compression' identifies and eliminates these unnecessary transactions. The number of cleared trades and the total cleared notional are thereby reduced.[72]

CCP initial margin models

1.128 CCPs require initial margin on cleared portfolios. Typically margin is the sum of several components. The largest is usually a 'models-based' requirement, where the task of the model is to estimate some property of the portfolio return distribution over the CCP's chosen margin period of risk. For OTC derivatives, this MPOR is required by regulation to be at least five days. The property must be at least the 99.5th percentile of the return distribution, and some leading CCPs set higher initial margin requirements than this.[73] Many CCPs then add extra requirements if the portfolio is large compared to market liquidity or if the clearing member is lower credit quality.[74] The additional requirements are sometimes called margin 'add ons'.

71 Strictly, this only applies within a given clearing service at the CCP. ('Clearing service' is defined in paragraph 1.137.)

72 Trade compression is also important because it reduces any burden, like the leverage ratio exposure measure, which depends on the notional of OTC derivatives. This is discussed further in Chapter 4.

73 Another choice some CCPs make is to use the expected shortfall of the return distribution rather than a quantile estimate.

74 Another situation where extra margin may be required is if the default of the clearing members is more likely in situations where the portfolio value increases. This is known as 'wrong way risk' and is particularly noticeable in credit default swap clearing.

CCPs as default managers

1.129 A core function of a CCP is to manage clearing member defaults. The CCP's rule book usually sets out guidance on how this process is to be conducted.

1.130 The first issue is when to trigger default management. There are usually automatic triggers which mandate close-out, and discretionary ones which allow but do not require it. A bankruptcy filing by the clearing member would typically fall into the former category, while a loss of confidence in the clearing member might be in the latter.[75]

1.131 If a clearing member defaults, the CCP has to close-out the trades in its house account. There is more flexibility with regard to client trades. If it is possible to port them, then clients will not suffer the costs associated with their trades being closed out and, presumably, having to re-establish them using a different clearing member.

1.132 Once a default has been triggered, the CCP no longer has a balanced position. The clearing member on one side of a trade has defaulted, but the CCP still has to perform to the clearing member on the other side. Therefore the CCP has to re-balance its position. If the defaulter was long, the CCP must sell; if it was short, it must buy. CCPs have a process for conducting this rebalancing. This usually involves convening a default management group, deciding on the liquidation strategy, and executing it. The group might for instance decide first to hedge the biggest risks in the defaulter's portfolio, then to auction the hedged portfolio; or to trade directly in the market.

1.133 The default management process will often involve losses: the CCP will have to pay more to exit the defaulter's position than its mark-to-market value at the point of default. CCPs hold financial resources to absorb these losses, as discussed next.

Resources for default management

1.134 The collection and availability of default resources, and the certainty about the CCP's right to use them, are fundamental to the safe operation of clearing.[76]

---

[75] CCP rules often grant a significant measure of discretion here. For instance, LCH's default rules say in part that the clearing house may begin default management in 'the event of a Clearing Member *appearing* to the Clearing House to be unable, or *to be likely to become unable* to meet its obligations in respect of one or more Contracts' (emphasis mine). See R. London Clearing House (2010).

[76] Indeed, as Braithwaite & Murphy (2017a) discusses, this is reflected in the definition of clearing in EU regulation as 'the process of establishing positions, including the calculation of net obligations, and *ensuring that financial instruments, cash, or both, are available to secure the exposures arising from those positions*' (emphasis mine).

1.135 The CCP's resources are organized into a 'default waterfall' with earlier resources being used first. Before a default, the CCP's book is matched: for every trade coming in to the CCP from a clearing member, there is one going out to another.[77] If there is a default, the CCP loses one leg of some trades. It closes out the defaulter's position to restore itself to a matched book, either by auctioning the position or by trading in the open market. This process will likely generate gains or losses. Any gains are returned to the defaulter's estate. Losses are absorbed in the order specified by the default waterfall. Typically the following resources are available in order:

- the defaulter's margin and default fund contribution;
- a layer of the CCP's own capital, sometimes known as 'skin in the game';
- non-defaulting clearing member's default fund contributions;
- further resources, usually including the ability to 'call' for additional clearing member contributions to the default fund.

1.136 After this, additional 'end of the waterfall' tools may be available to absorb very large default losses. Common tools are the ability to curtail positive variation margin payouts to clearing members, and the ability to 'tear up' trades, i.e. to terminate them at a price set by the CCP.

Services and netting

1.137 Another good reason to consider central clearing with multiple centres, as in Figures 1.12 and 1.13, is that often CCP legal entities contain a number of clearing services, with each service clearing only a single asset class or related collection of products. Thus, there might be an interest rate derivatives clearing service, a credit derivatives clearing service, and so on. Margin is calculated on a per-service basis, so there is no cross service netting of risk. Each service has its own default fund too, but the different services can share a common infrastructure for calling margin, making payments, and so on.

1.138 The term 'CCP' is used loosely for an entity or group of entities providing clearing services. There may be a legal entity housing one clearing service or several; there may be multiple legal entities providing clearing services within the same group; the legal entity with the clearing service may also engage in other activities, such as providing an exchange. In particular, securities CCPs typically have a related securities settlement system. The broader term 'financial market infrastructure' or 'FMI' is often used for CCPs and other market services such as payment systems, central securities depositories, and securities settlement systems.

77 If it goes back to the same account at the same clearing member, then it just nets out.

1.139 A major benefit of central clearing is the multilateral netting of bilateral exposures into a single exposure to a clearing service. But against this is the fact that even if all the trades between *A* and *B* and *A* and *C* were clearable, they would likely need to be cleared by multiple services. If we were dealing not just with *B* and *C* but with many counterparties, each with many trades, then the effect of clearing in practice will likely still be lower counterparty credit risk. However, this depends on the number of services and the balance of trades cleared at each of them. CCP fragmentation, and the fact that some trades remain uncleared, often because they are not clearable, reduces the benefit of multilateral netting from central clearing.[78]

1.140 This reveals one of the important policy issues in central clearing. The largest benefit comes from having a single global CCP, but the stress of such a party—or indeed any CCP which has a large share of clearing a given asset class—would create financial instability. This means that large CCPs must both be highly robust and be seen to be so. Realizing the full benefits of clearing requires accepting very large concentrations of risk in global CCPs.[79]

[78] For a fuller discussion of these issues, see Duffie & Zhu (2011).

[79] Different parties can reasonably differ on whether the benefits are worth the risks here, especially given the supervisory arrangements in place for such global CCPs. We return to this issue in Chapter 7.

2

The 2008 Crisis and the Regulatory Response to It

Introduction

2.1 David Cannadine, following Eric Hobsbawm's magisterial lead, has written an engaging account of how traditions came to be invented to support the power of the British monarchy.[1] He points out that the weddings, funerals and coronations of British monarchs in the centuries before Victoria were often scrappy, informal affairs with little of the pageant that is now associated with them. It was only when it became necessary to consolidate and amplify national power that royal ceremonies acquired their current pomp. Choirs became better drilled, Westminster Abbey better appointed, and preparations markedly more elaborate. Despite their recent (re)invention, these pageants were given a patina of antiquity as fictive as the King Arthur they evoked. Many of the 'traditions' practised in the funeral of George V had in fact been invented for that of Edward VII only 26 years earlier, for instance. This example illustrates how accounts of the past are often remade in service of present interests. Knowing this, it is important to examine critically any claims about the lessons that prior events hold for the present.

2.2 Financial regulation typically evolves in the shadow of a crisis.[2] It changed enormously in response to the crisis associated with the failure of the investment bank Lehman Brothers. This crisis peaked in 2008, so we will use the shorthand '2008 crisis' for it. It was very expensive, with large direct losses and even larger lost output: for the United States alone estimates of these losses range 'from a

---

1 See Cannadine (1983). Hobsbawm's 'lead' was his concept of invented tradition set out in the first chapter of the same volume in which Cannadine's chapter appears.

2 Coffee (2012) at 1029 describes the phenomenon whereby 'regulatory oversight is never constant, but rather increases after a market crash, and then wanes as (and to the extent that) society and the market return to normalcy'. This is discussed further in Chapter 11.

few trillion dollars to over $10 trillion'.[3] The crisis originated within the financial system, starting with residential mortgages, and spreading to become a crisis of confidence in financial institutions.

2.3 We begin by giving a short account of the phases of the crisis. The following section discusses how finance damaged itself, and the broader economy, so badly; how regulators reacted to the crisis; and how they have subsequently described that reaction.

The Phases of the 2008 Crisis

2.4 Momentous events may appear sudden and unforeseeable as they are occurring. But, in retrospect, it is often possible to see the factors and influences assembling well before the event itself. With the 2008 financial crisis, the precursors lie in the US residential property market of mid-2000s. Design and incentive problems in this market led to a dramatic and eventually unsupportable growth in credit extension: we begin with this part of the story.[4]

Phase 1: the mortgage boom and the 'power of yes'

2.5 Financial transactions have two parties, a buyer and a seller. Deleterious consequences can result if one of them is badly motivated or has incentives that create uncompensated and undisclosed risks. But really bad things result if the self-interest of *both* parties is to do bad things.

2.6 This was often the case in the US residential mortgage market of the early to mid-2000s. During that period in the United States, buying houses was an attractive proposition. House prices doubled from the start of 2000 to 2006, and mortgages were readily available. A mortgage is a leveraged investment in the property: the borrower pays only a fraction of the house price, and uses the property as collateral for the loan. When house prices are rising and finance is cheap, this is an appealing investment.[5]

---

[3] The quote is from the United States Government Accountability Office inquiry into the 2008 crisis: see USGAO (2013) at 2.

[4] Much of the material in this section is based on Murphy (2009). For other accounts, see Calomiris & Haber (2015), Mishkin (2011) or Shiller (2012).

[5] 'The power of yes' was an advertising slogan used by Washington Mutual or 'WaMu'. WaMu was the United States' largest savings and loan association until its subsidiary, WaMu Bank, was seized by its regulator on 25 September 2008. The firm had sustained substantial losses on residential mortgages. This caused a loss of confidence in the firm and a run on deposits which, when Lehman failed ten days earlier, had become large enough to threaten the bank. WaMu Bank was at the time the largest bank failure in American financial history: it was subsequently sold to JPMorgan Chase. The slogan 'Power of Yes' is therefore a good reminder of the risk of extending mortgage credit.

2.7 A feature of residential mortgages in some states makes them even more attractive to borrowers. Lender recourse to the borrower on a residential mortgage is a matter of state law, and some states, especially in the Western half of the US, do not permit it.[6] That is, the lender can only use the mortgaged property to meet the amount owed; they do not have a claim on the borrower. It is a heads I win, tails you lose situation; if property prices continue to go up, borrowers made money. If they fall, the borrower can, in a non-recourse state, walk away from the property with few other consequences.[7]

2.8 The US mortgage market historically had a loan structure that was relatively safe for borrowers: the 30 year, fixed rate, prepayable mortgage. This locked in borrowing costs in nominal terms for the duration of the mortgage. However, because this mortgage structure was based on long-term interest rates, it was relatively expensive.[8] Mortgage lenders therefore invented a variety of structures to make mortgages cheaper.

2.9 One of the most successful was the ARM, or adjustable rate mortgage: this was based on short-term interest rates, and had a substantially lower headline rate than the 30 year fixed rate mortgage at the cost of exposing the borrower to the risk of rising interest rates. These features were turbo-charged in the hybrid ARM, where borrowers had a short period, perhaps one or two years, of very low payments; but then these reset to payments based on a floating rate plus a (usually big) spread.[9] Essentially the borrower was delaying the true cost of their borrowing. If property prices went up the meantime, they could sell before the reset: but if they did not, then borrower might not be able to afford the higher rate, and hence was at a higher risk of default. These risks were hidden while house prices were rising: even mortgages made to borrowers of poor credit quality—those without verified income, or with a prior history of not paying their debts,

---

[6] Non-recourse states include Alaska, Arizona, California, Connecticut, Idaho, Minnesota, North Carolina, North Dakota, Oregon, Texas, Utah, and Washington. For an account of the role of recourse in mortgage defaults, see Ghent & Kudlyak (2011). Even in states with recourse, processes differ. Some states, such as Florida, require that a judge hear a foreclosing petition: this became a problem in 2007 when court capacity was inadequate to hear the volume of foreclosure petitions lenders wished to make. See Li (2009) for a discussion of the interaction between states' legal arrangements and the risks of residential mortgage lending.

[7] Other than a temporary reduction in their credit rating.

[8] Not only was this mortgage price based on long-term rates, the fact that it was prepayable meant that the borrower had, in effect, bought an interest rate option from the lender, and they had to pay for this option. If rates fell, borrowers could often refinance, depriving lenders of an asset just when it became more valuable, while if rates rose, borrowers would tend to hold on to their now-below-market loan.

[9] Relatedly, in the 'option ARM' the borrower could choose each month whether to make, e.g., a minimum payment, an interest-only payment, or a payment based on an amortization schedule.

say—looked good, because it was in the interest of all borrowers to pay their mortgages and thereby retain the rising equity they had in the house. Moreover, mortgage payments in the period before the reset were relatively cheap, so making these payments was relatively easy.

2.10 Some lenders were misled by these hidden risks. They misestimated the risks of mortgage lending, both in the dimension of the likelihood the borrower would repay and the value of collateral held if they didn't. Borrower credit quality and the average loan-to-value ('LTV') ratios of residential mortgages fell, especially in areas of high population growth such as much of Arizona, California, Florida, and Nevada. Risk misestimates led banks to make more—and more risky—loans. With more borrowers and cheaper finance available, more houses were built, some of them in marginal areas which were only considered viable because house prices in better locations were rising so fast.[10]

2.11 Why did lenders make these mistakes? Much of the answer lies in the disintermediated nature of the US residential mortgage market. One might think of a bank designing a mortgage, marketing it, assessing loan applications, lending funds, and holding the risk. But it was rarely this simple. A bank might design and market a mortgage structure, but that marketing was to mortgage brokers, who would advise borrowers on loans and in some cases fill in the loan application for them. The loan might well be sold on several times, and the ultimate holder of the risk might not even have access to the original loan application. This kind of specialization, where loans were made with the intent of selling them on, is known as the 'originate to distribute' model. It had the disadvantage that those making lending decisions did not always have a stake in the consequences of those decisions.

2.12 Two further features of the financial system were also important to the development of the crisis. First, the United States is unusual among advanced economies in the role that the government plays in residential mortgage lending. Government-sponsored enterprises or 'GSE's hold a significant fraction of residential mortgages, particularly high quality ones.

2.13 The most important GSEs in the residential mortgage market were (and are) Fannie Mae and Freddie Mac.[11] The GSEs had huge economies of scale, and highly diversified pools of mortgage risk. These pools were attractive to investors, so the enterprises created the mortgage-backed securities ('MBS') market to fund

---

[10] See Ellis (2008).

[11] These two GSEs backed roughly half of all home loan originations in 2002. As mortgage quality fell, so did their market share, so they were supporting about 30% of new loans in 2005 and 2006. This decline caused them to increase the risks that they took. For more details, see Frame et al. (2015).

themselves.[12] This market was deepened by the issuance of MBS by private entities. It made the originate to distribute model possible.[13]

2.14 The second feature of the financial system in the mid-2000s that was important as a crisis incubator was the huge demand for safe assets combined with their relatively scarce supply.[14] The financial system met the need by manufacturing pseudo-safe assets. It did this by pooling mortgages and tranching the resulting pool of risk into various tranches of MBS. One would suffer the first defaults up to a fixed maximum; the next would suffer if defaults exceeded this amount up to another maximum; and so on.[15] The higher tranches of these securitizations attracted AAA ratings due to the perceived low probability that default rates would be high enough to endanger them.[16] Meeting the demand for safe assets via tranching pools of residential mortgage risk had the side effect of increasing demand for these pools and hence decreasing the cost of mortgage borrowing. But as newly originated mortgages became riskier, the securities backed by them became riskier too.[17] At first this increase in risk was hidden by tranching: the AAA-rated MBS tranches were safe at average or even (what were thought to be) somewhat elevated levels of mortgage defaults.[18]

2.15 The use of tranching to break a pool of assets into a range of securities of various risk and return levels was not confined to residential mortgages. The term 'collateralized debt obligation' or 'CDO' is used for any structure where a pool of assets supports one or more tranches of liabilities. The terms originally used for the various tranches in MBS—senior for less risky, lower return securities; 'mezz' for those in the middle; and 'junior' for high return, first loss pieces—became

---

12 For convenience, we will conflate securities whose performance is based directly on the performance of a pool of mortgages, known as 'pass throughs'; tranched pass throughs; asset-backed securities some or all of whose assets are mortgages; and collateralized debt obligations based on these securities, calling all of them 'MBS'. For a much longer account of the tangled web of MBS in the 2008 crisis, see Gorton (2008).

13 Nadauld & Sherlund (2009) discusses the role of securitization in the growth of the US mortgage market from 1997 to 2007.

14 Caballero et al. (2017) identifies the high growth rate of emerging economies such as China as being a major contributor to this demand.

15 The lowest level was known as the 'equity' tranche of the securitization; the next tranche or tranches the 'mezzanine', up to the 'senior' and sometimes 'super-senior'. See Gorton (2008) for details.

16 For more on the rating of MBS, ABS, and CDOs of ABS, see Benmelech & Dlugosz (2010).

17 See Nadauld & Sherlund (2009) for details of the different loss levels on different vintages of tranched MBS.

18 This is the problem of default comovement discussed in the last chapter. When defaults are idiosyncratic, the loss distribution for a portfolio of mortgages has a relatively low unexpected loss. But if there is a common risk factor, such as house prices, and this falls, then there can be a wave of defaults and the UL is much bigger.

commonplace in securitizations of bonds, loans, and even securities that were themselves tranches of securitizations.[19]

2.16 The highly rated MBS created by tranching seemed attractive. However it was sometimes difficult or uncongenial for asset managers to do adequate due diligence on them.[20] There were three main classes of issues. First, the loans themselves were sometimes dishonestly obtained or created by predatory lending. In these cases, the loan documentation would not have given the full picture.[21] Second, even where the underlying loan documentation was available, buyers did not necessarily look at it.[22] Often, they outsourced their due diligence to ratings agencies.[23] Third, in some cases, the risk was passed on in such complex ways, and with such information loss, that the ultimate risk holder could not know exactly what they owned.[24]

2.17 Eventually easy credit and speculative house building led to a levelling off in house prices. There were too many houses and not enough buyers. Broad measures of US house prices started to fall in mid-2006.[25] Once house prices were no longer rising, there was a lower incentive for borrowers to perform on their

---

19 This was the origin of 'CDOs of ABS', where a first level securitization process created securities backed by asset pools, and some or all of these securities were in turn used to create a second level securitization.

20 A broad sketch of due diligence on an MBS would be: investigate the credit quality of the borrowers, the collateral quality, and the loan structure. Understand any systemic factors such as concentration in particular locations/states or types of borrower. From this, model the cashflows of the loan pool in a wide range of scenarios of varying probability. Then model how those cashflows are turned into cashflows on the security under consideration by the MBS structure. This results in a return distribution for the security. Assess whether the expected returns on the security are adequate compensations for its risks.

21 Fligstein & Roehrkasse (2015) discusses the causes of fraud in the 2008 crisis.

22 See, for instance, footnote 18 in Coffee (2012) or USPSC (2011) at 250.

23 Ashcraft et al. (2011) and Benmelech & Dlugosz (2010) discuss the role of the ratings agencies and their conflicts of interest in rating MBS.

24 A good example of this phenomenon occurred in CDOs of ABS. CDOs took pools of asset-backed securities, themselves representing sometimes complex claims on pools of risk such as mortgages, and structured these, issuing tranched securities. The problem for CDO structurers was that while there was a good demand from buyers for the riskiest tranches of the CDO and for the safest, the middle or mezzanine tranches were often not attractive. This problem was sometimes 'solved' by CDO *A* buying the mezz of CDO *B* and CDO *B* buying that of *A*. More complex structures of CDO cross-holdings were also observed. This cross-holding meant that the senior tranches of both *A* and *B* were less safe than would have been had the mezzanine been sold to third parties. It was, moreover, often invisible to the buyers of the senior tranches and to the ratings agencies.

25 The S&P/Case-Shiller 20-City Composite Home Price Index peaked in April 2006 and fell over 30% from there until May 2009. Some specific areas, such as greater Las Vegas, experienced substantially large falls. Las Vegas' state, Nevada, also had the highest per capital level of personal bankruptcy filings, at roughly twice the national average for both 2008 and 2009.

mortgages, and so defaults rose. Sales of the repossessed houses then contributed to further house price falls, creating a spiral of falling prices, rising defaults and foreclosures. The decline in the value of mortgages lowered the value of MBS, since MBS were composed of pools of these mortgages. These losses reverberated through the financial system, given how widely held MBS were.

2.18 In summary, four phenomena came together to create the boom in US house prices, the subsequent bust, and its impact on the financial system. Rising house prices made leveraged investment in houses attractive and incentivized house building. Cheap and readily available mortgages allowed many borrowers, including poor credit quality ones, to take advantage of this. Mortgage lenders' self-interest did not prevent them from making these loans because either they misestimated the risks, or they passed them on, or both. There was a huge demand for safe assets, some of which was met by MBS. These MBS were increasingly unsafe, but buyers did not and, in some cases, could not do sufficient diligence to discover this.

Phase 2: from losses to a liquidity crisis

2.19 By the summer of 2007, it was clear that US mortgage-related losses were substantial.[26] However, these losses were not a dominant part of the total cost of the 2008 crisis.[27] While residential mortgage lending was the cause of the crisis, the nature of the financial system at the time propagated and amplified the stress, turning a bad situation into something much worse.

2.20 A widely noted sign that mortgage losses were going to have broader effects came in August 2007 when the bank BNP Paribas suspended redemption of three

---

[26] A common term in the literature for lower quality mortgages is 'subprime', but this should be used with care. First, 'subprime' in the early to mid-2000s was only used to refer to mortgages where the borrowers' credit score was low: a common benchmark was a Fair Isaac Corporation or 'FICO' score of 620 or below. 'Prime' in contrast meant a FICO above 700, so there a middle ground of borrowers who were scored as neither prime nor subprime. There are also the categories of 'Alt-A' and home equity loans. Alt-A mortgages are characterized by borrowers with less than full documentation—so their FICO might not be known, or their income unproven—or higher LTV ratios, or who non-owner-occupiers. Home equity loans are second (or third, or fourth) mortgages which allow borrowers to extract equity from their properties. Total 1–4 family (which counts as 'single family') mortgage debt in the United States outstanding was \$10.4T, of which only about \$1.3T was subprime. Second, residential mortgage-related losses were by no means confined to subprime: default rates spiked in all classes of mortgages, including prime, as Meyer et al. (2008) discusses.

[27] IMF (2009) estimated total losses in April 2009 of \$2.8T, of which only half come from residential mortgages and securities backed by them. Earlier estimates were lower: Greenlaw et al. (2008) writing in a paper of January 2008, had 'only' \$500B.

funds[28] quoting 'complete evaporation of liquidity in certain market segments of the US securitization market' which 'made it impossible to value certain assets fairly regardless of their quality or credit rating'.[29] Market participants knew that things were bad, but not how bad, and many of them had become reluctant to trade as a result. This meant that by the autumn of 2007 there were no or few market prices for many MBS, and this intensified the uncertainty about the size and location of the ultimate losses.[30] This problem was driven home when Citibank, after announcing mortgage-related losses of $3.1 billion for the third quarter of 2007, was forced two weeks later to write down a further $5.9 billion.

2.21 Uncertain, but likely large, mortgage-related losses drove a decline in confidence in financial institutions and a broad increase in risk aversion. Trust was limited. It was not clear which firms would survive. There are two reasons that investors did not trust many financial institutions:

Leverage was high. Many firms, including many banks, had a relatively small amount of equity, and so could not withstand large losses.

Funding was short-term. Many firms relied on short-term borrowing to fund longer-term assets. This meant that if they could not roll over their funding, they would fail even if they were solvent.

2.22 A classic banking crisis involves an interaction between the opacity of financial institutions, high leverage, and short-term funding.[31] It goes like this. A bad thing happens. Investors are not sure how solvent a bank is because the bank's losses are uncertain and it is leveraged. Therefore they are reluctant to lend to the bank. Because the bank is funded short-term, this creates liquidity stress as the bank scrambles to replace the funding which has been withdrawn. If it cannot do this, it fails. Thus doubts about solvency create actual liquidity problems. Figure 2.1 illustrates the 'solvency/liquidity spiral', as this mechanism is known.

2.23 The vulnerability of the originate to distribute model of mortgage lending became clear in September 2007 with the distress of a British bank, Northern Rock. This entity had its origins in the UK mortgage market, and it had grown in large part by making and securitizing mortgages. The business model was to

---

[28] These funds were Parvest Dynamic ABS, BNP Paribas ABS EURIBOR, and BNP Paribas ABS EONIA: the names make it clear that they invested in asset-backed securities.

[29] Press release, BNP Paribas Investment Partners, 9 August 2007.

[30] The changing loss estimates over time described in footnote 27 are illustrative of this Knightian uncertainty. For a further discussion of the problem of Knightian uncertainty in finance, see Chapter 9.

[31] This is essentially the model in Diamond & Dybvig (1983). For more on the role of confidence in this setting, see Murphy (2012).

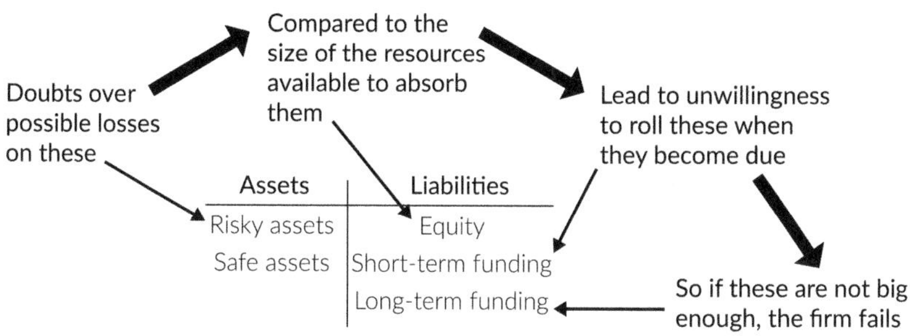

Figure 2.1– The classic bank solvency/liquidity spiral

build up a pool of mortgages funded by borrowing on the wholesale credit market then, once the pool was big enough to be attractive to investors, issuing a MBS backed by it. When the MBS market began to stall, investors became concerned that this business model no longer worked, and by 12 September many wholesale investors were refusing to lend to the bank. Northern Rock was forced to cover the funding gap with borrowing from the Bank of England.

2.24 After this news became public on 13 September, a general loss of confidence in the firm ensued. The design of the UK deposit protection scheme made matters worse as it did not guarantee 100% of funds above £2,000, nor did it promise speedy return of funds. Many retail depositors were therefore incentivized to withdraw their funds when they became concerned about the potential solvency of the bank. These concerns created a run on Northern Rock, with long queues of retail depositors forming outside its branches on 14 September 2007. The UK authorities were forced to announce a full guarantee of retail deposits, and the Bank of England extended further funding to Northern Rock to shore up its liquidity position. The bank was eventually nationalized in February 2008 after attempts to find an acceptable private buyer failed.[32]

2.25 Another class of entity was particularly exposed to the solvency/liquidity spiral: this was the US investment bank. There were five large investment banks in the United States, distinguished by the fact that they were lead-regulated by the Securities and Exchange Commission (or 'SEC') rather than the Federal Reserve, as the national banks in the United States were.[33] The big five were Bear Stearns, Goldman Sachs, Lehman Brothers, Merrill Lynch, and Morgan Stanley. These

[32] For a more detailed account of the distress and rescue of Northern Rock, see NAO (2009).

[33] This account glosses over some details: a bank's primary regulator in the United States can be the Office of the Comptroller of the Currency ('OCC'), the Federal Deposit Insurance Corporation ('FDIC') or the Federal Reserve ('Fed'). The Fed is the lead regulator for, among other entities, bank holding companies. Moreover, being an investment bank—and hence having a holding company which was lead regulated by the SEC—did not mean that deposits could not be taken: the large investment banks often had banks or bank-like entities within their groups.

firms were supervised under a regime introduced by the SEC in 2004 known as the Consolidated Supervised Entity program.[34] What distinguished the investment banks from their bank peers was the relatively large size of their capital markets activities, their relatively high reliance on short-term funding for these activities, and their lack of access to funding from the Fed due to their regulatory status.[35]

2.26 In particular, the investment banks were major bond dealers. They had significant inventory in order to provide liquidity to their customers: when you called an investment bank to buy a bond, you expected that they had an extensive range to sell you, and they did. Much of this bond inventory was financed by overnight collateralized borrowing known as repo. The investment banks would use their inventory as collateral, and hence only had to source a small fraction of their liquidity needs with more expensive unsecured borrowing. This was a profitable strategy, but it had risks. In particular borrowing via repo tended to be short-term, so the investment banks had to roll their funding frequently. This meant that if confidence was lost, repo funding could not be rolled, or could only be rolled at significant cost. Higher funding costs meant the investment bank might have to sell some of their bond inventory, or at the very least, suffer losses.

2.27 Bear Stearns was the weakest of the five in early 2008. It was the least well capitalized, it was a relatively large player in MBS, and it was reliant on repo funding. The problem was not its capital: it was its liquidity. The chairman of its primary regulator, the SEC, told the story of what happened like this:[36]

> *Bear Stearns' registered broker-dealers were comfortably in compliance with the SEC's net capital requirements, ... [the firm's] capital exceeded relevant supervisory standards at the holding company level... [and] the holding company had a pool of high quality, highly liquid assets of over $18 billion as of the morning of March 1.*
>
> *In accordance with customary industry practice, Bear Stearns relied day-to-day on its ability to obtain short-term financing through borrowing on a secured basis. Beginning late Monday, March 10, and increasingly through the week, rumours spread about liquidity problems at Bear Stearns, which eroded investor confidence in the firm. Notwithstanding that Bear Stearns continued to have high quality collateral to provide as security for borrowings,*

[34] See Sirri (2010) for details of the Consolidated Supervised Entity regime.

[35] Section 10B of the Federal Reserve Act allows any Federal Reserve bank 'under rules and regulations prescribed by the Board of Governors of the Federal Reserve System' to 'make advances to any member bank on its time or demand notes having maturities of not more than four months and which are secured to the satisfaction of such Federal Reserve bank'. The investment banks were not member banks and hence they did not have access to lender of last resort facilities via this route.

[36] The quote is from Cox (2008).

market counterparties became less willing to enter into collateralized funding arrangements with Bear Stearns. This resulted in a crisis of confidence late in the week. In particular, counterparties to Bear Stearns were unwilling to make secured funding available to Bear Stearns on customary terms.

2.28 In other words, Bear Stearns could not roll their repos.[37] The firm's surplus liquidity began to fall rapidly: to $11.5 billion on Tuesday 11 March and to $2 billion on the 13th. The end was nigh, and the firm was sold to JP Morgan on the 16th after they were unable to secure sufficient funding as a stand-alone entity.[38] The Federal Reserve Bank of New York was mindful of the systemic consequences should Bear Stearns file for bankruptcy. Therefore, it was supportive of the purchase, lending $12.9 billion to Bear Stearns through JPMorgan Chase Bank and setting up a special purpose entity, Maiden Lane LLC, to purchase roughly $30 billion of Bear Stearns' assets. This lightened the load on JP Morgan.[39]

2.29 The atmosphere after these events was febrile. There was a relentless stream of loss announcements over the summer of 2008 and, as a result, a steep decline of market confidence in financial institutions. Some banks announced large rights issues in an attempt to shore up their capital bases.[40]

2.30 Financial institutions were trying to reduce their exposure to the most affected markets, too. However, illiquidity in these markets made this challenging, so often they sold related assets instead. This caused a contagious spiral of price falls and illiquidity which went first from the US MBS market to the broader asset-backed securities ('ABS') market, then from there to lower quality credit markets more broadly, and finally to nearly all markets for risky assets.[41]

Phase 3: giants fall

2.31 The trigger for the third phase of the crisis was the failure of the two largest GSEs, Fannie Mae and Freddie Mac. These two entities were enormous: between

[37] Bear Stearns was unlucky with the news, too. A hedge fund specializing in MBS, Carlyle Capital Corporation, failed on 7 March, highlighting the problems in the MBS market that Bear Stearns was so exposed to. This cannot have helped confidence in the firm nor the willingness of the firm's counterparties to 'make secured funding available to Bear Stearns on customary terms'.

[38] See SEC (2008) for the SEC's analysis of the failure of Bear Stearns and the role of regulation in it.

[39] Section 13(3) of the Federal Reserve Act allows the Federal Reserve 'in exceptional and exigent circumstances' to authorize emergency 'advances': this was the authority which allowed the Fed to provide the funds to Maiden Lane LLC which it used to buy the unwanted Bear Stearns assets. The back-to-back loan intermediated via JPMorgan was extended under the authority of Sections 10B and 13(3). See footnote 35 for a discussion of section 10B and Weinberg (2013) for section 13(3).

[40] Good examples were rights issues of $15.5 billion from UBS in May 2008 and £12 billion from RBS in June 2008: the latter was the biggest in UK corporate history at that point.

[41] The contagion mechanisms and evidence of their size are discussed in Longstaff (2010).

them they had over $1.7 trillion of assets and they guaranteed an additional $3.7 trillion of mortgages. By mid-2008, falling house prices and the deteriorating economic outlook combined to reduce the private sector's interest in origination mortgages. As a result, Fannie Mae and Freddie Mac had a hand in over three quarters of new mortgages. Despite this central position in the mortgage market, their credit status was uncertain: while they were 'government-sponsored', it was not clear to the market whether the US government would stand behind them. Given the size of their losses since house prices started to turn down in 2006, their thin capital base, and their vast stock of debt outstanding, this was not good enough for investors.[42] They were reluctant to purchase more of the GSEs' liabilities or to recapitalize them, and without this, the GSEs might well have failed. The consequences of this would have been very serious not just for the mortgage market but for the wider financial system, given how widely held their debt was.[43] Therefore on 7 September 2008 these two entities were seized by their regulator.[44] The US Treasury injected funds, and both it and the Federal Reserve bought substantial amounts of the GSEs' debt. These actions allowed the GSEs to maintain, and even expand, their presence in the mortgage market, but at the cost not just of a bail-out but also of giving a clear public signal of the depth of the problems in the MBS market.

2.32 Firms which were exposed to this market were vulnerable. Financial institutions raced to reduce risk, raise capital, and improve their liquidity position while losses rose and investor confidence fell. The investments banks were particularly endangered given their reliance on repo and their exposure to the same business model that had failed at Bear Stearns. Lehman Brothers was the second smallest of the five investment banks, and it had the largest exposure to real estate-related risk relative to its capital. This put a spotlight on the firm. Understanding its vulnerability, Lehman Brothers had entered into talks with Korea Development Bank in the hope of raising new equity, but these were terminated on 9 September 2008 by KDB due to 'financial market conditions at home and overseas'. Lehman made other efforts to appease investors,[45] but these were not

[42] In the half year to June 2008, Fannie Mae and Freddie Mac together posted $14.2 billion in losses and saw their capital decline to $41.2 billion for Fannie Mae and $12.9 billion for Freddie Mac. By August, excluding deferred tax assets, Freddie Mac had negative net worth. For more details, see Frame et al. (2015).

[43] Treasury Secretary Henry Paulson said that 'there is a consensus today that these enterprises pose a systemic risk': see Paulson (2008).

[44] The terminology was 'put into conservatorship'.

[45] In its earnings announcement, the firm said that it had boosted its liquidity pool to an estimated $45 billion, decreased its gross assets by $147 billion, reduced its exposure to residential and commercial mortgages by 20%, and announced an intention to sell off a majority stake in its investment-management business.

enough in the light of a third quarter loss of $3.9 billion. When this result was announced on 10 September, Lehman's liquidity position began to decline. The fall from here was fast, as it was for Bear Stearns, and Lehman Brothers' holding company filed for bankruptcy on 15 September 2008.

Après Lehman, le déluge

2.33 Lehman's bankruptcy filing was the largest in US history. At the point of failure, the firm held over $630 billion in assets: over half as much again as Bear Stearns. But unlike Bear Stearns, there was no Fed-assisted rescue, so bankruptcy was inevitable when the firm ran out of money.[46] The consequences were severe for financial markets and institutions. Equity markets fell around the world. Credit markets froze. Wholesale borrowing was very difficult for even the best quality institutions, and impossible for everyone else.

2.34 The other three investment banks suffered further losses of confidence. Bank of America, with its huge base of stable funding from retail deposits and relatively low exposure to capital markets, saw an opportunity, and purchased Merrill Lynch at a discount of over 60% from its price a year earlier.[47] Morgan Stanley, without a rescuer in sight, suffered a 40% fall in its share price from Friday, 12 September to Wednesday the 17th.[48] It was clear that more large bank failures were likely without further action from the authorities, and news of bail-out plans started to appear on the afternoon of 18 September 2008.

2.35 Beginning on Friday 19th, central banks around the world flooded the markets with money in a coordinated action to ensure that the financial system has sufficient liquidity to continue to function.[49] In the US, the troubled asset relief program, or TARP, was proposed by the Bush administration. This allowed the United States Department of the Treasury to purchase up to $700 billion of

---

46 The question of why the Fed did not lend to Lehman as it had to Bear Stearns is interesting. The Fed chairman at the time, Ben Bernanke, insisted that unlike Bear Stearns, Lehman did not have sufficient collateral to back the required size of loan, but some commentators find that explanation unconvincing: see, for instance, Ball (2016).

47 The Board of Merrill Lynch approved Bank of America's offer of $29 per share on Sunday 14 September 2008, when it became clear that Lehman Brothers would file for bankruptcy the following day. This was a 70% premium to where Merrill stock had closed on Friday 14th, but a 62% discount to its price a year earlier.

48 The close on the 12th was $37.23; it opened at $33.30 on the 15th, then closed at $32.19, $28.70, and $21.75 on the 15th, 16th, and 17th respectively.

49 For an example, see the Bank of England press release *Coordinated Central Bank Action to Address Pressures in Global Money Markets*, 26 September 2008, available at https://www.bankofengland.co.uk/news/2008/september/coordinated-central-bank-action-to-address-pressures-in-global-money-markets-sep26.

troubled assets.[50] The funds were quickly put to use buying ABS and other assets from and injecting capital into nine large financial institutions.[51]

2.36 The two remaining investment banks, Morgan Stanley and Goldman Sachs, converted themselves into bank holding companies so that they could borrow from the Fed: Morgan Stanley was ultimately the largest single user of Fed emergency bank lending facilities during the crisis.[52]

2.37 The financial system was severely stressed outside the United States, too. In the days that followed Lehman's failure, the Belgium banking and insurance group Fortis, the Franco-Belgium bank Dexia, the Dutch bank ING, and the British banks HBOS, Lloyds TSB, and the Royal Bank of Scotland all received bailouts, among many more.[53] Governments around the globe fell as politicians took the blame for what had evidently been a system predicated on privatized gains but socialized losses.

Analyses of the 2008 Crisis and Policy Responses

2.38 The events of the crisis represented a fundamental disruption to the global economy. They were enormously costly not just to financial institutions but to billions of ordinary people and a vast range of non-financial institutions. Governments had to bail-out the financial system because the consequences of not doing so would have been even worse. It was odious to most people that so many financial institution employees had done so well before 2008, their actions had caused enormous harm, their personal suffering during and after the crisis was often minimal, and yet everyone else had to bail their firms out. Given this anger, it was appropriate that there was a thorough investigation into what went wrong.

2.39 The previous sections laid out the history of the crisis. The next ones turn to a summary of the lessons learned in the aftermath; what role the authorities contended derivatives played in the crisis; what they did in response; and how they talked about the post-crisis reforms.

---

[50] The TARP was enacted as part of the Emergency Economic Stabilization Act of 2008 on 3 October. It required financial institutions selling assets to the TARP to issue equity warrants to the Treasury, giving the state a stake in their recovery: see R. US Congress (2008). The TARP was eventually reduced in size to $475 billion as part of the Dodd-Frank Act.

[51] For a detailed account, see Calomiris & Khan (2015).

[52] See the news story, *Morgan Stanley at Brink of Collapse Got $107 Billion From Fed*, Bradley Keoun, Bloomberg, 23 August 2011, available at https://www.bloomberg.com/news/articles/2011-08-22/morgan-stanley-at-brink-of-collapse-got-107b-from-fed. The date of this story illustrates how long it took Bloomberg using freedom of information requests to get data from the Fed about who borrowed how much during the crisis.

[53] For an interesting study of recapitalization needs in the 2008 and other crises, see FSB (2015).

The financial crisis inquiry commission

2.40 The United States Congress set up a Commission to investigate the causes of the 2008 crisis. The Financial Crisis Inquiry Commission ('FCIC') was a bipartisan body, and it held an extensive series of hearings, so its conclusions reflect broad evidence gathering.[54] They were, in summary:

- *The financial crisis was avoidable.* The prime example of this was the Federal Reserve's pivotal failure to stem the flow of 'toxic' mortgages. It could have done so by setting prudent mortgage-lending standards, but it did not act. As the Federal Reserve was the principal entity empowered to set these standards, its inaction was decisive.
- *Widespread failures in financial regulation and supervision proved devastating to the stability of the nation's financial markets.* Regulators had the power to protect the financial system: they chose not to use it.
- *Dramatic failures of corporate governance and risk management at many systemically important financial institutions were a key cause of the crisis.* Many financial institutions acted recklessly, taking on too much risk, with too little capital, and with too much dependence on short-term funding.
- *A combination of excessive borrowing, risky investments, and lack of transparency put the financial system on a collision course.* Financial institutions and mortgage borrowers took on debt to acquire risky assets. The dangers of this were magnified because transparency was not required or desired. When markets cratered, the result was panic.
- *The government was ill prepared for the crisis, and its inconsistent response added to the uncertainty and panic in the financial markets.* Policy makers and regulators were caught off guard as the contagion spread through 2007 and 2008, responding on an ad hoc basis instead of providing a comprehensive and strategic plan. They lacked a full understanding of the risks and interconnections in the financial markets.
- *There was a systemic breakdown in accountability and ethics.* Mortgage borrowers took out loans that they never had the capacity or intention to pay. Mortgage brokers were paid by lenders to put borrowers into loans with higher lifetime costs, like hybrid ARMs, because these products paid them higher fees. There was a rising incidence of mortgage fraud: 'liar loan', the industry terminology of the time, is telling.

[54] They were not, however, unanimous. See FCIC (2011) for both the majority view and the dissenting ones.

2.41 This is an understandably critical account of the causes of the crisis. In order to understand where reform is needed, it is helpful to discuss the four different vulnerabilities noted by the FCIC: each is the subject of a following subsection.

Mortgage lending is risky

2.42 The first and most important vulnerability was in the US mortgage market.[55] This market was unusual in several ways. One was the lack of recourse to borrowers' assets beyond the property securing the mortgage in many states. Another was the large role played by the GSEs. Finally, there was the extent of the disintermediation between mortgage design, the lending decision, and the ultimate holders of the various risks. All of these features contributed to making residential mortgages in the United States uniquely risky.

2.43 The US was not unique in other ways. Mortgage lending everywhere is risky when house prices fall—which they do sufficiently regularly that it should be no surprise. Hong Kong property fell over 60% after the 1997 crisis. Swedish property fell more than 50% after the 1991–1992 crisis.[56] Japanese land prices fell by 80% during the 'lost decade' of 1990–1999 and property prices by more than 60%.[57] Given this, it would have been sensible to have more robust standards for residential mortgage lending[58]. However, while this would have been helpful, it would not have been sufficient. The potential for large house price falls means that, even when lending standards are high, residential mortgage lending should be considered risky. It should accrue meaningful capital requirements too, so that the financial system is protected. However, thanks to the bank capital reforms introduced in 2004 known as Basel 2, by 2008, residential mortgage lending was not considered nearly as risky as it was.[59] Instead, in run-up to 2008, regulators had cut their estimates of the risk of residential mortgage lending.[60]

2.44 Shockingly, mortgage lending is not considered to have materially higher risk by bank regulators now, either. The internationally agreed regulatory risk

---

55 As Peter Wallison and Arthur Burns put it in their dissenting statement to FCIC (2011), 'the *sine qua non* of the financial crisis was US government housing policy, which led to the creation of 27 million subprime and other risky loans—half of all mortgages in the United States—which were ready to default as soon as the massive 1997–2007 housing bubble began to deflate'.

56 See Jaffee (1994).

57 See Okina et al. (2000).

58 The standards would include more robust analysis of borrower debt to income ratios and minimum LTV levels for residential mortgage lending.

59 See R. BCBS (2004) and, in particular, the treatment of residential mortgages in paragraphs 328.

60 See the results of the third Quantitative Impact Study, or 'QIS' on Basel 2 of 2003. Risk-weighted assets, the regulatory measure of risk, for retail mortgages fall by an average 55% for banks using one of the sophisticated approaches to calculating capital (the Foundation IRB), and 60% by those using the other (the Advanced IRB): see BCBS (2003).

measures for residential mortgages have only changed in minor ways since the crisis, and these changes do not materially affect the largest banks.[61] Until the financial system is robust to the risk of large falls in house prices, the vulnerability remains.[62] This conclusion is politically uncongenial, because it makes mortgages more expensive, and politicians of many persuasions understandably support affordable housing.[63] But affordable housing does not have to mean subsidizing private wealth creation while increasing the risk of a banking crisis.

Regulatory organization and culture

2.45 Pre-crisis financial regulation in the United States was split among many authorities. As US Treasury Secretary Timothy Geithner put it, the structure of the US regulatory system was 'unnecessarily complex and fragmented' and it operated 'with large gaps in meaningful oversight'.[64] Many institutions had a choice of regulator for their whole business or for substantial parts of it. Regulatory competition, in turn, created a disincentive to be too tough.

2.46 This was not the only issue. There was an ideology, even among regulators, of deregulation. As the Fed's General Counsel, Scott Alvarez, put it:[65]

> *The mind-set was there should be no regulation; the market should take care of policing, unless there already is an identified problem ... We were in the reactive mode because that's what the mind-set was of the '90s and the early 2000s.*

2.47 It is difficult to recapture this culture, given how profoundly regulatory ideology changed after the crisis. One vignette might be illustrative: in 1998 Citicorp announced a planned merger with Travelers Insurance which would have been illegal under the then 65-year-old Glass-Steagall Act. In response, and with the support of Citicorp's supervisors, Congress enacted the Gramm-Leach-Bliley Act which repealed much of what remained of the Glass-Steagall Act restrictions and allowed the merger to proceed. In other words, the authority

[61] Compare paragraph 328 of R. BCBS (2004), the Basel 2 standard of 2004, with paragraph 118 of R. BCBS (2017), the Basel 3 standard of 2017. The typesetting is nicer in Basel 3, but the formula determining the regulatory risk measure is the same.

[62] One could argue that while the risk-weighted asset definition has not changed, the capital needed to meet it has increased because the minimum CET1 ratio has increased. This is true, but given the huge increase in risk-weighted assets in other areas of the capital framework, the relative contribution of mortgages to total risk as measured by regulators has fallen.

[63] See Calomiris (2010) or Calomiris & Haber (2015) for an account of how US politicians subsidized the inexpensive use of leverage by residential mortgage borrowers.

[64] See Geithner (2009). For a competing argument that fragmentation does not necessarily explain regulatory outcomes, see Awrey (2010a).

[65] See FCIC (2011) at 96.

response to Citicorp's announcement could be crudely summarized as something closer to 'hang on, we'll fix that bothersome law for you' than 'no, you can't do that, it's illegal'.

Incentives and risk transmission

2.48 It is self-evident that you cannot have a crisis involving billions of dollars of risky securities unless someone has bought billions of dollars of risky securities. Sellers are not enough: you need buyers too. The incentives for the sellers of MBS were obvious; but clearly it was not in the buyers' interest to pay good money for bad assets. The reasons that they did included the shortage of genuinely high quality assets and the fact that there was insufficient disclosure to allow them to do due diligence on the risks of the securities.

2.49 One policy response would be to require substantial *pari passu* risk retention at every step in the originate to distribute chain, to ensure that everybody has a stake in the risks that they are moving.[66] Another would be to require mandatory public disclosure in a common format of all of the details of assets being securitized (perhaps subject to a *de minimis* exemption for small private placements). Together these policies would ensure that everyone had skin in the game and no one should be able to say that they did not know what they were trading. The opportunity to do this was not taken.[67]

Confidence is key

2.50 The crisis demonstrated that the amount of capital a financial institution needs to retain confidence in good times is substantially lower than it is in stress. When the bad times come, investors usually become more sceptical. Firms found wanting under investors' newly raised standards will find it difficult or impossible to roll their funding. This means that they can fail if they are too reliant on short-term borrowing. The solvency liquidity spiral can be broken at any of the steps in Figure 2.1 by any of three means singly or in combination:

- *Increasing transparency on asset values*, so there is less uncertainty whether financial institutions are solvent.

[66] As Levitin (2013) points out, there are alternatives to risk retention, such as the ability to put badly performing risk to the originator, which have similar incentive effects. However we prefer risk retention because this has to be funded: participants have to buy some of the risk before they move it.

[67] The Dodd-Frank Act directs US regulators to make rules on credit risk retention requirements for securitizations. In October 2014 they did so, but the required retention was only 5%, and securitizations consisting solely of good quality (so-called qualifying) residential mortgages are exempt from it. This, and similarly meagre EU regulation, represents a failure to ensure that the interests of all the parties in the originate to distribute chain are aligned.

- *Increasing capital*, so that even when there is significant uncertainty in asset values, it is still likely that the institution has sufficient resources both to absorb further losses and to continue to inspire confidence.
- *Reducing reliance on short-term debt*, so that the consequences of the inability to roll funding are less severe.

2.51 After the crisis, bank regulators acted on the second and third of these, substantially increasing the capital required to support the same amount of risk[68] and introducing liquidity regulation with the aim of reducing funding liquidity risk.[69]

OTC Derivatives in the 2008 Crisis

2.52 OTC Derivatives were central to the authorities' response to the 2008 crisis. 'Making OTC derivatives markets safer' was one of four key reforms listed in a leading regulator's summary of the post-crisis achievements,[70] with others calling it 'a key element of our financial regulatory reform package'.[71] 'Improving over-the-counter derivatives markets' was one of the key objectives articulated by the G-20 after the crisis,[72] so clearly the authorities believed that they both could and should intervene. These beliefs were not wholly well founded. Derivatives were not central to the causes of the crisis, but neither were they blameless. In this section, we set out the case against blaming derivatives in general for the events of 2008; elucidate the role of one type of derivatives, CDS; summarize the post-crisis derivatives reforms; and, given this understanding of derivatives' real role, discuss which reforms were justified and which were not.

2.53 The immediate result of the post-crisis impulse to regulate was a wave of new public policy. This included the Dodd-Frank Act in the US,[73] the Basel 3 bank capital reforms,[74] global margin requirements, the CPMI/IOSCO principles

68 See R. BCBS (2010).

69 There were two main pieces of international liquidity regulation: the liquidity coverage ratio, R. BCBS (2013a), and the net stable funding ratio, R. BCBS (2014d). For want of space, these regulations and other issues in post-crisis regulation, such as too big to fail, are not treated in detail here. The leverage ratio is discussed in Chapter 4, while derivatives regulation is discussed further below.

70 Mark Carney, Chair at the time of the Financial Stability Board and Governor Bank of England listed this item alongside 'making financial institutions more resilient', 'ending the problem of financial institutions being too big to fail', and 'transforming shadow banking into resilient market based finance' as the key achievements of post-crisis regulation in Carney (2017).

71 The phrase is from Geithner (2009).

72 See G-20 (2009).

73 See R. US Congress (2010).

74 See R. BCBS (2010). The 'comprehensive' version was not published until 2017.

for financial market infrastructures,[75] and the European Market Infrastructure reforms known as EMIR.[76] This section then considers discusses the rationale the authorities might have had for contending that these enormous OTC derivatives policy changes were necessary.

What derivatives did not do

2.54 Most forms of derivative did not create losses in the 2008 crisis. This is a key point. Commodity, equity, FX, and interest rate derivatives markets performed well: problems were confined to credit derivatives, as we discuss later.[77] The exposures financial institutions had to each other via derivatives were typically not large either. As the FCIC report puts it,[78] despite a diligent search, the Commission 'never uncovered evidence that [derivatives were] a significant contributor to the financial crisis through interconnections'. So if most classes of derivative did not cause material losses or create overly large exposures, what were the issues that motivated so much derivatives reform?

Opacity and complexity

2.55 Pre-crisis, OTC derivatives were mostly traded bilaterally. There was no mandatory reporting of transactions, so there was no central record of the exposures between key market participants. This opacity meant that no one knew who owed what to whom. This, in turn, increased uncertainty about the true risks in the system. Even though OTC derivatives did not cause a cascade of failures—Lehman's exposures were contained for instance[79]—it was not clear until well after the fact that OTC derivatives exposures were not, in fact, large. When the crisis hit, regulators scrambled to understand the exposures, with mixed success.[80]

---

[75] See R. CPMI & IOSCO (2012). These were 'second wave' rules in the sense that, having decided to reform the derivatives markets, the authorities needed to ensure that the infrastructures supporting their new market structure were robust.

[76] See R. EC (2012a).

[77] Out of a total of $240 billion of losses in the 2008 crisis analysed by the UK FSA, only $3 billion came from interest rate derivatives and $5 billion from interest rate derivatives. All commodity and FX losses—not just those from derivatives trading in those asset classes—came to $1.5 billion. See Table 5.1 in FSA (2010).

[78] Dissenting statement, P. Wallison, at 447.

[79] The initial claims on OTC derivatives against Lehman entities were large: Fleming & Sarkar (2014) at 179 quotes $75 billion. However, these were substantially reduced through the bankruptcy process. Counterparties' eventual recovery depended materially on which Lehman entity they faced: for instance, counterparties facing Lehman Brothers OTC Derivatives Inc. received 100%, while those facing the holding company Lehman Brothers Holdings Inc. only got about 30% in nominal terms.

[80] See the FCIC (2011) at 326.

2.56 The opacity of the OTC derivatives market amplified the loss of confidence which hit the markets in 2008, potentially contributing to contagion.[81] However, while this opacity was implicated in financial institutions stress,[82] there is no evidence of how significant this issue was. There must therefore be a question whether a concern that the lack of transparency over OTC derivatives exposures *might* have been important in the crisis is sufficient to justify the massive transformation of OTC derivatives markets that was imposed. Given that the Dodd-Frank Act was passed well before the Financial Crisis Inquiry Commission had published their report—or even had had many of their hearings—there is a suspicion that the authorities acted first and analysed later.

2.57 A middle ground might be to agree that regulators need information about OTC derivatives exposures, and hence that reporting of exposures was necessary.[83] The G-20 required in 2009 that 'OTC derivative contracts should be reported to trade repositories'.[84] Sadly, the subsequent history of this policy raises questions as to how useful that reporting is.

2.58 The first issue is the plural: trade repositor*ies*. A recent Financial Stability Board ('FSB') report lists 34, ten of which were authorized in multiple jurisdictions.[85] OTC derivatives transactions are not reported to a single repository, nor are they in a single, easily aggregated format. Moreover, central banks reported in 2018 that the data had 'significant data gaps' and was of 'limited quality'.[86] Finally, because an individual authority only has access to the trades done by firms it supervises or, if it is a central bank, trades made in its currency, no authority has a consolidated view of the risks of the entire global derivatives market.

2.59 A different approach was possible. Instead of requiring reporting of OTC derivatives transactions (not, notice, risk exposures—which would be more

81 As Geithner (2009) put it: 'a lack of transparency in the OTC derivative markets' meant that 'the government and market participants did not have enough information about the location of risk exposures, or the extent of mutual interconnection among firms. And this lack of visibility magnified contagion as the crisis intensified'.

82 Thus, the argument in McNamara (2014) that one of the major post-crisis OTC derivatives markets reforms is a 'confidence-bolstering device that reduces the spread of contagion in the financial markets' is almost certainly true. This was, however, a very expensive device. We turn to the issue of cost-benefit analysis and the issue of the least onerous means necessary to achieve regulatory objectives in Chapter 9.

83 This argument would be more convincing if regulators had waited to get information about OTC derivatives before they made policy. Claiming that 'the government and market participants did not have enough information about the location of risk exposures', as Geithner (2009) does, but then enacting legislation before you have that information suggests that you do not care what the evidence might suggest is the optimal policy response.

84 See G-20 (2009) at 13.

85 See R. FSB (2019a) at 11 and Chapter 8 in Helleiner et al. (2018).

86 See IFC (2018).

useful), authorities could have relied on compulsory collateralization. If you know that systemic market participants are posting daily cash initial and variation margin to each other, then (as discussed in Chapter 1) you know that OTC derivatives exposures are small. Moreover, because margin policy is publicly disclosed, this approach is more confidence-enhancing than trade reporting, where only regulators know how big exposures are. In fact, regulators imposed margin policy *as well as* trade reporting: this is discussed further in Chapter 6.

Taking mortgage risk

2.60 The odd man out from the list of OTC derivatives asset classes which did not contribute to the crisis is credit derivatives. A credit derivative allows the protection seller to take credit risk without having to fund it. This can be on a single name, as in a credit default swap referencing a particular corporation, or a pool of names, as in a CDS referencing an index. Credit derivatives referencing MBS were important in the 2008 crisis.

2.61 The 'benign' use of CDS referencing mortgage risk was the assembly of some MBS in the originate to distribute model. A lender might identify a pool of mortgages which it wished to securitize. One way to do this would be for a vehicle to plan to issue MBS, and to source the risk of the underlying loans not by buying them, but by writing CDS to the original lender in exchange for a premium. The lender would be compensated for defaults on the mortgage pool via the CDS. This risk would be passed on to the investors who bought MBS issued by the vehicle.[87] This is benign in the sense that there is no reason that this structure is necessarily riskier than one where the lender keeps the risk: if the structure is diligently constructed, risk has not been created, it has just been moved. The MBS buyer *could* do due diligence on the mortgages; they might even be in a better position to assess it than the original lender.

2.62 One issue in the 2008 crisis was that a significant number of protection sellers not only did not understand the risks that they were taking, they also did not have sufficient capital to support them. Insurance companies were particular culprits here, as was their regulatory framework, which permitted them to take positions which were concentrated and outsized given their capital.

2.63 A more problematic case involving the use of CDS occurs when a protection buyer does not own the asset that they are buying protection on. The issue is the potential for there to be more protection sellers than there is asset to buy protection on.[88] This, in turn, can distort prices as, instead of the CDS market

[87] This is a synthetic securitization: see Gorton (2008) or Murphy (2009) for more details.

[88] In situations like single name CDS where the payout is determined by an auction of deliverable bonds, the problem arises when protection buyers cannot source enough bonds to deliver into

representing an alternative way of taking the same credit risk, it develops its own dynamics, potentially divorced from those of the underlying asset. Moreover, even when the CDS market is a small fraction of the total credit risk transfer market in the asset, it can pose pitfalls for the unwary. A group of insurance companies known as the monolines experienced this during the 2008 crisis, and we turn to their part in the story next.

Mortgage risk and the monolines

2.64 The origins of the bond insurers lie in the municipal or 'muni' bond market. Muni bonds are issued by sub-national actors such as counties, states, or sub-state sponsored agencies. They are generally used to raise money for a public project such as a hospital, a road, or a school, or to finance the ongoing provision of public services.

2.65 The muni market in the United States was substantial at the time of the crisis,[89] as it is today. A large fraction of these bonds were held by retail investors, partly because holding muni bonds gave them tax advantages that corporate or government bonds did not.

2.66 The muni market was relatively fragmented: rather than having a small number of very large bonds, as for instance the US Treasury market does, there are thousands of bonds, many of them small. To pick an example at random, Unified School District No. 409, Atchinson County, Kansas issued a $5.15 million bond in 2004 to finance improvements to its schools.[90] The Municipal Securities Rulemaking Board lists four trades in this bond ever, all of less of than half a million dollars.[91] Clearly bonds like this are relatively illiquid. Their small issue size makes it uneconomic for institutional investors to assess them, and retail investors usually did not have the skills or incentive to do so either.

2.67 This coordination problem was often solved by bond insurance: a small group of highly rated insurance companies grew up to serve the muni bond market. These insurers would do due diligence on issuers and their desired muni bond structure, then propose a fee for providing a financial guarantee on the bond. If the issuer agreed, the bond was issued with the insurer's guarantee or 'wrap'. This meant that it would only fail to pay if both the issuer defaulted and the (highly rated) insurer failed to honour the guarantee, so the wrapped bond was often

the auction. This can happen for a variety of reasons: see Cahill et al. (2019) for a discussion of a recent auction short squeeze and Fletcher (2019) for a perspective on 'innovative' uses of CDS.

89 The Securities Industry and Financial Markets Association report that $3.6 trillion of muni bonds were outstanding in 2008: see https://www.sifma.org/resources/research/fixed-income-chart.

90 The bond's Cusip was 046627DM4 for any reader who wishes to investigate.

91 See https://www.msrb.org for details.

AAA-rated. As a result, many retail investors took the view that they could buy the bonds without having to do their own due diligence.

2.68 A number of insurers came to specialize in this market: they are known as monolines.[92] At the time of the 2008 crisis, there were six large monoline insurers who dominated the muni wrap market.[93] One of these, the Financial Guarantee Insurance Company, insured the Atchinson County school board bond discussed above.

2.69 The monolines looked at the risk of the bonds that they insured on a hold to maturity basis. Typically, muni bond default rates were low and defaults were fairly uncorrelated, so the monolines' portfolios required relatively little capital to support them.[94] The upper tranches of MBS also seemed to be low risk and uncorrelated with each other based on their historical behaviour, so wrapping them appeared to be similar to wrapping muni bonds—and it too required relatively little capital.[95] Moreover, wrapping MBS diversified the monolines' portfolios of muni risk, and the premiums available from taking this risk seemed attractive. All in all, this proposition was too good for the monolines to resist, and providing bond wraps on mortgage- and other asset-backed securities soon became an important part of most monolines' business models.

2.70 The next step in the evolution of the monolines' business model involved a paradigm change. Instead of wrapping MBS, they started writing financial guarantee policies and CDS on MBS and other asset-backed bonds.[96] While this involved taking similar credit risks, it was different from wrapping bonds.

---

92 In the US, insurers are regulated by the states rather than federally. In New York State, bond wrap (or 'financial guaranty') insurance policies can only be issued by insurers writing that kind of policy alone: state insurance regulation does not permit insurers to write financial guarantees or most other forms of insurance. (This is known as the Appleton rule: see section 6902 of R. New York State Senate (2021) which prohibits New York State licensed insurers from writing business (much) beyond financial guarantees, and section 1106, which prohibits insurers operating in New York State but not licensed by the state from organizing themselves differently from state-licensed insurers.) This prohibition in New York State meant that financial guarantee insurers had to have just that single line of business: hence 'monoline'.

93 These were Ambac, Assured Guarantee, CIFG, Financial Guarantee Insurance Company, Financial Security Assurance, and MBIA.

94 In the language of Chapter 1, the UL was small. See Drake & Neale (2011), especially footnote 8, for more on the monolines' view on muni risk.

95 The regulatory requirements for the monolines at the time were unsophisticated: there was a fixed minimum requirement of only $140 million (comprised of capital and policyholders' surplus), and additional capital requirements of between 0.55% and 2.5% of the notional that protection was written on. These requirements achieve the difficult feat of making the investment banks' pre-crisis capital regime look relatively prudent.

96 As Drake & Neale (2011) reports, the monolines had significant exposures not just to MBS, but to other forms of structured finance security too. They wrapped asset-backed securities, they wrote

2.71 Two key differences between bond wraps and CDS are:

- A CDS, being a derivative, is a mark-to-market instrument whose value depends on the market price of the underlying bond. If the bond price falls, then (all other things being equal) the CDS writer suffers an immediate loss. In contrast, written wraps on bonds are usually not accounted for on a fair value (or mark-to-market) basis. Instead, the wrapper's liability usually only depends on their assessment of the bond's ultimate performance, not the bond's market price on the way.[97]
- CDS are usually documented under an ISDA Master Agreement with an associated CSA. The insurers were obliged to comply with whatever credit support terms that they had agreed to in these CSAs, and these sometimes required them to collateralize their exposure even when the underlying bonds were still performing.[98] Their wraps, in contrast, only obliged them to make payments if the underlying bond issuer did not. Taking risk via the derivative therefore sometimes had greater funding liquidity risk than writing insurance on the same bond.

2.72 The monolines' business was stable and profitable until 2007, but their exposure to MBS and related risks was substantial.[99] In the summer of that year, the beginning of what became an avalanche of downgrades of MBS tranches began. Some of these tranches had been protected by bond wraps or CDS written by the monolines, so this led to concerns about how exposed the monolines were.

2.73 The ratings agencies started to downgrade the monolines, and this in turn affected their muni business as it made their wraps less attractive to bond issuers. As losses rose and the prices of the securities the monolines were exposed to fell, confidence in the insurers fell precipitously and with it their credit quality.[100]

protection in the form of financial guarantees and CDS, and they invested some of the premiums they received from these activities in ABS.

97 This is closely related to the difference between risk-neutral probabilities of default and real-world ones discussed in Chapter 1. For a further discussion of the issues here, see Fender & Scheicher (2009), and note that we have glossed over the issue of when a price decrease is significant enough that it evidences a permanent deterioration in credit quality.

98 The monolines did not often agree to CSAs which forced them to collateralize their mark-to-market exposure, but another prominent insurer was less careful: this is the subject of the next section.

99 Drake & Neale (2011) quotes the percentages of structured finance risk in the portfolios of three of the leading monolines, Ambac, MBIA, and Financial Security Assurance, at their peak as 36%, 62%, and 51% respectively. Clearly these firms had moved a long way from their core muni wrap business.

100 To pick one example, Ambac was downgraded from AAA to Aa3 in June 2008 by Moody's; then to Baa1 in November 2008; then to Ba3 in April 2009; then to Caa2 in July 2009. A monoline with a credit rating below single A (and arguably higher) cannot credibly wrap bonds.

Some of the monolines did not survive, and most of those that did had a long journey back to sufficiently high ratings that their wraps inspired full confidence.[101]

Monoline CVA

2.74 Buying protection on MBS from the monolines seemed sensible in 2006. It was relatively cheap, the big monolines were highly rated, and the MBS market was starting to show signs of distress. Hedging with a good quality counterparty was an obvious move, even if that counterparty would not necessarily agree to collateralize the transaction.

2.75 The problem was that too many people made that move. By late 2008, when MBS prices had fallen much further, the liabilities most monolines had from writing protection were large compared to their capital bases. This caused their credit quality to fall. Protection buyers who had inadequate collateral suffered substantial CVA losses as a result,[102] because having protection from someone who might not pay is less valuable than having it from someone who is more likely to. For 12 of the most affected banks, CVA losses on monoline exposures exceeded $50 billion,[103] and analysis of crisis losses by regulators suggest that CVA was the third largest loss category, after direct holding of structured finance assets such as MBS.[104]

Derivatives and funding liquidity risk

2.76 The last section illustrated the problems that can arise in derivatives markets with weak or no collateralization. CDS buyers purchased protection against a fall in the price of an underlying asset. This means that the CDS decreases in value for the protection seller when the underlying asset decreased in value. If the protection seller had sold a lot of CDS, and they all fell in value at once, this could cause a decline in the creditworthiness of the seller. The protection buyer

[101] Ambac filed for Chapter 11 bankruptcy protection on 8 November 2010. Financial Guaranty Insurance Company was ordered by its regulator to cease writing any new policies and to suspend payment of all claims in November 2009. MBIA restructured itself, splitting its municipal bond business from its structured finance operations: National Public Finance Guarantee, its muni-focused monoline, was not upgraded back to A3 until May 2014. Of the big six, four—Ambac, CIFG, Financial Guarantee Insurance Company, and MBIA—discontinued writing financial guarantees after 2008, and FSA was acquired by the only monoline left relatively unaffected by the crisis, Assured Guarantee. To extend the comparison of footnote 95 above, while the investment banks' record of two survivors out of five looks bad, the monolines' record is scarcely any better.

[102] The mechanism whereby widening credit spreads create CVA losses on trades without sufficient collateral is discussed in Chapter 1.

[103] See ISDA (2011).

[104] See Table 5.1 in FSA (2010).

experienced two effects: an increase in the value of the protection they had bought if it was honoured, but CVA losses due to the increased chance that it would not be. But the situation is not necessarily better if a CSA is in place which allows for collateral calls. This reduces or even eliminates the CVA loss but at the cost of creating liquidity risk for the counterparty who has to meet the call. The failure of another insurer —AIG—is the paradigmatic example of this phenomena.

2.77 AIG was one of the world's largest insurance companies, with about $1 trillion in assets at the start of 2008. By the end of the year, it had lost nearly 10% of this amount and been rescued by the US authorities. During its rescue it borrowed over $180 billion from the Fed, more than any bank. The principal cause of its failure was writing protection: by the end of 2007, it had written CDS with a notional value of over $500 billion.[105] Many of these CDS were under a particularly pernicious kind of credit support agreement: a 'trigger' CSA. Here collateral was only required if the portfolio value fell below a trigger point. Worse, in some CSAs, this trigger point rose as AIG's credit rating fell.

2.78 The firm had already been downgraded earlier in 2008, so before Lehman failed, it was only one notch above the rating which would force it to post much more collateral. It was downgraded again on 15 September, and, on that day alone, was required to post over $8 billion more margin. It did not have enough liquidity to meet this call, and would have failed had it not been rescued.

2.79 The AIG subsidiaries that primarily conducted the business which caused their parent to fail were not insurance companies. Moreover, the consolidated AIG group was regulated as a thrift, by the Office of Thrift Supervision, rather than as an insurance company. The lack of an effective consolidated supervisor for the group was significant.[106] Moreover, for both AIG and the monolines, a regulatory framework which allowed these firms to build up large concentrations of risk with little capital was partly to blame for their distress. Despite this, little[107] of the focus of post-crisis regulatory reform was on insurance groups: rather, it was on the insurers' counterparties, the banks and broker/dealers.[108]

2.80 One more liquidity-related issue in OTC derivatives is worthy of mention: novation. Recall that in a novation, a counterparty can move a trade or a whole portfolio from one party to another. This can, depending on the credit support arrangements, create a funding liquidity risk, as the party losing the trade may

105 See McDonald & Paulson (2015) and Sjostrom (2009) for more details of the failure of AIG including an important part of the story not touched on here, AIG's securities lending portfolio.

106 The OTS was also responsible for regulating Countrywide, WaMu, and Indy Mac, large firms prominent in the residential mortgage market in the US, all of which failed during the crisis.

107 The Dodd-Frank Act did create the Federal Insurance Office. However, this was not a Federal regulator, and it does not replace the state-based system of insurance regulation in the US.

108 For a robust defence of the reasons for this, see Harrington (2009).

have to pay its value on novation. It has sometimes been claimed that this mechanism was important in the distress of Bear Stearns,[109] but the contemporaneous evidence supporting this mechanism speaks to a general loss of confidence in the firm rather than novation as a particular contributor to liquidity drawdowns.[110]

Derivatives Reform after the 2008 Crisis

2.81 The volume and impact of derivatives reform after the 2008 crisis was very substantial. The principal planks of the reform agenda for derivatives were:[111]

- *Bilateral margin requirements.* Rules were put in place to require bilateral derivatives participants whose portfolios were over a certain size to post initial and variation margin, subject to certain exemptions.[112] The minimum margin period of risk in these rules for bilateral derivatives is ten days, while it is five days for cleared OTCs. This means that clearing a portfolio of OTC derivatives typically reduces its margin requirement even without any benefit from multilateral netting, so the bilateral margin requirements incentivize central clearing.[113]

- *Mandatory clearing.* The authorities imposed the obligation that all in-scope OTC derivatives entered into or novated after a fixed date should be cleared by a CCP, again subject to certain exemptions. This is known as the clearing mandate.

- *Execution requirements for OTC derivatives.* Regulators decided that, where appropriate, standardized OTC derivatives contracts should be traded on exchanges or electronic trading platforms. As a result, execution requirements for certain types of OTC derivatives were introduced in various jurisdictions, including the US and the EU.

  The rules for bilateral margin, the clearing mandate, and the derivatives execution requirements are discussed in more detail in Chapter 6.

---

109 See, e.g., footnote 3 in Dudley (2009).

110 See FCIC (2011) at 287. The email referred to in footnote 57, from one regulator to another, reads in part: 'We have begun to see some buyside firms trying to move away from Bear as a prime broker counterparty. Also seeing some HFs [hedge funds] wishing to assign [i.e. novate] trades the clients had done with Bear to other CPs [counterparties] so that Bear "steps out" .... Snese [*sic*] that clients are more concerned about BS than the [other] dealers at this point.'

111 For a different perspective, see Zazzara (2020).

112 At the time of writing, the most recent version of the internationally agreed rules is R. BCBS & IOSCO (2020).

113 See section D of DAT (2018) for a discussion of this incentive.

- *Trade reporting of OTC derivatives.* As noted above, the authorities required reporting of OTC derivatives entered into or novated after a fixed date to trade repositories.
- *Enhanced standards for FMIs.* The clearing mandate meant that CCPs became more systemically important than ever. In order to mitigate the extra risks that they and other types of financial market infrastructure posed, various aspects of the prudent standards relating to FMIs were revised. The first major internationally agreed enhancement was the CPMI IOSCO Principles for financial market infrastructures, or 'PFMI's: these principles were subsequently extended in various ways.[114] They are discussed in Chapter 7.
- *Increased bank capital requirements for market risk.* Regulators' estimates of the market risk of portfolios were increased in two major steps: once with the so-called Basel 2.5 changes in 2011, then again with the (still largely unimplemented) fundamental review of the trading book.[115]
- *Increased capital requirements for counterparty credit risk.* The elements of models for estimating the counterparty credit risk of OTC derivatives were discussed in Chapter 1. Changes to both models-based and standardized methods for calculating counterparty credit risk were made after the crisis.[116] Regulators also brought in new rules for capitalizing bank exposures to CCPs, reflecting the increased size of these exposures now that OTC derivatives clearing was more commonplace.[117]
- *Increased capital requirements for CVA risk.* New prudential standards for CVA risk were imposed by bank regulators. The bank capital requirements for market, counterparty credit and CVA risk are discussed in Chapter 5.

2.82 In addition, OTC derivatives were affected by broader financial regulatory changes. These included the imposition of a leverage ratio (discussed in Chapter 4), bank liquidity regulation, higher capital ratios, changes to the definition of capital, and policies requiring additional capital for systemically important banks.

---

114 The extensions include guidance on recovery and resolution of FMIs, additional guidance on the PFMIs themselves, and mandatory disclosure obligations for FMIs: see https://www.bis.org/cpmi/info_pfmi.htm.

115 See respectively R. BCBS (2011a) and R. BCBS (2019a). There are also various other changes to the treatment of market risk in the consolidated Basel framework.

116 There were revisions to policy on backtesting counterparty credit risk models and on the treatment of collateral in the models-based approach, while a new standardized approach, the Standard Approach for Counterparty Credit Risk, or 'SA-CCR', was introduced. See R. BCBS (2014b) for details of the latter.

117 See R. BCBS (2014c).

Crisis issues and policy responses

2.83 At this point it is useful to stand back and compare the broad areas of reform with what the issues relating to OTC derivatives in the crisis were. The top half of Figure 2.2 does this. An alternative approach is to consider which of the issues which emerged in the crisis could be addressed by these types of policy: this is in the bottom half of the Figure. (The questions of whether the policy as implemented achieved its desired effect or were proportional responses to the issue are separate, and will be considered later.)

Policy	Justified by crisis?	Justified more broadly?	Treated further in chapter
Bilateral margin	Yes	Yes	6
Mandatory clearing	No	No	6
Standards for FMIs	No	Yes	7
Trade reporting	Yes	Yes	2
Higher capital requirements	Partly †	No	5
CVA capital	Yes	No	5
Execution requirements	No	Partly	6

Figure 2.2– A summary of the justifications for post-crisis derivatives policy initiatives (above) and an analysis of how far the policy reforms addressed crisis issues (below)

Issue	Addressed by policy?
Opacity and complexity in OTCD	Yes
Incentives in the originate to distribute model	Marginally ‡
Insufficient capital for mortgage lending	No
Liquidity risk in CSAs	No
Insufficient capital for CVA risk	Yes

† There was justification for higher capital for real estate lending, for default risk in the trading book and for uncollateralized written credit protection.
‡ The specified retention amounts are too small and there are too many exemptions to the requirement.

2.84 There are, of course, debatable judgements in this analysis, both in the analysis of the justifications for policy making and in the choice of issues. But the broad picture is clear: there is at least a reasonable case that much of what was done was not justified by the events of the crisis while some of the important issues which emerged during the crisis were not obviously addressed.[118]

[118] This assessment is part of a wider pattern. As Romano (2014b) puts it at 56, the 'iron law' of financial regulation is that 'enactment is invariably crisis driven, adopted at a time when there is

2.85 Many parts of this case have received separate attention. This book draws them together in order to understand why derivatives received so much regulatory attention, where that attention was justified, and how good the resulting policy making was. In spite of its many shortcomings, there has been relatively little over-arching analysis of the derivatives policy over-reaction. Before discussing it, it is worth examining how regulators talked about their response, as it gives some insight into the nature of the attention paid to this area.

Regulatory Discourse and the 2008 Crisis

2.86 One tool for analysing how regulators discuss the 2008 crisis and their response to it is to consider an ideal justification for reform. Different stakeholders will have differing views of this, but a reasonable table of contents might include:

- A historical account of the key events of the crisis;
- A discussion of a range of potential mechanisms which could have caused them;
- A detailed analysis of these mechanisms, including bounds on their size, leading to a shorter list of mechanisms which are judged significant and which could reasonably apply in the future;
- For each mechanism, a presentation of potential interventions which could reduce its severity or probability or both;
- An analysis of the 'best' intervention or interventions in each case; and
- A discussion of the tests which could be used in future to determine whether these interventions were working.

2.87 This would be, in the terms of Bruner (1986), a 'logico-scientific' approach: an attempt to provide a parsimonious description of the most important crisis phenomena, their causes, and how those causes might be disrupted at low cost. There is nothing like this for the regulatory interventions which were made after the 2008 crisis.[119] A detailed justification for the measures proposed is largely or wholly absent from the rule texts themselves. Instead it must be inferred from hints in introductory paragraphs or from policy makers' speeches and other marginal discourses.

a paucity of information regarding what has transpired; resulting in "off-the-rack" solutions often poorly fashioned to the problem at hand; with inevitable flaws given the dynamic uncertainty of financial markets; but arduous to revise or repeal.'

119 For a discussion of one limited counterexample to this, the Macroeconomic Assessment Group on Derivatives' Report, see Chapter 6.

2.88 In this section, a sample regulator's account will be considered. This is a speech by a senior regulator setting out his view of the progress made in financial regulation ten years after the crisis: see Carney (2018). Consideration of it will illuminate the nature of the claim being made by policy makers about their work.

Some claims

2.89 The justification for financial regulation after a crisis often takes the form 'because these things happened, these rules must be imposed'. The speech considered here makes that kind of claim. It begins with general observations: that before 2008 there was a sense that 'this time was different' because authorities finally understood how to 'do' financial stability; that markets are imperfect, but that this fact had been forgotten.

2.90 The story then pivots with the observation that the pre-crisis financial system had 'only spread risk, contingently and opaquely, in ways that ended up increasing it'. That 'only' is interesting. Had equity markets *only* spread risk when shares were traded? Were these markets 'contingent and opaque'? The strategy of extending a valid critique of one part of the structured credit market to the whole financial system is effective because it justifies a wider intervention than a more nuanced analysis would.

2.91 The speech then goes on to discuss market conduct issues, mentioning the Libor and FX market scandals. These episodes, and reforms to prevent them, are important, but they are separate from the 2008 crisis. Using them to introduce the call for reshaping the financial system is curious because while culture, incentives and market norms were important enablers of the 2008 crisis, they alone were not enough. You also needed too little capital for mortgage risk; market participants buying trillions of dollars of mortgage-backed securities that they did not understand; and lax regulation, especially of investment banks and some insurers. None of these issues are mentioned.

2.92 Next, rather at odds with the concern early in the speech about the dangers of 'this time is different' claims, there is the suggestion that if the right institutional framework is built, 'true finance', 'an enduring platform for strong, sustainable and balanced growth' will result. The suggestion is that this is not just a vision, but a path that, thanks to post-crisis policy making, we are already on. It is claimed that the 'reforms are having their desired effects'. However, the reforms touted are not to mortgage markets, nor to the originate to distribute model. They are trade reporting of OTC derivatives and 'encouraging' central clearing. Given that none of the OTC derivatives implicated in the crisis were or are clearable, this is a bold claim. Clearing had simplified the exposures between OTC derivatives markets participants, but it had done little to reduce the risks of mortgage lending, or to improve US insurance regulation, or to meaningfully address the vulnerabilities in the originate to distribute model. It is therefore natural to ask why the speech spotlights a policy that addressed one issue in the later part of the crisis—the loss of confidence in financial institutions caused by uncertainty about the derivatives exposures between them—while staying silent on so much else.

Regulatory attention

2.93 One answer comes from an analysis of the issues the speech mentions. These fall into two categories: either issues where post-crisis policy had already been agreed upon, or ones where it was being actively discussed. Bank liquidity standards, capital requirements and resolution fall into the former category; action on liquidity risks in asset management and CCP resolution in the latter.[120]

2.94 The speech does not waste words on areas where there was little chance of successful policy making.[121] The art of the possible is a clear constraint; or, rather, because most of the regulations being discussed are internationally negotiated, the art of the agreeable. Thus it is plausible that the contents of the speech reflect a sifting of the issues based not just on their salience but also on whether regulators have already acted on them, or are likely to in future.

2.95 There are broad claims in the speech which make for good slogans but which each deserve careful analysis. To pick just one example, 'regulation has made banks less complex and more focused' is not clearly true. Consider, as an example, JPMorgan. In 2007, this bank's balance sheet was $1.56 trillion: in 2019, it was more than a trillion dollars bigger. In 2007, the bank identified its principal business lines as investment banking; retail financial services; card services; commercial banking; treasury and securities services; and asset management. In 2019, the major contributors towards the firm's revenues were investment banking fees; principal transactions; lending- and deposit-related fees; asset management; investment securities; mortgage fees and related income; and card income. The bank has got bigger and its activity in 2019 seems to rather similar to what it was doing in 2007.[122] How then is this bank less complex and more focused?

Storytelling

2.96 The rhetoric in this speech is evidently far from Bruner's logico-scientific approach. Rather, it is the other form of discourse he describes: narrative mode,

[120] At the time of writing at least, the judgement that regulators would be willing to act on liquidity risks in asset management has not proved correct.

[121] This highlights the need for a regulatory attention theory, studying the regulatory agenda, much like political attention theory studies the political one: see Jones & Baumgartner (2005) for the latter.

[122] Respectively JPMorgan 2007 Annual Report at 27 and 2019 Annual Report at 48.

or storytelling. Discourses in the narrative mode are interpretive. They give a partial account of events and attempt to explain, persuade, and categorize. This mode helps listeners—especially listeners who share norms with the story teller—to understand things. However, many people would consider that a persuasive metaphor is not sufficient justification for re-engineering the financial system. The 2008 crisis was *like* a storm, but this metaphor does not tell us how high to build the financial dykes.[123] The financial system is *like* a group of people some of whom will sometimes get sick; but different illnesses require different treatments, and are contagious in different ways.[124] Metaphors often break down when they are followed too far, so there is reason to be cautious about the strength of the implication from metaphor to action.

A story disguised

2.97 The strategy of telling stories to persuade is very old. As the exercise of power has moved from physical coercion to more diffuse forms of control, so framing narratives have become more important. Gramsci points out the 'spontaneous' consent given 'by the great masses of the population to the general direction imposed on social life by the dominant fundamental group'[125] due to unquestioning belief in the narratives this group promulgates. Power, for him, is not just the right to do what you want, but also to shape how people think about it; to have the story you tell become the dominant one. This latter manifestation of power is sometimes called 'Gramscian' or 'cultural hegemony': we will just call it 'hegemony'.[126]

2.98 A key aspect of hegemony is manufacturing consent by promoting one narrative as objective, and hence one set of interests as universal. When this technique is effective, it becomes very difficult to imagine a different story with a different moral. It limits the boundaries of permissible discourse so as to discourage the consideration of alternatives.[127]

---

123 The metaphor is from Wellink (2008). For more on floods, and whether building higher dykes is a good idea, see footnote 268 in Chapter 9.

124 The 'contagion' metaphor is a commonplace of narratives about the 2008 crisis, including the one in this chapter. See, for instance, Carney (2018), and, for more on metaphors in narratives of the crisis through the lenses of Critical Discourse Analysis and Cognitive Linguistics, see Abdel-Raheem (2013).

125 The quote is from Gramsci (1971) at 145.

126 Litowitz (2000) characterizes Gramscian hegemony as power that 'induces people to comply with a dominant set of practices and institutions without the threat of physical force'.

127 See Lears (1985) at 570. This closely relates to Foucault's observation of the central role that producing and shaping discourse has in the exercise of power and Althusser's idea of an ideological state apparatus: see Foucault (2003) at 33. Also important here, as Lears points out, is the fact that hegemony is a continuous process: consent is continually reconstructed, partial, fluctuating.

2.99 The speech discussed above adopts the hegemonic strategy of presenting a partial, situated analysis as universal and objective. The claim that there is only one interpretation of the crisis and only one correct response serves to obscure potential alternatives.[128] As with the invention of tradition studied by Cannadine, an account of the past is being framed in the service of particular interests in the present. This suggests that we need to be alert to the nature of regulators' claims; to how regulatory knowledge is constructed; and to the potential responses which have been obscured by policy makers' stories.[129]

2.100 In this spirit, the four chapters in Part II present various aspects of post-crisis regulation in more detail. Each examines a policy, considers its effects, analyses the evidence for it, discusses the story told about it, and uncovers alternative responses. The final chapter brings these discourses together, presenting potential changes to post-crisis financial regulation and to the policy making process that they suggest. First, though, it will be helpful to analyse the performance of post-crisis regulation during a recent stress—that created by the Covid pandemic.

When there is an opportunity to extend and solidify it—for financial regulators, a crisis—then it is no surprise to see a new story emerge and be rapidly refined. As President Obama's Chief of Staff, Rahm Emanuel, said to the *Wall Street Journal* in November 2008: 'you never want a serious crisis to go to waste. And what I mean by that is an opportunity to do things that you think you could not do before.

128 As Rancière (2010) puts it at 144, the problem is the claim that 'there is one unique reality to which everything must be related, a reality that is experienceable as a sense datum and which has only one possible signification'.

129 Gramsci (1971), writing about an entirely different set of events, pointed out that while the phenomenon whereby a crisis 'creates situations which are dangerous in the short run', 'the traditional ruling class ... changes men and programmes and, with greater speed than is achieved by the subordinate classes, reabsorbs the control that was slipping from its grasp'. This phenomenon was clearly visible after 2008.

3

The Financial System during Covid: A Test of the Performance of the Post-2008 Regulatory Regime

Introduction

3.1 At the time of writing in the late summer of 2021, the coronavirus pandemic is still underway, so any attempt at analysing its impact on the financial system must be preliminary. One way to begin to uncover it is to consider how the financial system's ability to deliver its key functions was affected by the pandemic.

3.2 For our purposes, there are five core financial system functions. These are:[1]

1. To facilitate payments;
2. To provide safe stores of value which can be accessed quickly;
3. To facilitate investment at prices which are broadly reflective of their risk, and to provide funds for borrowers at suitable prices;
4. To allow risks to be transferred from those who do not want them to those that do, again at prices commensurate with the value of what is being traded;
5. To support public policy objectives, including the management of inflation and the maintenance of financial stability.

3.3 Together, these functions serve workers, consumers, producers, and investors, including those within the financial system itself.[2]

---

[1] See Merton & Bodie (1995) for an alternative, longer account.

[2] This division into functions is somewhat artificial: some instruments are issued to transfer risk, but bought as investments, for instance. Nevertheless, the distinction between short- and long-term funding markets, and between markets where most issuers' motivation is to raise funds and those where most transactions are motivated by a desire to transfer risk, is a useful one.

3.4 The Covid-19 pandemic, caused by the widespread transmission of a novel coronavirus, began in 2020. The disease itself, and the measures taken to manage the risks to health it created, caused an appalling loss of life. They present, as the health authorities put it,[3] 'an unprecedented challenge to public health, food systems and the world of work'.

3.5 Covid also represents the biggest challenge to the financial system since the 2008 crisis (and, arguably, ever). The impact of this stress test on the financial system's ability to provide its key functions gives insight into its nature and the effects of the post-2008 regulatory reforms.

3.6 This chapter examines the trajectory of markets and the extent to which the financial system facilitated the needs of the real economy. Covid created an enormous need for risk transfer, for credit, and for liquidity: how well were these needs met?

3.7 The answer will turn out to be 'not without problems and interruptions', so the interventions which authorities made to address these issues are considered. This naturally leads to a discussion of the aggregate performance of the post-2008 regulatory regime. Building on this discussion, the final section of the chapter previews how this regime will be analysed in the rest of the book.

Market Trajectory

3.8 A major indication of the looming threat of the coronavirus came when the central government of China imposed a lockdown in various cities across Wuhan province in January 2020. The World Health Organization had confirmed the potential for human-to-human transmission of the infection earlier that month, emphasizing the risk that the coronavirus infection posed to human health. The Wuhan lockdown was imposed in an attempt to control the spread of the virus.

3.9 Financial markets outside Asia were initially unaffected by this news, with US and European equity markets buoyant until the last week of February.[4] This would prove to be the high point of 2020 for global financial markets.

Covid spreads

3.10 By the start of March, it had become clear that the disease had spread to Europe, the Middle East, North and South America, and Australasia. In an

[3] See the joint statement by ILO, FAO, IFAD, and WHO, *Impact of COVID-19 on people's livelihoods, their health and our food systems*, October 2020, available at https://www.who.int/news/item/13-10-2020-impact-of-covid-19-on-people%27s-livelihoods-their-health-and-our-food-systems.

[4] US equity markets reached record highs on 19 February 2020.

early sign of what was to come for most countries, Italian authorities imposed lockdowns in a number of cities,[5] and various authorities enacted travel bans.[6]

3.11 A week later, thousands of cases and hundreds of deaths had been confirmed in Europe. Local lockdowns quickly became common. At this point, expectations of economic disruption rapidly increased. Financial markets reacted precipitously. Equity markets fell; volatility in many risk factors rose; and there was a flight to assets which are perceived as safe, such as US Treasuries. Figure 3.1 illustrates this with two key indicators, the yield on ten year US Treasuries and the level of the S&P 500 equity index.

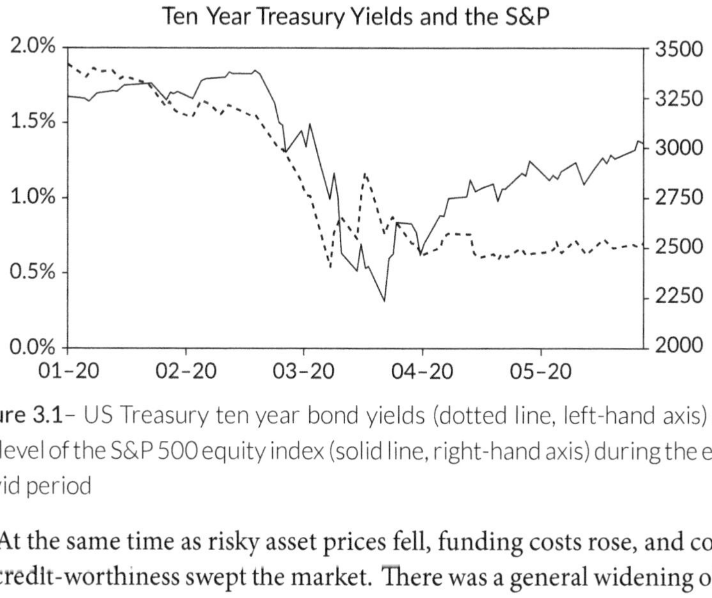

Figure 3.1– US Treasury ten year bond yields (dotted line, left-hand axis) and the level of the S&P 500 equity index (solid line, right-hand axis) during the early Covid period

3.12 At the same time as risky asset prices fell, funding costs rose, and concerns about credit-worthiness swept the market. There was a general widening of credit spreads and a withdrawal of leverage.

3.13 Commodity markets were acutely affected in this period. One of the most disrupted was the oil market, which was roiled both by the sudden fall in demand and by the failure of oil-producing countries to reach an agreement on output cuts as orders fell. Prices of both of the global oil benchmark futures contracts, Brent crude and West Texas Intermediate ('WTI'), fell, and storage facilities started to fill as refineries cut production.

[5] Quarantines of the northern Italian towns which were early coronavirus hot spots were announced on 21 February.

[6] The UK issued advice against all non-essential travel on 17 March, and extensive restrictions on entry at Germany's borders were imposed on the same day. The list of countries affected by travel suspensions and limitations on entry into the United States was extended from its initial scope—the People's Republic of China excluding Hong Kong and Macau—first to Iran on 29 February, then to the Schengen area on 11 March. The UK was added on 14 March.

The dash for cash

3.14 The WHO declared that Covid was a global pandemic on 11 March. At this point, it became clear that markets had severely underestimated the disruption that the measures to contain the virus would cause. Many market participants reduced their risk levels, causing further drops in the prices of risky assets.[7] Concern over the extent of the interruption in company earnings grew, and many firms began to increase their reserves and draw down on credit lines. There was very high demand for cash and near-cash assets: as the Fed's Randal Quarles put it in Quarles (2020), there was 'a historically unprecedented dash for cash', and few suppliers: many of those that had cash, hoarded it. The financial system's ability to withstand these demands and remain sound was, Quarles said, 'a damn, close-run thing'.

3.15 Meanwhile, investors in funding markets were becoming increasingly nervous. In the commercial paper market, an important venue for short-term corporate financing, investors would only buy the shortest-term and highest quality instruments. This, in turn, increased many companies' demand for cash from other sources. Many money market funds experienced high levels of selling as investors liquidated their positions to increase their cash reserves. Some funds could not liquidate their assets fast enough and suspended redemptions, forcing their investors to use other sources of liquidity.[8]

3.16 Stress was particularly evident in the market for offshore US dollar funding. Many companies outside the United States invest in dollar-denominated assets due to the range of opportunities available. The derivatives markets are often used to swap dollar flows from these investments back into local currency. A financial variable known as the cross-currency basis is a measure of the price of doing this.[9] Dislocations emerged in this market during March 2020: the US

[7] On 16 March, the S&P 500 index fell by 12%, the worst one day drop since 1987. The VIX index of equity market volatility reached an all-time high of 83.

[8] Many funds typically offer investors a price at which they can sell with little or no delay. This works well when outflows are low or fund holdings are liquid, but if there are substantial demands to exit a fund and low or substantially declining liquidity in the markets for the assets the fund is invested in, this can create issues. See ESMA (2020) for a further discussion.

[9] The cross-currency basis is the amount by which a cross-currency swap differs from the rate predicted by forward FX rates. It therefore, as Borio et al. (2016) put it 'indicates the amount by which the interest paid to borrow one currency by swapping it against another differs from the cost of directly borrowing this currency in the cash market'. In many currencies there are more investors wanting to swap back from dollars than risk capital available to profit from a non-zero basis, so the cross-currency basis vs US dollars tends to be negative. The dollar/yen basis is a good example of this. (Elsewhere, as for instance in Australian dollars, many companies pay US dollar coupons on bonds they have issued by swapping local currencies to dollars: here the basis is positive.) See PRA (2020) at 49 for a further discussion of the continuing arbitrage

dollar appreciated, and the cross-currency basis went more negative as non-US corporates were unable to roll over their dollar borrowing and hence were forced to sell dollar-denominated assets. This represented a substantial increase in the cost of offshore US dollar funding.

Market quality issues

3.17 Securities markets were unable to bear the extent of the sales being made in March 2020 without declines in market quality. Bid-offer spreads widened and market depth fell as waves of selling overwhelmed the liquidity available to absorb it.[10] This was particularly evident in markets that were largely intermediated by dealers, such as those for corporate bonds. In these markets, dealers typically warehouse risk, buying assets from sellers and waiting until they can find a suitable buyer. During March, they became less willing to do this and charged more for intermediation. Transaction costs rose precipitously, and trades were increasingly only done when dealers could find both a buyer and a seller. This 'agency' form of trading was slower and less certain.[11]

3.18 The US Treasury market is the most liquid fixed-income market in the world. US Treasuries play a central role in short-term funding markets. They are the single most common form of collateral in the repo market. Treasury bonds and bills act as a benchmark for most other dollar fixed-income securities, and they form a substantial part of many institutions' liquid asset buffers.[12] They often act as a safe haven in stress. This was not the case during the first two weeks of March 2020. Instead, a wide range of investors, including offshore corporates and leveraged investors, tried to sell US Treasuries.[13]

---

opportunity present in cross-currency basis and why it exists, and Avdjiev et al. (2020) for an account of movements in the cross-currency basis for various currencies during March 2020.

10 State Street (2020) suggests that US-listed ETFs saw average bid-offer spreads increase from 0.37% in 2019 to 1.09% in March 2020.

11 The reluctance of dealers to facilitate trading during the stress period by holding inventory is discussed by Kargar et al. (2020). As they put it, 'corporate bond dealers appeared unwilling to use their own balance sheets ... during the most tumultuous trading days, the dealer sector absorbed no net inventory'.

12 A liquid asset buffer is a stock of highly liquid financial instruments which many firms, including most banks, keep in order to be able to meet payments as they fall due. The minimum size of these buffers is set by international bank regulation. Current regulation assumes that the highest quality assets in banks' buffers can be liquidated at short notice and with minimal loss of value, so a material dysfunction in the US Treasury market represents a failure of regulatory assumptions. See PRA (2020) for a further discussion of bank liquid asset buffers.

13 Lorrie Logan manager of the System Open Market Account at the New York FED, reported that 'customer transaction volumes reported by primary dealers spiked from an average level of around $400 billion per day in February to a peak of around $650 billion per day in mid-March'. While this was a substantial increase, it was only an increase of a touch more than 50%: see Logan (2020).

3.19 This selling pressure reversed the usual flight to quality effect experienced in most stresses, including that in the first week of March. Instead, Treasury yields rose, as Figure 3.1 illustrates.[14] Market quality fell, with bid-offer spreads widening dramatically and market depth plummeting.[15] Trading was only possible in smaller size than usual, and with greater price impact, even for the most liquid Treasury securities. The situation was even worse for less liquid Treasuries.[16] Thus, while there was a substantial amount of trading activity, it cost market participants much more and took longer. For something as systemically important as the US Treasury market, these were alarming developments.

Failing relationships

3.20 Financial market participants often have precise risk transfer requirements. They want to buy *this* bond, or move exactly *that* risk. However, often, it makes sense to trade a related instrument. It may be that a bond from the same issuer with a different maturity is more liquid, or that a futures contract referencing the exact type of commodity the participant wants to sell is not available, but one referencing a different type of the same commodity is.[17]

3.21 The efficacy of this strategy of using related, more liquid instruments relies on financial relationships continuing to hold over time. If I buy an on-the-run five year Treasury bond, for instance, instead of the less liquid six year one that would precisely match my need, I do this in expectation that the difference between the prices of the two instruments will stay within relatively tight bounds. This, in turn, relies on other market participants being willing to step in should the difference become too big. Unless there is a good reason for the prices of these

[14] Investors did not behave as if US Treasuries were safe haven assets as have done in previous episodes of stress: they preferred cash. See Duffie (2020) for a discussion of this phenomena.

[15] Fleming & Ruela (2020) quote a six-fold widening in the bid-offer spread for the 30 year and a doubling for the ten year. They further state that the order book depth for five and ten year Treasuries fell as low as 10% of their post-crisis average.

[16] Logan's remarks discussed in footnote 13 include the observation that the bid-offer spread for less liquid off-the-run Treasury securities rose to almost 30 times their normal value, a historically unprecedented level.

[17] The crude oil market is a good example: the crude oil from different wells has slightly different chemical compositions. One key aspect of this is its sulphur content, as this affects the cost of storing and refining the oil, but other aspects are important too. The two benchmark crude oil futures contracts, Brent and West Texas Intermediate, refer to crude oil whose composition lies between narrow bounds. NYMEX's rulebook effective from 2018, for example, restricts crude deliverable into the WTI future to that with 0.42% or less by weigh of sulphur, with specific gravity between 37 and 42 degrees, and with various other limits on its properties: see Appendix A of the rules, R. CME (2017). A producer or consumer who has a specific risk transfer need for crude oil outside these bounds might nevertheless decide to use a WTI futures contract due to its liquidity, ready price visibility, and low transaction costs.

two instruments to diverge—and it is difficult to think of an event five and a half years into the future which we know now would be likely to affect the prices of US Treasury securities after it but not before it—market participants could reasonably expect large price deviations to be arbitraged away. This 'policing' of the yield curve ensures that the difference between the yields of treasury securities close to each other in maturity are usually small. Similar policing usually ensures that other financial relationships hold: commodity futures prices are usually closely related to the spot price of the same commodity, for instance.

3.22 Many of these relationships started to break down during the Covid period. There were two main reasons for this. The first was real-world disruptions or declines in demand caused by Covid.[18] A good example was the US crude oil benchmark futures contract on West Texas Intermediate Crude, or WTI. For the first time ever, this had a negative settlement price in March 2020. This was due to an already oversupplied oil market suddenly experiencing a massive reduction in the demand for crude oil, and limited storage available at the delivery point for the future, Cushing.[19] There was too much oil relative to the demand, and it was difficult for most market participants to store it, so there was quite literally the prospect of having to pay people to take it away. The importance of factors specific to the shortest maturity (or 'front month') WTI contract, such as the paucity of storage at Cushing, is underlined by the fact that other crude oil futures contracts, including longer maturity WTI futures, did not suffer the same fate.

3.23 The other main reason for the breakdown in arbitrage relationships was the dearth of market participants willing and able to take advantage of arbitrage opportunities compared to the volume of transactions pushing the relationships further apart. Consider the five year versus six year Treasury bond example again, and suppose that the five year bond is cheap compared to the six year. In order to profit from the arbitrage, a market participant would need to buy the five year bond and sell short the six year. Not only does that depend on the availability of capital to support the trade, given other competing opportunities, but it also relies on the six year being available to borrow at an attractive price.[20] If the volume of arbitrage activity is small compared to the volume of people selling the five year, perhaps because it is on-the-run and hence more liquid, and they want to sell anything they can to get cash, the arbitrageur will lose money on a mark-to-market basis as the relationship becomes more dislocated. They may even have to sell their position and lock in this loss if they experience too large a margin call, or the cost of borrowing the six year becomes too high.

[18] See PRA (2020) at 52 for a discussion of other the breakdown of some other relationships.

[19] See CFTC (2020) for a detailed account of the events leading up to this event and a much more comprehensive analysis of its causes.

[20] Typically this would be done via repo.

Treasury futures and repo

3.24 A particularly stark example of the failure of arbitrage relationships came in a complex of markets linked to US Treasuries. Before Covid, arbitrageurs commonly bought US Treasury bonds and sold futures on these bonds. This trade worked because the basis between the futures and the bonds was often positive, so there was money to be made as the future converged to the cash price towards expiry. However, the returns were not large, so this 'treasury basis' trade was usually leveraged by repoing the bonds out, allowing a far larger position to be taken with the same amount of cash.

3.25 In the dash for cash episode, arbitrageurs were competing with other market participants for repo capacity and facing a wave of selling in the Treasury market. As a result, their Treasury basis trades went against them, and they faced margin calls. Some arbitrageurs could not meet these calls and were forced to liquidate their positions, creating a further wave of selling. This caused the basis between the future and the bond to reach unprecedented levels.[21]

3.26 The result of this disruption was the imposition of real costs on market participants using futures to hedge Treasuries, the reason for having Treasury futures in the first place. While other markets suffered similar dislocations,[22] the events in the US Treasury market were 'especially notable', both due to its importance and because 'measures of market functioning deteriorated at unparalleled speed to levels not seen since the [2008] Global Financial Crisis'.[23]

3.27 This episode illustrates a key feature of the post-2008 financial system. Large banks have largely withdrawn from engaging in arbitrage and other forms of proprietary trading activity.[24] This activity now takes place mostly in non-bank market participants such as hedge funds and principal trading firms. Intermediation in securities and many futures markets—market making—now often takes place outside the banking system too. While this has had negative implications for market quality in less liquid instruments in ordinary conditions,[25] the biggest issues come in periods of stress. Unlike banks, many of these new intermediaries are relatively badly capitalized. They are often reliant on repo markets for funding,

[21] Duffie (2020) at 11 quotes a cash-futures basis of 'hundreds of basis points' while Schrimpf et al. (2020) quantifies the issue by examining the difference between the actual one month repo rate for Treasuries and the repo rate that is implied by the prices of Treasury securities and Treasury futures contracts. For five and ten year bonds, the difference between these two rates exceeded 7% in late March, a very large amount.

[22] See Hauser (2020) for a discussion of stress in GBP and USD government bond markets.

[23] The quote is from Lorrie Logan's speech discussed previously in footnote 13.

[24] See PRA (2020) for an extended discussion of this.

[25] CGFS (2014) discusses this trend in the nature of the entities conducting financial market intermediation and its implications. See also the analysis in Box 3 (at 42) of Bank of England (2019).

and they typically do not have access to central bank windows. This means that both the policing of arbitrage and the provision of market making has become more dependent on short-term funding markets such as repo. When funding markets become disrupted, so does market making. In this situation, arbitrage relationships often fall apart, and risk transfer becomes more difficult and more expensive.

Interventions and Their Effects

3.28 The events of March 2020 forced the authorities to take 'extraordinary action to stabilize markets'.[26] There were five main classes of measures:

- *Lending to the real economy.* Government programmes were established to extend credit to firms. Typically these were focused on real economy businesses which were in sound financial condition before the onset of Covid, but which required financing to 'bridge the gap' until they could resume normal activity.[27]
- *Liquidity provision.* Central banks made very large amounts of liquidity available to qualifying borrowers, sometimes against a wider range of collateral than hitherto accepted. The FED also opened or reduced pricing on dollar swap lines to other central banks, allowing them to lend dollars as well as their own currencies.[28] Additional liquidity provision was targeted at classes of entity or market particularly in need.[29]
- *Asset purchases and last resort market making.* Central banks bought securities to reduce risk-free rates and to improve market quality in government

[26] The quote is from Cunliffe (2020).

[27] See for instance the FED's Main Street Lending Program or HMT's Coronavirus Business Interruption Loan Scheme, Coronavirus Large Business Interruption Loan Scheme, Bounce Back Loan Scheme and Future Fund Scheme. These schemes were all targeted at firms without access to central bank liquidity support.

[28] By 19 March, this provision of dollars offshore had extended to 14 central banks: see Federal Reserve Press Releases, *Coordinated Central Bank Action to Enhance the Provision of US dollar Liquidity*, 15 March 2020 and *Federal Reserve announces the establishment of temporary US dollar liquidity arrangements with other central banks*, 19 March 2020, available at https://www.federalreserve.gov/newsevents/pressreleases/monetary20200315c.htm and monetary20200319b.htm.

[29] See Federal Reserve Press Release, *Federal Reserve announces extensive new measures to support the economy*, 23 March 2020 available at https://www.federalreserve.gov/newsevents/pressreleases/monetary20200323b.htm for a discussion of three of these targeted measures, the Primary Market Corporate Credit Facility, the Secondary Market Corporate Credit Facility and the Term Asset-Backed Securities Loan Facility.

bond and agency markets, absorbing sales onto their balance sheets when other parties would not do so.[30] They also intervened in a number of other areas, including corporate bond, repo, and commercial paper markets, providing market intermediation and price support.[31]

- *Rate cuts.* There were various cuts in interest rates by central banks in early and mid-March.[32]
- *Regulatory easing.* Authorities reduced the regulatory burden on banks. Some countries had capital buffers which were under the control of the authorities: many of these were released, reducing capital requirements.[33] Some bank capital rules were also eased,[34] and many authorities reduced compliance burdens on financial institutions and extended deadlines for the implementation of new regulations.

The strain abates

3.29 The disruption to financial system functions in mid-March 2020 lasted until the authorities intervened, and declined afterwards. This demonstrates that some of the measures discussed in the last section were necessary—and possibly they all were.

3.30 In any event, collectively, the interventions were highly effective. Market quality recovered and, by the summer of 2020, most risky assets had regained all or nearly all of their pre-Covid value.[35] Indeed, by July, the question was whether the markets were overly optimistic and, if so, whether excessive central bank liquidity had created an ultimately unsustainable bubble in asset prices.

---

30 Central banks acting as market makers of last resort has gone from an unconventional and innovative policy in 2007 to a key part of authorities' tool kit in 2020. For the historical perspective, see Buiter & Sibert (2007).

31 Cunliffe (2020) relates that in 'the UK, the MPC increased the stock of asset purchases by £200 billion to a total of £645 billion, and bought gilts at the fastest rate operationally possible.' There were similarly sizable programmes in the US and the EU.

32 The FED reduced the FED funds rate by 0.5% on 3 March and again by 1% on 15 March; the UK reduced the bank rate by 0.5% on 11 March.

33 An example is the countercyclical buffer. This is an extra amount of capital which some jurisdictions required in the 'good times' prior to Covid. Where this requirement existed, it could be removed in stress, improving banks' capital ratios. For more details, see the BIS's summary of countercyclical buffers at https://www.bis.org/bcbs/ccyb/.

34 One interesting easing by a number of authorities, discussed further in the next chapter, was the exemption of central bank reserves from the leverage ratio. US authorities, in addition, gave banks a means of exempting US Treasuries from the leverage ratio. See R. BCBS (2020a) for a discussion of various forms of regulatory easing.

35 US equity indexes were at all-time highs; many corporate credit spreads were close to their pre-Covid levels; oil prices had stabilized; and primary corporate bond markets had reopened. Bank equity prices, however, tended to lag the broad market recovery.

The nature of the interventions

3.31 It is insightful to tie the Covid interventions back to the functions of the financial system. This illustrates where the authorities thought that action was needed to assure the provision of critical economic functions. Figure 3.2 summarizes the effect of each of the major classes of authority action discussed above.

Intervention	Impact
Asset purchases and last resort market making	Improved market quality in risk transfer markets, stabilized funding markets, and improved the transmission of monetary policy
Real economy lending	Provided credit beyond that available from the banking system (and non-bank providers)
Liquidity provision	Met cash needs in excess of the private financial system's capacity; improved liquidity-dependent market intermediation and the policing of arbitrage relationships
Rate cuts	Reduced the cost of cash and hence had similar effects to liquidity provision measures
Regulatory easing	Improved banks' ability to provide capital and balance sheet constrained functions; reduced the probability of financial instability and forced deleveraging

Figure 3.2– A summary of the effect of Covid-related inventions on financial system functions

3.32 One problem with interventions is judging how much is necessary, and when. If the authorities wait until there is clear evidence of serious issues in the financial system before taking extraordinary action, then the problem is often pressing by the time they act. This, in turn, means that there is a strong incentive to succeed. In this case, central banks tend to bring a bazooka to a gun fight, taking substantial risks onto their balance sheets in the process.[36]

3.33 On the other hand, if the authorities act in a precautionary fashion, it is unclear if action is needed at all, nor how much is needed. Moreover, in both cases, official sector action will tend to crowd out private sector provision, and markets come to expect that it will be repeated in the next stress. This means that market participants do not adequately prepare themselves for trouble. A 'just

[36] European Central Bank president Mario Draghi's famous 'whatever it takes' comment at the height of the eurozone crisis in July 2012 is an example of this tendency. For a concrete illustration during Covid, note that on a number of days in March the FED bought more than $100 billion of US Treasury and Agency securities. Cumulative purchases between 13 March and 31 July amounted to more than $2.6 trillion, an extraordinary amount: see Logan (2020) for details.

right' intervention would minimize these effects, but this is difficult to judge given the imperative to maintain stability at all costs.

The Performance of the Post-Crisis Regulatory Regime and the Rest of this Book

3.34 The post-crisis reforms required banks to hold substantially higher levels of liquidity and loss absorbing resources. This meant that when Covid hit, they did not fail, and they (mostly) did not have to sell assets to stay liquid enough to survive. However, they were not well enough resourced that they could support socially desirable lending to the real economy. The financial system could not facilitate the economy's unprecedented demand for cash.

Function	Score	Notes
Making payments	⋆⋆⋆	No significant issues during Covid
Safe stores for cash	⋆	Bank deposits worked but commercial paper, Treasury, and repo markets were disrupted
Risk-priced investments and credit	⋆⋆	Bond and equity markets largely functioned but with dislocated prices
Risk transfer markets	⋆	Some risk transfer was possible but arbitrage relationships broke down
Public policy support	⋆⋆	No large firm failed, but monetary policy transmission was uneven, and invention was necessary to support lending

Figure 3.3– A scorecard for the performance of the financial system during the early Covid period: scores are out of three

3.35 Relatedly, the quality of many financial markets during the early Covid period was not socially optimal. Risk transfer was often expensive and sometimes impossible. There was insufficient risk capital to keep arbitrage relationships in line, creating costs and risks for hedgers. Given all this, the assessment must be that the core functions of the financial system were only inconsistently and inefficiently provided during Covid, as Figure 3.3 summarizes.[37]

The nature of the financial system in 2020

3.36 It would be unfair to take a wholly negative view of the post-2008 reforms. As we have noted, banks in 2020 had more capital and liquidity both absolutely

[37] The judgement pre-Covid would have been kinder: see, for instance, Crump & Santos (2018).

and relative to their risk levels than they did in 2007. This helped. Banks are seldom if ever involved in the egregiously structured transactions based on asset and mortgage-backed securities that created issues in 2008. Authorities are now more alert to macro-prudential risk, and the need for tools to address it, than they were. Their interventions during the first half of 2020 were, in general, speedy and effective.

3.37 However, there are concerns. The partial withdrawal of banks from financial market arbitrage and intermediation, and their replacement by non-bank players, has made financial markets, including derivatives markets, more fragile. The private market could not meet the liquidity needs of the real economy, so authorities were forced to create massive amounts of additional liquidity and to liquefy a wide range of assets to prevent a crisis. Covid demonstrated that the demand for market liquidity in stress has increased dramatically since 2008, while the capacity to provide it has not kept pace.[38] As one strategy piece put it, 'post-2008 regulations appear to have substituted a liquidity crisis for a credit crisis'.[39]

3.38 At the same time, while not central to the concerns of this book, the rise of the dollar as the currency of international trade, finance, and investment has made the global financial system very sensitive to dollar funding conditions.[40] Finally, credit risk is increasingly held outside the banking system, often on a mark-to-market basis. This has made credit provision more sensitive to market signals and more reliant on the investors' willingness at a given point in time to invest in credit risky assets, further increasing the importance of financial markets.

Some questions

3.39 Even before Covid, there had been signs that the system's ability to move liquidity to where it was most needed; to intermediate between savers and borrowers; and to transfer risk was questionable.[41] After Covid, the answer was clear: the steps taken to enhance financial stability after 2008 had resulted in a system that did not always work very well. This suggests the following questions:

[38] The future looks even worse in some cases. For instance, the support measures introduced during Covid have dramatically increased the size of the budget deficit. This will likely mean more US Treasury issuance, and hence more secondary market trading, a bigger repo market, and so on. It is unclear how intermediaries will keep up with this demand unless, as Duffie (2020) advocates, the market is re-designed to facilitate more efficient intermediation.

[39] JPMorgan, *Scary stories to tell in the dark*, North America Fixed Income Strategy, June 2020.

[40] See Correa et al. (2020) for a further analysis of the role of the US dollar and US banks in global liquidity provision.

[41] For issues with liquidity, see the discussion of the September 2019 repo market 'spike' discussed in Chapter 4. For risk transfer, see the issues with access to client clearing discussed in Chapter 6.

- What are the shortcomings of the current prudential framework for derivatives specifically and for market quality more generally?
- Why does financial regulation so frequently fail to meet its goal, or lead to unintended consequences, or both?
- How can the rule making process and the institutional arrangements of financial regulation be reformed to improve the quality of future policy?

Opening up these questions is the task of Parts II and III of this book.

Part II: The Regulations

3.40 We continue the discussion with the rules themselves. The next four chapters treat four key sets of post-2008 financial regulations: the leverage ratio; bank risk-based capital regulation; the rules around uncleared margin and mandatory clearing; and the requirements for CCPs. The focus will be on derivatives regulation, but it will sometimes be necessary to consider broader policy issues, such as the leverage ratio, where they have a substantial impact on risk transfer markets. In this sense, derivatives regulation will be a lever to expose a wider set of policy issues.

3.41 Part II of the book studies what the rules say and what their effect on the financial system is. 'What the rules say' is also a question whose answer often seems to involve a daunting corpus of interlinked concepts. The 2019 Basel 3 framework has seven pages of abbreviations alone, for instance, and a frightening number of defined terms. It is clear that financial regulation has its own logic, its own rhetorical rules.[42] Given this, it is important to ask how this system has been constructed and what, in a given context, counts as a 'valid' deduction within the logic of financial regulation. The methods by which regulatory knowledge is constructed illustrate 'the type of reality with which we are dealing'.[43] To pick one example from many, how mandatory clearing of standardized OTC derivatives came to be seen as the accepted solution to the 'problem' of derivatives during the crisis, despite the fact that almost none of the positions which caused substantial losses in 2008 were clearable derivatives, tells us a great deal about how financial regulation is made.

3.42 The response of the system to regulation is also important: imposing a prudential rule does not necessarily lead to the same activity being carried out in the same way by the same actors more prudently. Rather, it causes those

[42] Thus the study of financial regulation can be understood in part as the exercise of uncovering this (shifting) logic and its implications. This, in turn, opens the possibility of using tools that scholars have introduced in other (in many ways more socially important) loci of study to uncover its logic: see Baudrillard (1987).

[43] The quote and inspiration is from Foucault (1982), the former at 778.

actors to re-evaluate the activity. They change what they do in reaction to regulation. This means that policy changes can result in the entry of new actors; in the restructuring of financial system activities; or in changed costs for market participants, affecting their incentives to conduct a given activity. In some cases, it can even result in an activity no longer being conducted. These shifts are key to understanding the effectiveness of regulation.

Part III: Perspectives on Financial Regulation

3.43 Part I of this book has introduced derivatives and given accounts of the 2008 and Covid financial markets crises. Parts II and III adopt a two track strategy. The first line of enquiry is to map the contours of the rules and their effects on the financial system. The second is to investigate the kinds of knowledge claims the rules represent, how these claims are justified, and the what sort of system emerges from their consolidation into a systematic apparatus of control.[44]

3.44 Three ideas motivate and shape this approach. These are that:

- *The details of the rules matter.* It is not possible to understand derivatives regulation and its impact on financial markets without sometimes[45] delving down into the rule text.
- *It is insightful to ask how regulatory knowledge is constructed and how regulatory power operates.*
- *Probing these issues reveals alternative approaches to policy making that might better serve society, and that would otherwise remain hidden.* As soon as questions of power and authority are considered, it is obvious that different choices for how regulation is organized, legitimized, governed, and operated are possible.

3.45 Part III adopts this approach, using a number of areas of scholarship as searchlights, illuminating derivatives regulation from different angles. It begins with legal scholarship, and in particular the perspective of administrative law.

[44] Foucault (1982) at 778, which in turn is looking back in part to Foucault (1972), suggests that the first step in this 'archaeology' of power is 'to create a history of the different modes by which, in our culture, human beings are made subjects'. One way to proceed is by considering adaptations to power. These are not just oppositions to it in the sense of claims of its illegitimacy, ineffectiveness or unreasonableness. Rather they are the strategies that a system develops as it evolves in response to the exercise of external power. The financial system and financial regulation are mutually constitutive: each defines and steers the other. Thus financial regulation only makes sense in the context of the financial system it helps to create and which helps to create it. Once the process whereby the exercise of regulatory power leads to the evolution of the financial system is exposed, alternative structures for this discourse can be considered.

[45] 'Sometimes', not always. We do not aim to give a comprehensive account of all of the rules discussed, but rather to uncover their key features and effects based on the text itself.

Regulation is an administrative matter, so the questions of when administrative acts are legitimate and how they are held to account by the courts clarifies how the institutional arrangements and processes of financial regulation could be improved.

3.46 Financial regulation involves an enormously costly interference in the organization and behaviour of the financial system. A justification for this would require a demonstration that the benefits of regulation exceed its costs. Economists have developed the framework for conducting this kind of cost-benefit analysis and uncovered many of the issues in its application. This technology is used to investigate the features of a convincing economic rationale for and review of derivatives policy.

3.47 Much financial rule making can be understood as a modelling exercise: some features of the financial system are represented, and claims are made about how they change under regulatory intervention. Regulators have requirements for banks' use of models, so it is interesting to use these requirements as a mirror, investigating how regulation might see itself.

3.48 We then turn to the discourses between regulators, between regulators and governments, and between regulators and the regulated. This helps to uncover how the regulators' tribe behaves; why it was mandated and empowered as it was; how it is held to account; and how its dialogues with stakeholders are structured.

3.49 There are some sensible ideas in post-crisis derivatives regulation, and the financial system is stronger as a result of some of the new policies. However, there is much that should be improved at the level of the individual rules. Some of the most useful possibilities, inspired by the analysis in Part II of the book, are proposed in the last chapter.

3.50 These revisions are not enough. An investigation of post-crisis rule making reveals that regulation is no longer part of the logic of finance, but rather a separate power centre which constructs and promulgates a situated, partial narrative about it. The construction of an enormous, complex corpus of regulation was only possible thanks to the power that financial regulators have accumulated. Opaque rule making processes have too often led to inefficient, disproportionate, hard-to-change rules. The last chapter of the book also gives some suggestions for improvements to the institutional arrangements of financial regulation, based on the analysis in the prior chapters, which would lead to a more responsive, open rule making process. Failure to reform financial regulation may not just result in the relentless imposition of unjustified costs on the society—it may also mean that the financial system will once again fail to do its job when stress hits.

Part II

Regulations

4

Leverage Ratios and the Construction of Regulatory Knowledge

Introduction

4.1 A leverage ratio is a measure of the amount of loss-absorbing resources a firm has, relative to its size. Defining a particular leverage ratio requires determining what resources count as loss-absorbing and how to measure size. Thus, one example of a leverage ratio is shareholders' funds divided by balance sheet assets.[1] A firm with a 4% leverage ratio defined this way has one dollar of loss-absorbing resources for every 25 dollars of assets.

4.2 The post-crisis bank capital reforms known as Basel 3 contain a binding leverage ratio. There is a requirement that banks subject to the Basel framework—or, more properly, to the national or bloc implementations of it—must ensure that a particular leverage ratio is higher than a minimum level, with both the method of calculating the ratio and the minimum required level of it defined by regulators.

4.3 This standard has had a profound effect on the banking system. The 30 largest banks globally, according to regulators' calculations,[2] had a total size of €75.9 trillion in 2019. This size corresponds to a minimum capital requirement generated by the Basel 3 leverage ratio for these banks alone of over €2.7 trillion.[3]

---

[1] The use of balance sheet assets as a size measure is somewhat ambiguous as this measure depends on the choice of accounting standards and on particular bank and auditor interpretations of it.

[2] See R. BCBS (2020d). Chapter 8 deals with the formation and nature of the relevant international standard setter, the Basel Committee.

[3] This calculation uses a minimum leverage ratio of 3.63%, which is the weighted average international standard leverage ratio requirement for the 30 globally systemic important banks identified by the FSB at end 2019: see R. FSB (2019b). Without these additional requirements, which apply from 2022, the total capital required by the Basel leverage ratio for these banks is €2.2 trillion. Minimum leverage requirements in national implementations which are stricter than the Basel standard increase this number significantly.

4.4 The Basel 3 leverage ratio was not a binding constraint on all banks when it was introduced. However, those banks which were bound by it had to raise additional capital or reduce their measured size to meet the requirements. A 2017 EBA study, for instance, found that full implementation of the Basel standard, then planned for June 2021, would require EU banks to raise more than €3B of capital.[4] This study also found that leverage ratio requirements were, at implementation, binding on roughly one in five EU banks, despite most banks' capital positions significantly improving since the crisis.[5] Even those banks which were not bound by the leverage ratio at its point of implementation had to plan for the possibility that they might be in future, so the leverage ratio has had some effect on all large banks' behaviour.[6]

4.5 This chapter considers what the leverage ratio is both at the level of definition—(broadly) what it says—and of epistemology—the kind of knowledge it represents. The justification for it will be found to rest on claims about its efficacy in measuring bank size, the past riskiness of banks which were big compared to their capital base, the future benefits of restricting the ratio of capital to size, and the lack of sufficiently undesirable side effects to the new regulation. Each of these claims is examined.

4.6 The chapter then turns to the nature of the leverage ratio requirement, with the aim of uncovering the roots of its claims to legitimacy. In order to explore these questions, it will be helpful to examine the nature of regulatory knowledge, how it is constructed within regulation, and how it acts on the financial system. These insights will then prove useful later when we turn to other aspects of post-crisis rule making.

The Basel 3 Leverage Ratio and the Claims Made about It

4.7 The Basel 3 leverage ratio is at its heart the demand that a certain ratio, when calculated for each bank under its scope, must exceed a minimum

[4] See table 7 in EBA (2017).

[5] Acosta-Smith et al. (2018) finds that in 2006, 18.3% of a 'panel of 655 EU banks covering the years 2005–2014' were bound by a 3% accounting leverage ratio. Since the accounting leverage ratio is typically higher than the Basel 3 leverage ratio, this implies more banks would have been bound by the Basel version. Bound banks could either raise more Tier 1 capital or reduce their size as measured by the leverage ratio; the latter was the more popular choice.

[6] A related issue is that the leverage ratio exposure measure is used in the calculation of how systemically important a bank is: see R. BCBS (2014e). This, in turn, means that any bank which is or might be a G-SIB needs to manage this measure whether or not it is bound by the leverage ratio.

threshold. The numerator of the ratio is a measure of a bank's loss-absorbing resources, known as tier 1 capital. The denominator is a particular measure of bank size, known as the leverage ratio exposure measure, or 'LREM'. The minimum requirement for the ratio is set at 3%.[7]

4.8 At the time of writing, the leverage ratio requirement is defined in the updated version of Basel 3 known as Basel 3.1.[8] The leverage ratio section in these rules is 32 pages long, and it has changed materially over time.[9]

4.9 There are two principal reasons given by the Basel Committee for implementing a leverage ratio constraint. The first is to restrict the build-up of leverage in the banking sector or, to put it perhaps crudely, to stop banks from getting too big, given the capital they have.

4.10 Understanding the second requires some history: the first and second Basel capital accords contain a number of ratio requirements relating to notions of risk. Bank capital regulations define a measure known as risk-weighted assets (or 'RWAs') based on regulators' perception of the riskiness of banks' activities and positions. They enforce ratios of loss-absorbing capital to RWAs, so activities perceived as less risky require proportionally less capital. The 2008 crisis demonstrated that regulators' perceptions were, on occasion, inaccurate, so the second major motivation for the Basel 3 leverage ratio was to backstop risk-weighted requirements with a second, deliberately risk-insensitive measure.

4.11 The Basel committee implicitly makes four claims in imposing their leverage ratio requirement. These are:

Claim 1. The Basel 3 leverage ratio is a good measure of leverage, and, in particular, the LREM is a good measure of bank size.[10]

Claim 2. During previous crises, smaller banks which were safer than bigger ones for the same amount of loss-absorbing resources. The precise claim is that the Basel 3 leverage ratio had predictive power about bank safety, with larger leverage being associated with safer banks.

Claim 3. Once the standard is implemented, the beneficial effects of having a higher Basel 3 leverage ratio will continue.

Claim 4. Imposing this particular leverage ratio requirement will not have negative effects which overwhelm its benefits.

---

7 The minimum is higher in some national implementations and in some other situations, such as when the bank is systemically important.

8 See R. BCBS (2019b).

9 Compare, for instance, R. BCBS (2013b) with R. BCBS (2014a).

10 The claim that Tier 1 capital is a good measure of loss-absorbing resources is not completely uncontroversial, but it is not a focus here.

4.12 These claims differ in their epistemological status—the kind of knowledge claim they represent:

Claim 1 is general and timeless: its truth depends among other things on unpicking what 'good' means in this situation.[11]

Claim 2 is a factual claim which, with sufficient data, could be investigated.

Claim 3 refers to an indefinite period after implementation. The claim is impossible to verify as, if the standard is imposed, the population of internationally active banks which do not have a Basel 3 leverage ratio above 3% will be very small.

Claim 4 also looks to the future, and depends on what counts as an overwhelmingly bad effect.

Leverage ratio exposure measures and their consequences

4.13 The first claim for the leverage ratio concerns the efficacy of a complex set of definitions in measuring bank size. Banks are not like matchsticks: they cannot be lined up in a row to facilitate easy size comparison. Their business is complex and multifaceted, involving an enormous collection of relationships, financial instruments, and activities. Comparing HSBC's size with Citigroup's is in this sense like comparing the British Museum's with the Louvre's—there are many choices of size norm, and different choices lead to different outcomes.[12]

4.14 Definitions matter here not just because they are arbitrary, but because different choices have different outcomes in practice. Two examples suffice to illustrate this.

4.15 Figure 4.1 shows a scatter plot of the accounting leverage ratio vs the UK regulatory leverage ratio of four large UK banking groups, with one data point for each of the years from 2015 to 2020. Not only do the two measures of leverage differ significantly, their correlation with each other is imperfect.[13]

---

[11] Presumably the sense is 'better related to the probability of bank failure than other size measures'. If so, this claim is unproven.

[12] The Louvre has roughly three times the gallery space of the British Museum but its collection is over a 100 times smaller. The Parisian museum 'has' (itself not an unproblematic term) the *Mona Lisa* while the London one 'has' the Rosetta Stone.

[13] The correlation between the two measures for this group of banks over this time period is less than 15%. This finding is contingent on the banks chosen: in particular, one important driver of the difference between the two ratios is the treatment of securities financing transactions and derivatives in regulatory measures, and different banks have markedly different amounts of these activities. For 2020, Covid-related transitional measures, as discussed in Chapter 3, are also in place, further complicating the picture.

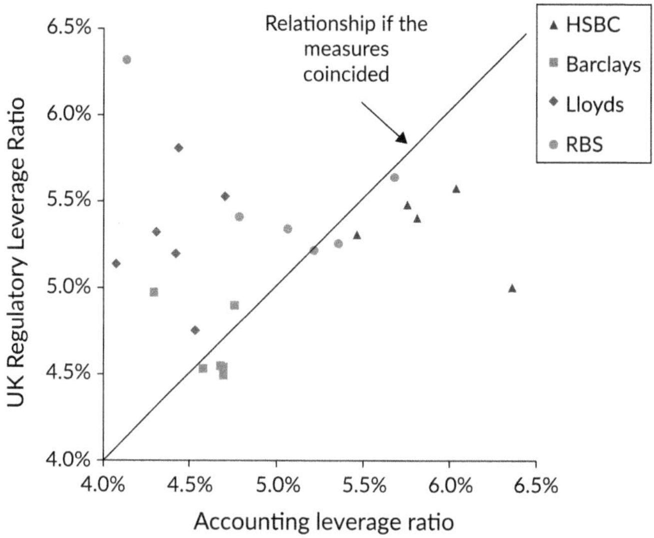

Figure 4.1– A scatter plot of accounting versus UK regulatory leverage ratios for selected banks 2015–2020

4.16 Moreover, even within regulatory definitions of leverage, there are notable differences. In 2019 RBS reported, for instance, that their end-point regulatory leverage ratio under UK definitions was 5.8%, but 5.1% under EU definitions.[14]

4.17 The different outcomes from different exposure measures mean that is ambiguous to speak of *the* leverage ratio for a bank. Instead, it is necessary to know the precise numerator and denominator in the definition, so it is clearer to refer to a particular set of definitions, as in 'the Basel 3.1 leverage ratio'.

The predictive power of leverage ratios

4.18 There is a significant literature on the predictive power of leverage ratios on bank failure. Broadly, this finds that banks with higher leverage ratios are safer. The statement from the abstract of Mayes & Stremmel (2014) is typical:

> *We find that the non-risk-weighted capital measure, the adjusted*[15] *leverage ratio, explains bank distress and failures best.*

[14] RBS Group Annual Report 2019, pp. 123. Another issue is that the UK definition uses the time average of the leverage ratio over a period, whereas some of the definitions, such as the EU one, use an end point measure. Since banks sometimes engage in behaviour which has the effect of reducing the size measure at the end of a quarter, the difference between these two approaches can be significant. This issue is discussed further in footnote 31.

[15] *Nowhere in the paper is the 'adjusted' leverage ratio defined, and indeed the term appears only in the abstract. However in Table 4 the authors define their leverage ratio as the ratio of 'Total Equity minus Estimated Losses to Assets', so it could be inferred that the 'adjustment' is the subtraction of estimated loan losses.*

4.19 However, because it is impossible to calculate a Basel 3.1 leverage ratio for prior periods given the publicly available information, researchers have almost exclusively used accounting assets as the size measure in these studies.[16] Acosta-Smith et al. (2018), Berger & Bouwman (2013), Betz et al. (2014), Estrella et al. (2000), Mayes & Stremmel (2014), and Vazquez & Federico (2015) all use a ratio of this type, for instance.[17] The broad finding in the literature could therefore be better stated as:

> *Banks with higher accounting leverage ratios, under then-in-force accounting standards, have in the past tended to be safer.*

4.20 There is evidence from Canada regarding the performance of a ratio that is closer to the Basel 3.1 definition, but even here it only dates from 1991,[18] and the population of Canadian banks differ substantially from the population of banks to which the Basel Accords apply.[19]

4.21 In short then, research does suggest that more capital has tended to make a bank of a given accounting size more stable, but it does not robustly support the claim that the Basel 3.1 leverage ratio exposure measure is the best, or even a good way, of differentiating between more and less stable banks. To pick an example that will be useful in the discussion later, the literature suggests that lychees[20] are good, but we have a longan.[21]

4.22 The gap in evidence supporting the imposition of the Basel 3.1 leverage ratio become more problematic when we examine why raising this ratio might make banks safer. This is not discussed in the Basel Committee documents. One, perhaps naïve formulation of it might be 'the smaller a bank is, relative to its capital, the less that can go wrong'. But this raises difficulties. It suggests that what matters is not size, but risk.

4.23 In this reading, if a leverage ratio is a better predictor of what can go wrong than the risk-weighted framework—which, as it says on the can, is meant to

---

16 Fender & Lewrick (2015) discusses an approach to reconstructing estimates of the Basel 3.1 leverage ratio from accounting ones using country-specific scaling factors. However, as Figure 4.1 illustrates, the correlation between these two ratios is not high even within one country, so this approach will not be very accurate.

17 As noted in footnote 1, this in itself is somewhat problematic as the definition of bank 'assets' (and, to a lesser extent, 'tangible equity') varies between different accounting standards and over time.

18 See Crawford et al. (2009) for a discussion of the issue, and, in particular, footnote 3.

19 The differences between the Canadian banking system and that of the United States are discussed in Bordo et al. (1993), in a paper dating from approximately the time of the implementation of the Canadian leverage ratio.

20 Lychees are the fruit of the *Litchi chinensis* tree.

21 Longan are the fruit of the *Dimocarpus Longan*. They are related to lychees and have a similar taste to them, but they are typically somewhat less fragrant and more bland.

measure bank risk—then this suggests deficiencies in the latter rather than the advantages in the former. It also suggests that if something cannot 'go wrong'—generate losses—then it should not be part of the size measure.

4.24 One question here is whether it is in society's interest for banks to increase their Basel 3 leverage ratio, given that they will likely do this by shedding low risk assets.[22] The turmoil discussed in Chapter 3 in the markets for safe assets, such as US Treasury bonds and Treasury repo, created by a lack of intermediation capacity, suggests that it may not be.

4.25 The issue becomes even more serious when the kinds of repo clients which dealer banks shed to reduce their LREM are considered. Repo with hedge funds and other dealers are much more likely to be nettable,[23] and thus less likely to be allocated a large LREM,[24] so these are less likely to be cut. Instead it is end-users who are likely to find their business unattractive to dealers. Regulation, in short, has made it more difficult for banks to serve the real economy while doing little about intra-financial system activity.[25] This tends to suggest that the claims that the benefits of having a high leverage ratio will persist, and that implementation will not have serious side effects, are problematic. In order to examine this further, it is helpful to consider how banks manage regulatory constraints.

Managing leverage

4.26 Suppose a regulatory constraint binds one bank in five, with four out of five not bound by it. This does not mean that it does not affect 80% of banks. This is because banks typically allocate regulatory constraints to business lines.

4.27 Many or all of the areas of a bank can be affected by a regulatory constraint: most business lines within a bank contribute to the LREM, for instance. Each business is typically managed separately, so its contribution to the size measure changes independently of other business lines. Even if a bank has a leverage ratio well above the 3% regulatory minimum now, it must have a mechanism for ensuring that it does not fall below that level in future. Indeed, given the

[22] It is easier to shed assets than to raise equity capital, so banks will tend to increase their leverage ratio by reducing their exposure measure. Low risk positions tend to be low return too, so they are the obvious things to reduce.

[23] A portfolio of repos and reverse repos with a counterparty is 'nettable' if repos can be netted with reverse repos. This requires them to be on the same security and with the same maturity, something which is more likely if repo is cleared.

[24] Netting reduces the leverage ratio exposure measure.

[25] See Kotidis & van Horen (2018) who at 29 'find that dealers subject to a tightening of the leverage ratio due to a change in its reporting requirements persistently reduced repo volume they accepted from their small clients compared to dealers not affected by the change'.

stigma associated with leverage ratios below 4%,[26] the fact that leverage ratios are disclosed, and the speed at which a bank's leverage can change, almost all large banks and many smaller ones will need to manage their leverage ratios even if they are not currently close to the regulatory minimum.

4.28 This management is usually done by allocating the regulatory measure to different business lines. Suppose that a bank has three business lines *A*, *B*, and *C*, regulatory capital of 6, and a size measured by the Basel 3 leverage ratio of 100, leading to a leverage ratio of 6%. If the contributions to the leverage ratio exposure measure are as shown in Figure 4.2, then the bank might impute capital required to support the leverage ratio of 3, 1.2 and 1.8 for *A*, *B*, and *C* respectively: these amounts would be allocated to each business.

Business line	LREM allocated	Capital allocated	LREM limit
A	50	3	60
B	20	1.2	24
C	30	1.8	36

Figure 4.2– An example of the allocation of the LREM

4.29 The profitability of each business would be judged based on its return on allocated capital.[27] The bank might also decide that a leverage ratio below 5% would attract criticism and so wish to keep its total LREM below 120. On this basis it might allocate size limits to each business of 60, 24, and 36 respectively.

4.30 The limit means that even if business *A* finds an opportunity whose return on equity exceeded the bank's target, it could not pursue it if it caused *A*'s size measure to exceed 60. Depending on how the limits were administered, this will often be the case even if businesses *B* and *C* were not using their full limit.[28]

---

[26] See, for instance, the Institutional Risk Analyst's 2018 discussion of Deutsche Bank ('DB'), available at https://www.theinstitutionalriskanalyst.com/post/2018/11/04/profile-the-challenge-for-deutsche-bank. R. Christopher Whalen blogs of the 'great difficulty constructing a bull case for the name ... On the list of concerns ... is capital. DB has just €61 billion or 4% capital to total assets of €1.5 trillion, one of the lowest simple leverage ratios of any major bank worldwide'. This is exemplary of the negative comments low leverage ratios attract even if the bank concerned is in compliance with regulatory requirements and even if it is well-capitalized on a risk-weighted basis.

[27] The capital allocated for a business is often the maximum of that allocated for each regulatory constraint.

[28] This is a simplified example, but it illustrates that while some management of individual business lines' size measures is necessary to ensure that the bank does not miss its target, it is not clear how to optimally ration multiple constraints, such as leverage ratio size and risk-weighted assets, without imposing constraints on business lines relating to requirements which do not bind the whole bank. For a discussion of how banks manage this process in practice see Bajaj et al. (2018)

4.31 It can be seen that the practice of allocating regulatory constraints means that each constraint can affect bank behaviour and constrain business activity, even when it does not bind the whole bank. Moreover, businesses who have poor returns on the capital they have been allocated are incentivized to reduce their allocation. For the leverage ratio, this would mean reducing their LREM.[29]

Side effects

4.32 Suppose a relationship is observed in finance whereby some phenomenon, *X*, tends to lead to another one, *Y*. If we want to reduce the incidence of *Y*, it might be tempting to regulate against *X*. Goodhart's well-known law is that as soon as we do this, the relationship tends to break down.[30] The reason for this phenomenon is that stakeholders start to manage the quantity once it is used for control, so its dynamics change. Thus, even if a particular leverage ratio was a good predictor of bank safety before regulators adopted it as a requirement, it might not be afterwards. Banks will change their behaviour to comply with the requirement, and the resulting financial system will be different.

4.33 The change in the financial system caused by regulation can have positive or negative effects. At one end of the spectrum, if behaviour changes in ways that reduce the risk of bank failure and there are no negative side effects, then the new regulatory requirement was a total success. At the other, if behaviour changes so that the financial system takes the same or greater risk in ways that are not measured, or the result of adaptation is unintended and severe side effects, then the attempt at control was a failure. The result of regulatory change is usually somewhere between these two poles.[31]

4.34 The allocation of regulatory constraints within banks is often the source of undesirable side effects. A good example of this phenomenon can be found in the 2014 leverage ratio exposure measure. The definition stated:[32]

or Goel et al. (2017). The number of the working paper in which the latter work is published is perhaps indicative of the complexity of the problem for many large banks.

29 See Acosta-Smith et al. (2018) for a demonstration of how the leverage ratio changed bank behaviour after its announcement in 2010. Banks did not wait for the rule to become binding, not least due to the stigma effects of being seen to be substantially further from the eventual target than their peers.

30 The original formulation relates to monetary economics and is stated in Goodhart (1975) as 'any observed statistical regularity will tend to collapse once pressure is placed upon it for control purposes'.

31 When banks game the quantity controlled, there is often an expression of pained disapproval from regulators. For an example in the context of the leverage ratio, see R. BCBS (2018).

32 The text is from R. BCBS (2014a). There is also a separate treatment of cash variation margin in the standard which does allow offset in some circumstances.

Collateral received in connection with derivative contracts does not necessarily reduce the leverage inherent in a bank's derivatives position, which is generally the case if the settlement exposure arising from the underlying derivative contract is not reduced. As a general rule, collateral received may not be netted against derivative exposures whether or not netting is permitted under the bank's operative accounting or risk-based framework. Hence, when calculating the exposure amount ... a bank must not reduce the exposure amount by any collateral received from the counterparty.

4.35 This is both a definition of the leverage ratio exposure measure (as including collateral received) and a claim justifying it, that collateral received 'does not necessarily reduce the leverage inherent in a bank's derivatives position'.

4.36 The effect of this definition was that transacting collateralized OTC derivatives led to increases in the 2014 leverage ratio exposure measure. This caused OTC derivatives activities to be allocated more capital than hitherto. As a result, these businesses were incentivized to reduce their LREM. Because the portfolios which had higher leverage ratio exposure measures and lower profits were those with smaller, usually non-financial end-users, this meant that real economy users of derivatives found it harder and more expensive to transfer risk, while most hedge funds and other large derivatives users were not greatly affected.

4.37 Thus, as with the repo example discussed in paragraph 4.25, the leverage ratio had the side effect of reducing the ability of the financial system to serve the real economy while doing little to discourage speculative trading.[33]

4.38 The claim that collateral received does not necessarily reduce the leverage inherent in derivatives positions in most situations was disputed.[34] The Basel Committee eventually modified the exposure measure to reduce (although not eliminate) the effect for client-cleared derivatives from 2022.[35]

4.39 This episode makes it clear that capital regulation needs not just to be correctly calibrated in total, but the contributions of each business to banks' total requirements also need to be right. If a business is overcharged, then banks will do less in this area, even if another business has a matching undercharge.

---

[33] For an extended discussion of the derivatives issues here and the evidence supporting them, see DAT (2018).

[34] One comment on the 2014 standard, Clearing House (2013), is particularly interesting. It says in part: 'requiring that cash collateral received or provided not be recognized [as reducing exposure]—meaning, effectively, a gross presentation insofar as collateral is concerned—elevates forms over substance'. In other words, the 2014 leverage ratio makes an arbitrary choice of how to measure the size of derivatives exposures that sees them as bigger than is suggested by their economic substance.

[35] See R. BCBS (2019c).

4.40 It has already been noted that overcharges from the Basel 3 leverage ratio to market making businesses are implicated in declines in the quality of financial markets. The broad problem is that efficient markets often need market participants who can deploy balance sheets to warehouse assets, intermediating between buyers and sellers. The leverage ratio is, among other things, a tax on balance sheet size, regardless of the risks involved, so it caused banks to reduce their intermediation. Frequently, non-banks have not been able to fill the resulting gap,[36] so buyers have to pay more and sellers receive less—and they may not be able to transact at all in stress.[37]

4.41 The Covid dislocations discussed in the previous chapter are not the only post-crisis episodes of stress in systemically important funding markets. US Treasury repo also suffered a severe dislocation in September 2019, with repo rates spiking far outside their normal range.[38] There were a number of interacting causes for this dislocation including large flows in the money market which reduced the supply of cash and increased the demand for repo financing of Treasury bonds;[39] relatively narrow 'pipes' connecting the swing providers of liquidity to the market and thus making it difficult for them to supply additional cash to meet the demand;[40] and, as in the Covid episode, an unwillingness of the banks to step in to serve market needs (and earn a very low risk profit in so doing).[41] It is highly likely that the treatment of repo in the LREM, and the use of this measure in G-SIB scoring (discussed in footnote 6) contributed to this unwillingness.[42]

---

36 Ample access to liquidity is important in some areas of the market, such as Treasury bond trading, so non-banks are badly placed in this market compared to institutions which have access to the Fed window.

37 Evidence for the impact of the implementation of the leverage ratio on the liquidity of US equity markets is given by Haynes et al. (2018), while Duffie (2016) discusses the leverage ratio's role in the declining quality of US Treasury repo markets.

38 On 17 September 2019, the secured overnight funding rate, which is based on repo transactions, hit 700 basis points intraday, behaviour that was highly unusual given it usually moved a few, or a few teens of basis points.

39 Tax payments due on 16 September were withdrawn from bank and money market funds, reducing the supply of both bank reserves and repo market liquidity (as money market funds often invest cash in Treasury repo to maintain a cushion against redemptions). A new issue of treasuries settled on the 16th too, reducing the reserves of primary dealers and increasing their demand for repo financing.

40 The market at the time was broadly split into triparty repo, which was largely settled by Bank of New York Mellon, and repo cleared by the Fixed Income Credit Corporation. The large dealers typically intermediate between these two segments.

41 As Anbil et al. (2020) put it, 'borrowing demand in the repo market proved to be highly inelastic': borrowers had no easy substitute source for cash, so they were forced 'to pay up significantly to secure the funding they needed'.

42 For a discussion of these events and the context surrounding them, see Avalos et al. (2019).

4.42 The interconnectedness of markets is important here. The repo market is not just systemically important in its own right: it is also used both as a reference for short-term rates in the interest rate swaps market,[43] and as the most important market for sourcing cash needed for margin posting.[44] Thus, dislocations in the US Treasury repo rate spread widely in the financial system.

4.43 The events of September 2019 in the repo market gave the authorities notice of its vulnerability in stress. When stress hit again during March 2020, they acted quickly. The Fed temporarily provided a route to remove leverage ratio-driven constraints on banks' ability to hold and repo Treasury securities and increased liquidity provision. After this, the market quickly recovered.[45] This action bolsters the case that the leverage ratio contributes to banks' reluctance to provide needed repo intermediation capacity in stress.

Referential Closure and Translation in Regulation

4.44 The previous section sketched the concept of leverage ratios, introduced the Basel 3.1 leverage ratio, and discussed the claims justifying its imposition. In order to open up the question of why regulations like this were imposed, it is helpful to consider the broader issue of the kind of thing financial regulation is.

4.45 This section uses ideas from critical and legal theory to give a short account of the epistemic status of financial regulation. The concepts of self-regenerating systems of knowledge, referential closure, and translation will turn out to be helpful, so we begin by giving a brief account of these ideas.

Regulation as an autopoietic system

4.46 The theory of self-regenerating systems is the work of two biologists trained in cybernetics, Maturana and Varela.[46] They coined the term 'autopoietic' for such systems. The characterization of law as an autopoietic system was spearheaded by Luhmann, Teubner, and other scholars,[47] and extended to regulation by Black among others.[48] The key elements of autopoietic systems for our purposes are that they are *referentially closed* and imbued with a *translation mechanism*. Referential closure means that the system can only refer to concepts within itself, and can only

[43] The replacement for US dollar Libor, SOFR, is a volume-weighted median of tri-party repo rates: see https://apps.newyorkfed.org/markets/autorates/SOFR for more details.

[44] This is discussed further in Chapter 6.

[45] See R. Fed Board (2020).

[46] See for instance Varela et al. (1974).

[47] Luhmann (1984) and Teubner (1982) are among the important early papers. See Rogowski (2015) for a recent review article.

[48] See Black (1995) and Black (2001) or, for a broader critical discussion, Moran (2002).

be changed internally. As Luhmann puts it, 'only the law can change the law',[49] so something outside the law must first be understood as legal before it can have an effect within the legal system.[50]

4.47 Financial regulation has the same nature: it deals only with items within itself, and the information which it possesses about exterior objects is only that which follows from its own processes. Thus, there is the regulatory balance sheet, which is not the accounting one (and often does not balance); the regulatory definition of CET1 capital, which is not the same as shareholders' funds; and capital adequacy, a property of a bank inferred from regulatory definitions.

4.48 There are various terms in the literature for the mechanism by which an autopoietic system is affected by its environment and creates internal representations; for instance, Black discusses the 'distorting lens' of a systems' 'perceptual apparatus'.[51] The term 'translation' will be used here as it emphasizes the creation of an object within the language of regulation representing something from outside. The key idea is that regulation must translate external objects into itself before it can recognize or act upon them.

4.49 Autopoietic systems like financial regulation or the law have their own internal rules or rhetoric by which internal knowledge is created. Whether a bank is considered well-capitalized follows, for instance, from the regulatory definition of capital, the definition of RWAs, and the required capital ratios for a given type of institution. This internal knowledge can then affect the world outside the system: regulators would likely demand that a badly capitalized bank raise more capital or reduce RWAs or both, for instance, and banks manage themselves to reduce the likelihood of this happening. The ability to control the outside world will be referred to as regulation's 'external power'.[52]

4.50 This analysis suggests that the mechanism behind Goodhart's law is a reflexive loop which depends in part on the external power of regulation: regulators observe what appears to be a regularity that they infer can be used for control purposes; they therefore attempt to define and control some quantity; the financial system, in response to this exercise of external power, adapts.[53]

49 The quote is from Luhmann (1984) at 113.

50 The evocative term 'self-referential closure' is Teubner's, from his description of the circular relationship between legal decisions and normative rules: see Teubner (1984), p. 195.

51 See Black (2001) at 107.

52 Teubner (1984) uses the term 'boundary trespassing processes' for both translations into the system and the effects of its inferences outside it, while Friedman (1975) talks of 'messages exchanged between legal and other coexisting social systems'. For our purposes, it is helpful to separate the input and output processes.

53 A reformulation of the law might be: 'whenever a financial quantity is used for control purposes by a system with external power over finance, the financial system tends to change in ways which reduce the utility of the control'.

Translations into the language of leverage

4.51 It is insightful to examine the translation process. Consider a bank's derivatives portfolio. This is an object outside regulation. It cannot be operated upon by the prudential framework until it is translated into a recognized format: the format regulation uses to represent portfolios of derivatives. There are rules in the relevant standards to tell us how to do this.

4.52 The comparison of a regulatory translation with an accounting one throws light on both. In the 2013 version of the Basel leverage ratio,[54] for instance, we find the following description of how to calculate the contribution to the leverage ratio exposure measure:

> *Derivatives create two types of exposure: (a) an exposure arising from the underlying of the contract and (b) a counterparty credit risk exposure. The leverage ratio framework uses the method set out below to capture both of these exposure types.*
>
> *Banks must calculate their derivatives exposures ... as the replacement cost for the current exposure plus an add-on for potential future exposure ... applying the regulatory bilateral netting rules ... and adjusting the exposure amount for the related collateral ...*

4.53 In contrast, the International Financial Reporting Standards ('IFRS') conceptual framework defines an asset as:[55]

> *A present economic resource controlled by the entity as a result of past events.*

where

> *An economic resource is a right that has the potential to produce economic benefits.*

4.54 So, to paraphrase, an accounting asset is something which you have now that is producing a benefit now, or might produce one later. The next step in the IFRS translation requires identification of the relevant resource. If it is just the portfolio of derivatives, then their current fair value is one reasonable choice of size: a portfolio's 'size' in this system is what it is currently worth.[56] If the right notion of 'resource' consists of a balance sheet item and a derivative hedging it, then the translation can involve a composite of the item(s) and its hedge(s) considered together.[57]

---

[54] See R. BCBS (2013b).

[55] See R. IASB (2018).

[56] The definition of fair value is given in R. IASB (2013).

[57] The details, including when a derivative qualifies as a hedge, what item or items can be hedged, and how to account for them together when permitted to do so are in R. IASB (2020).

4.55 While this terse account obscures much important detail, it does at least suggest that there is a clear connection between the concept of size and an IFRS balance sheet. The choice to define IFRS size as current fair value is a normative one, but it does not seem capricious or unreasonable.[58]

4.56 The Basel leverage ratio takes a different approach. Here the 'size' of a derivatives portfolio is not just its current fair value, but that value 'plus an add-on for potential future exposure'. In other words, its 'size' in this system is how big it might be in the future where it grows by a regulator-specified amount, not how big it is today.

4.57 Potential future exposure was a concept[59] that was originally introduced into the risk-based capital rules to capture the risk that a derivatives portfolio with a counterparty might fall in value between the current point (where the counterparty is assumed to default) and liquidation of the portfolio. The use of a risk-based measure in a framework whose avowed aim is not to be risk-based is somewhat peculiar.

4.58 This analysis shows that the internal representation of the size of a derivatives portfolio in the Basel framework has completely detached from the accounting notion of the size of an asset, and become a purely free-standing concept with its own logic.[60] There was a belief among rule writers that a different definition of size from the accounting one was justified.[61] Hence, one was constructed and imposed.

4.59 This action suggests that one way to see financial regulation is as a fictive strategy whose power derives from the ability to form and privilege its internal definitions at the top of an epistemic hierarchy entirely created, sustained, and reshaped by its own processes.[62]

---

[58] This is not to deny that accounting is a 'fluid and technically ambiguous practice', as Power (1989) puts it at 295, nor that it is a bureaucratic technology whose choices of translation and internal representation have profound social, economic, and political consequences.

[59] Or, more properly, a family of concepts, since there are various ways of estimating it in the Basel framework, including the Current Exposure Method, the Internal Models Method, and the Standardized Approach to Counterparty Credit Risk.

[60] This is evocative of Baudrillard's notion of simulacra. He writes: 'Abstraction today is no longer that of the map, the double, the mirror or the concept. Simulation is no longer that of a territory, a referential being or a substance. It is the generation by models of a real *without origin or reality*: a hyperreal' (emphasis mine). See Baudrillard (1988), pp. 166–184.

[61] See Lockwood (2020) for a further discussion of central role of regulator's beliefs about derivatives in shaping policy making.

[62] It is therefore a form of domination by naming. Haraway (1991)'s account of an activity that is (at 175) 'deadly serious', closed by exclusionary practices which obscure 'the apparatus of production' (at 200) of authority, sustains its power by claims of objective authority yet is really (at 181) a 'myth system', are uncannily true of financial regulation.

Regulatory categories

4.60 A central strategy in regulation's self-construction is the definition and use of categories. A category exists whenever two or more distinguishable objects or events are treated equivalently. Creating categories, in other words, necessarily involves erasing differences between things in the service of the claim 'all these things behave the same way' and hence 'all these things should be subject to the same treatment'.

4.61 One issue arises when 'behaving the same way' is not part of the definition of the category. If I create a category 'fruit for my fruit salad', that act has little import; but if there is also the rule 'buy fruit for my fruit salad, prepare the salad using them, and eat it', then a tension arises if the definition of 'fruit for fruit salad' does not include the requirement that the constituents are all 'fruit I want to eat'.

4.62 The problem is particularly acute if the membership rule—the definition of when a fruit counts as a fruit salad constituent—is fixed, but the population of objects it is applied to is open-ended. I might like lychees, and so have a definition of components of fruit salads which includes them, but which also inadvertently admits the somewhat similar longan, especially if I have never encountered the latter. If subsequently I try a longan and decide that I don't like it, can the rule be updated?[63]

4.63 Financial regulation has a long history of suffering from problems of this type. The phenomenon is:

- Regulators define a category of objects, their properties for regulatory purposes, and a relatively penal regulatory treatment of them based on those properties.
- The regulated invent an engineered object that is either:
  - not defined as in the category by the rules but behaves in economically meaningful ways as if it was; or
  - where the regulatory treatment is less penal due to the translation into regulation of one or more 'engineered' properties, but which otherwise behaves largely or exactly as before.
- This engineered object arbitrages regulation, as it achieves most or all of the desired effects of the original but at lower regulatory cost.[64]

---

63 A logician might say that the error is due to an invalid induction. As Hume put it, we are assuming that 'instances of which we have had no experience resemble those of which we have had experience', and that assumption sometimes causes an error.

64 See Gerding (2016) and Riles (2013b) for further discussions of regulatory arbitrage, and Funk & Hirschman (2014) for the specific issue of categorical distinctions in derivatives regulation.

4.64 A fascinating example of this occurs in the treatment of the maturity of derivatives in the leverage ratio (and in some risk-weighted capital rules). The rules define the charge for potential future exposure based on the maturity of a derivative. Broadly, the longer the maturity, the higher the charge. This reflects the intuition that the longer the maturity, the more time the instrument has to change in value, and hence the greater the potential future exposure which should be charged for. However, there is a technique for reducing exposure: the use of collateral. The rules allow for this by, broadly, allowing variation margin to reduce current exposure; but the potential future exposure charge is still determined by the maturity of the derivative regardless of credit support.

4.65 One way to engineer around these rules is to construct a structured derivative whose cashflows are:

- those of the original swap; netted with
- the variation margin payments that would have been made on that original swap under a daily cash-only CSA.

4.66 Because variation margin extinguishes current exposure, this engineered derivative never has any: each day it is settled to its market value.[65] Therefore it can be argued that its maturity is one day, as its exposure never has more than a day to move from zero until either there is a default or the current exposure is settled.

4.67 The short period between VM calls of the engineered derivative means that its potential future exposure is low. Regulation recognizes this, assigning a small PFE change. Hence, the engineered derivative contributes less to both risk-based capital requirements and the leverage ratio size exposure measure than the original swap.[66] The engineered swap and the original swap under a daily cash variation margin arrangement are economically identical, so it is hard to justify the difference in their treatment as anything other than evidence for the inadequacy of the arbitrary definitions that leads to it.

Arbitraging category definitions

4.68 There are numerous economically meaningful examples of this situation. For example, one of the major spurs for the development of the credit derivatives

65 Typically the settlement is based on the end-of-day value, and payment is due the following morning, so there is a delay between the calculation of the daily settlement value and its payment.

66 This regulatory treatment is confirmed in R. Joint Agencies (2017). The key paragraph states: 'Accordingly, for the purpose of the regulatory capital rules, if, after accounting and legal analysis, the institution determines that (i) the variation margin payment on a centrally cleared Settled-to-Market Contract settles any outstanding exposure on the contract, and (ii) the terms are reset so that fair value of the contract is zero, the remaining maturity on such contract would equal the time until the next exchange of variation margin on the contract.'

market was the realization that the translation into the Basel 1 framework of the 'risk of a corporate loan' into 'its rating' and 'its notional', and the resulting capital requirement as a fraction of the notional, meant that if a transaction could be developed which reduced notionals without a concomitant reduction in the default risk, then capital charges could be reduced much more than the risk they supported was.

4.69 The first well-known use of this insight was a synthetic securitization of a loan portfolio arranged by JPMorgan in 1997. This deal, known by the acronym BISTRO, allowed the bank which originated the loans to keep most of their risk (and hence return) through the retention of a relatively small junior tranche, but to reduce their regulatory capital requirements by buying protection on the (collectively, much larger) mezzanine and senior tranches.

4.70 The effectiveness of BISTRO[67] and subsequent similar transactions at reducing capital requirements was one of the major motivations for the revisions to Basel 1 which lead to the creation of the Basel 2 framework: see R. BCBS (2006). As the original consultative paper on Basel 2, R. BCBS (1999), puts it at 9:

> *Regulatory capital arbitrage [in Basel 1] can occur in several ways, for example, through some forms of securitization, and can lead to a shift in banks' portfolio concentrations to lower quality assets.*

The character of regulatory translations

4.71 We now turn from regulatory definitions to the nature of the system that they inhabit. Our contention is that the evolution of the language of bank regulation gives some insight into its present character. In Basel 1, from 1988, the tone is tentative, acknowledging within the text itself the imperfect nature of the translation from banks' exposures into the language of regulation:[68]

> *The Committee considers that a weighted risk ratio in which capital is related to different categories of asset or off-balance-sheet exposure, weighted according to broad categories of relative riskiness, is the preferred method for assessing the capital adequacy of banks.*

4.72 By the 2001 consultation on Basel 2, the tone becomes more confident:[69]

> *To secure the objective of prudentially sound, incentive-compatible and risk-sensitive capital requirements, the Committee is providing a progressive, evolutionary approach to the calculation of … capital charges.*

[67] For more details of the BISTRO deal, see Meissner (2009), pp. 55–56. Jones (2000) contains a broader discussion of the role of securitization in regulatory capital arbitrage from the time when Basel 2 was being created.

[68] The quote is from R. BCBS (1988) at 8.

[69] The quote is from R. BCBS (2001) at 7.

4.73 The vocabulary of finance is used here to claim equality: there is a sense of technocracy, that regulation has a goal of keeping up with the way banking talks and thinks about itself, and that this is as an ambition achieved in Basel 2.

4.74 By Basel 3, this has disappeared. Instead, bank regulation has become a separate power centre which does not rely on the authority of the rhetoric constructed by the industry, and indeed actively rejects it in favour of its own language:[70]

> *The Basel Committee is raising the resilience of the banking sector by strengthening the regulatory capital framework, building on the three pillars of the Basel II framework. The reforms raise both the quality and quantity of the regulatory capital base and enhance the risk coverage of the capital framework. They are underpinned by a leverage ratio that serves as a backstop to the risk-based capital measures, is intended to constrain excess leverage in the banking system and provide an extra layer of protection against model risk and measurement error ...*
>
> *One of the key lessons of the crisis has been the need to strengthen the risk coverage of the capital framework. Failure to capture major on- and off-balance sheet risks, as well as derivative related exposures, was a key destabilizing factor during the crisis.*

4.75 While finance might accept that, after the crisis, risk management practices and risk capture needed to improve, it would not suggest that an extra layer of risk-insensitive protection was needed: the ability to measure and thereby manage risk is central to the rhetoric of finance. The promulgation of a prudential leverage ratio requirement is thus evidence of the emergence of regulation as a distinct power centre.

4.76 One way to reflect on the nature of the powerful system that appears at the end of this evolution is to use some of the insights from studies of translation in other contexts. Translation studies—the study of the theory and practice of translation—is an obvious place to look. As Bassnett (1998) puts it at 135, this discipline is concerned with 'questions of power relations and textual production', exactly the questions that arise when attempting to understand the nature of contemporary financial regulation. As noted above, without the confidence that bank regulation can establish its own knowledge separate from that of finance, the leverage ratio would never have been enacted—so how should we think about this kind of knowledge creation?

4.77 Regulatory definitions exist to enforce the primacy of some particular means of knowing, while attempting to delegitimize others. Thus they assert

[70] See R. BCBS (2010) at 2. By this point, the desire to construct a simulacra of banking inside bank regulation referred to in footnote 60 is fully formed.

not just, for instance, that the leverage ratio exposure measure is *a* valid way of measuring bank size, but also that other measures, such as accounting assets, *are not*. In translation studies, this would be called epistemic violence, that is violence exerted against or through knowledge which privileges one form of knowing, in this case the regulatory one, while denying the validity of others.[71]

4.78 There are several aspects to this epistemically violent way of constructing regulatory knowledge. The first issue is in the act of making arbitrary translation that erases important differences.[72] Just as important is the system's assertion of the indisputable rightness of the translation even as it is disputed, and its failure to provide a mechanism for meaningful discourse.[73]

Dialogue and closed systems

4.79 The role of legitimizing discourse becomes clearer when it is remembered that some systems like regulation and the law are referentially closed. They need some internal representation of pertinent external events, and the only way of getting it is by translation.

4.80 The legitimacy of these translations depends on a discourse with those affected by them. In the criminal law, for instance, trial by jury facilitates such a discourse. Jury trials, as Devlin (1979) puts it, give 'protection against laws which the ordinary man regards as harsh and oppressive'. The exercise of their rights by juries have played a central role in the self-recreation—autopoiesis—of the criminal law as it reacts to changing societal norms.[74]

---

71 The approach taken here is informed by the profound analysis of Vázquez (2011). The abstract of the latter work is worth quoting at length: it 'focuses on the question of translation as erasure, that is, as a mechanism through which modernity expands and demarcates its proper place, its territory. This operation of translation renders invisible everything that does not fit in the "parameters of legibility" of modernity's epistemic territory ... Translation brings to view the epistemic borders where a politics of visibility is at play between erasure and visibility, disdain and recognition.' The stakes in Vázquez's discussion are enormous. Ours are much smaller, but Vázquez's epistemological analysis, and its insistence on exposing the role of fictive utterances in creating and sustaining power relations, is entirely apt.

72 All formal systems necessarily involve imperfect translations. The well-known aphorism attributed to George Box, 'all models are wrong; some are useful' captures this idea. But this does not absolve us from asking 'useful to whom?', 'useful in the furtherance of what agenda?', and 'what are the consequences of this use for all affected parties?'.

73 To paraphrase Habermas, a norm is justified if all those affected by it accept the consequences and side effects that could be anticipated to result from following it: see Habermas (1996) at 127. This justification emerges through a discourse between affected parties in which all can speak freely without being marginalized or ignored. We will return to this idea in Part III.

74 The term for verdicts where the jury finds opposite to a plain reading of the facts is 'perverse' (although, as Devlin (1979) discusses, this term could be seen simply as shorthand for disapproval by those who are not empowered to reach a verdict of the conclusions reached by those who are).

4.81 Importantly, the members of the jury are outside the law until they are selected, but then they become legal actors, and in doing so provide a mechanism for validating legal translations within the law by importing knowledge from outside it. Jury trials, in other words, allow the internal logic of the law to be tested by a dialogue with jurors, legitimizing the law in the process.

4.82 In marked contrast, disputes of regulatory translation are settled purely by regulatory fiat. The regulated are permitted to ask questions about regulatory definitions, and answers are provided in an oracular fashion. However, these questions are ones of implementation, not of foundation, and the answers are sometimes admonitory.[75]

4.83 An independent review of the post-crisis bank capital framework would, among many other things, examine each of the translations of bank activities into the language of the leverage ratio in detail. If there was some well-defined safety standard that the leverage ratio was designed to meet, this could be a 'truing up' exercise which better aligned the leverage ratio exposure measure to the desired standard. However, this is not possible, because there is no such standard. Indeed, the risk-insensitive-by-design nature of the leverage ratio means that there cannot be one.

4.84 An important task for reviewers is therefore the analysis of the need for a risk-insensitive standard at all rather than, say, revising the risk-based capital

A well-known example of a perverse verdict is the case of Clive Ponting, a civil servant who admitted leaking classified documents which showed that the Argentine battleship *General Belgrano* was heading *away* from the Royal Navy taskforce when it was sunk during the Falklands conflict. Ponting was prosecuted under the Official Secrets Act. His defence was that there was a public interest in making the documents public as they raised a question about the legality of the sinking and contradicted the account of the sinking the Prime Minister, Margaret Thatcher, had given to Parliament.

At the time there was no public interest defence to offences under the Official Secrets Act: there still isn't. The judge directed the jury that it was no defence that Ponting 'honestly believed that it was his duty to leak the documents in the interests of the state if, in fact, it was not his duty to do so'. Nevertheless, the jury acquitted Ponting. The case, as Lord Elwyn-Jones put it in the House of Lords soon afterwards, gave 'rise to many questions which call for an early answer' and thus can be seen as exemplary of the dialogue the law has with itself in its process of self-recreation. For a further discussion of the role of jury trials in the legitimization of the law, see Whittington (2015).

[75] See, for instance, Question 9 in R. BCBS (2016). The question asks if written options, which do not 'encounter' counterparty credit risk—the image of an afternoon stroll interrupted by a chance, unpleasant meeting is arresting—should be included in the Basel 3 leverage ratio exposure measure. The answer is 'As written options create an exposure, they must be included in the Basel III leverage ratio exposure measure'. This makes it appear as if the definition of exposure was a fact of nature rather than an act of construction by regulators. It could equally have been defined otherwise but, as it was not, a question from the regulated prompts nothing more than an assertion of the regulators' definition.

rules so that they do not need a backstop. The issue of whether this is possible is exactly the kind of question which, if it could be asked in a dialogue of equals, would legitimize post-crisis bank regulation.

Regulation as a System with External Power

4.85 The way that financial regulation constructs knowledge has been explored using the frame of autopoietic systems. It has been seen that in the passage from Basel 1 to Basel 3, financial regulation has changed from an adjunct to banking to an independent, powerful system. Banks' positions and risks are imprecisely translated into the system of regulation, erasing some of their features and creating others. This translation is necessary because financial regulation does not recognize anything outside itself: it is referentially closed. Moreover, regulation has its own rhetoric and its own notion of what counts as the construction of valid new regulatory information.

4.86 The inferences made within financial regulation matter because it has external power. Regulation creates change in the financial system, both through the management of regulatory constraints within regulated institutions and through reactions by the unregulated. This means that financial regulation is, to borrow a term from sociology, performative: rather than being true or false, it makes things happen.[76]

4.87 It is insightful to examine the claims used to justify this exercise of power. The status of these claims varies: some form judgements about the past; others are normative judgements which refer to the future behaviour of the financial system.[77] They are sometimes contentious both in themselves and because legitimizing external review—review from those outside the regulatory system—is rare.

4.88 The claims supporting the leverage ratio in particular are suspect in part because they do not justify the precise regulatory definition of bank size and they do not provide an account of the mechanism by which controlling this measure, rather than another one, would have been optimal. The allocation of the leverage ratio exposure measure has substantial side effects on the financial system's ability to do its job, and there is no convincing explanation of why these costs are necessary to achieve financial stability.

---

[76] The term 'performative utterance' is due to Austin. Foucault (1972) at 49 has 'practices that systematically form the objects of which they speak', which riffs on the idea. See Bamford & Mackenzie (2018) and MacKenzie & Millo (2002) for accounts of it in finance.

[77] The 'better' in 'things will be better if we do this' is a value judgement: the whole statement is a prediction, but one that is very difficult to test if there is no option not to 'do this'.

5

Risk-based Capital Regulation in the Trading Book

Introduction

5.1 This chapter considers four key areas of the risk-based bank capital rules which apply to derivatives:

- the market risk capital rules;
- the counterparty credit risk rules which capitalize the risk of the default or substantial decline in the credit quality of a counterparty;
- the rules capitalizing the risk of exposures to CCPs; and
- the rules which capitalize the risk of CVA increases.

5.2 Capital rules seek to ensure that the institutions which are subject to them have enough loss-absorbing resources for the risks that they bear. They are important for derivatives because they apply to most dealers and determine the economics of their activities. In particular, the capital required for a given amount of risk transfer in a particular form determines how attractive facilitating this transaction is compared to other activities with a similar return but different capital requirements.

5.3 Capital requirements can be divided into two types: minimum requirements, which institutions must meet at all times; and buffers, which can (at least theoretically) be used in stress, either by the authorities or by banks.

5.4 Buffers are needed because stress causes losses, and losses reduce capital resources. If a bank just met its minimum capital requirement before a loss, it would be in breach after it. The capital needed to meet minimum requirements is therefore not loss-absorbing on a going concern basis. It does, however, help maintain confidence in the firm, and thus mitigate against the solvency/liquidity spiral discussed in paragraph 2.22.

5.5 The Covid episode considered in Chapter 3 demonstrated that there is sometimes a public policy need for banks to provide an additional volume of financial services during stress. If the authorities release a buffer, by temporarily eliminating the need for this layer of capital, then additional capital resources are freed up to support extra activity and to absorb losses.

5.6 Risk-based capital requirements are often set based on the unexpected loss of an estimate of the return distribution, as discussed in paragraph 1.110. For market risk factors, for instance, the distribution of returns due to market risk factors is the object of interest. However, there is no single standard for the estimation of this UL. The time horizon over which returns are measured; the confidence interval used; and whether stressed conditions are assumed: all vary depending on the rule at hand.

5.7 This chapter surveys the four areas of capital regulation most relevant to derivatives. As with the leverage ratio in the last chapter, these rules make arbitrary definitions which incompletely capture the properties of the portfolios that they are applied to. As before, the regulatory inferences which follow from these definitions benefit some forms of financial system activity at the expense of others with the same or lesser risks, and sometimes lead to unintended consequences.

5.8 We then turn to the objectives of capital regulation and desirable properties for the rules, discussing some of the tensions between these desiderata. Given these conflicts, different countries can properly have different views on whether a given internationally agreed rule is right for their financial system. The final section therefore considers deviations from international standards and how they are policed.

Market Risk Capital

5.9 The post-crisis reforms to the prudential requirements for market risk can be divided into two main stages:

- the immediate response is known as Basel 2.5 as it comprised relatively contained revisions to the Basel 2 framework;[1] and
- a longer-term response, known as the Fundamental Review of the Trading Book or 'FRTB'.[2]

5.10 Before considering these, it is helpful to consider the domain of applicability of the various types of capital rule.

---

1 See R. BCBS (2009): Basel 2 is R. BCBS (2004), revised in R. BCBS (2006).

2 See R. BCBS (2013d). The final version of this has been integrated in the Basel 3 framework.

Trading and banking books

5.11 Broadly, a bank's trading book contains positions in financial instruments that it enters into with trading intent. Thus, derivatives will usually be in the trading book,[3] as will market making positions in securities, foreign exchange, and commodities, together with their hedges. Positions in the trading book are mainly accounted for using fair value. This means that the trading book generates profits and losses as market prices move. The market risk rules capitalize the risk of loss from these movements.

5.12 In contrast, a firm's banking book will consist of positions for which the firm does not have trading intent. In many cases this will be because the firm intends to hold them to maturity, or because they have no contractual maturity. Thus, most bank deposits and loans will be in the banking book. Many banking book items are accounted for on an amortized cost basis, so income from taking credit risk is recorded as it is earned.[4] As the predominant risk in most banking books is credit risk, the capital framework for the banking book, not discussed here, addresses both default risk and the risk that the credit quality of banking book items decreases, leading to an increase in provisions for loan losses.[5]

Basel 2.5

5.13 The Basel 2.5 changes represent a rapid response to fact that the trading book losses experienced in the 2008 crisis were large compared to the capital required for market risk. The Basel 2 paradigm was that there were two sets of capital rules. The first, known as the standardized approach, is the default. It is simpler, and produces, on average, higher capital requirements for a given portfolio. The second, 'models-based' or 'internal models' approach allows banks to use their own models to calculate capital requirements: these are value at risk ('VAR') models in the case of market risk. Banks must prove that they meet certain minimum quantitative and qualitative criteria before they are permitted to use an internal models approach, and their modelling is constrained by supervisory requirements.

5.14 Most large banks took advantage of the availability of the models-based approach for market risk under Basel 2. The resulting capital requirements were typically relatively small, and certainly smaller than the actual losses some dealers experienced on a number of days in 2008 and early 2009.[6]

[3] There are sometimes exceptions for derivatives that are entered into to hedge a bank's own risk, such as interest rate risk in the banking book.

[4] See the discussion in footnote 1.65.

[5] See PRA (2020) Box 1 for a further discussion.

[6] To pick one example from many, Citigroup's one day 99% market risk VAR in 2007 was $191M. In 2008, the bank recorded negative trading-related revenue on 109 of 260 trading days and, of these,

5.15 Bank regulators addressed the failure of the Basel 2 regime to capture market risk prudently by making four major changes. The first was to supplement VAR-based capital requirements with a stressed VAR methodology, so that banks had to use stressed market conditions[7] to calculate their VAR. This change dramatically reduced the tendency of market risk capital requirements to fall in placid times, something which can leave banks with too little capital when stress hits.[8]

5.16 The second change was to introduce an 'incremental risk charge' to capture default and credit migration risks in the trading book. Once a corporate bond defaults, it tends to be much less traded. This creates an adverse selection problem whereby the price history of the current contents of the trading book, which over-represents non-defaulted bonds, under-states the risk of future defaults.[9] The incremental risk charge corrected this issue.

5.17 The third change was to the prudential treatment of correlation trading portfolios, which will not detain us further, as the trading strategy they implemented is no longer commonplace in banks.

5.18 Finally, reflecting the fact that securitized assets were held in the banking as well as the trading book, the authorities changed the treatment of securitizations in the credit risk framework.[10]

5.19 The impact of these changes was substantial. Banks were required to hold significantly more market risk capital than hitherto.[11] There was still typically a benefit for using the models-based approach, but a somewhat lower one than under Basel 2. There was, in effect, a bargain being offered: meet the higher standards required for the models-based approach, and get (usually) lower capital requirements which are based on how you model risk.

---

on 21 days the losses were greater than \$400 million; \$191M was evidently not a good prediction of the market risk UL at 99% for Citi's portfolio during 2008.

7 The requirement is that 'model inputs [are] calibrated to historical data from a continuous 12 month period of significant financial stress'.

8 One issue with stressed VAR is what happens when current conditions are more stressed than the ones used in the capital calculation. There is no good answer to this: incorporating current conditions is procyclical, but failing to do so might mean that risk is under-estimated. We return to this issue in a different context—that of margin—in Chapter 7.

9 In particular, the time series of the past prices of non-defaulted bonds, which are used to calculate VAR, do not contain the large falls in price which tend to accompany default.

10 This is not strictly a market risk capital change, in that it affected the banking book, but it was introduced as part of Basel 2.5 and is trading book adjacent, in the sense that banks had transferred MBS and other securitized assets from the trading book into the banking book in 2008 and 2009 when liquidity disappeared in the market for these securities.

11 As an example, JPMorgan had the following breakdown for June 2013: (ordinary, Basel 2 VAR) capital requirement, \$909M; stressed VAR, \$2,727M; incremental risk charge, \$908M; comprehensive risk charge for correlation trading, \$4,209M. For this bank in this quarter, the Basel 2.5 market risk changes increased capital requirements for market risk by a factor of over nine times.

The fundamental review of the trading book

5.20 Basel 2.5 was a swift, targeted response to the crisis. The fundamental review of the trading book, in contrast, was an extended and extensive piece of policy making. The first consultation for it was published in 2012, and as of time of writing, it will not be implemented until 2022. As might be expected from this protracted gestation, the FRTB is more complex than the framework it will replace.[12]

5.21 The FRTB begins by establishing a clearer and more easily policed boundary between the trading book and banking book. Previously, trading intent was a determining factor in where positions were booked. This was inherently subjective and, given that there were large differences in the capital required for some positions depending on the booking location, it tempted some banks to optimize their capital by selecting an accommodating booking location.[13]

5.22 One of the main aims of the FRTB is to overhaul the models-based framework for market risk. The main changes are:

- a change to the calculation of unexpected loss, defining it as the expected shortfall of the return distribution rather than the VAR,[14] while carrying forward the charge for incremental risk from Basel 2.5;
- accounting for different levels of market liquidity in risk estimation;
- constraining the benefit for diversification between risk factors; and
- splitting the trading book into trading desks,[15] each of which has to separately qualify for the models-based framework. This involves two criteria: a profit-and-loss attribution test to determine if the risk factors models explain the desk's profit and loss;[16] and a 'backtest' to see if the models' statistical predictions about the desk's return distribution are accurate, and with the imposition of extra capital requirements if they are not.[17]

---

[12] For further discussion and analysis of the fundamental review of the trading book, see Farag (2018), Laurent et al. (2016).

[13] Banking book positions, because they are not usually subject to fair value accounting as trading book positions are, genuinely have different risks to trading book positions, so they *should* have a different capital requirement.

[14] This is a relatively technical change which better captures the risk in return distributions with fat tails by averaging over them: see Yamai & Yoshiba (2005).

[15] These are defined as a 'group of traders or trading accounts that implements a well defined business strategy operating within a clear risk management structure'.

[16] The idea is that each day it should be possible to decompose the total profit or loss on the desk into components arising from each risk factor (and other factors such as new trades or funding), in order to demonstrate that any risk factors not modelled are immaterial.

[17] Suppose a model predicts the 99th percentile of the one day return distribution. Thus, a loss bigger than this number—an 'exception'—should, on average, be experienced one day in 100.

5.23 The authorities also revised the standardized approach for market risk, updating the (somewhat) simpler rules for banks who did not have permission to use internal models. These revisions meant that the standardized approach captured more risks more accurately, at the cost of increased complexity. In particular, the new standard rules contain capital charges for default risk, giving the standardized approach an analogue to the incremental risk charge in Basel 2.5.

5.24 The FRTB will, on average, increase capital requirements for market risk substantially above Basel 2.5 levels.[18] But, as with many other aspects of post-crisis prudential policy, the impact is not just a simple turning up of the dial. The new standards are tougher on some asset classes than others: the standardized changes for foreign exchange risk, equity risk, and certain types of credit risk have attracted attention for their conservatism.[19]

5.25 Another aspect of the redistributive effects of the FRTB relates to its treatment of market liquidity risk. The liquidity-sensitive nature of the models-based change is reasonable from the perspective of ensuring the illiquid positions are properly capitalized, but it has the disadvantage of entrenching and perhaps increasing liquidity differences between markets. For example, many corporate bonds are already relatively illiquid, so trades in them will attract a relatively, as well as absolutely, higher charge under the fundamental review. This means that these bonds will be less attractive to intermediate than assets which are judged more liquid by regulators, and thus they will become even more illiquid.

5.26 Another impact relates to the gap between models-based and standardized capital requirements. In order to make the withdrawal of permission to use models a credible threat, the gap has been narrowed. However, this reduces the incentive to apply for permission to use models, given the high fixed costs involved: the bargain discussed in paragraph 5.19 has changed, and, in many cases, it is no longer so evident that there is a capital benefit for most banks to meet the standards for the use of internal models.

5.27 In stress, some issues with the desk-based qualification criteria in the FRTB became evident. Increased volatility causes market risk capital requirements to increase. This 'procyclicality' of capital requirements, as it is known, was damped by the stressed VAR component, but still demanded more resources from banks

---

A backtest analyses the number of days such an exception is actually experienced to determine whether there is evidence that the model can be rejected for inaccuracy. If there are too many exceptions, regulators impose capital multipliers or, at higher levels, withdraw permission to use models from the desk entirely.

18 Interim impact analysis in 2015—the latest available at the time of writing—suggests that it will 'result in a weighted average increase of 74% in aggregate market risk capital charges' based on a sample of 44 large banks: see BCBS (2015b).

19 See ISDA et al. (2018).

when they were least able to provide them. Market stress also increases the number of exceptions, which further increases capital requirements. This was one of the impacts of the Covid-related stress on the prudential framework discussed in Chapter 3 which were considered undesirable, and which authorities have acted to mitigate.[20]

The Standardized Approach to Counterparty Credit Risk

5.28 We now turn from market risk to counterparty credit risk. Chapter 1 discussed the measurement of this risk. It was seen how the return distribution of a portfolio could be used to estimate expected exposure at a given point in time, and how the time profile of these expected exposures could be used to define the effective expected positive exposure.

5.29 The models-based approach to setting capital requirements for counterparty credit risk uses these ideas. The exposure at default for regulatory purposes is a fixed multiple of effective EPE, with the proviso that there are two calculations, one based on current risk factor volatilities, and one based on stressed estimates, with the higher of the two being used. This approach, like other models-based approaches, is only available to banks satisfying various quantitative and qualitative criteria.[21]

5.30 This is not the only approach to setting capital requirements for counterparty credit risk. Standard rules have become relatively more important in the Basel Capital framework since 2008, in part driven by a lack of trust in the consistency and prudence of models-based approaches.[22] Basel 3 contains a new standard rule for counterparty credit risk, replacing a prior rule for estimating EAD which dated from the early 1990s.[23] Like most standardized rules, this was designed to be a relatively simple, conservative approach suitable for use by banks who did not meet the criteria for using a models-based approach. The EAD estimates the new rule produces are then used as an input to the prudential rules for capitalizing credit risk.

5.31 This new rule is the Standardized Approach for Counterparty Credit Risk, or 'SA-CCR'. It is not just used in the risk-weighted framework: after it had been

20 See, for instance, R. Fed Board & OCC (2020). Procyclicality is discussed further in Chapter 6.

21 See R. BCBS (2019b), §53.28–53.71.

22 See Behn et al. (2016), Mariathasana & Merrouche (2014) and the discussion starting in paragraph 5.66.

23 For a discussion of the issues with this earlier rule, known as the current exposure method, and criteria for the replacement, see R. BCBS (2013c).

developed, it was also adopted elsewhere in the capital framework. In particular, it is the only rule available for calculating the contribution of OTC derivatives to the leverage ratio. Thus, the SA-CCR is being applied not just to small portfolios in unsophisticated banks, but—at least for some purposes—to all derivatives portfolios in all Basel-compliant banks.

The method used in the SA-CCR

5.32 The SA-CCR has to perform a complex task. It starts with individual transactions and derives an estimate of their potential future exposure. These PFEs are combined in a way that is intended to reflect the netting of risk within a portfolio. The SA-CCR also has to consider the effect of collateral in reducing exposure.[24]

5.33 The SA-CCR attempts to do this in a way that balances between risk sensitivity and complexity.[25] However, it is difficult to judge this balance because both concepts are imprecise. Regulators have not stated the target risk measure which the standard rules should aspire to matching, so it is not clear how to measure risk sensitivity.[26] There is no obvious measure of complexity either. Is it textual length, number of free parameters in the rules, compliance cost, or something else?[27]

5.34 The SA-CCR estimate of the exposure at default of a derivatives portfolio is defined as a constant,[28] known as α, times the sum of the current exposure[29] and the potential future exposure. For portfolios subject to variation margin, the current exposure is (approximately) zero, so a major part of the SA-CCR is devoted to rules which define the regulatory notion of PFE.

5.35 The SA-CCR is compositional. It begins by defining particular risk types. Individual trades are translated into the SA-CCR by rules which set out how much of each of these risk types the trade is defined to have. The rules then provide a

---

[24] See BCBS (2014) for the official sector account, and Berrahoui et al. (2019), Kratochwil (2020) and Murphy et al. (2021) for independent analysis.

[25] For a discussion of this desiderata, see R. BCBS (2013c).

[26] The issues around the variability of models-based risk estimates are discussed further in paragraph 5.66.

[27] See Colliard & Georg (2020) for a discussion of regulatory complexity. In practice it may be that the complexity of individual rules matters less than the number of rules which simultaneously bind a business. A risk-based capital rule, for instance, might be a complex function of a number of parameters, but it only has to be coded in a firm's systems once, and it is only one constraint: in contrast, a suite of rules, even if they are all individually simple, might together be more limiting (and hence, potentially, better able to distinguish safe from risky banks, but more likely to lead to herding of business models, as Buckmann et al. (2021) discusses).

[28] See paragraph 1.103 for the issues around the setting of this constant, and paragraph 5.42 for the political economy considerations concerning it.

[29] 'Replacement cost' in the language of the rule.

recipe for combining those trade-level risk estimates into asset class risk estimates. These are summed to provide a portfolio (or 'netting set') PFE; this is then adjusted for the effect of collateral.[30]

5.36 The features chosen for the translation of individual transactions are, in sketch, notional and (adjusted) duration. The idea is to construct a measure of how sensitive the value of a transaction is to a risk factor move. This is then multiplied by a fixed amount which reflects regulators' estimates of what a big move in the relevant risk factor might be. For instance, for equity indices, the factor is 20%.[31]

5.37 The recipe for combining trade level risk measures into asset class risk estimates is based on buckets. A bucket is a collection of similar risk sensitivities, such as exposures to closely related interest rates in the same currency. First the net risk within a bucket is calculated, allowing positions within the bucket to offset each other; then regulator-specified correlations are used to calculate a net PFE for all of the buckets within an asset class.

5.38 The adjustment for collateral is based on the fact that there is a distribution of exposures, of which PFE is a tail estimate. Therefore, if we have an amount of collateral equal to the PFE, sometimes the exposure will be bigger than the collateral, and sometimes smaller.[32] The SA-CCR therefore gives benefit for collateral, but it does not allow it to extinguish exposure.[33]

The consequences of SA-CCR

5.39 In common with most standardized capital rules, the SA-CCR is in general conservative, overestimating the required capital compared to a choice of a truly risk-sensitive model based on the same assumptions.[34] More problematically, its conservatism varies across asset classes and trade types. It is relatively punitive towards equity and commodity derivatives and towards large, diversified portfolios.[35] Finally, it is not self-consistent.[36]

5.40 The biases of the SA-CCR have material effects. It discourages liquidity provision in some asset classes, by assigning relatively higher charges to them,

[30] The full calculation is (much) more complicated that we have space for: see R. BCBS (2019b) for the details.

[31] See R. BCBS (2014b), table 2, and note that this is not the percentage change in price of a trade with duration one year because the notional is also multiplied by an additional factor: see §164–171.

[32] See the discussion in paragraph 1.27.

[33] The SA-CCR provides a conservative approximation to the true effect of collateral under certain distributional assumptions: see Murphy et al. (2021) for details. In particular, it floors the effect of collateral at 5%, 'to ensure that some PFE is always recognized', as BCBS (2014) puts it at 13.

[34] See Murphy et al. (2021).

[35] Ibid. and Kratochwil (2020): the latter also discusses the issues with exotic options.

[36] See Berrahoui et al. (2019).

while providing less of a handicap to others. It penalizes diversification, through conservatively set correlation parameters. Finally, by overcharging for counterparty credit risk versus other risk types, it discourages derivatives activity for all banks subject to Basel-compliant regulation, especially large banks.[37]

Implementing the SA-CCR

5.41 The SA-CCR reflects the difficulty of being prudent throughout a rule. If we add a measure of conservativism in the trade level PFE measure, a pinch in the correlations, and a soupçon in the adjustment for collateral, the overall level of conservatism is impossible to state. It varies substantially depending on which trades are in a portfolio. A better approach would be to attempt to be as accurate as possible, given the complexity budget, then multiply the final EAD estimate by a fixed amount to tune to the desired degree of conservatism.

5.42 The SA-CCR does have an overall tuning parameter in addition to, rather than instead of, its various conservative (i.e. erroneous) modelling choices, α. Perhaps indicative of the issues with the SA-CCR's high but variable level of conservatism, this proved controversial, as we discuss later in this chapter.

Capital for Bank Exposures to CCPs

5.43 There were no capital requirements for counterparty credit risk exposures to CCPs in the Basel 2 framework. The post-crisis reforms to derivatives clearing, introduced in Chapter 1 and discussed in detail in the next chapter, increased the size of these exposures and the systemic importance of CCPs. Reflecting this increase, and the realization that 'zero' was typically not a good answer for most risk weights, regulators introduced a new rule for bank exposures to CCPs.[38]

5.44 They first distinguished 'qualifying' central counterparties—roughly, those compliant with the CPMI/IOSCO Principles for Financial Market Infrastructures[39]—from others. Most CCPs qualified, so this served more as a protection against regulatory arbitrage than anything else.[40]

5.45 There are two components to the requirement for exposures to qualifying central counterparties under the revised framework:

- A charge for (funded) default fund contributions, reflecting the fact that the default fund is a mutualized resource available for use by the CCP if

[37] This is due to the use of the SA-CCR in the leverage ratio discussed in paragraph 5.31. The G-SIB framework uses the leverage ratio exposure measure, so the SA-CCR is important here, too.

[38] See R. BCBS (2014c): the prior arrangement is in R. BCBS (2006), Annex IV, Section II, §6.

[39] R. CPMI & IOSCO (2012).

[40] One obvious arbitrage would have been to set up a thinly resourced CCP-like entity to clear those bilateral OTC derivatives which were not cleared by PFMI-compliant CCPs.

the losses from member default exceed the defaulter's resources, and thus the default fund contributions might be lost.[41] This charge declines as initial margin increases, corresponding to the fact that more initial margin reduces the risk of the default fund being used.

- A charge for 'trade exposures' to the CCP, capitalizing the risk of CCP default. This is comprised of a charge for the amount of initial margin at risk from CCP default[42] and a charge for the cleared portfolio. As in other areas of counterparty credit risk, the charge for the cleared portfolio is based on the sum of the current exposure and the PFE.[43]

5.46 These charges are interesting, because of what is not captured. Most CCPs have extensive powers in their rule books to call for additional default fund contributions and to allocate losses to members, discussed further in Chapter 7. The risk to clearing members created by these powers is not capitalized, whereas the more remote risk of CCP default without a resolution which preserves trade continuity, and where margin is lost, is.

5.47 Unlike many of the post-crisis policies discussed in this chapter, the rules for bank exposures to CCPs do not often generate very large capital requirements, as the risk weight assigned to CCPs is small.[44] However, because there is a one day gap between margin being called and being received, the contribution of the current exposure to the overall capital charge can be quite volatile.[45]

Capital for CVA Risk

5.48 The bank capital treatment of CVA risk is one of the most complex areas of the whole capital accord. It has changed on a number of occasions, both conceptually and in detail.[46] The current version is formidably complex, with two

[41] The default fund was discussed in paragraph 7.135.

[42] I.e. initial margin posted to the CCP and not held in a bankruptcy remote manner.

[43] The PFE for cleared OTC derivatives uses the SA-CCR, but with a shorter margin period of risk—five days—than the ten days specified for uncleared OTC derivatives.

[44] This risk weight, and the dependence of the capital charge on CCP margin levels, are also considered in Chapter 7.

[45] To see this, consider a cleared derivatives portfolio with a large payment due tomorrow. The current trade value, and hence the variation margin, will include this payment. However, after it is made, the trade value of the portfolio will change substantially. Variation margin will change to reflect this, but it takes a day for this to catch up, potentially creating a one day spike in exposure, and hence in capital requirements.

[46] See R. BCBS (2010), R. BCBS (2011b), R. BCBS (2017), and R. BCBS (2020c), noting also a consultation that did not result in the proposed changes, R. BCBS (2015).

standardized approaches, and over 50 free parameters in the rules.[47] This section reviews the journey, highlighting the twists and turns in policy evolution created as different regulatory objectives came to the fore. This leads to a discussion of the conflicting goals of capital policy in the following section.

The foundations of CVA risk capitalization

5.49 The motivation for introducing a capital charge for CVA risk was the observation that:[48]

> *While the Basel 2 standard covers the risk of a counterparty default, it does not address CVA risk, which during the financial crisis was a greater source of losses than those arising from outright defaults.*

5.50 Here a key distinction is being drawn. The CVA itself—the adjustment to derivatives pricing due to the potential for counterparty default—contains two components:

1. The adjustment due to the risk of default or significant increases in the risk of ultimate counterparty non-performance. This is driven by the real-world probability of default, discussed in Chapter 1.[49] It is capitalized by the counterparty credit risk charges in Basel 2 such as the SA-CCR or the models-based approach to counterparty credit risk.
2. The adjustment due to the changes in the credit spread for other reasons, such as changes in liquidity preferences. This is driven by the difference between the risk-neutral and the real-world probabilities of default.[50]

5.51 The Capital Accords before the advent of CVA risk charges already capitalized the first component of CVA, default risk. They did not capitalize the risk that non-default components of the credit spread would increase, leading to *necessarily temporary* increases in CVA.[51]

5.52 The CVA capital charge is intended to capture the risk of variation in the second of these two components. This, in turn, only arises because of the choice to apply fair value accounting to CVA. If CVA was an amortized cost item, then there would be no variation in value due to changes in the credit spread that did not

---

47 In contrast, the standard model in physics, which accounts for the four fundamental forces of nature so well that it is accurate to one part in ten billion, has (depending on exactly how CP violation is addressed) around 26 free parameters.

48 See R. BCBS (2010) at 3.

49 This is a measure in the real-world numeraire, and is (broadly) the data which would be used to estimate a lifetime expected loss provision in amortized cost accounting.

50 The term 'non-default component of the credit spread' is sometimes used here.

51 'Necessarily temporary' because if it was permanent, it would be an increase in the risk of ultimate counterparty non-performance and hence be capitalized in the counterparty risk charges.

lead to a permanent change in credit quality, because amortized cost accounting does not recognize this effect. Therefore there would be nothing to capitalize. Thus, there is a choice about what CVA is—something like an expected loss provision, or a fully market consistent pricing adjustment—which determines how it is accounted for, capitalized, and risk managed.[52] CVA capital requirements are only needed if the market consistent alternative is chosen.

Hedging CVA

5.53 The question of whether it is possible to hedge CVA is important, because CVA is valued as if it were a derivative, and derivatives valuation depends on hedgability. The CVA on a portfolio of OTC derivatives transactions with a counterparty varies as the market risk factors driving the portfolio valuation change and as the counterparty's credit spread changes. It is likely that the market risk factors can be hedged, as most portfolios depend only on tradable risk factors. The key issue, then, is the counterparty's credit spread. If liquid credit default swaps are available on the counterparty, then the CVA on their portfolio is likely to be at least approximately hedgeable, and the way is clear. Without this, valuation is more complex[53] because we cannot use a replicating portfolio approach.[54]

5.54 In short, it makes sense to treat a hedgeable CVA like a derivative, use fair value accounting for it, and capitalize the risks of the hedged portfolio (i.e. the CVA and its hedges). But if the CVA is not hedgeable, this becomes more problematic, and accounting for it as an expected loss provision becomes more attractive. If the market makes it quack, perhaps you should treat it like a duck.

5.55 The amount of liquidity needed to hedge the CVA with a given counterparty obviously depends on the size of the exposure, but given that only about 100 names globally are liquid in the CDS market, there is at least an open question

[52] Financial regulation is not the only framework that makes arbitrary definitions: accounting does too, among many others, as Nobes & Stadler (1989) discuss. A question that arises for regulation is the extent to which it should rely on accounting definitions. This is a source of tension, as reviewed by BCBS (2015a). Accountants and regulators have somewhat different aims, and indeed neither group is homogenous. There are substantial costs associated with regulators rewriting accounting to create, e.g., the regulatory balance sheet, so this should only be done when it is justified by highly undesirable behaviour from the regulators' perspective in accounting outcome. This happens both on an ongoing basis where the accounting approach is, in regulators' judgement, imprudent, and on an ad hoc basis when events demand it. The exclusion of the inverse of CVA—own credit or debt valuation adjustments—from the definition of capital is an example of the former, while the Basel Committee's transitional arrangement for expected credit loss accounting in light of the Covid-19 pandemic in R. BCBS (2019c) is one of the latter.

[53] See Jouini (2001) for a summary of the issues pricing derivatives in incomplete markets.

[54] Recall from paragraph 1.82 that derivatives are often priced as the cost of continuously hedging them.

as to how many counterparties have fully hedgeable CVAs. This set of hedgeable counterparties is much smaller than most OTC derivatives dealers' set of counterparties with significant CVAs.

5.56 Proxy hedges to credit spread risk in CVA are available, too. Just as the systematic risk in a basket of equities can sometimes be hedged by taking a position on an equity index, so some of the credit spread risk in a basket of CVAs with different counterparties can be hedged by taking a position in index CDS. The more the collection of CVAs a dealer has resembles a liquidly traded credit index, the better this hedging technique works.[55]

5.57 The discussion above makes it clear that if a bank mostly has CVAs with counterparties who are liquid in the single name CDS market, or has a collection of CVAs with counterparties which collectively behave like a traded CDS index, then the CVAs are at least broadly hedgeable. A large North American dealing bank would tend to be in this position, as the most liquid non-sovereign names tend to be North American corporates, and dealers' books are well enough diversified that index hedges would tend to work reasonably well. On the other hand, a regional bank in Europe or Asia would tend to be a worse position: fewer of their exposures are likely to be liquid in the CDS market, and their CVA book would tend to 'look' less like a tradable index.

CVA capital from 2008 to 2020

5.58 The evolution of the CVA capital rules demonstrate two phenomena which deserve unpacking:

1. the search for a definition of regulatory CVA that does not have serious disadvantages; and
2. the attempt, for a given definition, to say what should prudently count as a hedge to that regulatory CVA, and what the risks of that considered-hedged portfolio are.

5.59 The first CVA capital rules in R. BCBS (2010), surprisingly, do not motivate the definition of a regulatory CVA at all. They simply state: 'Regardless of the accounting valuation method a bank uses for determining CVA, the CVA capital

[55] The most liquid index CDS positions are five year trades on either the CDX North American Investment Grade (the 'CDX' for short) or the Markit iTraxx Europe Main index (the 'iTraxx'). Both of these indices consist of 125 equally weighted investment grade rated entities. Therefore if a dealer's book consists of many portfolios with roughly equal credit spread sensitivities, each with a higher credit quality corporation domiciled in Europe or North America, then CDX or iTraxx positions would probably be reasonable hedges. Hedging smaller, less diversified, or differently domiciled collections of CVAs using liquid CDS index positions would involve taking more basis risk.

charge calculation for each counterparty must be based on the following formula', before giving a definition. This version of the rules does not capitalize the risk that a bank's CVA changes. Instead, it capitalizes the risk that a different object, regulatory CVA, changes. The definition of accounting CVA, i.e. of the object that actually creates profits and losses for banks, has been replaced by an alternative regulatory definition.[56]

5.60 This regulatory strategy of arbitrary definition has already been discussed in Chapter 4: it suffices to note that 2010-era regulatory CVA bore the same epistemological relation to accounting CVA as the famous model of Khedive of Egypt's palace in the Paris Exposition of 1867 did to the real thing.[57]

5.61 By the time of the consultation on the second major revision to the rules in 2015, this strategy was acknowledged even as the representation was changed. R. BCBS (2015) states that the 'new regulatory capital treatment of CVA that is based *to some extent* on accounting CVA' but 'the proposal would impose several conditions on the accounting exposure models used ... reflecting best practice' (emphasis mine). In other words, they are defining a new object within regulation that is different from accounting CVA but which in some ways resembles it better than their prior representation: the model of the Khedive's palace is now in higher definition.

5.62 The use of internal models for CVA capital changed substantially as the CVA rules developed, too. The 2011 rules included an 'advanced CVA risk capital charge'[58] which was available to banks which already had permission to use models-based approaches for counterparty credit risk and market risk.[59] By 2015, this had been modified into 'an adaptation of the Internal Model Approach for market risk under the FRTB to the CVA book'.[60] The 2017 revisions to Basel 3

[56] The problem here is there has not been a matching change in earnings for regulatory purposes. Suppose there is a loss of 10 in accounting CVA. This creates a loss of 10 of capital. Regulatory capital requirements are supposed to protect against the risk of this. But the object whose risk of loss is being capitalized is not accounting CVA: it is regulatory CVA. So there is a fundamental disconnection between the risk of loss to capital and how capital requirements are being set.

[57] Mitchell (1989), in an insightful paper on some of the mechanisms by which the West creates distorted internal representations of the East which are then proclaimed as objective as part of a strategy of domination, discusses this representation. He recounts how the Khedive of Egypt visited the Paris model of his own palace and was induced to stay there. The viceroy was even persuaded to receive visitors in a simulation of the ancient manner, becoming, in the process, both a part of the spectacle and an imitation of himself. Mitchell points out the 'remarkable claim to certainty or truth' in this approach, 'the certainty with which everything seems ordered and organized, calculated and rendered unambiguous'. Power, in this reading, includes the power to define a representation which is then presented as real.

[58] See R. BCBS (2011b), §98.

[59] Specifically, the specific interest rate risk component of market risk.

[60] R. BCBS (2015), §71.

removed this approach entirely,[61] leaving banks with the choice between a 'basic' and a 'standardized' approach to CVA capital.

5.63 Another key aspect in the exegesis of the CVA rules is the regulatory definition of eligible hedges to CVA and of net CVA risk. The first CVA capital rules only considered the risk of increases in the counterparty's credit spread, and only allowed certain specified hedges to that risk.[62] Later versions of the rules included hedges to the market risk of CVA to some extent. The trend is towards treating CVA just like any other fair valued derivative in the trading book, although it has not yet fully converged to that position.[63]

Trade-offs in the Design of Capital Rules

5.64 It is helpful to take a step back at this point and consider the design goals of bank capital regulation. At the highest level, policy makers are striving to balance:

- *Risk sensitivity*: the capital requirements for a given risk should be proportional to the level of that risk.
- *Prudence*: that the rules generate capital requirements which are sufficiently high to absorb (most) losses.[64]
- *Confidence creation*: that the rules are seen to be prudent by bank investors and other stakeholders in the financial system.
- *Support for the provision of critical economic functions*, even in stress.
- *Proportionality*: that the response is appropriate, given the prudential goal. (This is discussed further in Chapter 9.)

5.65 This section explores the issues in the design of capital rules created by these primary objectives.

---

61 R. BCBS (2017) at 109.

62 Specifically, single name CDS and contingent CDS, and, to some extent, index CDS.

63 The version of the standardized approach to CVA in R. BCBS (2017) differs from the standardized approach for market risk in several ways: it 'features a reduced granularity of market risk factors'; it 'does not include default risk and curvature risk'; it 'uses a more conservative risk aggregation'; and it 'uses the conservativeness multiplier' to increase capital requirements. Only the first two of those differences survive in the version in R. BCBS (2020c).

64 The logic here is subtle as capital used to meet minimum requirements is not loss-absorbing on a going concern basis, as noted in paragraph 5.3. Haubrich (2020) calls this the 'last taxi' issue, based on the long-standing problem that if there is a rule that there must always be one taxi waiting at a station to serve travellers, the last taxi cannot actually serve anyone as, if it is used, the rule is violated. Instead, minimum requirements affect usable resources because capital buffers are usually sized as a fraction of them, and the capital ratio required to pass supervisory stress tests may be too. Capital requirements determine the amount of going concern loss-absorbing capital a bank has by these mechanisms rather than directly through minima.

Consequences of the primary objectives

5.66 An important motivation for the flurry of regulatory definition writing after 2008 was investors' loss of confidence in many banks' capital ratios. The capital requirements calculated using Basel 2's models-based approach were not found credible by investors once stress hit, for instance.[65]

5.67 Both academic[66] and official sector studies showed significant variation between different banks' estimates of the capital they require for the same or similar risks under the Basel 2 framework,[67] so this loss of confidence is understandable.[68] If capital requirements between banks were not comparable, what did a capital ratio mean?

5.68 Eager to restore confidence, regulators put precautionary constraints on the use of models in the post-crisis capital framework. The leverage ratio discussed in Chapter 4 is one such: so too are Basel 3's output floor[69] and the 'Collins floor' in the Dodd-Frank Act.[70] At the same time, some of the features previously allowed in bank capital models were withdrawn, constraining banks' modelling choices.[71] The desire is clearly to limit the capital benefit of models-based approaches.

5.69 The increasing importance of comparability, and precautionary measures supporting prudence, came at the cost of risk sensitivity.[72] There are two issues

65 Samuels (2013) discusses some of the issues here. They are not new: as long ago as 2006, a prominent US regulator was pointing to the 'lack of an objective process within the Advanced Approaches for producing similar capital requirements for similar risks'—see Bair (2006a).

66 See, for instance, Turk-Ariss (2017) and Plosser & Santos (2014), which find significant differences between, respectively, European and American banks' estimates of capital requirements across portfolios for the same country or counterparty.

67 'Significant variation' is perhaps an understatement. The hypothetical portfolio exercise reported in BCBS (2013b) at 28 reports that for exposures to the same corporate, the ratio of the 75th percentile of bank estimates to the 25th percentile is more than two. In other words, if a bottom quartile estimate of the risk of a corporate exposure was $4 million, a top quartile estimate for the same exposure might well be more than $8 million.

68 Estimating the high quantiles of financial return distributions is an inherently difficult problem and the results have wide confidence bounds, as Danielsson et al. (2016) discusses. This means that even without gaming, different banks cannot be expected to come to the same answer for the same portfolio.

69 See R. BCBS (2017).

70 Susan Collins was (and at the time of writing still is) a Republican Senator from Maine. She was friendly with Sheila Bair, the FDIC Chair whose views were noted in footnote 65 above. Bair encouraged her to introduce an amendment to the Dodd-Frank Act which placed a floor on capital requirements. The provision is that capital requirements shall not be 'quantitatively lower than the generally applicable risk-based capital requirements that were in effect for insured depository institutions as of the date of enactment of this Act', i.e. 21 July 2010: see §171(b)(2) of the Act.

71 A good example is the withdrawal of the Advanced Internal Ratings Based approach for exposures to large and mid-sized corporates and to banks and other financial institutions in Basel 3.

72 See Ahnert et al. (2018) for a model where some risk sensitivity is good, but not too much.

here: equal charges for equal risks at one point in time, and equal charges for the same risk at different points in time. In both cases, the idea is that there should be a clear goal, such as setting capital requirements to estimate the 99th percentile of a return distribution. The rules should not target the 98th percentile for one asset class and the 99.5th for another, as this would introduce incentives to trade more the first asset class and less of the second. Without parity of treatment, the rules will incentivize some activities over others which create the same risks, and hence discourage the provision of some economic functions. Moreover, over time, there should be some mechanism to recalibrate the rules as more information becomes available on risk factor returns.

5.70 The desire to have risk-sensitive capital rules is in direct tension with the desire for capital not to increase too much in stress—or to limit procyclicality, as regulators would put it. This is because volatilities increase in stress, and, with them, estimates of unexpected loss. One way of addressing this issue, without the danger of having capital ratios which are imprudent or which cause confidence to be lost, is to abandon the time dimension of risk sensitivity. Risk estimates would then be based on stressed conditions, as in the models-based approach to counterparty credit risk.[73]

5.71 Risk sensitivity is also in tension with the desire for simplicity in capital calculation. Simpler capital rules are easier for investors and other stakeholders to understand, but they create larger deviations from risk sensitivity, and hence bigger incentives for banks to change their activities to do more of the relatively cheaper things and less of the expensive ones.[74]

5.72 There are proportionality considerations here too. Are complex rules that are expensive to comply with a proportionate response to relatively small risks? For instance, by the time CVA capital charges were imposed, banks had few of the trades that generated significant CVA losses in the crisis. No one buys uncollateralized protection on MBS from insurers any more. Indeed, the bilateral margin rules mean that no bank buys substantial amounts of uncollateralized anything from anyone. For most banks, CVA capital is less than 3% of total capital requirements. Does this really justify the definition of a regulatory CVA and a complex set of capital rules for it which are almost, but not quite, the same as the market risk capital rules?

5.73 The desirability of creating incentives for good risk management, together with the idea that banks are better able to measure their risks than regulators

[73] A problem does however arise if the current conditions are more stressed than the stressed conditions used. This can be addressed in way that is sensitive to procyclicality by updating the model well after the stress has subsided.

[74] See Gai et al. (2019) for more on the balance between complexity and prudence in capital regulation.

are, was an important feature in Basel 2. Regulatory ideology has changed and this principle has been largely forgotten in Basel 3, with the balance swinging towards comparability[75] and against using incentives to encourage, rather than rules which mandate, good risk management. Traces of it can still be found in the models-based approaches to capital that persist, but they are growing fainter.

5.74 Finally, it should be noted that there is an efficiency in the design of prudential regulation if the same risk is measured in the same way in different areas of the rules. This uniformity property would suggest that the standard rules for capturing market risk, for instance, should be the same across the market risk, CVA and counterparty credit risk frameworks. This, though, is in tension with regulators' desire to have a larger measure of precaution in some settings than in others.[76] At very least, there should be a clear articulation of why these choices have been made.

The evolving tensions in capital rule design

5.75 At various points in the development of the capital framework, the relative importance of the different design goals seems to have varied. Immediately after 2008, precaution dominated, with the introduction of the leverage ratio and various floors to model-based capital approaches. Latterly, there were some steps towards uniformity, for instance in the steps toward convergence of the treatment of market risk in the CVA rules, but it remains the case that the same risk is treated in different, incompatible ways in different areas of the rules.[77] The market turmoil associated with Covid then brought the issue of procyclicality into prominence, and there are now signs that some authorities are becoming more concerned with aspects of the proportionality of the prudential framework.[78]

---

[75] Sheila Bair was an influencer here too. In Bair (2006b) she said that an 'issue of concern is a lack of an objective process within the Advanced Approaches [i.e. the models-based approaches] for producing similar capital requirements for similar risks ... The framework allows banks substantial flexibility in how they develop risk inputs. It remains unclear how to reconcile the twin goals of individual bank flexibility within the Advanced Approaches and regulatory consistency across banks.' This problem is insoluble: if banks do indeed look at risk differently, then their approaches will sometimes produce different estimates of the same risk. The real question is the balance between the value of having diverse views of risk and that of more comparable risk estimates. Regulatory minima are not the answer if they are set so high that there is no incentive for banks to develop their own models.

[76] There is also the issue that risk is not entirely the property of an instrument: the business model of the risk taker and how it is accounted for matters too.

[77] Compare, for instance, the calculation of PFE in the SA-CCR—which is essentially a market risk measure—with the standard rules for market risk in the 2019 version of Basel 3.

[78] One example can be found in Woods (2020) where a 'graduated regime' in which banks 'can migrate from a very simple regime, up through a series of steps towards the full Basel regime as they become larger and/or involved in more complex activities' is suggested.

5.76 Overall, between Lehman and Covid the impression is of the authorities ricocheting between the different design goals without an overarching theory which would suggest how to manage the tension between them. This, combined with the use of different safety thresholds in different areas, has meant that the framework has become more complex and its impact across different areas of activity has been more variable, with significant winners and losers.

Regulators' Modelling Claims, Oppositions to Them, and the Policing of Dissent

5.77 If our account of regulators' goals is broadly correct, then it follows that the overarching claim being made when a new capital rule is promulgated is that it appropriately balances these conflicting desiderata. One facet of this claim is that capital rules are accurate models, in that they use properties of banks' positions to produce good estimates of the risk of loss. It will therefore be helpful to consider the foundations of modelling claims such as 'this rule estimates this risk'.

5.78 Bank capital rules are internationally agreed. Sometimes, an individual country or bloc might have a sufficiently different view of the balance between objectives in a particular situation, given their financial system, that they do not wish to conform to the international consensus. This is often because they do not concur with the modelling claim made.[79] This section considers this issue, before turning to a discussion of how the regulatory community polices deviations from international standards.

Regulatory capital requirements as a modelling exercise

5.79 Since at least the work of Edmund Husserl,[80] the importance of considering the philosophical foundations of modelling exercises has been recognized. To summarize in a few words what is now a large body of scholarship, a model is a linked body of definitions or categories that is 'grounded in fact, is duly responsive to reasons or evidence, and enables non-trivial inference, argument, and perhaps action regarding the topic the information pertains to'.[81] The 'grounding in fact' implies a translation mechanism into the model's representation, while the ability to make 'non-trivial inferences' means that the model has an internal notion of inference: its own rhetoric. We return to this topic in Chapter 10.

[79] Typically international standards permit countries to adopt a more stringent approach, so when an issue arises, it is usually because the international standard is too tough rather than too lax.

[80] In Husserl (1913): see Guizzardia & Halpin (2008) and the subsequent chapters in the same volume for a discussion.

[81] The quote is from Elgin (2017) at 44.

5.80 The calculation of capital requirements within financial regulation is a modelling exercise. For banks, this exercise[82] involves two levels of representation and two levels of model. There is the level of what will be called a 'primary' capital model. Here the definitions are the sorts of things seen in Chapter 1: risk factors and portfolio return distributions and PFEs. A typical inference would be the estimation of a property of one of these distributions, such as a quantile.

5.81 The counterparty credit risk models discussed in Chapter 1 and the market, counterparty credit, and CVA models considered in this Chapter are all primary models. They make a claim similar to many modelling exercises; that their inferences, under some circumstances, are reliable estimates of 'real-world' facts. For instance, in Basel 2.5, there is the claim that, given certain risk factor histories, the sum of the VAR, stressed VAR and incremental risk charge is an accurate measure of potential losses on a portfolio due to market risk in stress.[83]

5.82 The use of primary models is constrained in contemporary bank regulation by a framing claim that the primary model's estimates of requirements are not always reliable, or will not be believed to be reliable. Hence, at a secondary level, there are precautionary interventions, such as floors, to address this. The status of the secondary model is difficult to verify because there is no account of when inferences in the primary model will be unreliable: rather, the claim is only that they might be.[84] Given that the aim of the interventions is not necessarily to make capital requirements more accurate, but perhaps to keep investor confidence in their prudence, their efficacy in part relies on the beliefs of an unspecified collection of individuals in an unspecified situation.[85] The actions of bank investors during the Covid stress are one of the few pieces of evidence available here.[86]

5.83 As noted in the previous section, constraints on models are a form of precautionary principle. In the context of financial regulation, this principle might

[82] Or, at least, the formal ontology of this exercise, in Husserl's terms.

[83] Latterly this claim has been modified by the introduction of capital for 'Risks not in VAR': see R. PRA (2020).

[84] The claim that there is a need for a constraint or ornament on a model is law-like or 'nomological': it is a brute contingency, unrelated to elements of the primary model.

[85] The doxastic claim that a particular individual or class of individuals believes something in a given situation would at least be susceptible to seeing if, in that situation, they behaved as if they believed it. The claim that investors will be more confident as a result of the floors on regulatory capital models is even less easy to verify than that as their behaviour without floors cannot be observed.

[86] Aldasoro et al. (2020) reports that 'from the onset of a generalized and severe stock market sell-off on 5 March [2020] banks joined the worst performers [in the equity market]. As a result, by the last week of April, banks' stock price declines were even deeper than those of the hardest-hit sectors of the real economy'. Bank CDS spreads in the early Covid period also increased by roughly the same amount as they did after the bankruptcy of Lehman Brothers. Banks did not fail, but they were not attractive to investors either.

be phrased as 'if an activity raises threats to financial stability or institutional resilience, precautionary measures should be taken even if some cause and effect relationships are not fully established'.[87] The problem is immediately obvious. Most forms of financial activity, and certainly most things recognizable as banking or financial risk transfer, involve *some* threats to financial stability or institutional resilience or both.[88] Which activities should the precautionary principle be applied to, and how much precaution is justified? Clearly a threshold should be exceeded before a certain measure of (pre)caution is justified.[89]

5.84 The evolution of the CVA capital rules are evidence of the problems that arise when there has been no characterization of this threshold: should the definition of CVA be precautionary, or the hedge recognition, or the treatment of market risk hedges, or all three? How much precaution is enough? The questions are not well-posed because there are no criteria for adjudicating between possible answers.[90] It is therefore impossible to judge the reliability of the secondary modelling claim about the necessity of precautionary interventions to the inferences of primary models.

Why deviate?

5.85 Different countries, or blocs with common standards such as the EU, have different financial systems. They also might reasonably have different trade-offs between regulatory objectives. The efficient provision of certain functions might be relatively more important to some jurisdictions. This means that there can reasonably be differing views on the suitability of a particular international standard to a particular financial system. In the language of the previous subsection, their secondary framing model might be different from the internationally agreed one.

---

87 The phrasing is a modification of the well-known precautionary principle in environmental science: see, for instance, Kriebel et al. (2001).

88 Fisher (2000), at 130, rightly makes the point that decision making about risk tolerance in the presence of uncertainty is complex and that simplistic accountability mechanisms can thwart effective policy making. However, as she also accepts, this is not a justification for the democratic illegitimacy that comes from a total lack of accountability. Rather, it is important that the goals of and evidence and criteria used to inform the setting of normative prescriptions like regulatory standards can be scrutinized by interested parties. The key issue is not that precaution is unnecessary, but rather that those imposing it must be accountable for their choices. We return to the issue of accountability in Chapter 8.

89 See Durnil (1999) for an analysis of the question in the context of environmental regulation, and Chapter 9 for a further discussion.

90 Fisher (2000) at 114 quotes the then-current UK pollution control standard as requiring the 'best available technique not exceeding excessive cost', which at least allows for a debate about what might be 'excessive'. Similarly, the Health and Safety Executive's statement that risk should be 'as low as reasonably practical', focuses attention on what is 'reasonably practical'.

5.86 This cuts both ways: a standard can be viewed as too lax or too constraining. A good example of the former was the implementation of stress testing in the United States after 2008: this provided a significantly higher capital requirement that internationally agreed risk-weighted capital requirements, effectively replacing it for most US banks as the binding constraint on capital.[91]

5.87 Derivatives have generated two prominent examples of standards which have been seen as too constraining by leading jurisdictions. These both relate to the impact of overly conservative rules on the cost of risk transfer for end-users. The European Union exempted certain OTC derivatives transactions with non-financial firms from the CVA charges, while the US reduced the capital requirements for counterparty credit risk generated by the SA-CCR by setting the multiplier, α equal to one rather than its Basel-approved value of 1.4. The next two subsections discuss these choices before turning to the international reaction to them.

The EU corporate CVA exemption

5.88 The details of the EU implementation of the early part of Basel 3 is in Capital Requirements Regulation or 'CRR': see R. EC (2013). Article 382 of the CRR contains an exemption from the CVA capital rules for exposures to corporates:

> *The following transactions shall be excluded from the own funds requirements for CVA risk: (a) transactions with non-financial counterparties ...*

5.89 This exemption is preserved in an update to the EU implementation of Basel 3 in CRR2 and is in force at the time of writing.

5.90 CVA capital charges affect the prices that counterparties are charged for OTC derivatives. In particular, transactions that lead to high CVA capital requirements are more expensive than ones with similar risk transfer characteristics that do not lead to such charges.[92] Therefore the CVA capital requirements affect the cost of transferring risk. The end-users who are most affected by this are those who generate significant regulatory CVAs. In broad brush, those are end-users who cannot collateralize their trades, either because they do not have access to sufficient liquidity, or because the operational costs of moving collateral every day are relatively large for them. These tend to be smaller non-financial end-users. The Basel CVA rules therefore implicitly discriminate in favour of hedge funds, who typically have ready access to cash for margin posting as part of their prime brokerage arrangements, and whose trades are typically not the long term,

91 The 2009 Fed stress test required bank holding companies subject to the programme to have capital levels in excess of regulatory requirements at the end of the eight quarter horizon of the test: see R. Fed Board (2009) for more details.

92 For an extensive analysis, see Part D of DAT (2018).

highly directional ones that generate large collateral requirements. They discriminate against smaller corporates trying to manage business risks using OTC derivatives.[93] The larger the CVA capital charge is for a given amount of risk, the more this discrimination bites.

5.91 In order to examine how high the capital charges for exposure to corporates are, consider the kind of OTC derivative a real economy end user might routinely trade to hedge its business risks, a five year interest rate swap. Suppose, as is likely the case for many end-users, that this CVA is not hedged. The charge capitalizes a movement of credit spreads for investment-grade end-users in typical sectors[94] of 3%.[95] How large is this?

5.92 The *Deepwater Horizon* disaster is a stress event which allows us to investigate the conservatism of the calibration of the CVA capital charge. This disaster involved an oil company, BP. Before it, BP was a very high quality credit, and hence exactly the sort of counterparty that a dealer might consider entering into a relatively 'light' CSA with, i.e. one that allowed considerable CVA to build up. BP does have single name CDS available, so CVA on it would be hedgeable, but we use it as an example as this very availability allows the conservatism of the CVA rules to be quantified.

5.93 The circumstances of the disaster were that BP had chartered a mobile drilling rig, the *Deepwater Horizon*, to drill a well in the Macondo prospect in the Gulf of Mexico. It was the principal developer for this prospect and responsible for its exploration. On 20 April 2010, there was blowout of a well in the prospect which led to an explosion aboard the *Deepwater Horizon* and a huge offshore oil spill. This spill is considered by many to be the largest marine oil spill in the history of the petroleum industry. Clean-up, litigation, and other costs eventually amounted to over $60 billion, and BP's market capitalization more than halved after the event.

5.94 The impact of the *Deepwater Horizon* disaster on BP is therefore an excellent test case for the potential credit spread changes to an investment grade corporation during and after a stress event. Figure 5.1 shows the distribution of ten day[96] changes in the benchmark CDS referencing BP. Even given that the company suffered a highly stressful event, the 99th percentile widening in the

[93] For a further discussion of the effects of CVA capital charges on corporate end- users, see the letter from the Chair of the European Association of Corporate Treasurers to the Chairman of the European Banking Authority, Raeburn (2014).

[94] Our argument will apply to what the rules define as sector 3—basic materials, energy, industrials, agriculture, manufacturing, mining and quarrying—and section 4—consumer goods and services, transportation and storage, administrative, and support service activities.

[95] See R. BCBS (2017) at 122.

[96] The standard margin period of risk for bilateral OTC derivatives is ten days.

spread is only about 50bps. The 99.5th percentile change is about three times that, 150bps.[97] It can be seen that the CVA capital charge capitalizes a spread movement which *twice* as big as the 99.5th percentile of changes for BP during this stress event.

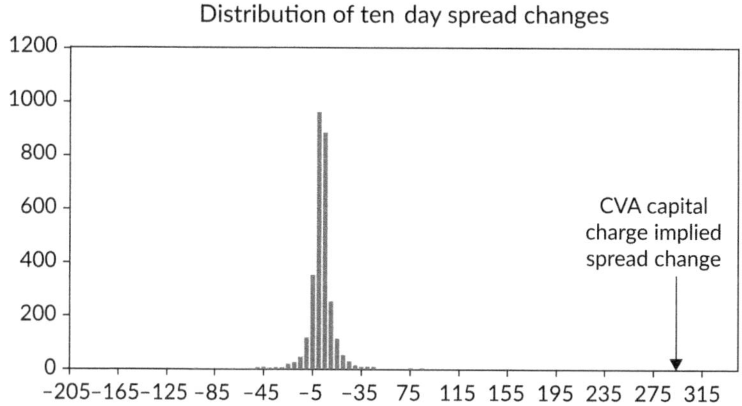

Figure 5.1– The distribution of ten day changes in the five year CDS spread on senior unsecured BP debt for a period including the Macondo oil spill

5.95 There is therefore reason to believe that the CVA capital charge might be excessive.[98] It appears to be set well beyond the safety standard in the market risk rules, in that the UL it requires capital for reflects a substantially higher confidence interval.[99]

5.96 The EU, then, had at least two good reasons for refusing to apply the Basel CVA charge to EU bank exposures to non-financial counterparties: it affected both their banks and their real economy end-users disproportionately, and its calibration seemed penal. EU legislators are to be applauded for this (sadly rare) example of refusing to apply a Basel standard whose costs to the EU would have been larger than its benefits.[100]

---

[97] Respectively 51.5bps and 153bps for the period April 2007 to February 2019.

[98] A detailed investigation of this question would examine the historical distribution of total CVA changes for a wide range of banks over a long period and compare a high percentile of this return distribution with the CVA capital requirement. The publication of the (anonymized) results of this exercise would provide some legitimacy to the likely-necessary recalibration.

[99] The fundamental review of the trading book uses a 97.5% expected shortfall with a stressed calibration. The *Deepwater Horizon* event was certainly stressful for BP's credit spread, but the expected shortfall above 97.5% for its return distribution is only 84bps. This is just 28% of the move imposed by the CVA capital rule.

[100] The EU treatment of corporate CVA is an example of a 'barn door' exemption to a policy that is considered excessively costly: as we discuss further in Chapter 6, a better approach is usually to rewrite the rule to be appropriately targeted and proportionate.

The US SA-CCR deviation

5.97 US authorities took a different approach to mitigating the impact of overly conservative capital rules on the risk transfer for end-users. Instead of providing a CVA capital exemption, they reduced the calibration of the SA-CCR.

5.98 The SA-CCR has an overall multiplier, α, discussed in paragraph 5.42. The Basel standard sets this at 1.4, but the US authorities chose to set it equal to 1 for contracts with commercial end-user counterparties.[101] Their choice is understandable, given the conservative calibration of the SA-CCR and its widespread use not just as a standardized risk-weighted rule but also in the leverage ratio framework and in the rules for cleared derivatives.

5.99 Deviations from internationally agreed capital regulations are relatively rare, so the fact that two leading jurisdictions have, in different ways, sought to offset the impact of bank capital regulation on derivatives is indicative of the strength of the case that the rules are damagingly over-conservative.

The policing of deviations

5.100 The Basel Committee has a Regulatory Consistency Assessment Programme, or 'RCAP' to monitor 'adoption of Basel 3 standards by member jurisdictions (timeliness), assess implementation across member jurisdictions (consistency) and assess implementation across banks (outcomes)'. The section of the Committee's website discussing this programme states:[102]

> *The lessons of the global financial crisis have highlighted the need for full, timely and consistent implementation of the Basel standards to underpin confidence in banks, prudential ratios and a level playing field.*

5.101 This statement is susceptible to challenge on multiple grounds, especially given the prior discussion in this chapter. The adoption of Basel 2 decreased confidence in banks: what reasons are there to believe that Basel 3 will be different? Full and consistent implementation only underpins confidence if the standards are appropriate wherever they are applied. One sense of the level playing field—equality of capital requirements for the same risk between banks in different countries—is being proposed. There are others. For example, there is a decidedly slanted playing field between those end-users of derivatives who can collateralize their exposures at low cost, such as hedge funds, and those that cannot, such as many non-financial end-users.

5.102 We should be suspicious of any totalizing claim for the universal rightness of an arbitrary construction. This is particularly so when the claim is accompanied by a disciplinary mechanism to delegitimate alternative perspectives.

---

101 See R. Joint Agencies (2020) at 4372.

102 See https://www.bis.org/bcbs/implementation/rcap_role.htm.

5.103 The RCAP is just such a mechanism. It makes jurisdictional assessments to 'review the extent to which domestic regulations are consistent with the minimum Basel requirements agreed by the Committee and help identify material gaps in such regulations'. Consistent with the view that these assessments are intended to bolster that Basel Committee's claim to a monopoly on truth rather than to assess the appropriateness of countries' arrangements for their own banking systems, the RCAP for the European Union identified the corporate CVA exemption as an issue of 'material non-compliance' which require legislative changes.[103] It is symptomatic of the extent of the power claimed by unelected regulators, despite the fact that their standards have no legal force, that they feel able to tell an elected Parliament to change a law which it has adopted with all due process.

5.104 The RCAP is a key tool in the hegemonic strategy of bank regulators. It enforces adherence to the Basel minimum, not to an approach tailored to a given country's banking system, given that country's definition of micro-prudential resilience and macro-prudential stability.[104] Moreover, its force is likely to fall disproportionately on smaller countries: the EU shrugged off its non-compliance verdict, but few jurisdictions risk such a rating.[105]

Improving bank capital rules

5.105 There is considerable reluctance among both authorities and the regulated to enter into yet more regulatory change after Basel 3.1.[106] However, if most countries continue to comply with Basel prudential rules, the case for reforming them is strong. Regulators should begin by defining the overall goals of capital regulation, and setting a single safety standard.[107] Clear, actionable principles for adjudicating between competing prudential goals should be set out

---

[103] See R. BCBS (2014f) at 21.

[104] See Acharya (2012) for a discussion of Basel implementation issues in India, or Frait & Tomšík (2014) and Gurrea-Martínez & Remolina (2019) for emerging, developing and small economies. This issue is considered further in Chapter 8.

[105] It is of course characteristic of a successful hegemony that deviation from the desired path is not often contemplated by the controlled. Young (2016) disagrees here, suggesting that the EU has 'selectively reshaped the content of Basel III in a variety of ways' and that this results in 'material non-compliance' of EU financial regulation with Basel 3. In fact, the only area receiving the lowest grade, non compliant, in the RCAP was the EU's implementation of counterparty credit risk, primarily due to its treatment of CVA. The surprise is not the deviation; it is the extent of the compliance.

[106] Discussing the Basel Committee's evaluation of the post-crisis reforms, its chair, Pablo Hernández de Cos, put it starkly: 'we are not reopening previously agreed standards': see de Cos (2019).

[107] One reasonable choice for such a standard would be a level of minimum capital that, even in stress, attracts the confidence of lenders in short-term funding markets, while allowing banks to continue to perform critical economic functions.

5.106 The trading book rules should treat market, counterparty credit, and CVA risk in an integrated and consistent way,[108] without biases against particular risk factors or products. This could be intellectually coherent, simpler than the current approach, and easier to calibrate. The aim in individual rules should be accurate risk capture for realistic portfolios,[109] with precaution only being imposed right at the end, as an overall multiplier.

[108] Counterparty credit and market-consistent CVA risks are just a combination of market risk and the incremental risk of default, so it makes sense to treat these three risks together.

[109] One important issue here is calibration: if the aggregation rules which combine the risks of single positions into those of portfolios are too conservative, capital increases too fast with portfolio size. In order to ensure that this does not happen—and that the rules do not grant too little diversification benefit—capital rules should be calibrated using realistic portfolios.

6

Clearing and Collateralization

Introduction

6.1 In Chapter 2 we saw how some areas of the financial markets—notably OTC credit derivatives linked to asset-backed securities—suffered stress during the 2008 crisis, and how the opacity of OTC markets was identified as one cause of financial instability. Policy makers used this to justify a huge swathe of OTC derivatives reform. In this chapter, two important planks of those reforms, the clearing mandate and uncleared margin requirements, are considered in detail. The execution requirements for derivatives are also briefly discussed.

6.2 This chapter describes these rules and considers potential justifications for them. We begin with the clearing mandate. Here our account considers both its use as political signalling and the claims for systemic risk reduction which might be used to justify it. The mandate has transformed the exposures between derivatives market participants: this transformation is surveyed. Regulatory theory—a body of inter-disciplinary scholarship concerned with the analysis of regulation—is deployed to understand the relationship between the mandate's purported benefits, its actual implementation, and the ensuing costs.

6.3 The rule for bilateral margin has a similar character to the clearing mandate: it is a 'bright line' regulation which requires something to be done with the intent of reducing counterparty credit risk. The chapter continues with a consideration of how these requirements are specified and how they might be rephrased to achieve similar benefits at lower cost. Finally, we consider the lessons that are suggested by a comparison of the pricing of clearing with that of other services mandated for public policy reasons.

What is a clearing mandate?

6.4 Clearing mandates are implemented slightly differently in different jurisdictions, but they are all essentially requirements that certain market participants clear certain OTC derivatives. A mandate includes a list of products which must be cleared, typically including the most liquid forward rate agreements, interest rate swaps, and credit default swaps; a definition of a size measure of OTC derivatives market activity; and a threshold such that, if a market participant's size measure exceeds this threshold, they must clear any trades in mandated products. Clearing mandates also often exempt certain classes of participant.[1]

6.5 In the United States, the Dodd-Frank Act required the Commodity Futures Trading Commission ('CFTC') and the SEC[2] to define clearing mandates,[3] while in Europe, the clearing obligation is set out in EMIR, with its detailed definition delegated to the European Securities and Markets Authority ('ESMA').[4] Many other countries have also implemented clearing mandates.

6.6 A key feature of clearing is that CCPs manage clearing member defaults. They rely on their members for most of their resources—including margin and the default fund—and these resources are sized assuming that CCPs will be able to close out a defaulter's portfolio within a prescribed period of time, the margin period of risk. This means that all the products in a cleared portfolio need to be sufficiently liquid that the CCP can reliably determine a price for portfolios containing them to use for variation margin calls each day, and in the estimation of initial margin requirements. They must also be liquid in stress, so that bids will be available if the CCP needs to close out a defaulter's portfolio. This, in turn, means that clearable products must be sufficiently standardized that a range of market participants can quickly understand and value them should they be invited to bid in a default auction.[5]

6.7 CCPs are acutely aware of the risks of clearing products which do not meet these criteria and are therefore reluctant to do so. Even if they proposed it, their regulator would likely have concerns. Thus, there is a hierarchy of OTC derivatives with the most standardized and liquid being mandated for clearing, a further set of slightly less liquid products being clearable at one or more CCPs but not mandated, then a long 'tail' of products which are not clearable.

---

1 For details of the clearing mandate in the EU see ESMA, *Clearing obligation and Risk mitigation techniques under EMIR*, available at https://www.esma.europa.eu/regulation/post-trading/otc-derivatives-and-clearing-obligation.

2 Broadly, in the United States, the CFTC has regulatory authority over commodity futures, options, and swaps, the SEC over security-based futures, options, and swaps, and the Commissions jointly regulate products which cover both bases. Thus, again in very broad brush, interest rate swaps and index products are under the CFTC's jurisdiction, while single stock-based derivatives and single name CDS are under the SEC. This split is part of the regulatory fragmentation in the US discussed in Chapter 2.

3 See Section 723 of R. US Congress (2010).

4 See article 4 of EMIR, R. EC (2012a).

5 For more on clearability see, for instance, EMIR, article 5, section 4.

Challenges in defining the clearing mandate

6.8 The intent of the threshold in the clearing mandate is that parties whose transactions create significant systemic risk should be required to clear standardized OTC derivatives, but that safer or smaller parties should not. As one rule puts it, the mandate 'should be set taking into account the systemic relevance of the related risks'.[6]

6.9 In part, the decision to use a threshold, and hence to mandate both clearing members and clients if they are big enough, was due to the motivating example of the distress of AIG discussed in Chapter 2. AIG was a client rather than a dealer, but it was a large enough OTC derivatives market participant that the potential for its disorderly failure troubled the authorities, and was likely a major reason for its bailout. AIG was an unusual client in that regard, though: most clients have relatively small OTC derivatives portfolios compared to dealers. The threshold should be set so that AIG-sized clients are mandated, but parties whose exposures are sufficiently small that their failure would cause a meaningful loss of confidence are not required to clear.

6.10 At this point, the policy choices made become less easy to motivate. The size measure used in current clearing mandates is the participant's gross notional of OTC derivatives in each asset class, excluding those that are exempt. A participant has to clear an asset class if their gross notional in it is over the threshold. The first problem is that gross notional is only very loosely related to risk, so it is a poor measure of an entity's contribution to interconnectedness or its threat to financial stability.

6.11 The thresholds are also rather low. For instance, they are currently €1 billion in both equity and credit derivatives and €3 billion in interest rate and FX derivatives in the EU. This means that some relatively small OTC derivatives market participants who are not plausible threats to financial stability are required to clear.[7]

6.12 The second problem is that hedging transactions are exempt from the size measure, and the definition of hedging for non-financial counterparties is broad.[8]

---

6 The quote is from R. EC (2012b) at 13.

7 In the EU, the thresholds are set by ESMA under article 11 of R. EC (2012b): see https://www.esma.europa.eu/policy-activities/post-trading/clearing-thresholds for details.

8 E.g. EMIR article 10(3) defines the OTC derivatives that count towards the threshold as those 'entered into by the non-financial counterparty or by other non-financial entities within the group to which the non-financial counterparty belongs, *which are not objectively measurable as reducing risks directly relating to the commercial activity or treasury financing activity of the non-financial counterparty or of that group*' (emphasis mine). For the (similar) position in the US, see §2(h)(7)(A)(2) of the Commodity Exchange Act and the discussion in the Federal Register Vol. 77, No. 139, 2012 at 42560.

This means that many non-financial entities with very large amounts of activity are not mandated to clear because all or nearly all of their activity is exempt.

6.13 The third problem is that the scope of the clearing mandate only covers a subset of clearable OTC derivatives. This is necessary to ensure that CCPs are not put at risk by clearing products which are difficult or impossible to manage in a default. However, as noted in Chapter 2, none of the OTC derivatives which caused problems in the crisis are clearable, let alone mandated. Even if the clearing mandate had been introduced well before 2008, the vast majority of AIG's portfolio would have remained bilateral.

6.14 Finally, the range of entity types that are captured by the clearing mandate is large. There are some types of OTC derivatives market participant who are unleveraged and of high credit quality. As such, their failure is unlikely, and hence the financial stability benefits of forcing them to clear are often small. Indeed, the 'benefits' may be negative: if the probability of their failure is nugatory, in a bilateral world they only lose their trades if the counterparties fail; while in a cleared world, trade continuity is not guaranteed if their clearing member withdraws from providing clearing services, as well as if it fails.[9]

6.15 Some pension funds are examples of unleveraged high credit quality derivatives clients. They form a particular problem for clearing policy partly because they do not naturally have significant cash balances. CCPs (and their regulators)[10] require variation margin in the form of cash on all cleared accounts, and pension funds' lack of liquidity makes it difficult for them to meet this requirement when variation margin calls are big. The revisions to EMIR have therefore repeatedly exempted pension funds from mandatory clearing. The latest exemption is for a further two years.[11] However, it is not clear that this carve out, together with that of small end-users and some governmental and international entities, covers all the parties whose participation in clearing is of debatable benefit to financial stability: no comprehensive analysis has been undertaken.[12]

---

9 Typical ISDA master agreements governing bilateral transactions do not allow for early termination by the dealer, or only do so at once point in time, such as ten years into a 30 year trade. In contrast, client clearing service agreements often allow the provider to give a short notice period, such as 90 days, and then withdraw the provision of clearing. Given the relative unattractiveness of many clients to their clearers, it is unclear if this period is sufficient for them to find a new clearing member. This point is discussed further in DAT (2018).

10 See, for instance, section 3.4.16 of R. CPMI & IOSCO (2012).

11 See paragraph 30 of R. EC (2019). This is in addition to a three year exemption set out in articles 85 and 89 of EMIR.

12 Exempted parties in the EU include multilateral development banks, public sector entities where they are owned by central governments and have explicit guarantee arrangements provided by central governments, the European Financial Stability Facility and the European Stability Mechanism.

6.16 The next section discusses the motivations for imposing a clearing mandate in more detail. Insights from other areas of regulation are then used to reveal the nature and vulnerabilities of rules like mandates. These are combined with data about the distribution of exposures in the OTC derivatives system to suggest how the mandate might be revised. Finally, compulsory margining, an alternative approach to reducing counterparty credit risks in OTC derivatives, is considered.

Transforming the System

6.17 The clearing mandate is a rule which transforms the network of OTC derivatives exposures. Before it, there was a complex web, with market participants mostly connected to each other: after it, connections intermediated by CCPs became more important. In this section, some stylized facts about the OTC derivatives network of counterparty exposures will be presented. These are important for understanding the effect of policies like the clearing mandate, as they reflect important properties of the object being regulated.[13]

- *Dense core.* Most OTC derivatives have one of a small number of dealers as a counterparty.[14] These dealers are highly connected with each other. They are also the largest clearing members of most CCPs, and often act in other roles at those CCPs too.[15]
- *Sparse periphery.* Clients typically transact with a single dealer or a handful of them: there are relatively few client-to-client links.[16]
- *Risk transfer from periphery to periphery across the core.* The derivatives markets facilitate risk transfer. It moves risks from parties who are less able to bear them to those who are more able, either because they are better resourced, or because the incoming risks offset their existing ones. Some dealer-to-dealer connections in the core are needed to facilitate this.[17]

---

13 For more information on the structure of the network, see Ascolese et al. (2017), Bardoscia et al. (2018), or Rosati & Vacirca (2019).

14 The exact number of firms who are generally considered to be dealers varies a little, but it is between ten and twenty. One moniker that is sometimes used is the 'G16': these are Bank of America, Barclays, BNP Paribas, Citigroup, Crédit Agricole, Credit Suisse, Deutsche Bank, Goldman Sachs, HSBC, JPMorgan Chase, Morgan Stanley, Nomura, Royal Bank of Scotland, Société Générale, UBS, and Wells Fargo.

15 For instance, as settlement and payment banks.

16 One could also make a case for a three-way classification: big dealers, smaller intermediaries, including many banks, and end-users.

17 Dealers warehouse risk, performing temporal intermediation. They standardize it, hedging non-standard risks with more liquid and (usually) correlated ones. Finally, they disperse risk, increasing the range of clients who can access it.

- *Power law of exposures.* It is common in financial markets to find that a small number of market participants reflect most of the activity or risk. If one were to plot a graph of exposure with the x-axis ordered from largest entity to the smallest, the curve would go steeply down, then level off close to the axis, reflecting a long tail of small exposures. Figure 6.1, which shows the distribution of initial margin by account at a leading CCP, illustrates this phenomenon.

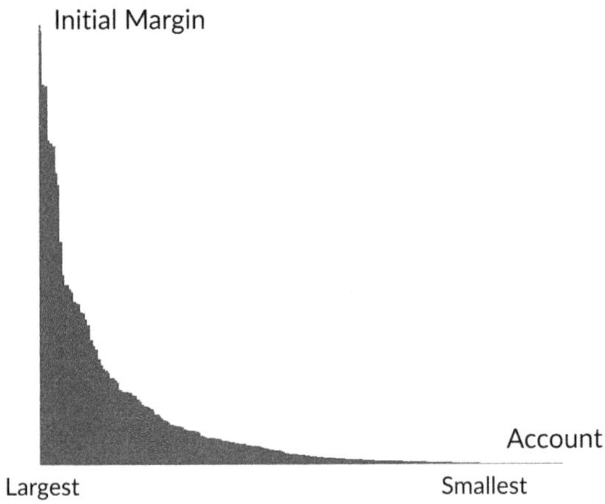

Figure 6.1– The distribution of initial margin by account at a leading CCP, ordered from largest to smallest

6.18 The clearing mandate and incentives to clear have had an impact on market participants' favoured trade form. Liquidity has moved from bilateral to cleared OTC derivatives for both interest rate swaps and index CDS. In other clearable products, such as inflation swaps, liquidity at the CCP is as good or better than that for bilateral transactions, even if clearing is not dominant. This 'turn to clearing' has drawn in market participants who are indifferent to the advantages of CCPs but who wish to transact in the most liquid form of the product available.

6.19 A combination of incentives, mandates, and these effects have transformed the OTC derivatives system from what was, pre-crisis, a mostly bilateral market into one where clearing has become important and, in some areas, dominant.[18]

Mandates, Huh, What Are They Good For?

6.20 Pascal once remarked that if Cleopatra's nose had been shorter, the face of the world would have been changed.[19] He probably meant that without such

[18] For a further discussion of the migration of liquidity to clearing, see DAT (2018).

[19] This is *Pensée* 162.

a feature—thought in Pascal's time to symbolize strength of character—her relationships with Julius Caesar and Marc Antony would not have been so destructive, and the fall of the Roman Empire would have been delayed as a result. Of course we cannot know, but the enduring appeal of speculations like Pascal's encourages us to explore the historical contingencies that lead to contemporary features.

A distance of 3,715 miles

6.21 Mandatory clearing represents a conundrum in financial regulation. In April 2009, soon after the failure of Lehman Brothers, the G20 met in London. At this summit, they declared:[20]

> *We will promote the standardization and resilience of credit derivatives markets, in particular through the establishment of central clearing counterparties*

6.22 In other words, they decided that *credit* derivatives should be cleared. Given the events of the crisis, this was at least somewhat reasonable. However, when the G20 met in Pittsburgh in September of the same year, their statement on clearing was rather different:[21]

> *All standardized OTC derivative contracts should be ... cleared through central counterparties by end-2012 at the latest.*

6.23 There is a big step from credit derivatives to all derivatives: credit derivatives were both much more implicated in the crisis and less than 10% of total derivatives outstanding at end 2008.[22] So why in the five months and 3,715 miles between the London and Pittsburgh summits did the clearing mandate get more than ten times bigger, and what were the effects of this policy change?

Confirmation bias

6.24 One of the things that happened between the London and Pittsburgh summits was the confirmation of Gary Gensler as Chairman of the CFTC. His confirmation hearings were not easy.[23] The Clinton administration, of which he

---

[20] G-20, *Declaration on Strengthening the Financial System*, London Summit, 2009, available at http://www.g20.utoronto.ca/2009/2009ifi.html.

[21] The quote is from the G20 Leaders' Statement, Pittsburgh, 25–26 September 2009, available at http://www.g20.utoronto.ca/2009/2009communique0925.html.

[22] Data from the BIS statistics warehouse, available at https://www.bis.org/statistics/index.htm. The total of all OTC derivatives notionals outstanding was €598 billion, of which €51.9 billion were credit derivatives.

[23] The transcript of his nomination hearing before the Senate Agriculture Committee (which oversees the CFTC) is available at https://www.congress.gov/111/chrg/shrg54564/CHRG-111shrg54564.htm.

had been a part, had dismissed attempts to regulate OTC derivatives. In the words of one of the senators in Gensler's hearing, Clinton's officials had been 'really quite dismissive' of claims that the risks of OTCs derivatives 'needed to be evaluated and appropriately regulated'.[24] Gensler was questioned about his personal role in the issue and expressed regret, saying that: 'looking back now it is clear to me that all of us that were involved at the time—and certainly myself—should have done more to protect the American public through aggressive regulation, comprehensive regulation'. Some senators, even from his own party, were inclined not to support his nomination, given his history: regret was not enough.[25]

6.25 In order to propitiate the objectors, the Obama administration needed to do something. On 13 May 2009 it did, with an announcement from the Treasury of a comprehensive regulatory framework for all OTC derivatives.[26] This is the first Treasury statement in which mandatory clearing of all OTC derivatives appears: it also announced the intention to give the CFTC and SEC 'clear and unimpeded authority' over OTC derivatives and the ability to impose 'a robust regime of prudential supervision and regulation' on OTC derivatives dealers. This was enough to appease the doubters, and Gensler was duly confirmed. Mandatory clearing, in other words, might not have been imposed because of a careful analysis demonstrating that it was a proportional response to the risks of OTC derivatives, but rather to signal that the Obama administration was serious about regulation and thereby to get their candidate CFTC chairman confirmed.

A rational reconstruction of the reasons for mandating OTC derivatives clearing

6.26 If clearing was actually mandated partly for political reasons, might it nevertheless have been the right policy from a prudential perspective? In this section, the benefits of clearing, and hence the conventional justifications for the clearing mandate, are considered.

---

[24] In 1998 Brooksley Born, a prior CFTC chairman, had advocated that her Commission should review its regulatory approach to OTC derivatives with a view to taking more action: see R. CFTC (1998) for details of Born's proposal, and McCaffrey (2006) for a longer discussion. Various Clinton staffers, and prominently Arthur Levitt of the SEC, Robert Rubin of the Department of the Treasury, and Alan Greenspan of the Federal Reserve all disagreed, and Born did not get her way. Gensler was a senior Treasury staff member at that time. By 2008, the suggestion that his background meant that he was a 'Rubin Democrat'—in other words, a believer in the 'light touch', market friendly regulation promulgated by Rubin—was a political problem.

[25] On 23 March 2009, Senator Bernard Sanders placed a procedural hold on the confirmation of Mr. Gensler: he was joined in this by Senator Maria Cantwell.

[26] See US Treasury, *Regulatory reform of over-the-counter (OTC) derivatives*, Press Release, 13 May 2009, available at https://www.treasury.gov/press-center/press-releases/Pages/tg129.aspx.

6.27 CCPs facilitate multilateral netting of exposures, as discussed in Chapter 1. They require both initial and variation margin for all cleared accounts. Together these two features mean that counterparty credit risk is substantially mitigated for cleared OTC derivatives. CCPs also enhance trade standardization and portfolio optimization (for instance via compression). This reduces the complexity of exposures. The management of defaults using a well-understood and documented process is another aspect which is central to the rationale for central clearing. By setting out the procedure for default management in their rule books, CCPs give certainty to the market about how defaulters' positions will be closed out and how the CCP intends to allocate any losses resulting from this process.[27]

6.28 Cleared trades are standardized and liquid. This means that their prices are readily determinable, even in stress, and that they can be closed out promptly. This, in turn, means that CCPs can demand lower levels of margin than would be required for the same risk in less liquid form.

6.29 A final feature of central clearing which deserves explicit mention is its role in enhancing the likelihood of trade continuity for market participants. If the clearing member of a CCP fails, then not only does the CCP attempt to manage the default while continuing to perform to the original counterparty of the trade,[28] it also seeks to preserve trade continuity for the defaulter's clients, through the process of 'porting' them to other clearing members. If porting works, participants in a cleared market are less likely to lose trade continuity than bilateral market participants.

6.30 Clearing has benefits, then. But why *require* it, rather than allowing these incentives to play out, and, if necessary, creating additional incentives to clear? To discuss this, insights from other areas of regulation will be helpful.

Regulatory Theory

6.31 The examination of how regulation arises and evolves; how it is and could be organized; and the benefits, costs and risks of framing it in various ways is a topic which touches on various disciplines. As a result, *regulatory theory* is an area of scholarship which gathers insights from economics, legal scholarship, political economy, and elsewhere.[29] It considers examples from a diverse range of situations including the regulation of airlines, telephony, and general trade, as well

[27] This allocation will be successful if the CCP does not suffer a legal challenge which affects it: as Braithwaite & Murphy (2017a) discuss, the ground is mostly, but not entirely, solid here.

[28] It is only in significant stress, if the CCP has to deploy 'end of the waterfall' tools such as tear up or forced allocation of the defaulter's positions, that trade continuity for clearing members is not assured. The issues here are discussed in Swerts & Van Cauwenberg (2016).

[29] Introductions can be found in, for instance, Drahos (2017) and Rose (2014).

as finance.[30] The regulation of environmental pollution in particular has proved a rich area of study, motivating consideration of both current policies and potential alternatives to them.[31]

Types of regulation

6.32 Regulatory theory identifies a typology of regulation. At the broadest level, regulations which define permissible or illegal activities, so called 'command and control' regulations, are distinguished from those which establish an incentive structure to encourage the desired outcome.[32] 'Bright line' command and control regulation is easier to monitor than incentive-based regulation, but a workable definition of permissible activities is obviously key. Command and control regulation also tends to be susceptible to watering down after some stakeholders argue that the proposed regulation accidentally captures or has a disproportionate impact on them, and thus they should be exempted.

6.33 A good example can be found in the Montreal Protocol. This is an international treaty on substances that deplete the ozone layer. During the negotiation of this treaty, farmers largely in the United States successfully argued that methyl bromide, a chemical which was used as a soil fumigant in strawberry and tomato production, should not be banned, as there were no similarly priced substitutes. This was despite methyl bromide being responsible for an estimated 4% of total ozone depletion.[33] The protocol entered into force in 1989, but, due to the success of the farmers' lobbying, methyl bromide remained available in the U.S. until 2016.

6.34 This episode demonstrates the vulnerability of command and control regulation to demands for exemptions from well-organized interest groups who can portray themselves as unfairly affected. If granted, these exemptions can substantially reduce the effectiveness of regulation.[34]

---

[30] For airlines, see, for instance, Levine (2006); for telephony and other examples from utility regulation, see Crew & Kleindorfer (2002); for trade and the problems of multilateral cooperation, see Trebilcock et al. (2013) and Hale et al. (2013).

[31] The literature ranges from discussions of theory, such as Keohane et al. (1998), through to quantifications of the costs and benefits of particular policies, as in Muller & Mendelsohn (2009).

[32] Command and control and incentive-based regulation are discussed extensively in the theory of environmental protection: see for instance Helfand & Berck (2013). They are moreover not the only types; there are models that define a self-regulatory framework (as discussed in Sinclair (2002)), or rely primarily on market discipline (as in Fung et al. (2004)).

[33] The farmers claimed that there was no economically feasible alternative; they also cast doubt on the underlying science of ozone depletion and predicted mass unemployment if the ban on methyl bromide was enacted.

[34] For a fuller discussion of the methyl bromide exemption, see Gareau (2010). Part of the problem is that exemptions tend to be large, or become so over time. Colloquially, they are 'barn doors'.

6.35 The flexibility of incentive-based regulation, in contrast, if properly framed, can mean that the largest impact is on the most marginal activity, and exemptions are less necessary. Once identified in the early 1970s, the comparative efficiency and theoretical cost-effectiveness of incentive-based regulation led to its increasing popularity.[35] The adoption of emissions trading was largely motivated by these insights, and it provides a substantial body of evidence about the performance of incentives-based regulation. In this case, the incentives created led to 'significant cost savings' but it did not 'even approximately achieve a cost-effective allocation of the control responsibility'.[36]

6.36 The emissions trading experience suggests that it is difficult to design good regulatory incentives, and that even effective incentives do not assure distributional equity.[37] Incentives need both to be fully transmitted to the party who decides how much to pollute, and not so sharp as to completely level the playing field between more and less polluting alternatives.[38] Moreover, both incentives-based and command and control regulation have the potential for unintended consequences, especially once affected parties modify their behaviour in response to regulation.[39]

Transplanting regulation

6.37 There is a rich literature on the use of one regulatory or legal construct in a different area.[40] A 'legal transplant' is a transposition of a rule or a sub-system of law from one from one country to another, or one domain to another. This approach has been used in many situations, but it can be problematic. One problem is cultural: the meaning of a transposed rule depends on the strategies of its implementers and their challengers. It does not 'take place in a legal cultural vacuum'.[41] Therefore if, as is often the case, there are substantial relevant cultural

[35] For reasons of space, the related 'comply or explain' approach to standard setting is not discussed here, as it has not been widely used in financial regulation.

[36] The quote is from Atkinson & Tietenberg (1991) at 18, where this case is discussed in detail.

[37] See Hahn et al. (2003) for an account of the shifts in environmental regulation during the Clinton era reflecting the evolving if contested understanding of the benefits, costs and risks of various styles of regulation.

[38] In the United States, the Clean Air Act's requirement for coal burning power stations to use the 'best available technology' made burning less polluting but more expensive coal from the Western states unattractive compared with the more polluting but cheaper alternative from Appalachia, as the same anti-pollution technology had to be used for both: see Ackerman & Hassler (1981).

[39] The phenomenon where the beliefs of market participants, as well as external information, affect firm behaviours and market dynamics, has been known at least since the work of Keynes (1936) on the Great Depression. It is sometimes termed 'reflexivity'.

[40] The classic account is Watson (1993): see Alshorbagy (2012) for an example in financial law.

[41] The quote is from Husa (2018) at 130.

or contextual differences between the original domain and the transplanted one,[42] the transposed rule can act very differently in the new soil it is planted in.[43]

Saying why

6.38 The need for a clear justification for the precise measures taken, given the desired policy goal, is an important insight from regulatory theory. To pick one example from many, deposit insurance can help to insulate depositors from the burden of doing due diligence on banks and the social costs of bank failure, but ill-designed deposit protection schemes can facilitate unsustainable growth by badly capitalized banks and still leave the financial system exposed to bank failure.[44] Regulatory outcomes, then, depend not just on the broad direction of policy, but on the existence of an effective mechanism which is utilized to achieve the public policy goal. A justification of a rule, then, should include an account of why its detailed design is optimal, given the mechanisms in action.

6.39 Policy making is more likely to lead to the desired outcome if that outcome is clearly specified. In emissions regulation, for instance, the total level of greenhouse gas emissions is a natural measure of outcome. The availability of an easily agreed measure of regulatory success is, however, the exception rather than the rule. More often, the definition of a measure often involves a normative choice. Thus, as discussed in Chapter 9, the definition of whose benefits and costs are accounted for, and how, is arbitrary, yet often determinative of policy choices.

Distributional issues

6.40 The last insight from regulatory theory that is relevant here is the importance of understanding the distributional aspects of regulation. By necessity, any effective regulatory regime 'affects the distribution of power and wealth'. Powerful interest groups frequently influence regulators, and benefit from the rents or influence that regulation affords them. Since regulators' power 'associated with framing issues and debates' is increasing, as we saw in Chapter 4, it is becoming correspondingly more difficult to check regulatory over-reach and question the arbitrary framing implicit in policy making.[45]

6.41 Regulators' propensity for hegemonic strategies, as Chapter 2 called them, make it likely that regulatory choices will be characterised as necessary whatever their redistributional effects. Thus, whether these choices are influenced by

[42] This is the situation in the example discussed in Alshorbagy (2012).

[43] For a further discussion of the part legal discourse plays in the interpretation of transplants see Graziadei (2009).

[44] See Calomiris (1989).

[45] The quotes are from Cafaggi & Pistor (2013) at 3.

lobbying or not, the need for fair, efficient and effective policy making requires that they are continually interrogated.[46]

6.42 Redistribution is not necessarily problematic, of course. In insurance regulation, for instance, the use of race, gender, and other buyer characteristics in pricing coverage is often restricted or prohibited to meet public policy objectives of equality.[47] Here the intent is explicitly redistributional, but even where these effects are a by-product of regulation, they can still be positive.

6.43 Environment regulation offers further examples. If correctly framed, this can correct the externality of the lack of pricing of pollution, and its benefits often accrue disproportionally to households in polluted areas.[48] The issuance of carbon permits, in contrast, is an example of an odious redistributional outcome. It has resulted in scarcity rents accruing to the (likely wealthy) owners of the firms they were issued to and higher costs for (likely poorer) consumers.[49]

Applying Insights from Regulatory Theory

6.44 Regulatory theory gives insight into various aspects of financial regulation. As an example of this, the insights of the last section are applied to the clearing mandate.[50]

Types of regulation

6.45 The clearing mandate is a 'bright line' command and control regulation. It brooks no flexibility: if a party is not exempt, and their OTC derivatives activity puts them over the threshold, they must clear all the products mandated. Regulatory theory would suggest that this kind of rule is susceptible to lobbying for broad exemptions which partially subvert the original purpose of the rule, and so it has proved. The pension fund exemption in the EU and the exclusion of hedging trades in both the EU and the US are good examples.

---

[46] As discussed in footnote 73 of Chapter 4, Habermas' definition of a valid norm as one 'that could meet with the approval of those potentially affected, insofar as the latter participate in rational discourses' is seldom satisfied by financial regulation.

[47] The issues here are complex. One problem is that this form of insurance regulation typically generates 'within market' transfers from the less risky to the more risky. As such, some of their effect can be undone by adverse selection whereby the less risky purchase less coverage: Clemens (2015) discusses an example of this situation.

[48] These households tend to be poorer, because the wealthy can often buy their way out of polluted neighbourhoods. See Bento et al. (2013) for an analysis of the redistributional effects of the Clean Air Act.

[49] This is one of six examples quoted by Fullerton (2011) of the potential distributional effects of a carbon permit system.

[50] For an alternative, more in-depth analysis, see Beylin (2015).

6.46 Not content with just having a command and control regulation, regulators also imposed incentives: a cleared OTC derivatives portfolio typically has lower margin requirements than the same portfolio uncleared, and capital requirements are lower too, as discussed further below.[51] It is interesting to contemplate whether incentives alone would be sufficient to achieve the desired effect: is a system with mandatory clearing of some trades—even when leaving them bilateral might reduce risk—and with substantial exemptions, safer than one with strong incentives to clear but no compulsion to do so?[52]

6.47 Regulatory theory suggests that a key part of the answer lies in the transmission of incentives. The process for allocating regulatory constraints described in Chapter 4 is important here. It passes capital and funding costs down to trading desks, and thus allows firm-wide incentives to affect the decisions about individual transactions. Regulators need to understand how it works, given that its effects are vital for achieving policy objectives. Such an understanding might clarify that having *both* a clearing mandate *and* incentives to clear is unnecessary.

Transplanting clearing

6.48 Clearing has been a key feature of exchange-traded derivatives markets for many years: if you trade a future or an option on an exchange, it is cleared by an associated CCP.[53] The clearing mandate represents the transplantation of a policy that works well for one market to another.[54]

6.49 Exchange-traded and OTC derivatives markets differ in important ways. Futures are typically shorter term, and individual trades are smaller; futures market participants are often of lower credit quality; and futures market intermediation is often less concentrated. There must therefore at least be a question as to whether the fact that exchange-traded derivatives markets developed clearing voluntarily, while OTC derivatives ones did not, is indicative of issues that the transplantation and imposition of clearing will have to address.

---

51 See also Section D of the DAT report, DAT (2018), for an analysis of these effects.

52 There is an alternative whereby systemic market participants could be mandated to have, say, at least a third of their margin requirements coming from CCPs. This would encourage them to reduce the risk in their bilateral netting sets, and to trade standardized products which could be cleared. It would also create a disincentive to use CCPs with relatively more aggressive margin requirements, and reduces the attraction of the potential arbitrage whereby transactions can be restructured so as not to be clearable. Of course, the fraction required would need to be carefully calibrated—'a third' is just a guess—and the parties to whom such a requirement was applied should only be those with genuinely systemic exposures.

53 For an account of the history of clearing houses growing up alongside futures exchanges, see Moser (1994).

54 Well but not perfectly: the only examples of CCP failure all involve futures clearing. See, for instance, Cox et al. (2016).

Why mandate clearing?

6.50 There are a number of properties of central clearing that recommend it for OTC derivatives, as discussed earlier in the Chapter. But there is no authoritative account of which of these features necessitates mandatory clearing—or of which problem exactly mandatory clearing is a proportional response to.

6.51 The difficulty of understanding the need for the mandate is compounded by the lack of an account of the mechanism by which it creates financial stability. Such a mechanism would need to explain not just why clearing improves financial stability, but also why *mandatory* clearing is necessary rather than, say, incentives to clear or a requirement for systemically risky parties to clear a certain percentage of their counterparty credit risk.

6.52 The need for a justification for the mandate is highlighted if the advantages attributed to clearing are considered together with the policies or means that realize them. These are summarized in Figure 6.2. Most of the benefits do not require clearing: it is only multilateral netting and trade continuity for clearing members which are most easily achieved through the use of a CCP.[55] This raises the question of whether mandatory clearing is a proportional policy response.

Benefit	Means of achieving it
Transparent and consistent pricing of OTC derivatives	Pricing services, capital disincentives for valuation uncertainty
Exposure reduction	Compulsory margining
Widespread knowledge that exposures are low creating confidence	Statement of who is captured by margin requirements
Risk reduction via multilateral netting	Central clearing
Standardized default management	Policies for default management
Trade standardization	Capital penalties for exotic trades
Trade continuity for clearing members	Central clearing
Trade continuity for clients	Porting or novation after default

Figure 6.2– The benefits of clearing and the policies which lead to them

Distributional issues

6.53 Mandatory clearing and the compulsory posting of margin have redistributional effects, like most regulations: these are considered next. The requirement to clear obviously has benefits for clearers: they are monopoly providers of a legally required service. These benefits have not accrued equally: because

[55] The need of the latter is, moreover, less pressing given that most clearing members are now covered by a resolution regime.

the key advantage of central clearing is the ability to net a new exposure with your prior cleared portfolio, there is a winner-takes-all effect. The result of this is that a single CCP has a dominant position in OTC interest rate derivatives clearing. Similarly, a single CCP group dominates in credit derivatives clearing. OTC equity derivatives are less standardized than interest rate or credit derivatives, so there is significantly less clearing here. This means that two CCPs globally have benefited greatly from mandatory clearing.

6.54 Client clearing involves splitting what would have been a bilateral contract between client and dealer into a cleared trade from client to clearing member, one from the clearing member to the CCP, and then one on to the executing broker, as discussed in Chapter 1. Figure 1.14 illustrated this. This structure opens up the opportunity of executing OTC derivatives without having to face clients. Acting as an executing broker is an attractive niche for some intermediaries: because the EB only faces the CCP, it does not need to do client due diligence, deal with client needs for margin finance, or monitor and manage client credit quality. When combined with trade execution on electronic platforms, a pure EB can be highly automated.[56] This has allowed new entrants to win significant market share in OTC derivatives execution, something that would have been substantially more difficult without mandatory clearing.

6.55 Another distributional issue arises due to porting. It is very difficult to port to a clearing member that you have no prior relationship with, so clients have to maintain clearing agreements with multiple clearing members if they want porting to be likely. This increases costs and reduces the benefits of multilateral netting for clients.

6.56 Larger clients benefit from the liquidity and standardization of clearing. They can afford to use multiple clearing members, and their portfolios are big enough that the loss of netting benefits from this practice may well be relatively insignificant. Smaller clients are in a worse position. They are unattractive to clearing members, as their activity is not sufficient to generate substantial clearing fees, and they create significant fixed costs. They can, at most, afford a single clearing member, so they are more exposed to the risk of the inability to port. Finally, they have to bear the costs of complying with client clearing obligations, including posting margin, and the fixed portion of these costs is shared over fewer trades. This all means that there is a minimum amount of activity below which OTC derivatives clearing makes little sense.[57]

[56] The extent to which this helps clients is debatable: they get better execution from efficient broking, but they also have to pay their clearing member for all the services that the executing broker is not providing.

[57] For more on client clearing, see Braithwaite (2016) or Murphy (2020b).

Trading Requirements

6.57 When the G20 agreed to mandate clearing, it also decided to impose a 'trading requirement' (sometimes known as an 'execution requirement'). The G20 Pittsburgh communique states that[58] 'all standardized OTC derivative contracts should be traded on exchanges or electronic trading platforms, where appropriate'. This section discusses the implementation of this requirement in the United States and the European Union.

The features of trading venues

6.58 Exchange-traded derivatives and securities have long been traded in organized venues, and, more recently, on electronic platforms which replicate many of their features. The definition of a 'regulated market' from the relevant EU regulation, the second Markets in Financial Instruments Directive, or MIFID 2,[59] captures many of the properties physical and electronic trading venues share:

> *A 'regulated market' is a multilateral system operated and/or managed by a market operator, which brings together or facilitates the bringing together of multiple third-party buying and selling interests in financial instruments in the system, in accordance with its non-discretionary rules, in a way that results in a contract, in respect of the financial instruments admitted to trading under its rules and/or systems, and which is authorized ...*

6.59 Regulated markets, and their analogues in other jurisdictions, share several features which can benefit market participants:

- *Pre-trade transparency* is the availability of bids and offers at which market participants advertise they would consider entering into a transaction.
- *Post-trade transparency* is the availability of the prices of transactions after they have been executed.
- *The prevention of market abuse* are steps taken by the market operator to prevent and facilitate the prosecution of insider dealing, unlawful disclosure of inside information, and market manipulation.

6.60 The standards of transparency in the pre-crisis OTC derivatives market were questionable, so the authorities introduced execution requirements to increase them. However, it was not appropriate to transplant exchange-trading conventions directly to OTC derivatives, due to differences in market liquidity.

---

58 G20 Leaders' Statement, Pittsburgh, 25–26 September 2009, available at http://www.g20.utoronto.ca/2009/2009communique0925.html.

59 See R. EC (2014).

Liquidity and order books

6.61 The volume traded on the New York stock exchange, at the time of writing, exceeds 1 billion shares per day,[60] of average value less than $10. In contrast, the CFTC reports roughly 40,000 interest rate swaps are traded each day by persons reporting to them, with an average notional of $190M.[61] At one extreme, then, there are securities markets where very large volumes of quite low value instruments are traded; at the other, there are OTC derivatives markets with relatively low volumes of quite high value instruments. Exchange-traded derivatives markets often lie between these two extremes, with lower volumes traded than stock exchanges, of higher value.

6.62 Securities markets are often characterized by a central limit order book: in order to trade, a market participant submits an order to a trading platform, and this is displayed to all other market participants in the order book. Transactions occur by matching bids and offers in the order book, and the full depth of liquidity in the market is visible.

6.63 In contrast, in a request-driven market, intermediaries stand ready to answer requests to trade from market participants. They may advertise indicative prices either publicly, or to favoured counterparties, and there may be little or no post-trade transparency.[62] The central limit order book facilitates anonymous trading: this has efficiency benefits when the identity of the counterparty does not affect the price of the transaction, which is only true when there is minimal counterparty credit risk.

6.64 The public policy issues here are nuanced.[63] A complete lack of pre- and post-trade transparency creates market inefficiencies and potentially allows a small group of dealers to extract rents as they—and only they—have accurate information on market prices. It may also facilitate discrimination, with some counterparties getting better prices than others. However, the requirement to trade at a quoted price may discourage intermediaries from quoting at all, especially in less liquid products, and the knowledge that large trades will be immediately disclosed to the market, before they can be hedged, might reduce market depth. Moreover, while request-driven markets do have information advantages for intermediaries, they also allow end-users to avoid the negative impact on

[60] This is across a number of venues: see https://www.nyse.com/markets/us-equity-and-equity-options-volumes for details.

[61] See https://www.cftc.gov/MarketReports/SwapsReports/index.htm.

[62] See Ruffini & Steigerwald (2014) for a further discussion of central limit order book versus request-driven trading.

[63] Reflecting the issues here, the FSB suggested that 'authorities *should explore the benefits and costs* of requiring public price and volume transparency of all trades, including for non-standardized derivative' (emphasis mine) rather than telling them to impose a requirement: see R. FSB (2010).

market prices that would come from advertising their interest in conducting a large transaction—and most OTC derivatives transactions are large.[64]

6.65 Mandatory clearing policy involves drawing a boundary. On one side are products which are safely clearable and where there are systemic benefits to clearing; on the other, are ones which can be permitted to remain bilateral, either because they are not clearable, or because the benefits of mandating clearing for them would be small. Liquidity is often determinative, with the most liquid products being mandated. In a similar vein, the trading requirement requires drawing a distinction between products which are liquid enough that there are benefits to requiring pre-trade transparency, and those which are so customized or illiquid that requiring parties to broadly advertise their interest in trading would likely increase their costs, without bring significant benefits.

OTC derivatives venues

6.66 Reflecting the issues associated with the fact that OTC derivatives trade much less frequently and in larger sizes than the typical instrument transacted on pre-crisis trading platforms, new categories of trading venue were introduced for OTC derivatives after 2008. In the United States, these are known as swap execution facilities or 'SEF's.[65] A market participant can avoid executing trades on a SEF if they are swaps which are not required to be cleared, or if the trades are large.[66] In the EU, under MIFID 2, the new execution venues are known as multilateral and organized trading facilities.[67] As with a regulated market, these venues facilitate pre- and post-trade transparency and the prevention of market abuse. Regulation requires non-discriminatory market access to trading facilities and enhances the transparency of venues through the requirement that their rule books be published.[68]

6.67 Despite these policy changes, OTC derivatives markets are still characterized by contingent liquidity: intermediaries are often willing to trade, but trade volumes are low and sizes are large, at least compared to securities markets. Most OTC derivatives trading continues to be conducted by a party sending a request for a quotation to a small number of dealers, now typically on an electronic derivatives trading platform rather than purely bilaterally.

---

64 If I want to buy some fruit salad, being able to research different choices in the market is helpful; but if I want to buy a painting by Gerhard Richter, and I am a credible buyer, letting the world's art dealers all know might cause the few dealers that have one to mark up their prices. See Riggs et al. (2020) for a discussion of how this phenomenon plays out in index CDS markets.

65 SEFs are a type of regulated market place created under §733 of the Dodd-Frank Act.

66 This would be analogous to wanting to buy 100 kg of fruit salad: the price for 300 g is not relevant to this transaction.

67 See Valiante (2012).

68 See MIFID 2, articles 18, 27, 48, and 53.

Margin Requirements

6.68 We have seen how mandatory clearing went from a policy just for CDS at the London G20 summit in April 2009 to one for all OTC derivatives at the September 2009 Pittsburgh summit. By the time of the Cannes summit in 2011, another commitment had been added to the OTC derivatives reform agenda: margining for bilateral OTC derivatives.[69] The idea was two-fold. First, belatedly, the authorities acknowledged that many OTC derivatives were not suitable for clearing, so clearing mandates were incapable alone of eliminating the risk of loss of confidence caused by uncertainty about OTC derivatives exposures. They therefore claimed that 'Margin requirements for non-centrally cleared [i.e. bilateral] derivatives would be expected to reduce contagion and spill over effects by ensuring that collateral is available to offset losses caused by the default of a derivatives counterparty.'[70]

6.69 Second, again rather late, policy makers reacted to the fact that clearing imposes costs, including margin, and hence that without an incentive, the clearing of non-mandated products might be rather limited. By imposing higher minimum margin requirements for bilateral OTC derivatives than for cleared ones, an incentive to clear was created.

Defining bilateral margin requirements

6.70 Bilateral margin requirements are in many ways a better risk reduction tool than clearing mandates as they can be applied to all OTC derivatives, not just clearable ones.[71] The industry developed a standard initial margin model or 'SIMM',[72] so a common measure of portfolio risk was available for all portfolios. The threshold for requiring margining could therefore be based on how much risk a market participant had rather than the gross notional of their portfolios. Sadly, the authorities did not take advantage of this possibility. Instead, the requirements are set much as for the clearing mandate: there is a threshold defined by gross notional, with certain exemptions. Counterparties above the threshold are required to exchange initial and variation margin on OTC derivatives transactions entered into after a fixed date.[73]

---

69 See G20 Leaders' Statement, Cannes, 4 November 2011, available at http://www.g20.utoronto.ca/2011/2011-cannes-declaration-111104-en.html.

70 The quote is from R. BCBS & IOSCO (2013) at 2.

71 In another 'barn door' exemption reminiscent of the case of methyl bromide discussed above, the bilateral margin requirements regulators imposed do not require initial margin for physically settled FX forwards and swaps: they could do.

72 This has gone through various versions: see, for instance, ISDA (2019).

73 There are additional product exemptions and delays: not only are physically settled FX forwards and swaps exempted from initial margin, but in the EU, variation margin only applies to those

6.71 The date after which margin must be exchanged by affected parties depends on the size of the party's exposures: roughly speaking, dealers (strictly, parties with a group notional amount, excluding exempted trades, over €3 trillion—but these were all dealers) have been captured since 2017, with the threshold dropping and more and more firms coming into scope of the requirement each year. The ultimate level is set rather low, just as it is for the clearing mandate: entities with a group notional amount (excluding exempted trades) over €8 billion will have to exchange margin with their counterparties by September 2022.[74]

6.72 There is no official sector account of why it is necessary to set the threshold at this level and, as a result, capture so many smaller counterparties.[75] Indeed, 95% of market activity would still be captured if it was set over ten times high.[76] This fact makes intuitive sense given the concentration of exposures in a small number of large market participants, as illustrated in Figure 6.1.

Bilateral resources vs cleared resources

6.73 Regulations require that initial margin for cleared OTC derivatives is calculated to a minimum safety standard. It must be at least as big as the VAR at a 99.5% confidence interval and with a five day MPOR under European regulation. The standard is 99% and ten days for bilateral derivatives, so the SIMM calculates margin to this safety standard. Simple theory would suggest that initial margin should be roughly 30% smaller for cleared portfolio than if the same portfolio were traded bilaterally.[77] In reality, the ratio of bilateral to cleared margin for a given portfolio is sensitive to the portfolio concerned, the CCP used to clear it, and market conditions.[78] One study found that, on average, bilateral margin requirements exceed those the same portfolio would generate if centrally cleared,

counterparties that are investment firms or credit institutions. There is delayed implementation for equity options, an initial margin exemption for certain covered bond swaps, and an intragroup exemption. See R. EC (2016) for details.

74 The date for the smallest entities captured was originally 2021, but this was extended by a year in response to the Covid-19 outbreak.

75 In partial mitigation it should be noted that the rules do permit initial margin not to be exchanged if the total requirement is less than €50 million, so some smaller parties whose activity is low risk but over the threshold—or at least lower than €50 million as measured by the SIMM—will not have to post initial margin if their counterparty allows it.

76 Condat et al. (2018) find that a threshold of €100 billion would capture 95.4% of market activity.

77 This assumes that the return distribution scales as the square root of time and has a normal tail, neither of which are likely to be precisely true.

78 As noted in Chapter 1, different CCPs use different initial margin models and treat different additional risks—such as the 'concentration' risk of large portfolios—in different ways. Moreover, the SIMM is a parametric model with a stressed calibration, while many CCPs use some form of filtered historical simulation or 'FHS' model. FHS models tend to produce lower requirements than parametric ones with stressed calibrations in placid times, but higher ones in extreme

but also that there was significant dispersion in the ratio of bilateral margin to cleared margin from portfolio to portfolio.[79] Thus margin requirements do, on average, create an incentive to clear, but this does not hold for every portfolio.

6.74 The previous chapter discussed the risk-based capital framework for derivatives exposures. This contains some incentives to clear, thanks to the low risk weight for exposures to CCPs discussed in paragraph 5.43 and the lower margin period of risk for house exposures. The incentive to clear from the risk-weighted capital rules is more difficult to assess for client exposures.[80]

Collateralization as a process

6.75 Mitigating risk by raising capital is like emigrating: if it is done properly, the effect lasts. Mitigating counterparty credit risk by margining, on the other hand, is like commuting: you have to keep doing it.

6.76 If initial margin requirements are calculated to cover 99% of the portfolio return distribution using a ten day margin period of risk, then the margin taker can only be sure that exposure will exceed collateral less than one day in 100 if both initial and variation margin is correctly calculated and moved every day.[81] Margin also needs to be calculated correctly for each counterparty's portfolio, while capital is fungible across exposures.

6.77 Thus, while there is some substitutability between capital and margin as tools for mitigating counterparty credit risk, it is not obvious that the balance would favour always using margin. Requiring some degree of collateralization does have the appealing quality that the defaulter pays, rather than the survivor. However, capital's fungibility and stickiness give it advantages over margin which suggest that it is sensible to have some amount of capital to support counterparty credit risk too. Capital becomes an even more attractive part of the answer given that the requirement to collateralize exposures creates greater risks for the poster the more is required, as discussed next.

---

stress. All of these factors contribute to the differences between bilateral and cleared margin requirements.

79 See DAT (2018) at 40.

80 A bilateral trade only attracts one measure of counterparty credit risk capital because there is only one trade: client to dealer. In contrast, a client cleared trade has three legs: client to clearing member; clearing member to CCP; and CCP to executing broker. Of these, the client to clearing member leg is treated as if it was bilateral with a five day MPOR. The clearing member to CCP and CCP to executing broker legs are treated using the exposures to CCPs rules.

81 There are also the issues of the gap between when variation margin is calculated and when it arrives; whether the collateral can change in value and what allowance is made for that; whether the margin can indeed be taken and used promptly if the counterparty defaults, among others: see Andersen et al. (2017).

Procyclicality of margin

6.78 In stress, markets tend to move more. This means that variation margin calls are bigger, and risk factor volatility is higher. Higher volatility, all other things being equal, means higher estimates of risk. This means that margin requirements based on current estimates of risk tend to be procyclical: they are usually higher in stress, when the financial system is less able to bear them.[82]

6.79 The SIMM model used for bilateral margin does not suffer from this problem as it uses a stressed calibration, thereby adopting a similar approach to procyclicality mitigation as the models-based approach to counterparty credit risk discussed in the last chapter. CCP initial margin models, in contrast, are usually at least somewhat procyclical, as they estimate risk based on current conditions.

6.80 The type of entity being asked to post additional margin by the CCP affects the liquidity risk borne:

- *Banks* are usually less severely affected by margin calls than other types of market participants. They tend to be liquid, as they usually take deposits. They are also subject to liquidity regulation, so they are required to have substantial liquidity buffers.[83] Moreover, as noted in Chapter 1, their derivatives risks tend to be hedged with other derivatives, so a big variation margin call from one counterparty is often offset by variation margin coming in from another. Finally, banks often have access to liquidity from the central bank if required.
- *Non-banks*, and especially non-financial entities, are often in a less favourable position. They are not naturally liquid, and they are typically not subject to liquidity regulation, so they do not have large cash buffers. They often use derivatives to hedge business risks such as commodity prices or interest rate risks embedded in non-margined products.[84] This means that a margin outflow on a derivative with one counterparty will often not be offset by an inflow from a different counterparty. Moreover, non-banks do not usually have access to central bank liquidity insurance.

[82] Even R. BCBS & IOSCO (2013) acknowledges this, saying that the 'potential benefits of margin requirements must be weighed against the liquidity impact that would result from derivatives counterparties' need to provide liquid high quality collateral to meet those requirements, including potential changes to market functioning as a result of an increased aggregate demand for such collateral'.

[83] Unfortunately, the regulatory required liquidity buffer is both procyclical—thanks in part to the treatment of derivatives margin—and hard to use, as there is stigma associated with dipping into it, even in stress.

[84] One example of the latter situation are pension funds who have to provide inflation-linked pensions: if these are hedged with cleared inflation swaps, the pension liability is not margined but the hedging swap is.

6.81 Chapter 7 discusses the liquidity demands clearing and bilateral margin posting place on derivatives market participants, and how they are met, in more detail. It suffices to note here that margin-procyclicality-driven liquidity risk is one of the consequences of mandatory clearing.

Revising Clearing and Collateral Policy

6.82 Clearing and collateralization policy has an interest in reducing the interconnectedness created by OTC derivatives, and in giving stakeholders confidence that exposures are manageable. The clearing mandate and the margin rules both address these issues. They are also similar types of rule. Both are 'bright line' regulations that require something to happen if a threshold is crossed. Both define the threshold in a similarly unfortunate way. Moreover, in both cases, there is a broad exemption for hedging trades in the calculation of the threshold.[85]

6.83 The similarities extend to some questionable policy choices in these rules:

- The mandatory clearing and bilateral margin rules use a measure to decide who the policy applies to which is at best loosely related to risk: total initial margin would be a better choice than gross notional.
- They capture some smaller market participants who are not systemic.
- They exempt some larger ones who may well be.[86]
- They rely on porting to achieve contract continuity for clients, but this is less likely for cleared OTC derivatives than for exchange-traded positions.[87]
- Neither rule justifies why IM is needed in addition to VM.
- Both policies place heavy reliance on collateralization to reduce risk for both bilateral and cleared transactions. However, collateralization depends on a highly robust repo market,[88] and on substantial legal and operational infrastructure.
- Finally, the benefits of clearing for very large clients are blunted, as these firms often have to use multiple clearing members. Their portfolios are also difficult to port, but risky to close out if one of their clearing members fails.

---

85 See EMIR, article 10.

86 This is due to the hedging exemption in the clearing mandate and the exclusion of physically settled FX derivatives.

87 A client cleared OTC derivatives portfolio has more margin per unit of risk than an exchange-traded one, due to the higher MPOR. This means that its leverage ratio exposure measure contribution is bigger. The higher MPOR also means higher counterparty credit risk capital requirements.

88 For a discussion of issues in the repo market during Covid, see Chapter 3 and He et al. (2020).

6.84 This suggests that the efficiency and proportionality of the clearing mandate and bilateral margin requirements should be reviewed together, with the political considerations of the past no bar to future change. Consideration should be given to optimizing the scope of affected parties, given the large number of non-systemic clients who use OTC derivatives to transfer risk; reducing the liquidity risk of collateralization for non-financial OTC derivatives users; making portability more likely; and performing a holistic analysis of the role of margin versus capital in mitigating counterparty credit risk.

The postal analogy to client clearing

6.85 If mandatory clearing makes sense, it would be because clearing is a public good. That, in turn, implies that clearing should be available to anyone who wants it at an affordable price. In fact, only market participants with substantial amounts of derivatives activity enjoy easy and reasonably priced access to clearing services.[89] We end the chapter with some insights which follow from a comparison of price regulation of clearing services with that of other public goods.

6.86 In the EU, there is a notion of services of general economic interest, or 'SGEI's. These are economic activities that public authorities identify as being of particular importance to citizens and that would not be supplied, or would be supplied under different conditions, if there were no public intervention.[90] Transport networks, postal services, and social services are all examples of SGEIs.

6.87 Member states have some discretion concerning what they deem to be a SGEI, although this is bounded by EU law.[91] A common feature of SGEIs is that providers are often subject to some form of price regulation.

6.88 One early example of SGEI policy was the penny post in the UK. By the 1830s, the postal service was an important mechanism for the distribution of knowledge. Most newspapers, pamphlets, and periodicals were distributed by mail. However, postal rates in this period were typically based on the distance from sender to receiver as well as the contents: a single sheet sent less than 15 miles in England would have cost around four pence in 1829, but the same correspondence sent the 400 miles from London to Edinburgh would have cost fourteen. As many publishers were based in or near London, this pricing structure created a disincentive for knowledge transmission the further one travelled from the capital. The deleterious effects of this, and the importance of cheap and rapid postal communication 'so that the distant parts of the country shall possess

[89] See Part E of DAT (2018).

[90] See European Commission (2013) for more details.

[91] See European Commission (2013) at 23–24.

the same advantage in obtaining knowledge as those more connected with the metropolis',[92] were a concern.

6.89 There was an evident public policy interest in changing the economics of the postal system. Rowland Hill had agitated for change for some time,[93] and his proposals for a uniform postal rate independent of the distance between sender and receiver were influential. After a brief experiment with a four-penny rate, the uniform penny post was established throughout Great Britain and Ireland was introduced in January 1840.[94]

6.90 The penny post was a considerable success. Lower prices stimulated activity, so increased volume more than made up for the loss in revenue from price cuts. The public policy goal of eliminating differentials in the cost of access to knowledge in the UK based on distance from London was largely achieved.[95] Another key achievement of the penny post was the demonstration that uniform price regulation for SGEIs was effective, and similar policies for other services became commonplace after 1840.[96]

6.91 The analogy with client clearing is that it has been argued that there is a public policy benefit in clearing OTC derivatives and the marginal cost of clearing additional trades from clients is often low.[97] However, some clients find it difficult to access clearing, or can only do so at a high price, so there is a case for uniform price regulation of client clearing services.

6.92 This argument is not convincing. Most stakeholders would take the view that requiring the provision of derivatives clearing at a uniform price would represent regulatory overreach. The flaw lies in the premise: the strength of the public policy benefit in client clearing in 2021 is far lower than that in the provision of postal services at a uniform price in 1839. If the benefits were larger, then uniform price regulation would be a proportional way to achieve them. But given that they are evidently too weak to justify such a step, why is mandatory clearing justified at all?

92 The quote is from Bulwer-Lytton (1834).

93 The first edition of his pamphlet, *Post office reform: its importance and practicability* appeared in 1837.

94 The relevant legislation was the Postage Act 1839. Some of the policy details in this Act have been elided: other issues covered by the legislation included moving primarily to a sender pays system and removing free franking rights.

95 For more on Rowland Hill and the penny post, see Coase (1939).

96 The success of the penny post was partly because, while the fixed cost of running a postal network was high, the margin cost of provision of an extra letter was close to zero: see Coase (1939) at 433.

97 In contrast, the fixed cost of on-boarding a client is high.

7

Central Counterparties and Their Regulation

Introduction

7.1 Central counterparties are not new: something recognizable as a CCP has been a feature of futures markets for a least 100 years.[1] Intermediaries in early commodities markets naturally formed associations as their markets grew, and these associations created infrastructure which suited their members' needs. CCPs were originally creations of these clubs, and their development reflects this.

7.2 The post-crisis reforms changed that club-like character. Derivatives CCPs became tools of public policy. Their use was mandated in many cases, as we saw in the previous chapter, and the role that they were assigned by regulators was extended far beyond the bounds of serving their members' needs.[2]

7.3 This change in the character of CCPs had profound consequences. It meant that the part that they play in the financial system became substantially larger, and that market participants could not avoid being exposed to them. This, in turn, meant that derivatives CCPs had to be very robust, and that the risks that they imposed on their users and the wider financial system had to be carefully judged against the benefits of clearing.

7.4 In this section, the development of derivatives clearing is sketched to illustrate the club-like nature of early CCPs. This is contrasted with the hybrid character of many post-crisis derivatives CCPs as private entities used for public policy purposes. The principal rules which define minimum standards for CCP robustness are considered: these will be seen to be more principles-based than many of the regulations discussed in prior chapters.

---

1 See Moser (1994).

2 See, for instance, Hermans et al. (2013) which suggests at 8 that 'it is important that CCPs view themselves and are viewed as systemic risk managers'.

7.5 The discussion then turns to the risks created by derivatives CCPs. The most important of these is liquidity risk, as we saw in the discussion of the Covid-related events in Chapter 3. Regulation around this risk, and others, is sketched.

7.6 Some CCPs are now so systemically important that their disorderly failure could be very damaging. This spurred the authorities to develop policy for the recovery and resolution of failing CCPs. The chapter ends with a discussion of this policy and the implications of the existence of globally systemic CCPs for regulators.

7.7 Our aim is to map how infrastructure which was originally developed for one purpose has been hastily co-opted for another, and how regulation at both the transnational level of international standards, and at the level of national or bloc law, has been deployed in controlling the resulting hybrids. Jurisdictions' prudential rules for CCPs differ more than they do for banks, as the relevant international standards are less detailed: therefore, it will be helpful to consider both US and EU approaches. As before, the aim is not to give a comprehensive account,[3] but rather to illustrate key features of the different regulatory frameworks.

Early commodity market evolution

7.8 The origins of central counterparties lie in nineteenth-century commodities trading. Initially, merchants interested in particular commodities formed informal gatherings. They found that their interests were best served by codifying some of the aspects of how their business was done, and so they formed associations with written constitutions and laws.[4] Members of these associations typically had better access to the market and better information about prices and order flow. Against this, they had to obey the rules of their association, with the threat of expulsion as sanction.[5]

7.9 Commodities trading then, as now, involved contracts which were extended in time: parties would contract to deliver a commodity in the future for a price agreed now. In England, forward contracts in a various commodities were common by the early 1800s. The most important commodity derivatives market of the time was the Liverpool cotton market. By the early 1840s, this market had 100 broking firms, and it grew further as the volatility in the cotton price created by the American Civil War increased the demand for hedging.[6]

7.10 Forward trading involves counterparty credit risk, as discussed in Chapter 1. The early trade associations were concerned with the mitigation of this risk.

---

[3] See Turing (2021) for a thorough account of the UK position.

[4] For a longer discussion of this and all the cases cited in this section, see Cranston (2007), Cranston (2021), and Simpson (1991).

[5] This was soon joined by the lesser penalties of fines, reprimands, and membership suspensions.

[6] See Hall (2000).

Initially the focus was on the credit quality of members. By the 1880s, the rules of the Liverpool Cotton Brokers Association, for instance, provided for automatic expulsion for insolvency, and for the investigation of members suspected of having bad debts.

7.11 The Liverpool Cotton Brokers Association's concern over performance on market contracts deepened as the markets grew. A good example is their 1909 rule book, which states that wilful and intentional non-fulfilment of contract, frivolous repudiation of contract, refusal to refer a question in dispute to arbitration, or refusal to abide by an arbitration award were dishonourable (and hence sanctionable) conduct.[7]

7.12 Brokers in nineteenth-century English commodity markets typically made trades in their own names. Client trades were typically not segregated, and often not disclosed as such. This led to the question of when a contract made by a broker could be set off against another. In particular, could 'house' trades be netted against client ones? The early cases are nuanced, with the outcome depending upon whether the client had enquired about the basis of the transaction.[8] There were other growing pains too, including the questions of whether a client was bound by market (i.e. association) rules in dealing with a broker, even if they were ignorant of them[9] and whether the claim for non-performance on a futures contract could be affected by other, fungible but unrelated contracts.[10]

7.13 The modern model of standardized, fungible futures contracts with separate client and house accounts developed slowly.[11] Cotton trading is again a paradigmatic example. There was a natural forward market, given the volatility of cotton prices and the time needed to ship the product from where it was

[7] See Cranston (2007) at 5.

[8] The case of *Cooke and sons v. Eshelby* (1887) LR12 App Case 271 is important. Here, the House of Lords held that if a party dealing with a broker desired the right of set-off, they should enquire whether the broker was acting for their house account or for a client as undisclosed principal: only in the former case was set-off available. As Derham (1985) discusses, this evidences the anomalous position of undisclosed principals in the law of set-off.

[9] The key case is *Robinson v. Mollett* (1875) LR 7, HR 802, where market rules were found not to be binding on a client who was not informed of them. This doctrine led to the development of documentation for client trades explicitly binding them to the rules.

[10] In *Williams v. Reynolds and another* EngR 595, (1865) 6 B and S 485, (1865) 122 ER 1278 it was held that the claim was only for the difference between the contract price and the market price at the time of delivery. This lack of linkage between one contract and another was important for establishing the extent of the counterparty credit risk in a futures contract.

[11] See Cranston (2021) for a discussion of the incremental and cooperative evolution of market infrastructure in England. He discusses how brokers slowly evolved the rules of their club to suit their interests. These interests often led to the promotion of market efficiency and integrity, and there was seldom a public policy imperative to intervene. The law often followed behind these practical considerations, only formalizing them well after the fact.

produced to where it was used. Cotton was also uniform enough that the market could standardize on a system of grades, allowing trading of a generic commodity rather than a specific set of bales. Finally, there was a trade association who was able to standardize contracts and set rules for market participants which reduced the sorts of legal uncertainty discussed in the last paragraph, and hence mitigated counterparty credit risk. From 1863 to 1873, the Liverpool cotton market slowly coalesced around trading standardized futures as these advantages became apparent.

Clearing in the early Liverpool cotton market

7.14 The early Liverpool cotton futures market suffered from chaotic expiries. Contracts had often been bought and sold in long chains of settlement, and the losers to a contract sometimes delayed settlement, creating problems down the chain. In 1873 a clearing committee was proposed to mitigate these problems. This was simply a special committee of the Cotton Brokers Association which oversaw a meeting on a specified day at which all contracts falling due in a particular month were presented for settlement. The Committee initially met on a trial basis. It was sufficiently successful that it soon became permanent and formalized its rules. All futures contracts had to be settled at its clearing meeting, and fines was imposed on any brokers which did not send a representative to the meeting at which contracts it was party to were cleared.[12]

7.15 The Liverpool market was an innovator in mandating the clearing of futures; the same cannot be said for margin requirements. Proposals for compulsory initial margin were discussed as early as 1863 and repeatedly thereafter,[13] but it was only when an American speculator in Liverpool cotton, Morris Ranger, went bankrupt in 1883 with debts of the then-enormous sum of £650,000[14] that the brokers accepted that the increase in costs created by margin obligations were worthwhile, given the benefits in counterparty credit risk reduction.[15]

7.16 The same pattern of a successful voluntary trial leading to a permanent compulsory arrangement was followed here. The practice of posting bilateral performance bonds on large transactions was already common in the Liverpool market by 1825.[16] This was formalized in 1882 when a group of around 60 brokers

---

12 See Hall (2000) at 110.

13 Ibid.

14 Hall (2000) quotes £400,000 for Ranger's liabilities in Liverpool and *The Times*, 5 January 1884, gives the larger sum for his total indebtedness at bankruptcy.

15 Ranger's failure caused widespread distress and the failure of a number of Liverpool cotton merchants. The most prominent of these was Hollinshead, Tetley and Co., 'one of the oldest and most respected houses in Liverpool' (*The Times*, 3 November 1883) which failed soon after Ranger's collapse with debts of £130,000.

16 Moser (1994) at 11.

began exchanging variation margin every two weeks on their joint trades. After Ranger's failure, the benefits of this arrangement were obvious, and the successor to the Liverpool Cotton Brokers Association, the Liverpool Cotton Association, adopted the practice of requiring the periodic exchange of variation margin.

7.17 This account suggests that the development of futures market infrastructure was incremental, experimental, and guided by the interests of those market participants who were members of the relevant association. In the case of the Liverpool cotton market, the narrow interests of the brokers often won out over the concerns of wider stakeholders, especially in the market's early days.[17] The incremental character of market infrastructure changes means that identifying a precise date for the 'foundation' of the clearing house is difficult: rather, there were a series of developments over roughly 25 years from 1865 which led to the emergence of something which was recognizable as a CCP.

The public policy turn in clearing

7.18 The first 125 years of derivatives central clearing were characterized by developments which were promulgated by one or more groups of market participants. The 2009 Pittsburgh declaration on mandatory central clearing of OTC derivatives, discussed in Chapter 6, altered that character. Instead of developing infrastructure incrementally (and with occasional mis-steps), a step change was imposed.[18]

7.19 OTC derivatives central clearing was not new: LCH's SwapClear services had been launched in 1999, and a CDS CCP was under development before the 2008 crisis, spurred by regulatory concern over the backlogs in outstanding CDS confirmations.[19] However, the scale of change mandated by post-crisis regulation was fundamentally different from anything that came before.

7.20 The regulatory turn in clearing, whereby CCPs became tools of public policy, had profound consequences. In 2009, ICE opened the previously planned two CDS clearing services, one in the US and one in Europe; the following year CME started clearing interest rate swaps in competition with LCH SwapClear.

[17] The initial design of the clearing house is a good example here. All futures contracts had to be settled through clearing house, but only members of the Brokers Association could use this facility. This meant that merchants who dealt in futures could only operate through a broker, which increased their costs and the brokers' profits. This conflict was eventually resolved with the formation of the Liverpool Cotton Association including both the brokers and the merchants.

[18] This, in turn, meant that CCP membership criteria became a regulatory matter: the club now had to be open to everyone who qualified. See R. CPMI & IOSCO (2012), Principle 18.

[19] See the Federal Reserve Bank of New York's two statements *Regarding Progress in Credit Derivatives Markets*, September 27, 2006 and February 16, 2006 and statement *Regarding Meeting on Credit Derivatives*, September 15, 2005, all available at https://www.newyorkfed.org/markets/otc_derivatives_supervisors_group.html.

Liquidity slowly moved to cleared products in OTC interest rate and credit derivatives: clearing levels for these asset classes were around 24% and 5% respectively in 2009, while by Q1 2018, this had risen to approximately 60% and 38%.[20] At the time of writing, the vast majority of newly traded interest rate swaps are cleared, and the most liquid market quotes are for cleared contracts.

7.21 As OTC derivatives clearing grew, it became clear that it was a winner-takes-(nearly)-all business: more than 90% of interest rate swaps were cleared by SwapClear service in 2017,[21] and ICE's two CDS services were similarly dominant in cleared CDS, as we noted in the previous Chapter.

7.22 CCPs' credit support arrangements are one way: clearing members post initial margin to CCPs, but CCPs do not post initial margin back to clearing members. This is in contrast to bilateral margin arrangements under the uncleared margin rules, where there is two-way posting. The result of this is that, even before the crisis, clearing members had significant exposures to CCPs. Post-crisis policy dramatically increased these exposures, both because there was more clearing, and because many of the newly cleared products had relatively high initial margin requirements.[22] As a result, clearing member exposures to CCPs grew significantly, and are now among their largest counterparty credit risk exposures.[23]

7.23 The increasingly systemic nature of CCPs was recognized by regulators. Their first step in 2012 was to set higher international standards for CCP risk management: these are the 'Principles for Financial Market Infrastructures', or 'PFMI's.[24] These rules are intended to reduce the probability of CCP distress by imposing minimum standards in various areas including CCP financial resources,

---

20 DAT (2018) at 17.

21 See Clarus FT, *2020 CCP Market Share Statistics*, 13 January 2021, available at https://www.clarusft.com/2020-ccp-volumes-and-market-share-in-ird/ for details. The market share of non-dominant CCPs in OTC derivatives clearing is partly due to regulatory barriers requiring the use of 'local' CCPs.

22 Most of the liquidity in exchange-traded derivatives is concentrated in short-dated futures, whereas OTC derivatives, notably interest rate swaps (which are the largest single OTC derivatives cleared product type), are much longer dated. This tends to mean that initial margin requirements are higher for the 'average' cleared OTC derivative than for the 'average' exchange-traded derivative.

23 To pick an example at random, HSBC's exposures to CCPs at the end of 2018 were $42.3B out of a total of $131.5B of counterparty credit risk exposure. (Of this, roughly two thirds comes from derivatives: the other third, approximately, from securities financing transactions such as repo.) See *HSBC Holdings plc Pillar 3 Disclosures at 31 December 2018*, available at https://www.hsbc.com/-/files/hsbc/investors/hsbc-results/2018/annual/hsbc-uk-bank-plc/190219-pillar-3-disclosures-31-december-2018.pdf.

24 See R. CPMI & IOSCO (2012), R. CPMI & IOSCO (2014), R. CPMI & IOSCO (2015), R. CPMI & IOSCO (2017), and R. CPMI & IOSCO (2020).

governance, and the management of counterparty credit, liquidity, operational, legal, and other business risks.

7.24 No prudential regulation can reduce the probability of CCP failure to zero. Because, in the words of Benoît Cœuré, 'the disorderly failure of a major CCP would be disastrous',[25] the authorities also introduced measures to address clearing house stress. These are known as recovery and resolution policy.[26]

7.25 The broad structure of public policy in this area is best understood, then, as several waves of regulation. First, as discussed in Chapter 6, there was the clearing mandate. As a result, CCPs became more systemically important, so higher standards were required for them: the PFMIs, and the subsequent guidance on and elaboration of them. But CCPs could still fail, so CCP recovery and resolution policy was needed. Each wave was a reaction to issues created by the prior one: the original choice of using CCPs, which had been designed for their members, to meet a public policy objective, was never revisited.[27] Many of the tensions in CCP policy result from this choice.

CCPs and Counterparty Credit Risk

7.26 The key role of a derivatives CCP is to mitigate counterparty credit risk. Bilateral derivatives expose the two contracting parties to the risk of each other's non-performance: by stepping between them, a CCP acts as a buffer, guaranteeing contract performance to each party. In this section, the mechanisms by which it does this, and the forms it takes, are investigated.

Types of CCPs

7.27 The corporate form of a CCP is an important aspect of its robustness, as this determines who controls it; who sets its resource levels; its incentives; and who it can call upon should it need support. The literature identifies five types of CCPs. The first two are government owned and government-mandated monopoly CCPs: these are self-explanatory. The next three form a spectrum. At one end is the purely private CCP, with all the risks being borne by the CCP's shareholders. At the other end is the purely mutual CCP, which is owned by its members and with all its risks being allocated to them. In between sit the partially mutualized

25 See Cœuré (2012).

26 Tucker (2013) summarized the motivations here as follows: '[t]he reforms of global capital markets put clearing houses at centre stage. The system will not be resilient unless the CCPs themselves are safe and sound and capable of orderly resolution.' Work is progressing here at the international level via a Financial Stability Board work programme, and at the national and EU levels.

27 See Genito (2019) for a framing of mandatory clearing based on the idea of changing structures of power and legitimacy in global finance.

CCPs, where some risks are borne by CCP shareholders and others by members.[28] This is the most common form in practice, and all the currently dominant CCPs in derivatives clearing take this form.[29] Not only are some risks borne by the members of these CCPs and others by their shareholders, their shares are wholly or largely owned by a single for-profit operator of an exchanges or exchanges.

The default waterfall

7.28 Suppose a clearing member of a CCP defaults. Typically the defaulter will have a house portfolio with the CCP: in addition, it may have one or more client accounts. The CCP is the counterparty to these portfolios. It has to close out the defaulter's house portfolios and either port or close out the client accounts. A number of different layers of resources are available to absorb any losses resulting from this. This default waterfall, as explained in Chapter 1, first uses resources provided by the account holder, then the defaulter's default fund contribution. After that, there is a layer of resources provided by the CCP—its 'skin in the game'—followed by the mutualized default fund. Then comes the CCP's power, documented in its rule book, to call for additional default fund contributions. Figure 7.1 summarizes these resources.

Resource	Contributor
End of the waterfall resources	Various
Default fund 'top-ups'	Non-defaulting clearing members
Remainder of the default fund	Non-defaulting clearing members
Skin in the game	CCP
Defaulters' default fund contribution	Defaulter
Account holders' initial margin	Account holder

Figure 7.1– A typical derivatives CCP default waterfall: losses flow from the bottom up*

* This is because waterfalls were first introduced in GSE-issued MBS, where prepayment risk went from the top down. When private label MBS were first issued, these had both prepayment risk and default risk: the former went from the top down as before; the latter from the bottom up. Hence the convention developed that default risk rises through the waterfall, despite the implication in 'waterfall' of downwards flow.

---

[28] Cox & Steigerwald (2016) call these 'demutualized' CCPs, but since some of the CCPs of this form did not arise from demutualization of a previously mutual CCP, we prefer the term 'partially mutualized'.

[29] Which CCPs dominate derivatives clearing is of course debatable; at the time of writing, we would include at least the CCPs in the CME Group, Eurex, the ICE Group, the HKEX Group, the LCH Group, and the Options Clearing Corporation.

Initial margin

7.29 The initial margin on a cleared account is intended to cover the potential losses which might arise on an account if it had to be liquidated over a period no longer than the margin period of risk.[30] It is typically estimated using a model of the return distribution of the portfolio, with some confidence interval of the distribution used to determine the base margin account. This 'model margin' is then often supplemented by extra margin for other risks, such as low clearing member credit quality or concentrated positions in the account.[31]

7.30 The PFMIs mandate that the confidence interval used to estimate the distribution of potential future exposure on the account should be at least 99%.[32] In addition to the choice of safety standard, the design of a margin model for a derivatives CCP involves several other delicate balances. The issues include:

- *Reactiveness.* Financial markets display periods of calm, often for extended periods; but they can become more volatile. The same portfolio displays less risk in calm periods than in volatile ones. How reactive should the margin model be to changes in conditions?
- *Memory vs staleness.* Relatedly, how much memory should the model have of past periods of stress? If it has too little, then new periods will always surprise it and margin will jump: but if it has too long a memory, then it will only adapt very slowly to paradigm changes.[33]
- *Margin period of risk.* Regulation sets a minimum MPOR of five days for OTC derivatives portfolios and either one or two days for exchange-traded derivatives.[34] When should model designers use longer periods? In particular, the choice of one day for ETD is aggressive, and leaves very little time

[30] See Carter & Cole (2017), Gurrola Perez & Murphy (2015), and Lin & Surti (2014) for more on CCP margin models.

[31] A position which is large compared to available market liquidity might be more expensive to close out than an initial margin model suggests, as these models typically do not account for market liquidity. See Cruz Lopez et al. (2017) and Menkveld (2017) for a discussion of some of the issues around 'crowded' trades.

[32] EMIR raises this to 99.5% and imposes further requirements on how this calculation is performed: see article 27 of R. EC (2012c), henceforth the 'EMIR RTS'.

[33] An interesting question arises here with the events of the 2008 crisis. The riskiest period in recent history for many outright positions occurred in late 2008. When will this period be so long ago that it can be discounted? EMIR gives the tentative answer 2038 (in that article 30 of the EMIR RTS refers to 'periods of extreme market movements observed over the past 30 years'), but this is obviously an arbitrary choice. The volatility experienced in the 1979 Gulf War would have been a good guide to the behaviour of the oil market during 2008, but the equity market now has very different dynamics to those it had in the 1987 crash, due to the rise of algorithmic trading.

[34] The original EMIR RTS set two days for both house and client exchange-traded derivatives accounts. The United States, however, had one day, and the issue threatened to create competitive

to port client portfolios, so model designers may wish to consider the base level choice here. This will interact with concentration margin policy: the more conservative the MPOR choice, the larger positions can get before requiring concentration margin.

- *Safety vs estimation error.* It might be tempting to think that a margin model with a higher confidence interval is safer than one with a lower interval. In the sense that having more money is better than having less money, that is true. However, the higher the confidence interval, the more difficult it is to estimate. Checking whether a model correctly estimates the 99th percentile of a portfolio return distribution is relatively straightforward: checking a model that claims to hit 99.9% really does so is more difficult, simply because one in a thousand events do not happen very often.

7.31 This brings us to model validation. Regulation requires CCPs to 'conduct a comprehensive validation of its models, their methodologies and framework for calculating liquid financial resources'.[35] For initial margin models, the intent is to determine the strength of the evidence that the model misestimates the target risk level. As with internal models used for capital estimation, a key element of this is the comparison of the actual pattern of losses bigger than a given threshold with the statistically expected pattern.[36] This backtesting process was discussed in paragraph 5.22: an initial margin model which cannot be rejected on the basis of it is said to have 'passed backtesting'.

Skin in the game

7.32 Which resources are used in which order matters for the incentives present in clearing. The doctrine that the defaulter's margin is used first means that the cost of failure is often born entirely by the defaulter. However, setting initial margin requirements high enough that they are always adequate would be prohibitively inefficient.

---

distortions, especially in commodity futures where EU-domiciled CCPs were in direct competition with US CCPs. The claim that CCPs can determine that a default had happened, go through the required default management process, and close out a large defaulter's portfolio all within one day is relatively implausible, as the account of the management of Lehman's exchange-traded positions in Valukas (2010) at 1841 evidences. Despite this, the EU backed down and adopted a one day MPOR for exchange-traded derivatives client accounts: see R. ESMA (2013).

[35] See article 47 of the EMIR RTS. This review must include 'an evaluation of the conceptual soundness of the models and framework', 'a review of the ongoing monitoring procedures', ' a review of the parameters and assumptions made', 'a review of the parameters and assumptions made' given the instruments they are applied to, 'a review of the appropriateness of its stress testing scenarios', discussed later in this section, and 'an analysis of the outcomes of testing results'. This is broadly similar to the requirements for bank internal models discussed in Chapter 10.

[36] Gurrola Perez (2018), Zhang & Nadarajah (2018), and Chapter 5, footnote 17 discuss this further.

7.33 In order to incentivize the CCP to set margin levels reasonably high, to ensure that its operational process and documentation are robust, and to set prudent membership requirements, a convention has evolved that CCPs should have some of their own capital at stake immediately after the defaulter's resources.[37] This 'skin in the game', as it is known, is usually not a material amount compared to the potential losses on liquidation of a large house account: rather, it is intended to be big enough to hurt the CCP if it is used, but not so big as to cause the CCP to fail should it be lost.[38]

7.34 The argument that skin in the game gives CCPs incentives for good risk management is reasonable at the level of the entity. However, it is also important to note that many CCPs, including most systemic CCPs, are members of groups with much larger levels of capital and with substantial earnings from other sources, such as running an exchange and selling data. The risk of a loss which is a material fraction of the CCP's earnings might not necessarily always motivate the CCP's owners if the CCP is a small part of the group. Instead, the argument is that the loss of reputation associated with failing to set margin accurately incentivized the CCP. In the past, this has not always ensured margin was set high enough to be robust,[39] so there is a question whether skin in the game requirements should be higher for the most systemic CCPs.

7.35 CCPs, all other things being equal, prefer higher levels of IM on cleared portfolios as it makes their skin in the game less risky. Clearing members prefer it too, as the costs of higher IM for them are relatively low and the larger IM is, the safer their default fund contributions are, given that skin in the game is not large.[40] This preference for more IM is strong when the cost of funding additional margin for most clearing members is low, as it is in the current environment of abundant central bank liquidity. It means that CCP and clearing member incentives are aligned to prefer higher initial margin.[41]

7.36 Clients often have more directional cleared portfolio than clearing members, because their cleared positions are often hedges against uncleared exposures. Clients' funding costs will on average be higher than those of banks, and most

---

[37] 'Should' rather than 'must': while there is a requirement for CCPs to put their own capital at risk in the default waterfall in EMIR, there is none in the PFMIs.

[38] See Lewis & McPartland (2018) for a development of this argument.

[39] For example, the adequacy of the margin required by the Nasdaq clearing house on a large position on the spread between German and Nordic power came under scrutiny after the position taker, Einar Aas, defaulted in September 2018: see Saguato (2020).

[40] See Murphy (2017) for an analysis of these incentives.

[41] When mandatory clearing policy was being written, regulators were concerned at the potential for CCPs to set low initial margin in order to attract business. 'Predatory' margin practices, as Krahnen & Pelizzon (2016) call them, have not materialized: the incentive to set margin higher rather than lower proved more powerful.

clients will not have access to central bank funding. All of this means that much of the cost of the choice to have higher initial margin requirements falls on clients.[42]

7.37 This example shows that there is a potential for conflict between CCPs and different classes of CCP users. Depending on the issue, this can align CCPs with a particular class of users and against another, or in conflict with most or all of its users.[43] These conflicts play out through CCP governance mechanisms.

7.38 The governance of CCPs is a controversial area. The title of one paper in the area—'Governing Systemic Risk'[44]—encapsulates the problem. Some CCPs have been co-opted into a systemic risk management role, but central clearing did not develop to support this requirement. Policy makers have taken existing CCP ownership and institutional arrangements as a starting point, and added rules designed to mitigate the tensions that arise when the systemic risk management role is added to the CCP's prior mission. In the case of governance, these interventions add certain consultation and disclosure requirements, but they do not change the fact that private, for-profit CCPs are run for the benefit of their shareholders.[45]

The default fund

7.39 CCPs maintain a pre-funded fund to cover any losses which arise from closing out accounts cleared by a defaulter that exceed the funds provided by the failed clearing member and skin in the game. The sizing of the default fund is based on two key ideas:

- *An extreme but plausible market move.* This is a large change in risk factors which causes losses on cleared accounts in excess of those contemplated in initial margin models, but which is not implausibly large. These losses

---

42 It is interesting to note that when CCP initial margin regulation was being designed after the crisis, the focus was on ensuring that margin levels were not too low: rather little thought was given to the question of the consequences, and especially the distributional consequences, should CCPs choose to set margin too high.

43 The literature on firm governance understandably concentrates on the conflicts between shareholders, creditors, employees, and other stakeholders that affect typical corporations. CCPs are different in the nature (and sometimes of the extent) of the conflicts between different creditors, and in the mechanisms by which equity holders and CCP managers can affect the risk borne by them. See Cox & Steigerwald (2016) and Saguato (2017) at 637 for a further discussion of this perspective and, in particular, the challenges that arise from the fact that CCP equity holders are, in many cases, not the ultimate risk holders.

44 See Griffith (2011).

45 For the argument that this choice is a debatable, see Saguato (2017), who suggests that 'the ownership structure of clearinghouses is a matter of public importance, due to the ways in which that structure affects the incentives of the firms' main stakeholders, which in turn affects systemic financial stability'.

are sometimes termed 'stressed losses over IM'. The CCP determines then based on a suite of scenarios, each of which contains risk factor moves in various extreme conditions. These include both historical scenarios—risk factor moves that were experienced in previous volatile periods, such as September 2008 or the early Covid period—and hypothetical situations which might generate substantial losses for cleared portfolios.[46]

- *Cover 2.* The default fund must be at least as large as the sum of the losses caused by the simultaneous default of the two clearing members with the largest stressed losses over IM.[47] It is then said to be sized at 'cover 2', reflecting its ability to cover the loss resulting from the failure of the two largest clearing members in the worst extreme but plausible scenario.[48]

7.40 The convention of providing further resources to absorb counterparty credit risk losses via a default fund, and sizing that default fund using cover 2, is a relatively recent innovation.[49] Nevertheless, it had become widespread in exchange-traded derivatives CCPs by 2008, so it was adopted in the PFMIs.

The default waterfall as a CDO

7.41 The default waterfall consists of various layers of resources which are used one after the other to absorb any losses caused by closing out a defaulter. This

[46] Article 30 of the EMIR RTS sets out the requirements for the selection of these scenarios. As Murphy & Macdonald (2016) discusses, the key issue is to find not just those scenarios which contain the largest moves in risk factors but, to the extent that they are different, the scenarios that create the largest losses for cleared portfolios.

[47] Specifically, a clearing member's loss in a scenario is the sum of the losses on the house and client accounts, with client account gains not being available to offset house account losses. The 'cover 2' loss in a scenario is the sum of the largest two clearing member losses in that scenario, and the overall 'cover 2' requirement is the largest cover 2 loss across all the scenarios: see Murphy & Nahai-Williamson (2014).

[48] Cover 2 is a somewhat peculiar measure of required financial resources because it does not depend on the total amount of counterparty credit risk in the clearing service, only that of the two largest clearing members. Ibid. shows how this results in relatively less prudent resourcing of the CCP when the distribution of exposures among clearing members is more uniform. It is also obviously imprudent if the probability of more than two clearing members failing in a short period of time is meaningfully more than zero. This happened during the Morris Ranger episode cited in the previous section and in the Hong Kong stress 104 years later discussed in Cox (2015), so it is not impossible.

[49] CPMI (1997) describes the diversity of resources derivatives clearing houses used in the 1990s for losses over IM: they included 'capital and reserves, clearing guarantee [i.e. default] funds, committed lines of credit, insurance policies, guarantees provided by members [and the] authority to make assessments on members'. Kroszner (2000) also mentions one CCP—the Board of Trade Clearing Corporation—having the right to demand that clearing members contribute additional shareholders' funds.

suggests that it is like a collateralized debt obligation or 'CDO'. Here too there are various tranches from the low return, (usually) low risk senior tranche at the top of the CDO to the high return junior tranche which takes the first losses at the bottom, as discussed in Chapter 2. This analogy motivates the application of tools originally developed to analyse CDOs to investigate the safety of CCP default funds.[50]

Regulatory requirements for sizing CCP resources

7.42 The default fund encapsulates the club-like nature of CCPs. In order to protect the CCP, whose services benefit them all, clearing members agree to jointly contribute funds which will be used to absorb losses in excess of the resources provided by the defaulter and the CCP, so that the CCP can provide trade continuity to non-defaulting club members. In other words, if the protection provided by the defaulter is inadequate, the clearing members all suffer the consequences.

7.43 The risk of default fund losses creates an incentive for the members to pressure the CCP to take steps which limit the extent to which any individual member can create extraordinary losses. Clearing members have a strong interest in the adequacy of margin for portfolios which could create such losses, such as those containing concentrated positions.

7.44 Loss mutualization, then, speaks to CCP governance: if the clearing members are responsible for nearly all of the loss absorption capacity above IM, then they should have a say in how the CCP manages risk.[51]

7.45 CCP governance structures facilitate the dialogue between stakeholders here. These structures typically include a board of directors elected by shareholders, and various committees, often including representatives from the CCPs' clearing members and, perhaps, clients.

7.46 The CCP's risk committee is particularly important, as it advises 'the board on any arrangements that may impact the risk management of the CCP, such

[50] See Murphy & Nahai-Williamson (2014). The result from that paper, discussed in footnote 48, that CCPs with less uniform member risk distributions are safer, was derived using CDO analysis techniques.

[51] Cox & Steigerwald (2016) and Cerezetti et al. (2019) set out this argument in more detail. The authors point out that it works to the extent that a derivatives market participant has a choice as to whether to become a member of a CCP: joining the club should be voluntary, as it was before 2009 when these conventions were developed. The incentives to clear in capital regulation, the concentration of OTC derivatives clearing—and hence liquidity and netting opportunities—in a small number of CCPs, and the clearing mandate, mean that membership not just of a CCP, but of the global, systemically important CCPs is nearly impossible to avoid. It is hard to argue that if a clearing member does not like these CCPs' rules or governance, it should not join. Thus, there is a tension between CCPs as originally conceived as club goods and their current status as largely private corporations but whose use is mandatory.

as a significant change in its risk model, the default procedures, the criteria for accepting clearing members, the clearing of new classes of instruments, or the outsourcing of functions'.[52] Risk committees must include representatives of the CCP's clearing members, independent members of the CCP's board, and representatives of the CCP's clients. This governance mechanism gives the bearers of the risk of the CCP's risk management decisions some say in them. However, it remains advisory: the ultimate authority rests with the CCP's Board.[53]

Resource	Sizing
End of the waterfall resources	Multiple approaches
Default fund 'top-ups'	Multiple of default fund
Remainder of the default fund	'Cover 2'
Skin in the game	12.5% of annual expenses
Defaulters' default fund contribution	Pro rata share of total DF
Defaulters' initial margin	At least 99% confidence, 1 day MPOR (ETD); 99.5% confidence, 5 day MPOR (OTC)

Figure 7.2– Minimum requirements and common CCP standards for sizing of the elements of the default waterfall for systemic CCPs

7.47 Figure 7.2 summarizes the regulatory requirements and common conventions for sizing the various elements of the waterfall. Default fund contributions are often allocated by share of IM, so while the total DF is sized based on the cover 2 loss,[54] each clearing member is required to contribute the same fraction of that amount that their IM is of the total initial margin at the CCP. There is no international standard for sizing SITG, so the European requirement is shown.[55]

Beyond the funded default waterfall

7.48 Most CCPs' rule books allow them to call for amounts in addition to the paid in default fund, should that be eroded by default losses. These calls are usually limited in some way. For instance, clearing members might be required,

[52] The quote is from article 28 of EMIR.

[53] EMIR does however require that CCP regulators are informed 'of any decision in which the [CCP's] board decides not to follow the advice of the risk committee'.

[54] The PFMI only require that CCPs which are 'involved in activities with a more complex risk profile or that is systemically important in multiple jurisdictions' should meet cover 2. For others, the regulatory minimum is cover 1.

[55] The EMIR RTS sets CCP SITG at 25% of the CCP's capital requirement in article 35, while R. EC (2012d) sets the capital requirement as a minimum of six months operating expenses plus various additional requirements which are often in practice small.

if called upon, to make additional contributions up to twice their share of cover 2. After this, there are various 'end of the waterfall' tools which different derivatives CCPs' rule books sometimes provide. Two of the most common are:

- *Variation margin gains haircutting, or 'VMGH'*. This is a process whereby a CCP can reduce or eliminate variation margin payments that would otherwise be due. It is envisaged as being used where the variation margin inflows to the CCP have not been received due to default, and where making the full payment due might endanger the CCP.
- *Tear up*. This is the elimination of one or more cleared contracts by the CCP at a price the CCP determines. Tear up is the ultimate default management tool in that a CCP using it can eliminate positions opposite the defaulter and so return itself to a matched book at a cost it defines. Obviously tear up is highly coercive, as it involves terminating contracts without consent, and typically without full compensation.

CCP resources and public disclosure

7.49 Three of the largest and most systemically important groups involved with derivatives clearing globally are the Chicago Mercantile Exchange, or 'CME', the various CCPs in the Intercontinental Exchange or 'ICE' group, and the London Clearing House CCPs within the London Stock Exchange Group. These different groups organize clearing in different ways: for instance, CME clearing is a 'division' within the CME group; ICE clears both exchange-traded and OTC credit derivatives within the ICE Clear Europe entity; and LCH Limited is a legal entity containing the SwapClear, EquityClear, ForexClear, RepoClear, and exchange-traded derivatives clearing services. Further complicating the mapping between clearing services and legal entities, ICE and LCH both have additional legal entities offering clearing services in the United States.

7.50 In 2015, regulators mandated that CCPs should 'provide relevant information to participants, relevant authorities and the broader public'.[56] These disclosures provide a variety of useful information on various aspects of CCP operation and risk. They are sometimes difficult to interpret, because some resources are held at the legal entity level, and hence sometimes shared between multiple clearing services, whereas others are dedicated to a particular service.

7.51 Figure 7.3 sets out some of the key quantitative disclosures from five large derivatives clearing services. The first part of the table concerns the CCPs housing clearing services. CME 'Base' is CME's exchange-traded derivatives clearing service, while 'IRS' is its OTC interest rate swaps service. ICEU CDS is ICE's

[56] See R. CPMI & IOSCO (2015).

European CDS clearing service, while 'FF&O' clears futures and options. LCH SwapClear is LCH's interest rate derivatives clearing service. Where available, (a proxy for) CCP equity is given, as is end 2019 shareholders' funds for the group the CCP is part of. The second half of the table considers the most important clearing services in each CCP, setting out the total number of clearing members, the total initial margin, the skin in the game and the default fund size. Finally, the percentage of total margin attributable to the largest five members is given.

Clearing service	CME Base	CME IRS	ICEU CDS	ICEU F&O	LCH SwapClear
Type	ETD	OTC	OTC	ETD	OTC
CCP	Chicago Mercantile Exchange Inc.		ICEU		LCH Limited
EFLA[1]	N/A[2]		$691.4M		£649.7M
Shareholders' funds	$26.3B		$19.5B		£3.7B
No. of CMs[3]	57	28	30	78	87
Initial margin[4]	$190.4B	$40.3B	€10.8B	$62.8B	£161.5B
Skin in the game[5]	$100M	$150M	€44.5M	$150M	£59.8M
Default fund[6]	$4.7B	$4.2B	€1.2B	$3.2B	£6.0B
% OI from top 5[7]	50%	66%	52.5%	30.4%	22.3%

Figure 7.3- Quantitative aspects of some large derivatives clearing services

The relevant sections of the CPMI IOSCO disclosures and their summary definitions are noted in the following. [1] 15.1.1 Equity funded liquid assets, a proxy for the equity capital in the CCP. [2] CME does not disclose this item, referring instead to the group's financial statements. [3] 18.1. Sum of direct and general clearing members. [4] 6.1.1 Total initial margin required. [5] 4.1.1 Prefunded—own capital before. [6] 4.1.4 Prefunded—aggregate participant contributions—required. [7] 18.2.2 Percentage of open positions held by the largest five clearing members. All disclosures are taken from the H2 2020 disclosures and are rounded to one figure after the decimal point.

7.52 There are a number of observations which follow from this data:

- The largest derivatives clearing services have very substantial amounts of initial margin, but differ somewhat in their number of clearing members.
- For these CCPs, skin in the game is, on average, over a thousand times smaller than initial margin, reflecting its lack of material loss absorbency. It is much smaller than the shareholders' funds available in each CCP's parent company.
- Default funds vary materially in size and are much smaller than the total initial margin in these clearing services.

- The ratio of initial margin to default fund varies from nine times to over forty times. This is partly due to different margin model designs, and hence margin levels, in different services, but it also depends on the degree of concentration in the service.
- Some services are quite concentrated, with most of the open positions held by the biggest five clearing members; others are less so.

7.53 Mutualization is most effective and a dollar of default fund goes further in highly diverse services, where the top five members are a relatively small percentage of the total margin. In contrast, services with relatively few total members, and where the risk of the top five members dominates, require default funds that are a higher percentage of total initial margin. In the limit, if the top two or three clearing members hold most of the risk, this might indicate a market which is not suitable for clearing at all.[57]

CCP default management

7.54 The PFMI are silent on how CCPs should close out defaulting clearing members' portfolios, confining themselves to stating that they should have 'effective and clearly defined rules and procedures' for it.[58] This is partly due to the diversity of reasonable approaches: an exchange-traded derivatives CCP might place orders in the market to 'buy or sell contracts identical but opposite to the net positions held by the defaulting participant', while an OTC derivatives CCP would be more likely to first roughly hedge the defaulter's positions using liquid instruments, then auction the hedged portfolio, as discussed in Chapter 1.[59]

7.55 CCPs usually take the auction approach if the portfolio was large or illiquid enough that placing market orders to liquidate it might not be successful, given the resources available.[60] The design of the auction is then important: CCPs would want to have those market participants who are most likely to make credible bids on the portfolio participating, but to exclude those who might trade against the CCP's position should they gain knowledge of it.[61]

---

[57] The issue is the plausibility of a successful liquidation of a large clearing member's portfolio after a default if there are only one or two parties who could potentially take it on.

[58] This is Principle 13.

[59] See R. CPMI & IOSCO (2020) for a further discussion of the issues in CCP default auctions. This paper rightly stresses the importance of documenting and testing processes for each stage of the default management process, while suggesting that there is a balance to be struck in practice between flexibility and predictability.

[60] Entering market orders for all the positions in a large portfolio will likely trigger substantial price changes before the portfolio can be fully liquidated.

[61] One of the reasons for the difficulties experienced in the liquidation of Einar Aas's position discussed in footnote 39 was that the first time the CCP tried to auction the portfolio, there was no

7.56 Between the dangers of having too many and too few auction participants, the latter is probably worse. In order to ensure sufficient participation, the PFMIs contemplate the possibility that CCPs 'may need to consider requiring participants to agree in advance to bid on the defaulting participant's portfolio'. An additional incentive for participation is sometimes given by 'juniorization', a process whereby the default fund contributions of clearing members failing to make a credible bid in a default auction are put at risk before those of members making competitive bids.

7.57 The participation of clients in default auctions is neither required nor prohibited by regulation, reflecting the fact that it may sometimes be desirable, particularly when clients are substantial liquidity providers in a market,[62] but that clients will not have the same incentives to bid as clearing members, given that they do not have default fund contributions at risk.[63]

Segregation and porting

7.58 A CCP's default management problem will be larger and more complex if it has to close out the portfolios of a defaulting clearing member's clients as well as the house account. Both CCPs and clients want to avoid this, and prefer instead to port client positions. Higher levels of segregation can help: the easier it is to identify and move a client's portfolio and margin, the more likely they are to be ported. The PFMIs therefore require that CCPs 'should have rules and procedures that enable the segregation and portability of positions of a participant's customers and the collateral provided to the CCP with respect to those positions'.

7.59 One of the reasons that international regulation is relatively silent on how CCPs should achieve client segregation—and thereby enhance the likelihood of portability—is that these questions are intimately bound up with both the clearing model and with national insolvency law. Another is that there is a tension between the cost of segregation arrangements and their safety: using a segregated account is more expensive than sharing an omnibus one, and different clients will reasonably take different views of this trade-off.

7.60 The different approaches taken in the US and the EU illustrate these issues. In the US, two segregation models coexist: the older, less secure[64] but cheaper futures model, and the 'legally segregated but operationally commingled'

credible bid. When the auction was repeated, the best bid still used more resources than had been provided by the defaulter.

62 This is common in commodity and energy derivatives markets.

63 R. CPMI & IOSCO (2020) also identifies issues of operational and legal readiness for client participation in default auctions.

64 This model is less secure because there is fellow client risk: one client of a clearing member can suffer a loss if another client of the same clearing member fails to satisfy their obligations.

or 'LSOC' model introduced by the Dodd-Frank Act for cleared swaps.[65] This is combined with the obligation to use 'best efforts' to port,[66] and the substantial powers facilitating porting granted under the Securities Investor Protection Act.[67] Porting is also made more likely by the fact that the client funds are (or at least, if margin posting and receipt has been properly conducted, should be) individually distinguishable under LSOC.

7.61 EU regulation[68] requires that CCPs at least offer the choice between omnibus client segregation and individual client segregation, and many CCPs offer a bewildering variety of segregation models in addition to these two. Each model offers a different balance between the likelihood of porting, client asset protection, and cost.

7.62 Another issue in the EU context is that porting is potentially more difficult in a principal-to-principal model, as the cleared portfolio flows through the clearing member. Client margin may well be the property of the clearing member too, with the clearing member having posted conceptually distinct assets to the CCP to meet margin requirements on client accounts. The implications of these facts for portability depend on the details of the account structure, the nature of any deficiencies in the account or accounts, and the quality of the record-keeping.[69]

Investigating CCP stress

7.63 Clearing member defaults can stress CCPs, especially if they generate losses or demands for liquidity which are larger than the resources immediately available to manage them. Other events can create problems too, as we discuss further

---

65 The US futures segregation model is an omnibus one. It requires that clearing members—futures commission merchants, or FCMs, as they are termed—must hold customer funds separate from house funds, and that this 'segregated funds pool' always contains at least as much as is required to cover the FCM's liabilities to its clients. In the LSOC model, the FCM must in addition assure the CCP that, when it meets a margin call for client positions, it never uses funds provided by one customer to meet the obligation of another. In other words, if a customer is in deficit with the FCM, this must be met by the FCM's own funds, not by an excess from another customer. FCMs must in addition identify each customer's positions to the CCP at least daily.

66 Under Part 190 of the CFTC's rules.

67 See Chamorro-Courtland (2016) for a description of the US position with regard to the porting of client cleared derivatives, and Fleming & Sarkar (2014) for a comparison of this with the situation for uncleared derivatives.

68 See EMIR, article 39 for the regulatory requirements and Braithwaite & Murphy (2021) for a further discussion of issues in EU client clearing.

69 This last is key. Collateral is constantly flowing to and from any large clearing member, so segregation should be thought of not as the labelling of a static block of assets as belong to a client, but rather as the continual process of keeping track of what belongs to whom as assets move. As Giddens (2012) discusses in the case of MF Global, when this process is not properly carried out, the consequences for clients can be severe.

below. In order to probe the consequences of potential stress, both CCPs and CCP regulators conduct stress tests.

7.64 The stress testing carried out by CCPs is used to size their default funds: these tests are essentially asking how big the loss could be in extreme but plausible circumstances if the most dangerous two clearing members default. CCPs also examine various other stresses and conduct default 'fire drills' to test the operational readiness of default management arrangements.

7.65 Stress tests conducted by regulators are useful to the extent that they go beyond those of CCPs' own testing in one or more directions:[70]

- The test can examine more severe stresses than the CCP does, for instance involving the failure of more than two clearing members; or it can examine the size of market moves needed to exhaust the default fund contingent on a given default scenario.[71]
- The test can examine a different dimension of stress than just default, such as the liquidity needs of CCPs in different situations.[72]
- The test can examine interactions which cannot be captured in an individual institutions' stress test, for instance including second-round effects whereby CCPs' default management causes further market moves which potentially cause further defaults.

7.66 The objectives that regulators could pursue with a CCP supervisory stress testing programme can be split into those primarily concerned with the robustness of individual CCPs—micro-prudential objectives—and those that are about the resilience of the clearing system and wider financial markets—macro-prudential objectives. The former provide assurance that the CCP's resources are indeed sufficient, while the latter consider interactions whose impact can only be reasonably estimated from data which is only available to the authorities.

Stressed CCPs

7.67 Stress tests are forward looking exercises, but the past can be informative too. There have been a number of events of historic CCP stress, and two of them are particularly instructive. The first was the stress of the Hong Kong Futures Exchange (or 'HKFE') during the equity market crash of 1987. The causes of

70 Anderson et al. (2019) discuss authority stress testing of CCPs in more detail.

71 A test which examines the size of the stress needed to exhaust the available resources is known as a reverse stress test. Size can be defined either in terms of the size of the market moves or the number of clearing member defaults needed.

72 CCPs by their nature have substantial flows of cash in and out each day: these are discussed further in the next section of this chapter.

this stress were complex. There was a precipitous market fall after years of rising prices. This caused losses at both clients and clearing members, but the size of these losses was uncertain as the exchange's settlement infrastructure had been unable to keep up with the volume of activity generated by the market turmoil.

7.68 After the market crashed, it was generally believed that the CCP would be unable to honour contracts with non-defaulters, as default resources were too low to cover the size of the losses, given the market fall. When a long closure was announced to allow time to resolve the situation, the already significant loss of confidence in the CCP intensified.[73]

7.69 Of particular modern interest was the continuing uncertainty over the losses and the controversy over who should meet them. Once the settlement infrastructure caught up with the trading and payments made during the crash, it became clear that many clearing members, especially smaller clearing members primarily serving retail customers, had failed to pay. These were all technically defaults, but it was evident that some of them were strategic: many clearing members could pay, or at least could pay something, but they were unwilling to, given that the CCP was not obviously a going concern.[74]

7.70 The ability to put many clearing members into default may not be useful if the threat is not credible: in 1987 in Hong Kong, it wasn't, given the number of members failing to pay. One reason for this behaviour was conflict over who should meet the default losses and how to re-resource the CCP, with most parties taking the view that the answer was 'not me'.[75]

7.71 Eventually, a proposal was assembled to re-resource the CCP using a combination of public money, funds from shareholders in the CCP, and contributions from the clearing members. This failed, partly because the resources promised were not clearly sufficient, which, in turn, was due to government reluctance to commit more public money. As the crisis deepened, this unwillingness was overcome, and a revised, larger proposal was accepted by key stakeholders. The CCP was saved, albeit with the injection of 2 billion Hong Kong dollars of public funds. This outlay was recouped by the imposition of a transaction tax.

[73] Cox (2015) gives a detailed account of this event of CCP stress. It should be noted in this event that the 'CCP' was not a single entity: a separate corporation, the Futures Guarantee Corporation, provided a limited guarantee of derivatives translations cleared by the HKFE's CCP, the International Commodities Clearing House Hong Kong Ltd.

[74] Clearing member reluctance to meet default fund top up calls at KRX in December 2013 after the default of HanMag securities are another more modern instance of this phenomena: see McPartland & Lewis (2017) for more on the HanMag default.

[75] The market had fallen a long way, so holders of long positions were losers. They wanted their losses capped, with contracts torn up at a price above the current market price. The shorts opposed them, wanting instead that the CCP be re-resourced. This would allow them to hang on to their profits, as Cox (2015) explains.

7.72 The second CCP stress with clear lessons for today was that of the New Zealand Futures and Options Exchange (or 'NZFOE') in 1989.[76] Here, a large position in the benchmark government bond futures contract was built up an individual, Stephen Francis, through the use of several clearing members. This was a 'corner', where Francis attempted to drive the price of the future lower and lower by selling both the future and the bonds which were deliverable into it.[77] Inadequate market surveillance had failed to identify the aggregate risk borne by Francis thanks to his tactic of clearing through multiple clearing members and because he falsely (and fraudulently) claimed that he was trading on behalf of clients, a claim that was not properly probed. Moreover, relatively low margin requirements had allowed Francis to accumulate this position cheaply: the NZFOE had no requirement for concentration margin at the time.

7.73 When the position started to move against Francis, he could not meet variation margin calls, and defaulted. The CCP was left to default manage a position comprising over 90% of the short open interest in the future. It did not have much margin to meet the costs of doing this. Its response was to propose a tear up. The members had to agree, as the only obvious alternative was the insolvency of the CCP. The tear up price determined the allocation of losses between the longs opposite Francis and shorts clearing his position and alongside him. This proved controversial, and was only agreed upon once the New Zealand Debt Management Office agreed to issue more bonds which could be delivered into the future, alleviating the squeeze Francis had created.

7.74 These salutary episodes indicate the extraordinary steps that were taken to prevent CCP failure in the past. In the HKFE case, the contractual rights of the CCP and the authorities' powers of suasion were not sufficient to avoid the use of a substantial amount of public funds, while the NZFOE was only saved at the cost of contract continuity and large losses for some clearing members. In both instances, inadequate CCP financial resources and oversized positions were partly to blame, and in both, default management descended into an argument over who could and should pay.

[76] This event is analysed in detail in Cox et al. (2016). The story is an extraordinary one: Francis was a charming man who managed to amass an enormous position, then went on the run, finally being arrested at Tunbridge Wells railway station with a suitcase full of cash.

[77] A corner is an attempt to control enough of the stock of a financial instrument or related instruments that the price can be manipulated. Corners are well-known in futures markets. They can occur either on the long side, where the cornerer buys the future in the hope of driving its price up, or—as with Francis—on the short side. In both cases the final settlement mechanism is key: if the future is settled by delivery of something, then the stock of that thing available for delivery is often a determinant of the success of the attempt. Cornering would now likely be market manipulation, but earlier standards of market conduct were more lax. For a historical discussion dating from the period when standards were changing, see Perdue (1987).

CCPs, Collateral, and Liquidity

7.75 Central clearing is a dynamic business. Portfolios change as new transactions are entered into and old ones mature. Markets move, and many contracts, such as interest rate swaps, have contractual flows during their life. CCPs make initial margin calls and exchange variation margin with their counterparties based on the current risk and market value of cleared portfolios, and these movement have to take place quickly. Clearing members and clients also sometimes make discretionary transfers of additional margin amounts above the minimum required, or request excess margin be repaid to them. CCPs regularly recalculate default fund contributions. They also often invest cash paid to them and receive the proceeds of maturing investments.

7.76 For all of these reasons, large CCPs are involved in a substantial number of cash or collateral asset flows each business day. There are issues at either end of the flows: clearing members need to have sufficient liquidity to meet demands from CCPs, and CCPs need to invest cash provided by clearing members safely. There are also unexpected liquidity demands on CCPs, for instance if there is a default of one or more clearing members. In order to provide contract continuity, CCPs must continue to meet their payment obligations even as they are managing defaults, and this requires cash.

7.77 The ability of clearing to mitigate counterparty credit risk therefore depends on liquidity. One could even say that clearing transforms counterparty credit risk into funding liquidity risk. In order to investigate the nature of this clearing-related liquidity risk, this section considers expected and unexpected cash movements related to clearing and the regulation pertinent to them.

Liquidity flows ordinarily

7.78 The payment flows into and out of a big derivatives CCP on a typical day are often in multiple currencies, and they can happen throughout the global trading day. As noted in Chapter 1, variation margin flows across the CCP, so provided that all clearing members are performing, the total VM flow into the CCP is equal to the total flow out of it.[78]

7.79 CCPs and clearing members are responsible for managing their liquidity in each relevant currency so that they can make payments when they are due. As an operational matter, payments happen either in central bank money[79] or using one or more payment banks. The CCP and the clearing members maintain accounts

[78] Some CCPs' intra-day variation margin arrangements allow them to call for losses but not to pay out on gains. For clearing member responses to the liquidity stress intraday VM calls in general and this process in particular create, see FIA (2020) at 3.1.3.

[79] PFMI Principle 9 states that CCPs should do this 'where practical and available'.

at the payment bank or banks, and a required movement occurs as an internal transfer on books of these banks.[80]

CCPs' investment of cash

7.80 Many initial margin payments and default fund contributions are made in cash and on a title transfer basis, meaning that the cash becomes the property of the CCP. This is advantageous for the clearing house, as the cash is immediately available to meet any other obligations it might have.

7.81 CCPs typically pay interest on cash posted to them.[81] To generate the required return and to keep their cash safe, CCPs make various investments. The principal choices are:

- Deposit the cash in an account at the central bank. This has the advantage of being very safe, but it requires that the CCP is permitted to have such an account in the relevant currency.
- Deposit the cash at a commercial bank.
- Use the repo market. Reverse repos on government bonds are often considered a safe investment. They are usually most liquid on a short-term basis, so the invested cash is available again quickly, but their use necessitates regularly rolling the repo.
- Buy a security, such as a government bond. Cash is only available from this strategy once the security has been sold and that trade settles.

7.82 The CCP's need for liquidity and its low tolerance for risk on its investments often results in a conservative investment strategy largely using central bank deposits, if available, and government bond reverse repo if not.[82] At the moment, this strategy typically gives a low or even negative return.[83]

7.83 Commercial bank deposits resulting either from the use of a payment bank or from cash margin investment are often credit risky, as they are typically not

80 Few banks can offer payment services in all the currencies that a global CCP serves, and using one bank for all payments might anyway be an unacceptable concentration risk, so multiple payment banks are common.

81 In the case of negative interest rates in the currency concerned, they may receive it.

82 Article 45 of the EMIR RTS requires that 95% of invested cash is held in one of these two forms. Several large US CCPs have been granted accounts at the Federal Reserve, and these offer an attractive rate of interest and complete safety. Thus, European and US CCPs predominantly invest cash in repo markets or at central banks. Asian CCPs, in contrast, tend not to have central bank access and tend to have more cash in currencies with less liquid and/or safe repo markets: they therefore often make more use of commercial bank deposits.

83 Excess return on cash collateral investments above the rate promised is the property of the CCP. Historically, this would have been valuable to CCPs, but it is much less so in the current interest rate environment.

covered by deposit protection schemes. CCPs may therefore be exposed to the performance of some banks in multiple roles—as a clearing member, as a deposit taker, as a repo counterparty, and as a payment or settlement provider.

Collateral taking by CCPs

7.84 Most CCPs accept some types of securities to meet initial margin requirements.[84] Usually only high quality liquid assets, such as highly rated government bonds, are eligible collateral assets. The 'high quality' requirement means that the value of the asset is stable, so it is unlikely to drop substantially in value between the default of a clearing member and the liquidation of the collateral. The presence of a deep and liquid market for a collateral asset is important, as it means that there is a high chance that a posted security can be sold in a short period of time. These desiderata are encouraged by regulation.[85]

7.85 Many collateral assets can change in value between a default and their liquidation, especially if markets are stressed. For this reason, collateral takers—including CCPs—often attribute less value to collateral assets the larger this change can plausibly be. This is typically done by the imposition of a percentage value reduction in the benefit given for securities collateral known as a 'haircut'.

7.86 Haircuts are typically set by asset type, so they might be zero for cash in the same currency as the exposure, a small amount for short-term government bonds in that currency, and a larger amount for longer term government bonds or bonds in a different currency.[86]

7.87 It might be thought that it was most prudent for CCPs (or other collateral takers) to restrict the assets that can be posted to only the highest quality and most liquid assets. This is not necessarily true when required collateral amounts are large. No asset is perfectly liquid, nor is any asset completely free of credit risk.[87] Moreover, the higher the criteria for acceptable collateral are set, the smaller the list of assets that qualify, and hence the more concentrated collateral pools will be.

---

84 See Holden et al. (2016) for a longer discussion of CCP collateral. Most of the discussion in this section also applies to bilateral collateral taking: see Chapter 7 in Gullifer & Payne (2011).

85 The PFMI say that CCPs 'should generally limit the assets it (routinely) accepts as collateral to those with low credit, liquidity, and market risks'. There is, however, no objective standard for any of these three requirements.

86 EMIR article 41 requires in part that haircuts 'recognize that collateral may need to be liquidated in stressed market conditions and take into account the time required to liquidate it'. They should be set 'taking in consideration the relevant criteria, including: the type of asset and level of credit risk associated with' the collateral asset; its maturity, price volatility and market liquidity, and any foreign exchange and/or wrong-way risk.

87 Some government bonds are often cited as credit-risk-free, but no financial construct is perfect. For instance, the United States defaulted (for a short period) on T-bills in 1979 and came within a few days of defaulting during the debt ceiling crisis of 2013, as Ozdagli & Peek (2013) discuss.

This means that market liquidity is more likely to be challenged by the volumes of collateral being liquidated if a large poster becomes stressed. It also means that a large volume of collateral will have to be substituted if a previously-eligible asset is deemed suddenly ineligible, again creating liquidity stress.

7.88 Therefore, it will typically be sensible for CCPs to accept a wider range of acceptable collateral than just those assets currently viewed as of the highest credit quality, adjusting for the additional risk involved using haircuts. This, in turn, allows CCPs to set prudent concentration limits on the amount of a particular collateral asset that can be posted while leaving collateral providers with some flexibility in how to meet collateral calls.

The collateral system

7.89 Many counterparties do not have large cash balances waiting in case they receive a margin call. Rather, their cash is invested in assets, many of which are not eligible for posting as margin. When a risk factor moves, portfolio values change, and there is a flow from losers to winners across the CCP for cleared trades, and directly from losers to winners for variation-margined bilateral portfolios. Portfolio changes or reactions of initial margin models to changing conditions can create margin calls too. These are also sometimes met with cash.

7.90 Thus, a margin call often triggers the need to convert an asset into cash, either through a sale or using a repo transaction. Moreover, as discussed above, once cash arrives at a CCP or a bilateral counterparty, it is often invested. This means that margin posting at CCPs and in the bilateral market should be seen as part of a broader system of flows, as illustrated in Figure 7.4. This collection of flows of cash and securities is known as the collateral system.[88]

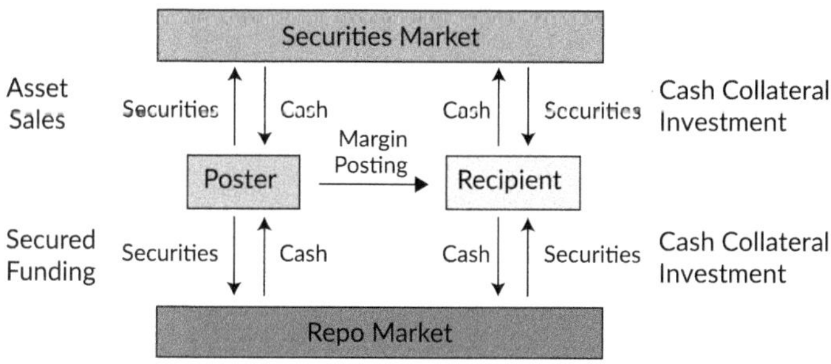

Figure 7.4– The collateral system

7.91 In key currencies, notably US dollars, the repo market is the most important part of the collateral system: those called for margin often repo securities to

[88] This figure is taken from Holden et al. (2016), where the term is introduced. A more comprehensive version of this figure would include the banking and custodial arrangements—including, often, the central banking arrangements—which facilitate the posting of margin.

obtain it; those it is posted to reverse repo the cash to invest it.[89] This, in turn, means that orderly margining relies on a healthy repo market.[90]

Liquidity risks created by CCPs

7.92 Margin models are risk-based, and risk estimates are lower in placid markets than in tumultuous ones. Therefore, more margin is often demanded by CCPs for the same portfolio when markets become stressed. Analogously to the same issue in capital requirements, this phenomenon is known as the procyclicality of margin. In the next few subsections, it is explored using a history of price changes from 1984–2020 of an example foreign exchange portfolio which is sensitive to the US dollar/Japanese yen ('USD/JPY') exchange rate.[91]

7.93 Figure 7.5 shows how three different risk estimates for a USD/JPY portfolio increased during the early Covid-related market stress in March 2020.[92] The three estimates have quite different degrees of reactiveness: the most sensitive (the solid line) increases by a factor of more than three from the start of 2020 to its peak on 22 March, while the least reactive (the dashed line) only increases by a factor of about 1.5.

7.94 If the increase in the margin required for a portfolio is too large, then the counterparty to it may not be able to meet the margin call, and may have to reduce its position or—in extremis—fail. Counterparties might not be prepared to post more than three times as much margin as had been required a week prior, for instance. Thus, the funding liquidity risk created by a change in margin requirements can be destabilizing, as discussed in Chapter 1.

7.95 The extent of the variability of margin depends on the design of the margin model. There is no a priori 'right' degree of reactiveness to market conditions which perfectly measures risk. Rather, it is necessary to test the performance of different margin models for various portfolios in a range of conditions and see how well they perform: this is backtesting, discussed in paragraphs 5.17 and 7.31.

---

89 Asset sales typically do not settle fast enough to meet CCP collateral calls, so if the asset sale is necessary to meet the call rather than to top a cash buffer back up, then same day repo might be the only choice available.

90 This is another reason that the repo market dysfunction referred to in Chapter 4, footnote 38, was so problematic. Derivatives markets have become more reliant on repo as funding markets have evolved and the size of cleared risk—and hence of margin flows—has increased. This became particularly noticeable during the Covid stress of early March. As Brainard (2021) put it, this 'generated exceptionally large flows of cash through CCPs from market participants with mark-to-market losses to those participants with corresponding gains'.

91 See Murphy & Vause (2021) for further details of the portfolio and the analysis conducted.

92 The three estimates are all exponentially weighted moving average volatility estimates: the reference numbers shown in the figure are the decay constants used. In each case, a ten year estimation window is used.

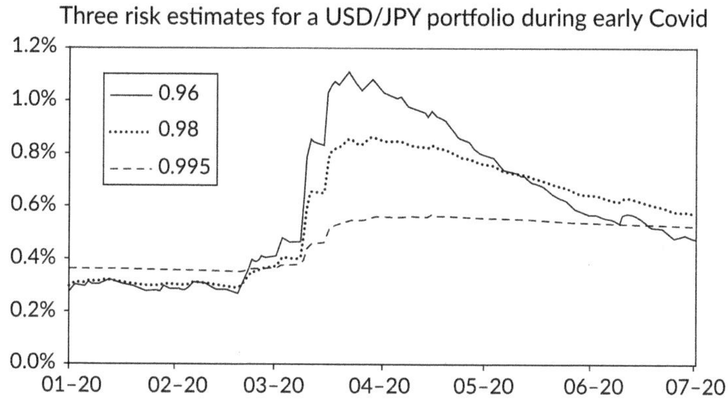

Figure 7.5- Three different risk estimates for a USD/JPY portfolio for the period January–July 2020

7.96 Backtesting is a relatively undiscriminating tool: models with quite different margin requirements in stress can pass it. Indeed, initial margin models based on all three of the risk estimation approaches in Figure 7.5 pass backtesting.[93] Tests of the accuracy of risk estimation, in other words, do not tell us much about how high margin should go in extreme stress.

7.97 Liquidity stress on market participants can occur in two broad classes of situation. First, after a period of prolonged market placidity, when markets become somewhat stressed. Here the issue is that the era of calm has become normal, and some market participants may have taken on positions which are outsized compared to their capacity to post additional margin. It is therefore important that margin does not go too low during placid periods.

7.98 The second aspect of procyclicality policy relates to reactions to extreme stress scenarios. Here, we want to avoid calling for an excessive and unnecessary amount of margin.

7.99 The relative frequency and risk of placid vs stressed markets is important to this discussion. Figure 7.6 shows the distribution of these three risk measures for the period studied. A number of stylized facts can be gleaned from this figure:

- All three risk measures vary to some degree, with all displaying readings at least as low as 0.32% (reflecting placid markets) and as high as 1.2% (reflecting stressed ones). The more reactive models have a wider spread of estimates.

93 Specifically, the hypothesis that they correctly estimate volatility for the portfolio concerned is passed at 99% confidence using the Berkowitz test on the residuals, and filtered historical simulation value-at-risk models based on them pass the Kupiec test. For a further analysis of the power of backtesting and references to the various backtests in common use, see Gurrola Perez (2018) and for the Berkowitz test specifically, Berkowitz (2010).

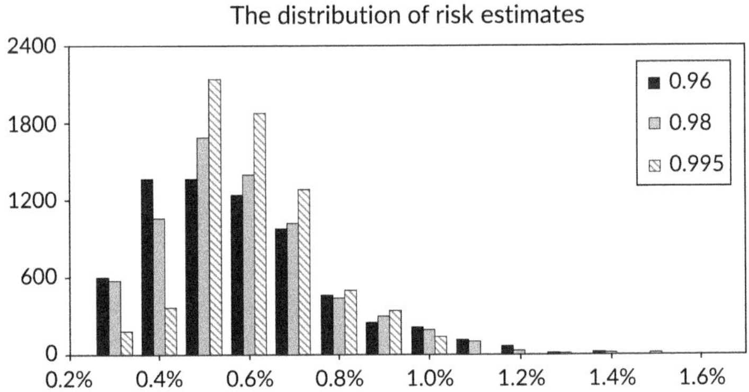

Figure 7.6– The distribution of each of the three different risk estimates, March 1994–October 2020

- The market is placid, with a risk estimate below 0.65%, more than half the time.[94] Risk estimates during these extended placid periods vary significantly. The most reactive measure is less than 0.4% on 770 days, but the least reactive measure only goes this low on 390 days.
- Stressed markets are relatively rare but much riskier than average markets. The most reactive measure is less than 1.3% 99% of the time, but it has 20 readings above 1.5%, and peaks above 1.85%, for instance.
- The most reactive model produces higher risk estimates than its two peers on days of extreme stress.
- The distributions of the three different risk measures have similar shapes, but different parameters. The most reactive one, in hatched grey, has a lower minimum and higher maximum, while the least reactive is more clustered around its average value.

Mitigating the procyclicality of initial margin models

7.100 The need to regulate initial margin model procyclicality follows from the choice to use mandate OTC derivatives clearing. Before the mandate, CCPs were free to choose margin models in consultation with their risk committees, and market participants were free to decide whether to clear with them or not, given all of the obligations involved, including posting the margin demanded. After the mandate, this freedom disappeared. CCPs now had a public policy purpose, and hence there was a need to ensure that they did not create too much systemic risk through their margin policies.

[94] The unconditional volatility during the whole period is 0.655%: the median conditional volatility for the three different exponentially weighted moving average models are 0.59%, 0.6%, and 0.63% respectively.

7.101 EU regulation requires that CCPs use tools to reduce margin model procyclicality, whether they behave too procyclically or not. Specifically, CCPs are required to apply one of three 'anti-procyclicality' or 'APC' tools.[95] They must either:

Floor margin requirements in all conditions at the level they would have 'using volatility estimated over a ten year historical lookback period';[96] or

Take an additional buffer of at least a quarter of the calculated margin, which can be released 'in periods where calculated margin requirements are rising significantly'; or

Weight stressed observations by at least 25% in the calculation of margin.

7.102 The first tool aims to ensure that margin does not go too low in placid periods. Figure 7.7 shows the impact of the ten year floor on the risk estimate from the most reactive model used in the previous section.

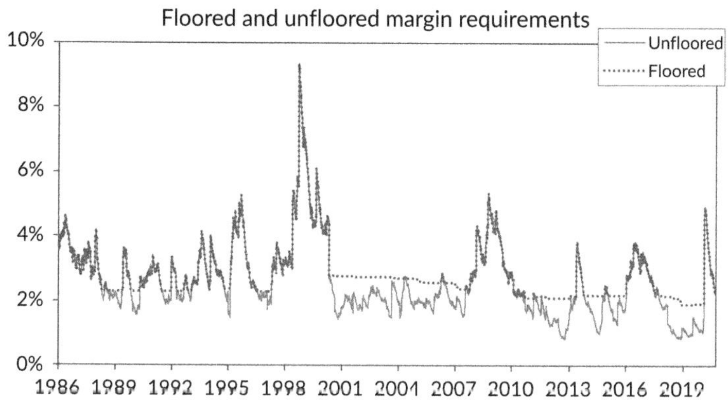

Figure 7.7- The behaviour of the ten year floor on margin

7.103 It can be seen that the floor is effective at its intended job, but that it does nothing to prevent margin from spiking in highly stressed periods, such as those around the Lehman default in late 2008 or early Covid in early 2020.

7.104 The behaviour of the buffer tool is impossible to determine without knowledge of when it will be released. If it is released too early, before high stress hits, then it is relatively ineffective at reducing the biggest liquidity demands: but if it is only released in extreme conditions, it simply has the effect of increasing margin demands by a quarter nearly all the time. The existence of rare but very

[95] See article 28 of the EMIR RTS. For a further discussion of these tools and their behaviour, see Murphy et al. (2014) or for a different perspective, Raykov (2018a).

[96] This is commonly interpreted as 'using the *unweighted* volatility estimated over a ten year period', and that is probably the intent.

highly stressed markets, with correspondingly high margin requirements, makes an optimal buffer release rule difficult to determine. For the sake of illustration, suppose that the buffer is released if the volatility estimate is over the 90th percentile of historical estimates,[97] and consider the period from the start of 1998 to September 1999.

7.105 Figure 7.8 shows the initial margin calls from models with this buffer and without it. It can be seen that the buffered model was effective at reducing some calls, for instance in June 1998 as the yen plunged. However, some calls are bigger than they would have been without the buffer, for instance during most of the first half of 1998. Worse, the buffer has been exhausted by the time very high stress hits in October 1998, so it can do little to mitigate the large call early in that month. The buffer imposes costs by demanding more margin most of the time, but it is not big enough to meaningfully mitigate the size of the calls in high stress.

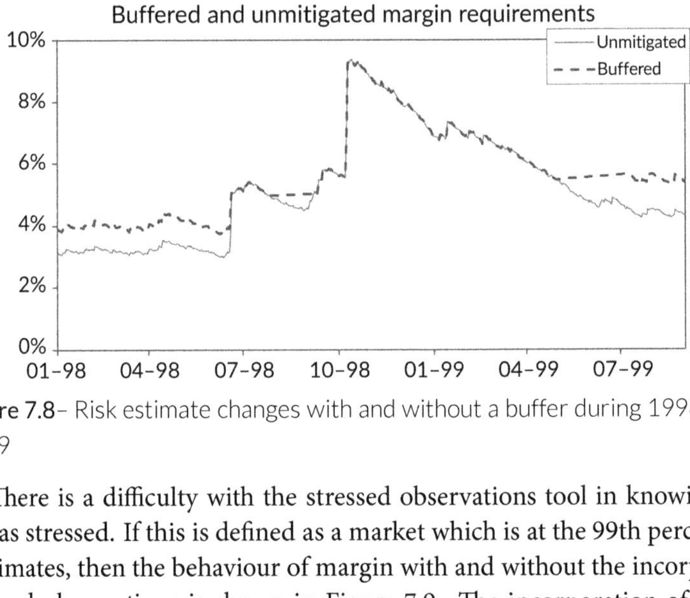

Figure 7.8- Risk estimate changes with and without a buffer during 1998 and 1999

7.106 There is a difficulty with the stressed observations tool in knowing what counts as stressed. If this is defined as a market which is at the 99th percentile of risk estimates, then the behaviour of margin with and without the incorporation of stressed observations is shown in Figure 7.9. The incorporation of stressed observations keeps margin a bit higher than it would otherwise be in early 1998.[98] The issue with this is evident at the end of 1998: here, because the current conditions are more stressed than the stressed period used, the anti-procyclicality

[97] The calibration of this threshold is delicate because before the buffer is released, the buffer is in place. Therefore, if we always want the buffer to cover highly stressed margin calls up to some maximum level $m_{\max}$, the threshold for releasing the buffer, m_0 say, should satisfy $m_{\max} - m_0 \approx 0.25m_0$.

[98] This effect is more pronounced in really placid markets, such as those of 2004–2007. Here, margin is about 30% larger than it would have been without the incorporation of stressed observations.

tool *reduces* the margin requirement. This is only prudent if the estimate before mitigation is overstated in these periods of high stress.

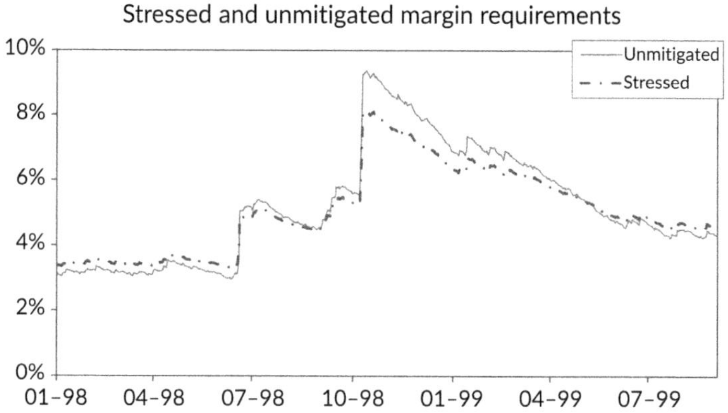

Figure 7.9– Initial margin with and without stressed observations during 1998 and 1999

Appraising European anti-procyclicality regulation

7.107 A review of the anti-procyclicality tools in EMIR produces a mixed scorecard. On one hand, EMIR goes beyond the PFMIs, identifying the procyclicality of initial margin as something that requires consideration, and imposing the requirement to use a tool. The floor is effective at reducing the risk of margin falling too far in placid markets. On the other hand, EMIR requires the use of a tool whether the underlying model is excessively procyclical or not. The effectiveness of the buffer at reducing the impact of highly stressed markets is dependent on when it is released, and the requirement to include 25% stressed observations can be imprudent in some cases. Worst of all, these three tools are hard-coded[99] in difficult-to-change legislation, so if a CCP had a better approach to procyclicality mitigation, it would not be EMIR compliant, and the route to making it so would be long.[100]

7.108 One way to open up the policy question here is to consider the nature of the market participants involved. Non-bank end-users have less access to liquidity

[99] 'Hard-coded' meaning that the required tool is specified in the text of legislation, in this case article 28 of the EMIR RTS, and so modifying it would require changing the legislation. The process for changing Level 2 legislation, such the RTS, is difficult: for level 1, such as EMIR, it is even more complex and time-consuming.

[100] Murphy et al. (2016) suggests that an 'adaptive stressed' approach whereby more stressed observations are used in placid market and fewer in more volatile conditions. This approach outperforms the non-adaptive approach, acting more like a floor when risk is low but offering some mitigation in market turbulence without the same reduction in risk estimates in the most stressed markets.

than banks, typically, so services where most of the risk is borne by clients should probably have more constraining procyclicality requirements than one where the risk transfer is primarily between banks. Policy should therefore set limits on the variability of initial margin requirements in particular situations, based on the composition of the clearing service. One could, for instance, require that margin varied by no more than a factor of two between placid markets (perhaps defined as those in the bottom 10% of risk estimates) and highly stressed ones (those in the top 1% perhaps) for services where non-financial clients contribute more than a quarter of the total margin, while setting the limit at a factor of four for bank-oriented clearing services. These numbers are crude estimates which would require calibration, but the general principal of setting procyclicality policy based on the impact of potential margin calls on posters is an interesting one.[101]

7.109 Disclosure is also an important aspect of procyclicality policy. If market participants are aware of the potential margin calls which might be made on their portfolios should the market become stressed, then they can reasonably be expected to prepare for them. Thus it is important for CCPs to make tools available which allow market participants to estimate what the margin required for their portfolio might be in various conditions.

CCP liquidity needs in default management

7.110 If a clearing member defaults, contract continuity means that CCPs should continue to make variation margin payments to non-defaulters despite potentially not being in receipt of inflows from the defaulter. The opposite situation can occur too: the CCP may owe a variation margin payment to the defaulter. CCP rule books typically permit it to withhold that payment. Moreover, a clearing member may technically be defaultable, perhaps because it is likely to breach one of the conditions of membership, but may nevertheless continue to make payments to the CCP when they fall due. The CCP then has to decide whether to actually place the clearing member in default. One situation where this may be particularly delicate is when the clearing member is a bank in resolution.

7.111 A CCP may require liquidity to manage a default, for instance to pay auction participants. Where a portfolio is auctioned in several pieces, or where the CCP has to buy in long positions before it is paid for shorts, the resulting liquidity need can be greater than the net value of the portfolio.[102]

---

101 See Murphy & Vause (2021) for a further discussion of this proposal and a cost-benefit analysis of various approaches to procyclicality mitigation: we return to this in Chapter 9.

102 Thus, the liquidity needs in default management of repo and securities clearing services are often larger than those of derivatives CCPs: see King et al. (2020) for a further discussion of these and other aspects of CCP funding liquidity risk.

7.112 Regulation requires that CCPs plan their liquidity arrangements to meet their potential needs.[103] This includes ensuring that the maturity profile of a CCP's investments gives it access to sufficient cash to meet unexpected liquidity demands, and obtaining lines of credit or other sources of liquidity where necessary to supplement this.

7.113 EMIR mandates that CCPs have access to a pool of liquidity. The sizing of this pool is done analogously to cover 2 for default risk. CCPs are required to calculate daily their potential liquidity needs caused by 'the default of at least the two clearing members to which it has its largest exposures'. The regulation defines the liquidity need caused by the failure of a clearing member as the sum of the shortfalls generated by its non-performance in each of its roles at the CCP.[104] This 'cover 2 liquidity' requirement entails ranking members by the total size of liquidity shortfall their failure in all roles would cause, and ensuring that the CCP has access to sufficient liquidity to meet the sum of the two largest such shortfalls.

7.114 The resulting need for contingent liquidity can be very substantial. Indeed, it is so large in some cases that it is surprising that CCP liquidity risk receives relatively little attention in the literature compared to CCP counterparty credit risk. For some CCPs, especially those clearing securities and repo markets, it can be the more important of the two risk classes.

7.115 Some CCPs have access to central bank liquidity backstops,[105] which reduces 'their dependence on commercial banks and repo markets for liquidity'. A reasonable view is that the 'availability of such a safety net in times of market strain is critical to financial stability',[106] but practice is variable globally.[107] Moreover, globally systemic CCPs might require emergency liquidity in multiple currencies, so this would require central banks to be able to provide liquidity outside their currency of issue.

7.116 This discussion demonstrates the delicate interplay between counterparty credit risk and liquidity risk in clearing. Using collateralization to reduce the first of these risks usually has implications for the second.

---

103 For instance, article 44 of EMIR states that a 'CCP shall at all times have access to adequate liquidity to perform its services and activities'.

104 Note that payment netting is not assured in this context.

105 For instance, at the time of writing, the Bank of England provides access to its Sterling Monetary Framework to central counterparties 'operating in the UK markets either authorized under EMIR or recognized by ESMA': see R. Bank of England (2020) at 3.

106 The quotes are from IMF (2018) at 21.

107 A prominent example of a central bank which has a high bar for lending to CCPs is the Federal Reserve: Section 806 of the Dodd-Frank Act allows advances in 'unusual or exigent circumstances'. The same section does however permit the Fed to open deposit accounts for CCPs that are designated as systemically important in the United States, so CCPs named as such can leave cash at the Fed but cannot easily borrow from it.

Risks in and around CCP Operations

7.117 CCPs are designed to take and mitigate counterparty credit risk. In the course of doing that, they also take other risks. Liquidity risk, discussed above, is the most prominent of these, but there are more. This section discusses these other risks arising from central clearing.

Operational risks at CCPs

7.118 The PFMIs require that a CCP should 'identify, monitor, and manage its general business risk'.[108] Prominent issues here include:

- *Cyber risk.* Central clearing is an almost completely computerized activity. This means that inadvertent or deliberate programming, systems or connectivity issues can disrupt it. The potential damage a hacker could do were they able to control a large CCP's payment or settlement flows, even for a few minutes, is enormous.
- *Investment risk.* CCPs invest large amounts of cash. This can create losses either through fraudulent activity, as in a rogue trader incident, or simply through unfortunate investment selection.
- *Custody risk.* Very large quantities of assets are held by custodians or central securities depositories in CCPs' names or the names of their clearing members or clients. The PFMIs[109] require that a CCP 'should safeguard its own and its participants' assets and minimize the risk of loss on and delay in access to these assets', but doing so may not be straightforward. In particular, collateral pools are often added to or subtracted from, and there are often multilevel, cross-border holding chains involved in the use of securities collateral.[110] The needs for convenience, the ability to optimize collateral, low cost, and high safety are in conflict with each other here.

7.119 CCPs' operational risks are mitigated in a variety of ways. The first line of defence are 'appropriate systems, policies, procedures, and controls', as the PFMIs put it, which are 'designed to ensure a high degree of security and operational

[108] See Principle 15.

[109] See Principle 16.

[110] Custodians do not typically accept liability for negligence by sub-custodians, and they may not grant the right of action of the ultimate beneficiary against them: this makes custodian risk more problematic. For a further discussion, see ISSA (2017) and, in particular, the table at 9. Given this, there is merit in extending the currently uncommon practice of CCPs (and indeed other systemically important collateral takers) having accounts in their own name at central securities depositories.

reliability'.[111] These should be supplemented by highly robust business continuity arrangements. However, losses can still occur and, if they do, they must be absorbed, or the CCP will fail.

7.120 Some CCP rule books permit the clearing house to allocate certain types of operational risk losses to clearing members. This is most common for investment and custody risks, where the argument is that the clearing members have a say in the policy, both through their participation in the CCP's risk committee and through their decision of which assets to post as collateral, so they should bear the consequences of their decisions. Many clearing members do not find this argument persuasive,[112] but it is supported by some CCP regulators.[113]

7.121 For other risks, the CCP is largely or wholly responsible for any loss. CCP equity is the only resource available to absorb losses which are not allocatable or insured.[114] However, many large CCP's equity capital bases are relatively small,[115] especially compared to the operational risk capital requirements of some comparably systemic banks,[116] and to the sizes of substantial operational risk loss events,[117] so it is difficult to conclude that the equity in the CCP entity is sufficiently large to absorb extreme but plausible non-allocatable operational risk losses.[118]

Legal risks

7.122 Legal risks at CCPs are broadly based, and include the conduct of their business (including issues of *ultra vires*), cross-border and conflict of law problems (including those created or modified by Brexit), and questions of contractual enforceability. The PFMI recognize the issue here. Principal one requires CCPs to

111 See Principle 17.

112 For a discussion of the clearing member position, see FIA & ISDA (2020).

113 See Regulation 3 of the Financial Services and Markets Act 2000 (Over the Counter Derivatives, Central Counterparties and Trade Repositories) (No. 2) Regulations 2013 amending the Financial Services and Markets Act 2000 (Recognition Requirements for Investment Exchanges and Clearing Houses) Regulations 2000 for the requirement for UK CCPs to allocate investment losses.

114 For a further discussion of non-default losses, see Lewis & McPartland (2017).

115 They are typically in the hundreds of millions of dollars range.

116 HSBC's and Morgan Stanley's operational risk RWAs at end 2020 were coincidentally both around $94B, so the capital supporting them at 8% was about $7.5B. This size is typical for a large bank.

117 The loss for the JPMorgan 'London Whale' event was about $6B; for Société Générale's Jerome Kerviel event, about €4.9B.

118 There is also potentially the problem of knowing what the allocatable vs non-allocatable part of a loss is, given that potentially non-allocatable losses may occur when a large financial institution has failed; that that institution will likely have multiple relationships with the CCP, some of which may be covered by the default waterfall, and some not; and that there may be full netting of claims against a defaulter in bankruptcy.

have 'a well-founded, clear, transparent, and enforceable legal basis for each material aspect of its activities in all relevant jurisdictions'. This is easier to regulate for than it is to achieve, as some of the issues involved are subtle.[119]

7.123 In this section, we concentrate on legal risks in default management, as these are among the most dangerous challenges for CCPs. Typical clearing members of derivatives CCPs are large financial institutions. These kinds of firms rarely default. This means that most of the time, the ability of the CCP to meet its fundamental purpose—to protect non-defaulting clearing members from defaulters—is untested. It is only occasionally that definitive information on CCPs' ability to manage defaults emerges.

7.124 Partly thanks to the clearing mandate, clearing members' portfolios at derivatives CCPs are getting larger. Therefore, if a default does happen, the amounts at stake are enormous. It is difficult to imagine that the default of substantial clearing member, or indeed a large client, will not result in litigation.[120]

7.125 The legal position regarding default management is complex partly because the law in these areas has evolved slowly and piecemeal. The position in English law of some of the key aspects of CCP activity is sketched below.

- *Contractual issues.* Clearing members enter into contracts with CCPs: the contractual framework includes the CCP's rule book, as well as the terms of cleared contracts, and any other relationships the clearing member has with the CCP. As with other contractual arrangements, there are issues of capacity, construction, and waiver. In particular, CCP rules define the events of default which would allow a CCP to begin the default management process. It is essential that if a CCP starts this process, its rules provide valid grounds for the commencement, and that other requirements, such as resolution regulations, do not supervene. The default must then be managed according to the rules, reasonably, and rationally.[121]
- *Are there general protections for CCP action?* CCPs benefit from some of the most extensive safe harbour provisions found anywhere in the financial system. These protections provide special treatment under insolvency law for many of the things CCPs do in default management.[122] However, it is

119 Braithwaite & Murphy (2017a) and Turing (2021) give longer accounts of the questions here.

120 See Braithwaite (2020) for an account of many of the derivatives-related cases relating to the default of Lehman Brothers: simply putting a CCP in the middle of risk transfer arrangements does not eliminate the possibility of all of these kinds of challenge.

121 See Braithwaite & Murphy (2017a) at 304–316.

122 Part VII of the Companies Act 1989 expressly protects market contracts, market charges, and market property from specific provisions of insolvency law, and also provides, at section 159, a general disapplication of insolvency law where it conflicts with market contracts and the default rules of recognized clearing houses (among other protections).

not a perfect shield against all challenges, not least because it interacts with and is overlaid by other legislative instruments.[123]

- *Settlement finality.* The PFMIs require that CCPs 'provide clear and certain final settlement, at a minimum by the end of the value date'. CCPs, of course, are unable to do this without a supportive legal framework[124] which eliminates the risk that a purported settlement is unpicked in bankruptcy. CCPs have substantial legal defences in major jurisdictions here, but they are not 'certain'.[125]
- *Collateral enforceability.* The enormous amounts of initial margin at leading derivatives CCPs discussed above suggest that there are potentially substantial resources available to manage a default. This is only certain if the CCP can take the collateral and sell it when necessary without fear of challenge. Supporting this, certain financial collateral arrangements, as they are known, are protected from delay, or the unpicking of netting, caused by insolvency or reorganization of a counterparty.[126] While these provide substantial protection for qualifying arrangements, there is always the question whether specific CCP collateral rules qualify for them.[127]
- *Public law challenges.* Market participants with experience of derivatives trading will be familiar with many private law challenges.[128] The issues that arise from the application of public law standards to CCPs may be more

123 Arias-Barrera (2018) points out that the legal protection for CCP action in default management may be too strong. Her point is that if the purpose of OTC derivatives reform is to reduce the losses to the defaulter's estate on close-out of OTC derivatives—as discussed for Lehman Brothers in Fleming & Sarkar (2014)—then having a legal framework for default management where the only limit on CCP action is 'utmost negligence' is not necessarily optimal.

124 The relevant UK instrument here is the Financial Markets and Insolvency (Settlement Finality) Regulations 1999/2979, which was implemented the EU Settlement Finality Directive 1998/26/EC.

125 Among the issues where the walls are lower than might be wished in English Law are the treatment of settlements which extend over the day of insolvency, foreign insolvency challenges, and the inability to guarantee certainty of settlement even if matching instructions have been submitted to the relevant settlement system: see Turing (2021) at 13.32.

126 The Financial Collateral Arrangements (No. 2) Regulations 2003/3226 implement the EU Financial Collateral Arrangements Directive 2002/47/EC.

127 One important class of issues relate to CCPs understandable commercial desire to give clearing members flexibility over collateral substitution and withdrawal of excesses. However, English Law requires that the collateral taker has possession or control of securities collateral. Exactly which rights to manage their collateral pool a CCP can grant before breaching this requirement are unclear, but certainly the collateral taker must have a legally valid right to prevent withdrawal of collateral: see Braithwaite & Murphy (2017a) at 316–321 and Turing (2021) at 13.42.

128 These can loosely be grouped under the headings of capacity and suitability; interpretation of contractual terms; valuation and close-out mechanisms; interaction of close-out provisions with

novel. However, given that CCPs now exercise their functions to meet a public policy purpose, a challenge on this basis is possible.[129] This may result in CCP decision making being held to a substantially higher standard than would be the case in a private law setting.

7.126 These challenges are complicated and often intensified by the cross-border character of most derivatives clearing, the intermediated nature of many of the relationships, including collateral holding and client clearing, and the potential for conflict of CCP default management arrangements with local insolvency law and resolution policy.

7.127 Legal risk forms another challenge to the adequacy of CCP equity levels. While such challenges are rare, if one were to succeed, the loss will likely be large. Indeed, even the filing of a credible case against a CCP could be enough to trigger a precipitous fall in confidence in the clearing house, given the paucity of resources most CCPs have available to absorb the loss.

The Organization of CCP Regulation

7.128 In previous sections, tensions have been seen to arise from the use of a financial market infrastructure designed for one purpose to meet a different purpose. The same kind of tension occurs in the reuse of supervisory architecture.

7.129 Clearing services are housed in legal entities. A legal entity has a domicile: LCH Limited is a UK company; CME Group Inc. is an American one. The supervision of financial institutions, including FMIs, was originally based on domicile, so the lead supervisor of the activities conducted in LCH Limited is the Bank of England,[130] while the CFTC has authority over CME. Different CCP regulators have different rule sets, although all the principal ones implement the PFMI.

7.130 Some of the functions of financial market infrastructures, including derivatives clearing, are mostly efficiently carried out in a single global entity. This achieves the full benefit of multilateral netting, but it means that institutions in many countries deal with the leading derivatives CCPs. SwapClear's 87 clearing members are spread across globe, as are CME's 57. Therefore, actions at either of these CCPs, and at others, can spread far beyond their domicile. This section deals with the regulatory consequences of that spread.

insolvency law; choice of law and cross-border issues; collateral enforceability and settlement finality: see Braithwaite (2020) for a thorough discussion.

[129] Indeed, it has happened: see *United Co Rusal plc v. London Metal Exchange* [2014] EWCA Civ 1271, discussed in Braithwaite & Murphy (2017b). The related issue of the amenability of financial regulation to judicial review is discussed in the next chapter.

[130] This supervisory authority is granted by Part XVIII of the Financial Services and Markets Act 2000.

Supervisory nexus and cooperative oversight arrangements

7.131 The term 'supervisory nexus' refers to the authority that a supervisor has over an entity, if any.[131] Typically, legislation grants powers to national supervisors which give them supervisory nexus over domestic entities.[132] However, the fact that someone is regulating does not always fully address the concerns of all supervisors. This is the case for many pieces of global financial market infrastructure, where the supervisors of various countries may wish to establish a nexus over an offshore entity, especially when this entity provides services which are, or plausibly could be, systemically important in the country concerned.[133]

7.132 One potential solution to the issue of supervisory nexus is a 'cooperative oversight arrangement'. Here, a group of regulators, typically led by the relevant national supervisor of an entity, agree to assist each other in pursuing their mandated responsibilities.[134]

7.133 EMIR defines a related type of arrangement. An EMIR 'college' consists 'not only of the competent authorities supervising the CCP but also of the supervisors of the entities on which the operations of that CCP might have an impact', and ESMA.[135] EMIR colleges have a key role in the authorization and ongoing evaluation of European CCPs.

---

131 See Budding & Murphy (2014) for a further discussion.

132 CCPs typically have a single prudential supervisor. They are not often separately supervised for their conduct of business. The division of bank supervision into prudential and conduct of business, with, for instance, the former being conducted in the UK by the PRA and the latter by the FCA, represents a helpful separation of concerns: the conduct of business supervisor can address how clients are treated, without being concerned about the implications of their challenge for the robustness of the entity. The lack of a supervisor focused on how the CCP treats its users and protects their assets is therefore potentially concerning, as Arias-Barrera (2018) discusses.

133 See Turing (2021) at 7.23 and 7.54ff for a discussion.

134 One of the early examples of this was the supervision of CLS, an entity providing settlement services in the global foreign exchange market. This entity is regulated by the Federal Reserve, but such is its importance internationally that a number of authorities from various countries have come together in a cooperative oversight arrangement which provides the members of it with 'a mechanism for mutual assistance in carrying out their individual responsibilities in pursuit of their shared public policy objectives for the safety and efficiency of payment and settlement systems and their focus on the stability of the financial system'. Somewhat opaquely, though, the Protocol for the Cooperative Oversight Arrangement of CLS, available at https://www.federalreserve.gov/paymentsystems/cls_protocol.htm, states that 'The Federal Reserve's *supervisory* role and responsibility for CLS are distinct from and complement the Federal Reserve's *oversight* role and responsibility for CLS' (emphasis mine), so questions naturally arise on the boundary between 'supervision' and 'oversight', and the extent of the supervisory nexus available to foreign authorities on supervisory matters.

135 See articles 18, 19, and 49 of EMIR and article 15 of EMIR 2.2 for more on the membership and role of colleges.

Equivalence

7.134 Cooperation is often helpful, and it may provide sufficient supervisory nexus in some situations. It is easier if the rules that a risk-posing entity is supervised under are equivalent to those that would apply were it located in the country it poses risk to. This 'equivalence' of regulation comes in two flavours. 'Textual equivalence' means that the rules are syntactically identical. This only applies where multiple countries use the same rules, as in the EU. 'Outcomes-based equivalences' turns on the idea that, while two rule sets have different provisions, they can lead to (broadly) the same outcomes.

7.135 The issue here is who determines whether outcomes are the same and on what basis. Equivalence is instantiated in a particular way when the baseline for the comparison is EU requirements.[136] Here, an equivalence determination is often needed before a firm domiciled outside the EU can access the internal market. For instance, when a CCP outside the EU wishes to clear for EU clearing members, ESMA provides technical advice on equivalence of the rules it is supervised under to the European Commission. The Commission then makes the decision as to whether to deem the rules in the CCP's jurisdiction equivalent.[137] Without this decision, EU counterparties cannot clear at the foreign CCP.

7.136 It appears that EU equivalence decisions are based not just on comparability of outcomes, but also on the materiality of the risk posed: positive decisions were made quickly by the Commission on equivalence for Australia, Hong Kong, and Singapore, but it took somewhat longer to sign off the United States.[138]

7.137 More generally, the adoption of an equivalence decision can be influenced by political considerations.[139] The relative power of the home and host country are important for the outcome. A good example here is the CFTC regime: while these rules do permit foreign CCPs to apply for exemption from the obligation to register with the CFTC, and hence give it full supervisory nexus, the CCP's ability to access the (enormous) US market relies not just on the CCP's home country being regulated under an approach which is comparable to that in the US: it also requires the CCP to accept various restrictions on its business activities.[140]

---

136 See Ferran (2017) for a discussion of equivalence and, in particular, its role post Brexit.

137 For an analysis of the application of US and EU derivatives rules to transactions involving a foreign party, see Knaack (2015), who takes this view that the extraterritorial application of these rules demonstrates a 'coordination failure'.

138 In particular, there was a delay in recognizing that the SEC's regime for US central counterparties led to equivalent outcomes to the EU's.

139 See the discussion of the withdrawal of Switzerland's equivalence in Turing (2021) at 7.2.

140 Foreign CCPs find it difficult to provide client clearing for swaps with US persons without CFTC registration. See Coffee (2014) and Yadav & Turing (2016) for discussion of the extraterritorial reach of US derivatives regulation.

7.138 Situations like this demonstrate that supervisory nexus requirements can be a bureaucratic technique to project a particular regulatory approach beyond national borders.[141]

7.139 The geopolitics of equivalence reveal some of the tensions behind global standards. The regimes being judged all implement the PFMIs,[142] and the PFMIs were negotiated by the same countries as are judging equivalence. But this—and by implication the PFMIs—was not enough to prevent a tussle for supervisory nexus, for the right to make definitions and have them stick. As Cotterrell (2009) puts it in a different context at 5, authority over global CCPs is unsettled, 'a matter of conflict to be resolved—perhaps only provisionally and temporarily for particular purposes in particular contexts—by negotiation, power or influence.'[143]

Location policy

7.140 It is possible to go even further than the US position of gaining supervisory nexus over offshore CCPs by requiring onshore registration. This is the requirement to domicile in the country concerned. A 'location policy' requires that certain clearing services are carried out in a certain jurisdiction, perhaps because of their systemic importance to the country or bloc concerned.

7.141 In 2011, the European Central Bank ('ECB') attempted to impose a location policy requiring the clearing of Euro-denominated instruments within the eurozone. This was challenged at the European Court of Justice, resulting in the ruling that the ECB had did not have the competence necessary to impose such a requirement.[144]

7.142 This was not the end of the story. Revisions to EMIR[145] introduced a distinction between non-systemically important, or 'Tier 1' CCPs and systemically important, or 'Tier 2' ones, with a requirement that Tier 2 CCPs grant ESMA a significant supervisory nexus. Brexit then brought back the prospect of an EU location policy. The contention was made that some Tier 2 CCPs might be so

[141] Brummer (2010) emphasizes that this technique is most effective when the threat to constrain access from offshore parties who refuse to grant the desired nexus is a powerful one.

[142] This is true in broad brush: there was an issue for the SEC when its implementation of the PFMIs was reviewed by CPMI/IOSCO: see R. CPMI & IOSCO (2018) at 24 which found that 2015 SEC regulations were 'consistent with *some* elements of the PFMI' (emphasis mine).

[143] This is especially true when conflicts between CCP regulators, clearing member regulators, and resolution authorities are considered. The last of these is considered in the next section: see also Baker (2016) and Guseva (2016).

[144] *United Kingdom v. European Central Bank* [2015] 3 CMLR 220. The judgment is interesting in that the court only examined the ECB's competence to impose clearing requirements for securities, and decided that it did not have such competence because it lacked responsibility for the regulation of securities settlement systems. As a result, derivatives clearing issues were not considered.

[145] These are known as EMIR 2.2: see Regulation (EU) No. 2019/2099 [2019] OJ L322/1.

systemically important to the EU that *regardless of equivalence*, it is unsafe for them to be domiciled outside the EU.[146] This is a question of the benefits of participating in efficient but offshore arrangements versus the risks of so doing. It is fundamentally a political judgement, and thus one for each jurisdiction to take its own view on.

7.143 At the time of writing, it is unclear whether any Tier 2 CCPs will be required to onshore (and indeed whether the UK CCP regulatory framework will be deemed permanently equivalent to that in the EU).[147] In the next section, an issue which might be important in this question is considered: who deals with CCPs which are close to failure, and how.

CCP Recovery and Resolution

7.144 Bad things can happen to good CCPs—and indeed to less good ones. A (very much non-exhaustive) list of events that could cause stress at a CCP is:

- the default of one or more clearing members causing losses larger than the defaulters' resources plus the default fund;
- the inability to close out a defaulter's portfolio, leaving the CCP with unknown but likely large losses;
- hacking of the CCP's systems which results in the CCP having inaccurate records of cleared positions or collateral, and/or suffering a theft;
- the failure of one of the CCP's custodians followed by the revelation that it had not properly segregated assets;
- a successful legal challenge to a CCP default management action resulting in a large liability for the CCP.

7.145 Each of these events would have a significantly different trajectory: in some, the losses are known; in others, not. In some, the contractual responsibility for bearing them lies mostly away from the CCP; in others, it is the CCP's problem. Finally, some reflect better on the CCP's management than others. The problem of addressing stressed CCPs is therefore a complex one, as there is no panacea for every type of event. Even before the clearing mandate, it would have been problematic to let a large CCP fail: now, the impact of a disorderly failure would be much worse.[148] This means that a range of tools to stabilize troubled CCPs are needed.

---

146 See Moloney (2020) for a further discussion.

147 ESMA has recognized three UK CCPs as third country CCPs eligible to provide their services in the EU until 30 June 2022.

148 See Tucker (2013) and Wendt (2015) for a discussion here.

7.146 We have already seen that there are many classes of stakeholder in clearing, beyond the CCP's clearing members, and that a common position among all stakeholders is that someone else, and not them, should pay to address the issue if a CCP is failing. The first stage of adjudicating between these competing interests and rights is contained in the CCP's rule book. This contains various 'recovery' provisions aimed at stabilizing the CCP after stress.[149]

7.147 These private powers may not be sufficient. The total (default and non-default) loss across might be too large to be absorbed by the resources available under recovery arrangements; it might not be fixed, perhaps because the CCP cannot fully liquidate the defaulter's portfolio; or confidence might have been lost in the CCP, and market participants are reluctant to fully cooperate with the recovery plan.[150]

7.148 In these cases, it may be in the public interest and/or in the interests of financial stability for the authorities to step in. This 'resolution' process is intended to enhance the likelihood of continuity of provision of clearing and reduce the risk of close-out of currently cleared trades. It is carried out by a public 'resolution authority' who may or may not be the CCP supervisor: the rest of this section discusses it in more detail.[151]

Recovering stressed CCPs

7.149 Regulation[152] requires that CCPs should have recovery plans to 'address circumstances that may give rise to any uncovered loss, liquidity shortfall or capital inadequacy'. They would typically be triggered if a CCP cannot close a defaulter's position; if the losses on so doing were beyond the funded waterfall; or if there is a non-default loss which is not immediately covered without causing capital inadequacy. For default losses, this means that the beginning of recovery is a failed auction or a loss which requires a default fund call, variation margin gains haircutting, or other end of the waterfall resources to address.[153]

7.150 In a given episode of stress, it is important to judge whether confidence in the CCP has been lost. If so, this may suggest triggering resolution sooner

[149] The traditional dictum that those who have the most at stake in a corporation have the most say in its affairs is difficult to implement because who has what at stake in a CCP is highly state dependent. This means that the governance issues around recovery plans are particularly delicate.

[150] In practice, there is a likely to be a significant gap between 'cooperating to the extent contractually required' and 'being as helpful as reasonably possible'.

[151] For further analysis, see Baker (2019), Cerezetti et al. (2019), Lubben (2017), Singh & Turing (2018), Raykov (2018b), Turing (2019), and, for the international consensus authority view, R. FSB (2017a) and R. FSB (2020b).

[152] See R. CPMI & IOSCO (2014).

[153] This process may have contagious effects, in that it can push losses or liquidity stress or both onto members: see Roe (2013).

rather than later. In contrast, if the recovery plan seems to be working, it is harder to justify the authorities stepping in. The EU recovery and resolution regulation, henceforth the R&R regulation,[154] suggests that intervention may be justified 'where a CCP infringes, or is likely to infringe in the near future, the capital and prudential requirements' of EMIR, or 'poses a risk to financial stability in the Union or in one or more of its Member States, or where the competent authority has determined that there are other indications of an emerging crisis situation that could affect the operations of the CCP, in particular, its ability to provide clearing services'.[155]

7.151 These criteria are somewhat subjective. For a resolution authority, the tension is between triggering resolution before most of the CCP's financial resources are used, thus leaving something for them to work with, but risking the challenge from CCP shareholders that they have unjustifiably interfered with their property rights; and waiting until resolution is more evidently necessary, but there are fewer resources left.[156]

Resolving CCPs

7.152 A key question in resolution is what useful, new tools the authorities have that were not already present in recovery. There are several answers to this, depending on the situation.

7.153 The first advantage a resolution authority has is that it is not the CCP. If the events that led to stress caused a loss of market confidence in the CCP, then simply erecting an 'under new management' sign may be enough. Second, resolution authorities, as *authorities*, have greater powers of suasion. They may, for instance, be able to persuade clearing members to make better bids at an auction than a CCP could. Third and relatedly, they may often have access to central bank liquidity to support CCP operations while a stress is being addressed.[157]

7.154 Resolution authorities are typically also granted particular tools in legislation. The R&R regulation mentions position and loss allocation tools; a write-down and conversion tool; a sale of business tool; and a bridge CCP tool.[158]

[154] See R. EC (2021) and, for a further discussion, Binder (2021).

[155] Article 18.

[156] See Braithwaite & Murphy (2017b) for a further discussion and in particular a treatment of the 'no creditor worse off' principle, which is intended to protect against arbitrary action by resolution authorities, but which is potentially more problematic for CCPs than it is for banks.

Note also that this is another area of potential regulatory conflict, especially where the resolution authority is different from the CCP regulator. The former may encourage a delay to resolution to allow the recovery plan to work, while the latter may prefer a precautionary early intervention.

[157] It is possible to imagine situations where it would not be credible to extend central bank liquidity to a CCP without resolving it.

[158] At article 37.

However, these are tools largely transplanted from bank resolution, and their applicability to CCPs is limited.

7.155 The position and loss allocation tools are likely to be the ones already present in the CCP's rule book, so their force in resolution lies in the fact that the resolution authority, with its incentive structure, reputation, and powers of suasion, is applying them, rather than in the strength of the tool itself.

7.156 The write down tool allows the book value of CCP equity to be reduced, absorbing losses through the use of shareholders' funds. This may be useful at the margin, but as CCPs' equity bases are small and—unlike banks—they do not typically have meaningful liabilities which can be converted to equity upon resolution, it leaves the problem of how to recapitalize the CCP.

7.157 The sale of business and bridge CCP tools envisage taking a clearing service and either selling it or moving it to a new entity. The sale of business tool might be useful once a CCP is stabilized, if there is a credible buyer, but this is unlikely to be a quick solution to a stressed CCP, especially a stressed globally systemic one, given that such a CCP would not have many, or indeed any, credible buyers.

7.158 Both sale and bridge are difficult given many CCPs' legal entity structures. Globally systemic CCPs—for whom resolvability is most important—are typically members of larger groups. Services to the CCP, including vitally important IT services, are often provided by other companies in the same group.[159] There are often multiple clearing services in one legal entity. If one of these clears exchange-traded derivatives, there may be difficulties in separating this from the associated exchange. For all these reasons, isolating a clearing service for resolution and selling it or moving it to a bridge entity is likely to be a challenge.[160] In practice, then, resolution of a globally systemic CCP is likely to involve a recapitalization in place, where the authority persuades someone to inject extra loss-absorbing resources into the relevant legal entity.

7.159 The problem here is intensified by CCP concentration: it is most efficient having a single, global CCP for each asset class, due to the benefits of multilateral netting.[161] But this means that there is no credible competitor to provide clearing services if the global CCP becomes stressed. Moreover, some recovery tools—such as tear up—could be contagious, especially if used by a globally systemic

[159] See article 51 of the R&R regulation for the enforcement of service agreements.

[160] Articles 15–17 of the R&R regulation require an assessment of resolvability and give authorities powers to address barriers identified by this assessment, so it will be interesting to see if CCP legal entity structure is deemed to represent such a barrier, or whether the other powers in the regulation are considered effective without such an action. See Braithwaite & Murphy (2019) for a longer discussion of these issues.

[161] See DAT (2018) and Krahnen & Pelizzon (2016) for more on the facts and implications of CCP concentration.

CCP.[162] It is difficult to conceive of the circumstances in which the full tear up of a globally systemic clearing service would represent the least worst solution to a problem, even given that there are no good solutions.[163]

7.160 None of these tools, then, go to the nub of the problem: who is going to inject extra resources in resolution to absorb losses and recapitalize the CCP? A partial answer is a resolution cash call.[164] This is a tool which allows the authorities to require non-defaulting clearing members to make additional default fund contributions. It therefore provides additional default loss absorbency and the ability to refill the default fund.

7.161 Recapitalizing the CCP is more difficult. Even where the authorities have the power to write-down or transfer instruments of ownership and to issue new equity,[165] they cannot force third parties to subscribe to an equity issue. The lack of a sure recapitalization device poses a particular challenge for large, non-allocatable, non-default losses. Hence, the R&R regulation does permit government or public support of a CCP in resolution,[166] but this is an odious solution, as it involves a taxpayer bailout. For globally systemic CCPs, a better answer might be an arrangement to 'pull down' more capital from the ultimate holding company into the CCP.[167]

7.162 The challenges created by CCPs domiciled in one location but posing systemic risk to another come to a particular focus in CCP resolution. The problem is that a CCP will be resolved by one particular authority.[168] The FDIC describes its

[162] The R&R regulation in article 27 permits resolution authorities in certain circumstances to force a CCP 'to compensate non-defaulting clearing members for their losses stemming from the application of loss allocation tools'.

[163] The rule book power of tear up raises an issue in the assessment of the no creditor worse off safeguard discussed in footnote 156. After a full tear up, there are no cleared claims left. Therefore, if the cause of CCP resolution was partially or wholly a default loss, it would likely be a going concern after full tear up—not insolvent. Given that the safeguard is an analysis of whether a creditor is worse off in insolvency, it is problematic if this state cannot occur. A further issue is that in insolvency, there would likely be full netting of cleared claims from all clearing services in the CCP legal entity (if any) with other claims, for instance from the CCP's investment and settlement activity. This again makes the assessment of whether the no creditor worse off condition has been met difficult, especially in the heat of a resolution action.

[164] See article 31 of the R&R regulation.

[165] Articles 33–35 and 48 of the R&R regulation.

[166] Articles 45 and 46 of the R&R regulation.

[167] In bank regulation parlance, this would be 'internal total loss-absorbing capacity': see R. FSB (2017b).

[168] The EU CCP recovery and resolution regulation goes to considerable lengths to address these issues via requirements for resolution colleges, the ESMA Resolution Committee, provisions for cooperation between authorities, and an extended set of principles for decision making and procedures during resolution.

role as to 'preserve and promote public confidence in the *U.S.* financial system',[169] while the Dodd-Frank Act[170] gives the FDIC the authority 'to liquidate failing financial companies that pose a significant risk to the financial stability *of the United States* in a manner that mitigates such risk and minimizes moral hazard' (emphasis mine).

7.163 These provisions are not unusual. Most resolution authorities, understandably, have mandates based on the financial systems of the countries they operate in.[171] The difficulty is that it is not clear that promoting public confidence in one country's financial system will always produce results which are optimal for another's. If a resolution authority acts to protect taxpayers in its country, will the effect of this be to push losses onto institutions in another country? Concerns like this stimulate the desire from authorities for greater supervisory nexus over systemically important offshore entities.

A CCP regulation is a CCP regulation is a CCP regulation

7.164 CCPs are not banks, as the title of Cox and Steigerwald's well-known paper *A CCP is a CCP is a CCP* emphasizes,[172] and bank regulation should not be blindly transposed to CCPs. But this does not that mean that there is nothing to learn from comparing bank and CCP regulations.

7.165 Financial regulation is historically contingent, as we have seen, and often largely driven by reaction to crisis. CCPs have not been at the centre of an episode of financial instability this century: indeed, after 2008, they were seen as a key part of the solution to financial instability.[173] CCPs have not had a justificatory crisis which would allow their regulators to consolidate into a separate power centre, as bank regulators did after 2008. This of course does not mean that CCPs are robust against all crises: just that a bad one has not happened yet.[174]

7.166 At the level of the rules, bank regulation is focused on loss absorbency and the adequacy of resources. CCP regulation focuses on counterparty credit risk loss absorbency, the allocation of certain non-default losses, and the adequacy

169 See Section 1 of R. FDIC (2020).

170 See R. US Congress (2010) at 204.

171 But see the R&R regulations, article 21: 'The resolution authority shall seek to minimize the cost of resolution *on all affected stakeholders*' (emphasis mine).

172 The paper is Cox & Steigerwald (2017): Hughes & Manning (2015) and Cerezetti et al. (2019) make similar points about the importance of taking into account the 'club-like' nature of CCPs in clearing house regulation.

173 Evocatively, Robert Steigerwald describes this as the 'outsourcing' of financial stability to CCPs.

174 The early Covid period discussed in Chapter 3 is an exemplar of a motivating period of stress. This was intense enough to highlight some issues, including the procyclicality of margin and certain vulnerabilities in the WTI futures market, and to provide an impetus for change, but not so intense that it created a systemic crisis.

of resources supporting liquidity requirements. Comparing this to bank regulation, the gap is non-allocatable non-default losses. A question must therefore arise whether, given their systemic importance, regulation requires CCPs to have enough funded resources to address such events.

7.167 One problem here is the category 'CCP'. This is inhabited by a large range of institutions, some of them rather small, and some global and highly systemic. Given the wildly differing impact of the failure of different sizes of CCP, there is a case for a more differentiation in standards for CCP robustness, so that globally systemic CCPs are held to higher standards of risk management, resourcing, governance, and resolvability, among others, and supervisory nexus over them is widely held.[175]

7.168 The fact that CCP regulation has not yet emerged as a separate power centre from clearing means that its conceptual framework is notably closer to how CCPs describe themselves than bank regulation is to bank definitions: it has tended to follow, or encourage, rather than lead industry practice.[176] The PFMI formalize good practice at CCPs, but they seldom go far beyond it.[177]

7.169 Global CCP regulation is also looser than bank regulation, as the 'P' in 'PFMI' indicates. The principles allow for a wider range of practices to be compliant than the Basel Accords do.[178] Indeed, CCP regulation is closest to the prescriptive style of bank regulation in areas which have been transplanted from it, such as resolution policy. Elsewhere, and especially where implementation of a standard depends on practices which have grown up in divergent ways in different jurisdictions, as with segregation and portability, the PFMI rightly concentrate on what must to be achieved but are often not prescriptive as to how.

7.170 A final suggestion motivated by the comparison of bank and CCP rules is therefore that global financial regulation can be more principles-based, more alert to local conditions, and less coercively policed than the Basel Accords. If it works tolerably well for globally systemic CCPs,[179] then it can work for banks too.

---

175 EMIR 2.2 introduced the concept of Tier 2 CCPs, foreshadowing this differentiation. However, it only imposes incrementally higher standards in a small number of areas.

176 The intent is not to suggest that the current loose tethering of CCP regulation to clearing practice is either a good or bad thing.

177 This is not true of individual CCP regulatory frameworks, which are sometimes prescriptive, as we saw with EMIR's APC tools earlier in the chapter.

178 This is a value judgement, but one that seems reasonable given the difficulty of agreeing that particular implementations of the PFMIs give equivalent outcomes discussed in paragraph 7.135.

179 One caveat here is CCP resolution policy, which cannot yet be said to inspire broad confidence, in part because it is a transplant from bank regulation rather than a standard which builds upon CCP best practice.

Part III

Perspectives on Rules and Rule Making

8

Legal Perspectives on the Legitimacy of Financial Regulation

Introduction to Part III and to the Chapter

8.1 The last four chapters discussed the key elements of regulation applicable to derivatives which were introduced after the 2008 crisis. The next four will use a number of different areas of scholarship to uncover aspects of these rules. These areas are law; the economics of cost-benefit analysis; the theory of modelling; and—as a unit—international political economy and social science. Each area is used as a searchlight, illuminating a different view of financial regulation. This multi-disciplinary approach is helpful precisely because of these differences: while the perspectives overlap, each area gives its own insights.

Insights from different areas

8.2 Legal scholarship provides criteria for analysing the legitimacy of financial regulation and for when it could be subject to review by the courts. It allows us to get a sense of the limits of administrative discretion and when they might be overstepped.

8.3 Cost-benefit analysis is useful because it provides a tool for investigating the effects of a particular rule. It allows us to probe the details of a rule. We could, for instance, ask not whether *some rule* requiring bilateral margin is worthwhile, but whether *this particular rule* requiring bilateral margin for certain specified market participants in particular circumstances is justified, and how the costs and benefits of the rule vary as the specification and circumstances are changed.

8.4 Regulation necessarily involves modelling: it constructs idealized categories into which the financial system is translated, and makes inferences using its own logic based on those categories. When banks use of quantitative models, regulators set requirements for addressing the limited applicability of models, assessing their ongoing performance, and ensuring that their users remain alert to the risks of their use. The models within regulation are prone to the same issues, motivating the need for similar precautions, and suggesting criteria for judging both rules and claims made about them.

8.5 Financial regulation is a community activity. It arises from the actions of a network of individuals sharing a culture and competing for professional status. Regulation is also a technique of government: it arises through a decision to empower an agency under a particular mandate. Investigating the dialogues within and between regulatory agencies, with legislators, and with the regulated, gives insight both into how regulation is made, influenced, promulgated, and defended, and how the choice of institutional arrangements affects these processes.

8.6 In short, derivatives regulation is part of financial regulation, so to understand and improve it, it is helpful to investigate the larger object using a variety of tools which probe its various aspects.

The law

8.7 Our first perspective comes from the law. Financial regulation is formed at two principal levels. The first is created by transnational institutions such as the Basel Committee on Banking Supervision, who were responsible for most of the regulation discussed in Chapters 4 and 5, the Committee on Payments and Market Infrastructure ('CPMI'), and the International Organization of Securities Commissions ('IOSCO'); who, with CPMI, had a large hand in the rules considered in Chapters 6 and 7.

8.8 The transnational approach to prudential standard setting has become commonplace since the late 1980s. An area of legal scholarship, global administrative law, has grown up to study it and related cooperative techniques of global government.[1] This chapter discusses how transnational rules are made, reviews the basic principles of global administrative law, and uses them to probe the nature of modern financial regulation.

8.9 Transnational regulation is law-like: it makes law-like claims; uses law-like techniques; and, in some cases, has law-like enforcement mechanisms. Therefore, the standards of legitimacy developed for global administrative law provide a useful benchmark for evaluating transnational regulation. Much of this chapter is devoted to this assessment and its implications for the institutional design of financial regulation and for its rule making processes.

8.10 The second level of rule making is that of national or bloc rules. Laws, such as the Dodd-Frank Act or EMIR, and the rules of regulatory agencies, such as the

[1] See Csatlós (2019) at 234 for a more detailed description of the architecture of transnational rule making in terms consistent with the perspective of this chapter.

CFTC or ESMA, fall under this heading. The relevant administrative law limits and legitimizes the actions of these regulators.[2]

8.11 A key feature of administrative law in England and Wales, as in many other countries, is the potential for judicial review. Courts can review the actions of public bodies, including financial regulators, and, under some conditions, reverse them. The final section of the chapter considers the amenability of financial regulation to judicial review and the grounds upon which courts will reverse regulators' actions—in this case, actions by the PRA or the Bank of England.[3]

8.12 Judicial review is available for rules implementing transnational regulation, but not for the agreements themselves. As such, it is a useful safeguard against egregious failures by individual regulators, but a poor substitute for a more legitimate transnational policy making process.[4]

Transnational Financial Regulation

8.13 While financial institutions' activities stretch across borders, each institution is based in one country. Regulatory authority is primarily vested in national authorities, or in EU institutions, as discussed in the previous chapter. These authorities regulate local institutions, but the financial system they are responsible for is affected by events elsewhere. Some financial crises, such as that of 2008, influenced economies across the globe. Cross-border financial flows are large. Moreover, it is relatively easy for a bank to lend outside its home country, so there is a danger that a 'lax' jurisdiction could attract financial institutions to redomicile there. If banks subject to lighter regulation become distressed, this could cause instability outside their home country. For all these reasons, financial regulators are incentivized to cooperate and to create common standards. Cooperation also facilitates the sharing of best practice and reduces regulatory development costs.

[2] For instance, in the United States, this would include the Administrative Procedure Act, Pub.L. 79–404, 60 Stat. 237, while in the EU it would include articles 2, 4, and 5 of the Treaty of the EU, article 41 of the Charter of Fundamental Rights, and articles 5, 263, and 298 of the Treaty on the Functioning of the EU.

[3] The Prudential Regulatory Authority, or PRA, is the part of the Bank of England which is responsible for the prudential regulation and supervision of banks, building societies, credit unions, insurers, and major investment firms in the UK. The Bank of England is directly responsible for the supervision of CCPs.

[4] This is not to say that 'legitimacy' is itself an uncontested norm. As Brassett & Tsingou (2011) point out, while questions of legitimacy are a useful tool in uncovering the practices of global governance, we should not defer 'the deeper question of how far those practices are themselves implicated in relations of power that regard certain standards of legitimacy as appropriate'. One person's expert advice from an independent working group is another's elitist stitch-up.

8.14 This section begins with a discussion of the development of regulatory co-operation and outlines the coordination mechanisms which have developed in recent years. We then turn to the process by which cooperating actors jointly develop regulation. A consideration of this process raises questions of governance and legitimacy: the section concludes with these issues.

Motivating coordination

8.15 The Bank of International Settlements, or 'BIS', is a key locus of transnational financial regulation. The origins of this institution lie in sovereign debt, and specifically in German reparations after the First World War.[5] It was set up to incentivize states to adhere to their debt commitments.

8.16 The BIS became a coordination mechanism for bank regulation thanks to episodes of financial stress on either side of the Atlantic. The UK suffered a secondary banking crisis from 1973 to 1975.[6] A little later, in the late 1970s and early 1980s, the United States saw a wave of bank failures as the Fed acted to control inflation and the Latin American sovereign debt crisis of 1982 bit.

8.17 By the mid-1970s, there were concerns that bank supervision had not kept pace with the increasingly cross-border character of banking. The failure of Bank Herstatt in 1974 was a motivating example. This bank had accumulated large foreign exchange positions. It failed late in the trading day, after Herstatt had received large Deutschemark inflows on physically settled FX positions against the US dollar, but—in a classic example of settlement risk—before it was due to pay out on the dollar side. Herstatt's failure to make contractually required USD payments left several New York correspondent banks with substantial losses and created turmoil in the FX market. This highlighted the risks of cross-border activity and the need for supervisory cooperation to address common threats.

8.18 The result was the formation of an international bank regulatory forum. The Basel Committee on Banking Supervision, or simply the 'Basel Committee',

[5] Borio & Toniolo (2006) describe the creation of the BIS as motivated by the challenges arising from the decision to package some of Germany's post War reparations into bonds. Some governments who held this debt wanted to monetize it, and private bankers were keen to help them do so. But, in order for the resulting bonds to be worth very much, given that they were very long term, an enforcement mechanism for sovereign obligations was needed. The BIS was created both to act as a bond trustee, and to provide an incentive for continued bond performance via an agreement to reinvest some of the proceeds in German reconstruction provided that payments of interest and principle continued.

[6] As Schenk (2011) puts it at 3, 'In mid-1974, a sharp monetary expansion and lax regulation prompted a wave of failures across the so-called "fringe banking" sector in London. Property lending based on short-term money market borrowing was at the heart of the liquidity crisis that struck the system … When the real estate boom broke in the autumn of 1973, many institutions were left illiquid.' In short, this was another real-estate-driven banking crisis.

was established by the central bank Governors of the G-10 at the end of 1974, based at the BIS.[7] Early publications from the Committee focused on promulgating sound practices and on supervisory cooperation, notably of banks' foreign operations,[8] evidencing its role as a forum for the central bankers of the leading financial centres to make agreements on topics of common interest. To this day, one half of the Basel Committee's charter is to provide 'a forum for cooperation on banking supervisory matters'.

8.19 The episodes of financial instability in the late 1970s and early 1980s convinced both US and UK central banks that a higher standard of bank capital regulation was needed, and in 1987 they came to a bilateral agreement on common rules.[9] However, the increasing internationalization of banking meant that, if it was going to be effective, the UK and the US needed other countries to agree to their bank capital standard too:[10] otherwise, there was a risk that they would simply lose their large banks to more accommodating jurisdictions. The Basel Committee was the ideal body to coordinate discussions. Negotiations began, based on the US/UK agreement, and these eventually resulted in the international accord on bank capital known as Basel 1.[11] This is the first example of the other half of the Committee's mandate: to act as the 'primary global standard setter for the prudential regulation of banks'.

The features of transnational financial regulation

8.20 Basel 1, like subsequent bank capital Accords, had a number of key features:

- it was a transnational agreement created by negotiation and representing a consensus within the group;
- it did not have the force of a treaty, but nevertheless represented a commitment by the participants to implement the agreed standard;
- this commitment was (at first loosely) policed by exhortation;
- it was constructed by bank regulators; and
- it was not subject to parliamentary scrutiny.

[7] The impact of the failure of Bank Herstatt on the FX market was also the motivation for the introduction of measures to reduce settlement risk.

[8] See R. BCBS (1983).

[9] See Goodhart (2011) at 167–171.

[10] As Goodhart (2011) describes at 550, a major motivation for the joint US/UK push for harmonization was the rapidly increasing size and reach of Japanese banks in the 1980s. Both jurisdictions were concerned about the risk that a Japanese banking crisis could pose to the global economy, and—in a precursor to the supervisory nexus discussion in the last chapter—they were prepared to use the threat of excluding Japanese banks from their markets to incentivize cooperation.

[11] Basel 1 is R. BCBS (1988).

8.21 The term 'soft law' has been introduced for agreements like these.[12] For our purposes, it will be helpful to consider both the transnational regulatory standards and the community and processes that create them.

8.22 The soft law mechanism for coordinating bank capital standards developed in Basel 1 was widely seen as successful at creating a common standard and discouraging countries from weakening their regulations to win business. This method of rule writing has continued and expanded, and there are now a number of transnational regulatory networks in various areas of financial regulation.[13]

8.23 The Basel Committee's origin in cooperation on supervisory issues caused by cross-border banking are reflected in the focus of Basel 1: it was designed for internationally active banks, not for banks in general. Moreover, as an accord, it required implementation: each BCBS member had to enact domestic regulation to make it a binding standard.[14]

Transnational supervisory consensus

8.24 Regulatory accords, like any international consensus, reflect what is agreeable. Deals have to be done; support on one issue is traded for deference on another. Issues which cannot be agreed upon are not addressed.[15] Their negotiated character is important for understanding them.

8.25 Another key issue in any agreement is who is at the table and what they say.[16] The Basel Committee's accords have been agreed by the members represented, and the content of the accords reflects their collective interests and relative influence.

---

12 See Guzman & Meyer (2010) for more on soft law in general, and Brummer (2011) and Hale et al. (2013) for the Basel Accords as soft law.

13 These include the Committee on Payments and Market Infrastructure, the Financial Stability Board, the International Association of Insurance Supervisors, and the International Organization of Securities Commissions.

14 The scope of application carries over to Basel 2, but the sense of it being an agreement rather than a requirement does not: the first full paragraph of R. BCBS (2004) reads 'This Framework *will* be applied on a consolidated basis to internationally active banks' (emphasis mine) rather than, say, 'Competent authorities have agreed to consider updating their regulatory frameworks to implement the following prudential principles for internationally active banks'.

15 The negotiated nature of transnational regulation is very clear in the passage from the 1987 UK/US agreement on bank capital to the 1988 Basel Accord: in order to get an agreement, it was necessary to accede to French proposals on the inclusion of subordinated debt as an element of bank capital. Similarly, the PFMI do not discuss skin in the game requirements for CCPs because they were not internationally agreeable when the Principles were being negotiated.

16 Smaller and less developed countries are excluded from full participation in the transnational standard setting process. This is both through formal means—the lack of an invitation to participate—and soft powers ones, whereby countries with large financial systems control the agenda which is then imposed on all. See, for instance, Grynberg & Silva (2006).

8.26 There has been criticism of the Committee for its under-representation of developing economies and the inappropriateness of its prescriptions for them.[17] In partial response, it has somewhat broadened its representation in recent years. Nevertheless, the Committee remains dominated by the interests of the countries which had the largest banking systems when it was founded,[18] and the countries with the largest financial sectors tend to take the lead in chairing working groups and steering the policy agenda, giving a 'minilateral' flavour, as Patrick (2015) calls it, to decision making.

8.27 The vast majority of the Basel Committee's work is conducted by bank supervisors. Its subcommittees and working groups are staffed by them and its secretariat has a number of secondees from them. Some of the represented authorities have macro-prudential responsibilities, and some are also resolution authorities, but the unifying competence of Basel Committee members is the micro-prudential supervision of banks. Market regulators are largely absent, and thus the impact of the Committee's actions on market quality or resilience are not foremost among its considerations. The Basel Committee, then, is an elite consolidation mechanism[19] for bureaucrats focused on making banks robust.[20]

The policing of transnational financial regulation

8.28 The spread of the Basel Accords has been wide: not only have all 27 member jurisdictions implemented the main planks of Basel 3,[21] but there has been substantial adherence even among lower-income countries who are not members of the Committee.[22] Moreover, even where a member country opposed a policy in transnational negotiations, they often implemented it once it was agreed.[23]

---

[17] See Acharya (2012) and Beck & Rojas-Suarez (2019).

[18] The EU and its constituents have roughly twice as many seats on the Committee as the entire Global South.

[19] The term was originally coined by Bartolini (2005) in a discussion of EU decision making.

[20] The absence of market and broker/dealer regulators at the Basel Committee, and their relative lack of influence at the FSB compared to central bankers, skews the policy agenda towards bank resilience.

[21] BCBS (2020b) reports that as at 'end-May 2020, all 27 member jurisdictions have risk-based capital rules, Liquidity Coverage Ratio regulations and capital conservation buffers in force. Twenty six member jurisdictions have final rules in force for the countercyclical capital buffer and the leverage ratio based on the existing (2014) exposure definition.'

[22] Jones (2020) reports some measure of implementation of 'the latest and more complex international standards' by 22 out of 45 such countries.

[23] A good example came in September 2016. In a speech to the European Banking Federation Conference, EU Commission Vice-President Valdis Dombrovskis, talking about Basel 3, said that 'A solution we could not support is one which would weigh unduly on the financing of the broader economy in Europe. At a time when we are focused on supporting investment, we want to avoid changes which would lead to a significant increase in the overall capital requirements shouldered

8.29 Compliance with transnational financial regulation is policed by exhortation and by regulatory consistency assessment programmes. The Basel RCAP was discussed in Chapter 5: other international rule making bodies have similar approaches. For more principles-based regulation, such as the PFMI, the control is necessarily looser, but it still has the same character: an organization which was formed as a coordination mechanism now enforces.[24]

8.30 This policing occurs in an environment characterized by fragmentation, complexity, and contested boundaries. There are multiple power centres at transnational and national levels, including bank and market regulators, financial stability authorities, regulators of non-banks, resolution authorities, and finance ministries.[25] In the language of Chapter 2, different actors are competing to tell their version of the story.[26] The general form of the regulators' story is often shared, but the emphasis, meanings, and implications vary depending on the teller. Regulatory consistency assessments serve to limit divergence.

8.31 The centre has other disciplinary mechanisms, too. One, as described in Chapter 2 is hegemonic: regulators' declarative authority to say 'this is the answer, and there is no alternative', and be largely believed, is used to close down discussion. The risk of reduced status within the transnational regulatory community serves to control dissent, as we discuss further in Chapter 11. There are also hard power mechanisms, such as the imposition of higher capital charges on counterparties which are deemed non-compliant.[27] These mechanisms also serve as additional means for the centre to control how far the local narratives can drift.

---

by Europe's banking sector … the proposals Basel has issued for consultation [on Basel 3] would imply significant capital requirement increases in all areas.' Yet the EU still agreed to the Accord when it was finalized the following year.

[24] The origins of the BIS in the enforcement of sovereign debt obligations, discussed in paragraph 8.15 perhaps help to explain its disciplinary character. Sovereign debt enforcement is fundamentally about ensuring time consistency of behaviour: an RCAP programme similarly ensures that regulators consistently implement what they agreed to. However, there is an important difference: sovereigns have untrammelled authority to borrow, while regulators' authority is constrained by administrative law requirements, mandates, and political oversight, all of which may be short-circuited in the Basel process.

[25] Black (2008) discusses polycentricity in the context of financial regulation.

[26] Local version are shaped by local traditions: the US version of post-crisis derivatives regulation must be seen as rooted in the Commodity Exchange Act of 1936, for instance. Even if greater harmonization of the regulation of OTC derivatives was desirable—as Knaack (2015) argues but I dispute—it would be very difficult in the face of these long-rooted differences between the definitions, translations, and rhetorics involved in different jurisdictions.

[27] The notion of a 'qualifying' CCP in the capital rules for bank exposures to CCPs in an example of this kind of mechanism: beneficial treatment is only given to CCPs which are supervised under 'domestic rules and regulations that are consistent with the CPSS-IOSCO Principles for Financial Market Infrastructures': see R. BCBS (2014c) at 1.

8.32 Jurisdictional power matters in this context:powerful regulators can drift further from the agreed narrative without severe consequences than those from smaller financial centres can.[28]

Making the sausages

8.33 The process by which international regulatory accords are made might be a surprise, given the strength of the narrative[29] around the necessity of complying with them. It typically works something like this:

- The consensus forming body has a forward policy agenda. Absent a crisis, members jockey for power over its contents. In stress, much or all of the agenda may be imposed externally by government(s).[30]
- Once agreement is reached to try to make policy, a working group is formed. Members again compete for influence, volunteering staff where they want power to shape the narrative, and stepping back when an issue is not deemed to merit a commitment of resources.
- The working group gathers evidence. They may conduct hearings or invite written submissions, but there is no requirement to do so. Where there are hearings, they are typically by invitation rather than open to the public.
- A quantitative impact study ('QIS') may be conducted, and the coordinating body will probably issue a consultation paper proposing a draft rule.
- The working group tries to find a consensus on a final rule. There are no formal standards for consideration of evidence or requirements for justification of policy proposals. A proposed rule does not have to be accompanied by a regulatory impact analysis, and most are not, so estimates of the effect of the proposed rule are not available. Working group members, and especially the chair, if they are so minded, can have a large influence on the text: dialogue within the group, rather than objective evidence or external comment, is key to shaping the outcome.
- Once a proposal is finalized at the working level, it passes up through a hierarchy of committees. Members of higher-level committees typically have neither time nor resources to repeat the discussion conducted at the

[28] A good example of here is the lack of consequences resulting from the SEC's failure to implement the internationally agreed cover 2 standard for all its systemically important CCPs: see 17 C.F.R. 240.17Ad–22(b)(3).

[29] For the strength of the claim, see paragraph 5.100.

[30] The G-20 communique after the 2008 crisis discussed in paragraph 2.57 should be seen as mandating policy making by the relevant standard setting bodies.

working group level, so decision making is usually confined to the broad sweep of the proposed new rule, rather than its details.

- After the rule text has been agreed upon, the final standard is published. Neither a substantive justification, nor an account of how it was calibrated are typically provided, although there may be a QIS.[31]
- There is no body which has the authority to review transnational regulatory accords and to require that changes are made to them.[32]

Questioning transnational financial regulation

8.34 The advantages of the transnational soft law rule making process for the authorities involved are obvious. Rule development costs can be shared, jurisdictional arbitrage avoided, and best practices disseminated.

8.35 Less positively, there are normative costs: the accord made by working group members might not be appropriate for the financial systems of all of the Committee's members. That would be fine if what happened in Basel stayed in Basel. Instead, it is exported widely, with an obligation to comply with the by-now-agreed international rule. Moreover, once a standard is agreed, it is hard to change: the burden of proof for changing an international regulatory rule is much higher than for initial adoption. This means that, absent a crisis, standards tend to petrify.

8.36 These features of transnational financial rule making have understandably raised questions about its legitimacy:

- The Accords have a profound impact on the banking systems of all the countries they are applied to. In each of these countries, authorities are presented with rules as a near fait accompli.[33] These rules are made by an opaque process; they are extremely complex and difficult to assess; they come without any account of their optimality for the financial system they are being applied to or of the risks around their adoption; and they are devoid of an effective, independent review mechanism should they have unintended consequences. Whether this is an acceptable price to pay for international standardization is questionable.[34]

---

[31] See, for instance, BCBS (2015b).

[32] See paragraph 8.53 for a discussion of the FSB's monitoring framework, perhaps the closest proxy to an independent review process.

[33] Tarbert (2001) suggests that 'home country enactment is simply a formality', which is not quite true—as we saw with the examples of alpha and the corporate CVA exemption in Chapter 5—but it is certainly close.

[34] To pick one example, if politicians in emerging markets and developing economies accept reduced access to and higher cost of financing for small and medium-sized enterprises in their countries

- For the Basel Accords, these questions have become more pressing as international standards have become more binding. When the Accords exercised limited influence over most banks' business models, the work of the Committee could be construed as information sharing and the promulgation of best practice, but this is no longer the case.
- For principles-based regulation such as the PFMI, the concerns are less serious as the second level process of writing implementing rules is more substantial. There is more room for transparency and dialogue, for regulation to be adapted to local circumstances, and for it to be reviewed.

Global Administrative Law

8.37 The term 'global administrative law' is used for the norms, rules, principles, and processes of administration which stretch beyond national borders.[35] Examples of these kinds of 'bureaucratic technologies'[36] have multiplied in recent years, and arise in a diverse range of fields, including measurement standards, health, and climate change, as well as financial regulation.[37]

8.38 No assumption is made that a given transnational bureaucratic technology is law:[38] rather, global administrative law studies areas which make law-like claims,[39] use legal reasoning, and have law-like enforcement mechanisms,[40] without arising from the authority and norm-defining power of the state. Thus, global

as an acceptable price for international consistency, as Fišera et al. (2019) describes, that would be legitimate. For it to be imposed upon them by regulators is more contestable.

[35] See Cassese (2005) and Kingsbury (2009) for a further discussion of global administrative law. Somek (2010) emphasizes that in this area there 'is neither system nor centre, but merely a number of family resemblances among different processes', so scholarship in this area should be sensitive to these differences.

[36] Rose & Miller (1992) at 281 use the term 'technologies of government' for this. Foucault (1982) at 792 calls for uncovering 'the means of bringing power relations into being': bureaucratic technologies are a prominent example of these means, as Chapter 11 discusses further.

[37] Respectively, the International Organization for Standardization, the World Health Organization and the Intergovernmental Panel on Climate Change. See Hale et al. (2013) for a comparative analysis of various transnational administrative bodies.

[38] Indeed, whether they are is contested: see Kingsbury (2009) and Somek (2010) for some of the arguments.

[39] Kingsbury (2009) at 31 identifies as a key property whether the policy 'has been wrought by the whole society ... [and it] addresses matters of concern to the society as such'.

[40] The animating principle might therefore be said to be the will to govern. The growth of these mechanisms is an example of the growth of Foucaultian governmentality: see Rose & Miller (1992) at 273.

administrative law would consider the Basel Accords, while their implementation in an EU regulation would be a matter of European administrative law.

8.39 The kinds of bureaucratic technology studied by global administrative law have been confronted by demands for more transparency, stakeholder consultation, evidence of reasoned decision making, and review. On this basis a body of scholarship has developed which articulates legitimating principles for global administrative law-like actions.[41] These, in summary, are:[42]

- *Legality and accountability under the law.* This is the principle that authority has been delegated under the (hard) law to a bureaucratic agent, that the agent's authority is constrained by that delegation, and that the law will hold them accountable for their actions.[43] In particular, it means that there should be a process for holding the agent to account for their work, given their mandate.[44]
- *Transparency and predictability of process.* This principle requires that there is an agreed and publicized process for administrative action: stakeholders should know what is being done, by whom, based on what evidence, for what reasons, and on what timescale.
- *Rationality of decision making based on evidence presented.* The idea here is that decisions should not be arbitrary or capricious and should be rooted in an analysis of conscientiously gathered evidence.
- *Proportionality and protection of rights.* An interference with rights must be justified, and that interference must be proportional to the authorities' goal. This principle is discussed further below.
- *Participation from affected stakeholders.* A focus on the public good, with participation possible by all of society, is 'a necessary element in the concept of law under modern democratic conditions'.[45] If transnational regulation is to be legitimate, it too must inform all stakeholders on proposed

[41] Black (2008) argues that 'legitimacy is rooted in the acceptance' of an organization by others but, as Somek (2010) points out, that rather depends on them having a genuine choice not to accept, given the disciplinary mechanisms in play. Moreover, acceptance can be nuanced: a stakeholder might, for instance, accept the legitimacy of a state or bloc-level regulator without recognizing the legitimacy of a transnational body.

[42] Other scholars suggest similar if often shorter lists: see, for instance, Barr & Miller (2006), Cassese (2005), or Kingsbury (2009), and note, the implicit (and Westphalian) normative assumptions in this project.

[43] See Habermas (1996) at 364.

[44] See Gonzalez-Watty (2016) and Chapter 11 for a further discussion of the accountability of financial regulators.

[45] Kingsbury (2009) at 31 calls this 'publicness'.

changes, give them all an opportunity to comment, and act on the comments received.

- *Independent dispute resolution mechanisms.* A process for independently adjudicating disputes, such as a court or an ombudsman, provides some protection for stakeholders that the rules made are interpreted reasonably and coherently.[46]
- *Review mechanism.* None of the other principles are effective unless there is some mechanism to challenge potential failures to observe them, and to review the continuing appropriateness of the actions taken. This requires the existence of an independent body with the power to enforce change if standards of good administration and effectiveness are not met.

8.40 Rules made by transnational regulatory bodies such as the Basel Committee, CPMI and IOSCO clearly fall under global administrative law: these acts have authority, the standard setting bodies are public and international, and their actions are made on the basis of a competence handed down to each of their constituent public authorities. But are they *legitimate* global administrative law? We address this question next, considering each of the principles outlined above.

Legality and accountability under the law

8.41 This is typically straightforward for transnational financial regulation: the authorities involved have been delegated authority to make rules, and they are not prohibited from cooperating with one another.[47]

Transparency and predictability of process

8.42 The origins of much of transnational regulation are opaque. There is no public agenda of topics under consideration.[48] Often, the first time stakeholders

---

[46] For an example, see the Dispute Settlement Panels of the World Trade Organization described at https://www.wto.org/english/tratop_e/dispu_e/disp_settlement_cbt_e/c6s1p1_e.htm and note that Habermas (1996) at 125 goes further, demanding a 'guaranteed legal remedy' for those who feel that their rights have been infringed.

[47] For a different view on whether authorities can cooperate, see the 2017 letter from Vice Chair of US House Financial Services Committee to the Chair of the Board of Governors of the Federal Reserve System, where the writer states that it 'appears that the Federal Reserve continues negotiating international regulatory standards for financial institutions among global bureaucrats in foreign lands without transparency, accountability, *or the authority to do so*' (emphasis mine): see McHenry (2017).

[48] See the Basel Committee's press release of 31 March 2021, available at https://www.bis.org/press/p210331.htm, for a typical example of this opacity. It states 'The Group of Central Bank Governors and Heads of Supervision (GHOS), the oversight body of the Basel Committee on Banking Supervision, has today endorsed the strategic priorities and work programme of the Committee for

outside the Basel club learn of the intention to make new rules is when a consultation paper is issued: at that point, it is very difficult to make more than minor alternations to the direction of travel. Thus, there is a process by which transnational regulation is made, but it is only predictable to many stakeholders once new rules are almost inevitable.

8.43 There are further transparency issues with transnational financial regulation. First, no details of who is responsible for a rule are disclosed. Stakeholders do not know working group membership, membership of the higher-level committees such as the Policy Development Group, nor who was consulted during policy development. Minutes of meetings are not typically published. Finally, and problematically for the proponents of the claim that 'consultation builds legitimacy', there is no disclosure of which comments the Committee accepted, which it rejected, and why.[49]

Rationality of decision making based on evidence presented

8.44 A legitimating account of decision making in rule making would start by presenting the evidence to support the desirability of a particular regulatory goal, a mechanism to achieve that goal, and an analysis of the effectiveness of that mechanism, compared to other choices.[50]

8.45 The account of decision making would then present a potential rule, and show how each part of it was determined. The net effect of the rule would be examined for a wide range of realistic portfolios. This would demonstrate that the rule choice was indeed a rational outcome of an evidence-based approach.[51]

8.46 As a sketch, for CVA capital margin, such a justification might start with the claim that CVA risk was uncapitalized, and that it could cause significant losses for banks. This would be supported by analysis of current CVA risks in large banks and the losses that these risks could plausibly cause at the chosen safety standard. Anonymized, averaged exposure data of banks' total CVA risk would be presented. Capital would be compared to margin as a mechanism for addressing

2021–22.' Three priorities are given in the accompanying document, and all are very general: one is 'strengthening supervisory coordination and practices', for instance.

49 Barr & Miller (2006) tellingly says 'the Committee issued background papers to inform the public about its thinking on key issues': not, the reader will notice, to stimulate a debate, nor to gather evidence. We are granted insight into what is going to be done, not being asked whether it should be done, or what might be better.

50 This is regulatory theory's notion of justification discussed in paragraph 6.38.

51 Kingsbury et al. (2005) state that the 'Basle [sic.] Committee and IOSCO, have developed web sites that contain abundant material on internal decision making and the information and considerations on which decisions are based' but give no evidence of this. Indeed, it would be an interesting challenge for the reader to select a rule in Basel 3 and try to find the 'material on internal decision making' supporting the precise rule text, including the calibration chosen.

the risk, and the costs, macro-economic effects and redistributional consequences of the proposed capital rule would be analysed, and compared to the benefit in enhanced bank safety.

Proportionality and protection of rights

8.47 The concept of proportionality is an old one in administrative law. Its origin lies in Prussian court review of police actions that infringed the rights of individuals. It has become a key feature of EU administrative law,[52] and is now 'the most important doctrinal tool in constitutional rights law'.[53]

8.48 The form of the argument justifying the proportionality of a policy is, in sketch, four-fold.

1. There must be a stated, legitimate goal that the policy is pursuing.
2. There must be a rational connection—what we called in paragraph 8.44 a mechanism—between the policy and the achievement of the goal.
3. A demonstration that there is no less intrusive but equally effective alternative policy is required.
4. There must be a balance evidenced between the importance of rights affected by the policy and the importance of the goal.

8.49 Much transnational financial regulation is on difficult ground here. The goals, to the extent that they are stated at all, are diffuse ones, like financial stability or the robustness of financial institutions. The rights interfered with are not just the property rights of the regulated, but also those of their clients and potential clients: the latter are typically not considered. There is often a general mechanism, such as the loss absorbency of capital, supporting the need for the proposed policy, but the 'no better alternative' leg of the justification is typically missing, as is a careful justification for the scale of the intervention chosen. Moreover, there are sometimes countervailing mechanisms so that, in some cases, the goal is not met at all.[54]

Participation from affected stakeholders

8.50 'Input legitimacy'[55] refers to the representation of all interested parties in administrative decision making, if that decision is to be regarded as legitimate.

[52] See article 5(4) of the Treaty of the EU.

[53] See Möller (2012), whose discussion this subsection follows.

[54] The impact of the leverage ratio on repo market intermediation in stress discussed in paragraph 4.25 is an example of this.

[55] The term is from Csatlós (2019): in contrast, 'output legitimacy' occurs when a system of governance produces results which are deemed by stakeholders to efficiently cater to the public interest and meet the assigned mandate.

This implies not just consultation—inviting comment—but also listening to and acting upon the replies. In a dialogue as imbued with power imbalance as that of financial regulators with the firms they regulate, it would be helpful to have a mechanism for levelling the playing field. Without such a mechanism, the regulated become so dependent on the favour of the regulator that they fully submit to the latter's discursive authority and self-censor to avoid conflict.[56]

8.51 Defenders of the legitimacy of the transnational financial rule making process[57] argue that its rule making includes significant participation from stakeholders and that, over time, improvements in transparency have 'permitted a wider range of actors to comment'. The suggestion is that standard setters' work 'appears to have been responsive to suggestions made during the notice and comment process'. This may be a reasonable characterization of the rule making process for Basel 2,[58] but there is less evidence of input legitimacy in the regulatory counter-reformation that produced Basel 3.

Independent determination of disputes

8.52 Any disputes about the meaning of transnational financial regulation are resolved by the rule maker, so the requirement for an independent dispute resolution mechanism is problematic for transnational banking regulation. The principles-based approach of CPMI-IOSCO scores better on this criterion because it is less proscriptive.

Review mechanisms

8.53 The closest thing transnational financial regulation has to a review mechanism is the FSB's Framework for Monitoring the Implementation of Agreed G20/FSB Financial Reforms.[59] However, this not an independent review of good administrative and effective rule making. It takes as its starting point that 'the success of the financial regulatory reform efforts ... depends on the complete

---

56 In Murphy (2020a), I used the term 'inverse regulatory capture' for this. Another aspect of this self-censorship is the need for the regulated to ensure that their invitations to stakeholder consultation meetings keep coming. Inverse regulatory capture, together with the more familiar regulatory capture, as discussed by Levitin (2014) and Stigler (1971), are important features in the dialogues of financial regulation. Analysis of the legitimizing nature of a discourse in the presence of inverse regulatory capture should consider who can say what to whom, and the power relations created by speaking and listening, or not listening.

57 Such as, for instance, Barr & Miller (2006), from whom the following quote comes at 26.

58 Barr & Miller (2006) cites as an example of the Committee's attention to stakeholder comment during Basel 2 that they 'yielded somewhat on capital charges for operational risk'. Perhaps the Committee did, that concession disappeared in the final version of Basel 3: compare R. BCBS (2004) §§655–659 with paragraph 2, page 128 of R. BCBS (2017).

59 See R. FSB (2011).

and globally consistent implementation' of the agreed policies.[60] There is no mandate to review the policy making process, and the review of the effectiveness of the reforms is confined to identifying 'useful lessons from experience … on the effectiveness of the policy reforms and the associated standards as well as on any unintended consequences'. Moreover, FSB review under the monitoring framework is not independent, in that many of the same authorities sit on the FSB and on the transnational standard setting bodies being considered. It also has no power to enforce its recommendations.

Global administrative law perspectives on the legitimacy of transnational financial regulatory accords

8.54 The discussion above suggests that global administrative law criteria supports the idea that transnational financial regulation has a legitimacy problem.[61] The methods adopted in regulatory cooperation often largely or completely bypass home state administrative law requirements. Moreover, these methods are unnecessary: there is no need for opacity, for such unequal stakeholder dialogue, for the lack of independent dispute adjudication, or for the absence of an effective review mechanism. These features are convenient for the authorities involved, but, as Csatlós (2019) politely puts it at 245, it does mean that the 'guarantees that protect individuals against authority powers are under construction'.

8.55 If the choice is between legitimate rule making with fewer, better justified rules, and the current process with its enormous and rapidly growing corpus of ill-justified regulation, then reform is attractive.

8.56 As noted above, these problems are more severe for the Basel Accords than for more principles-based regulation, such as the PFMI.[62] Transnational rule making, then, is most legitimate when it is abridged and contingent on local

[60] This premise is only true if the agreed policies are effective—something that a genuine review would probe.

[61] Kingsbury et al. (2005) suggest that the requirement should be 'adequate standards of transparency, participation, reasoned decision, and legality, and … effective review of the rules and decisions' made. Of these, only 'legality' is difficult to contest for transnational financial regulation. See Gonzalez-Watty (2016) for a further discussion.

[62] The PFMI are not fully principles-based, in the sense of Black et al. (2007): they contain some harder standards, such as initial margin covering at least of 99% of possible movements over the margin period of risk. They do however mostly say what must be done but not how, as in Principle 14: 'A CCP should, at a minimum, have segregation and portability arrangements that effectively protect a participant's customers' positions and related collateral from the default or insolvency of that participant'. No method of segregation is required, and appropriately so, given the diversity of legal systems the PFMI must apply to.

circumstances,[63] and most problematic when it is strongly normative, detailed, and inflexible.

8.57 Transnational regulatory communities are self-governing: the ultimate authority on a transnational agreement is the body which made it. Moreover, as we saw above, the decisions of these communities have questionable legitimacy.[64] This means that challenging transnational regulation directly is difficult. Perhaps the solution is to go down a level. Can regulation acquire legitimacy through the possibility of external challenge when comes to be implemented in national or bloc law? In the next section, this question is considered.

Judicial Review

8.58 The rule of law demands that courts police the boundaries of administrative power. If this form of review were impossible, it would be more likely that regulation is illegitimate, illegal, unfair, or unreasonable. Administrative action, whether regulatory or deregulatory, should 'be animated by the legislative purposes', as Garland (1985) puts it at 512, and not arbitrary or capricious. The potential for it to be reviewed by courts assists this. It creates legitimacy by offering a means by which improper or illegal regulatory action can be checked.

8.59 Judicial review is the process by which this occurs in English law: it is the local version of global administrative law's review mechanism. Echoes of many of the same concepts, including the need for the legality, rationality, and procedural fairness of regulatory action, will be found within it. Because public bodies implement transnational regulatory agreements, judicial review provides a potential constraint on the local rules which implement such agreements.

8.60 Different stakeholders have different perspectives on the efficacy of the judicial review of regulation. A median position might perhaps be that it is an imperfect but nevertheless vital guardian.[65] Indeed, one way to see this area of administrative law is as a legitimizing discourse: the potential for judicial scrutiny restrains regulatory power and encourages (somewhat) more open rule making. Before discussing that, though, it is necessary to consider in more detail what court intervention is for and when it can happen. The judicial review of financial regulation is then considered, revealing how vulnerable the policy making process might be to challenge. The chapter ends with an example of a court striking

---

63 To see the difference, compare the gap between the PFMI and EMIR with that between Basel 3 and CRD IV.

64 There is also a balance between the risks created by non-harmonization and the deleterious effects of imposing ill-fitting global accords in particular, local situations which would warrant discussion, if there were space.

65 For discussion and critique, see Cross (2000), Daly (2017) and, in the US context, Sunstein (1989).

down derivatives rule making and a discussion of potential remedies for the issues identified earlier in the chapter.

The purpose of judicial review

8.61 Judicial review is a constitutional protection to 'increase the incidence of legality' in public decision making.[66] Most regulators are keen to avoid illegal action. It can nevertheless arise because legality has an unclear boundary. Public bodies sometimes operate in this liminal zone, taking risk and making decisions 'which are, at least arguably, of doubtful legality'.[67]

8.62 The second reason for having judicial review is to constrain administrative decision making to produce reasonable results from a reasonable process. At least in English Law, the motivation is not to revise 'incorrect' decisions, even if they have inefficient or odious outcomes,[68] but to guard against bad administrative practice.

Grounds for judicial review

8.63 The grounds for judicial review broadly follow from its purposes, but they have evolved over time as the norms for administrative practice have changed. A statement of the starting position for this evolution is 'whether sensible decision makers, properly directed in law and properly applying their minds to the matter, could have regarded the conclusion under review as a permissible one'.[69]

8.64 The power to conduct administrative action is typically granted under an Act of Parliament or secondary legislation, so one route to review is the argument that the action being disputed is not within the power of the authority to make: this is the 'properly directed' point.

8.65 The 'sensible' and 'properly applying their minds' criteria are rooted in the nuanced concept of reasonableness. The classic standard here is the well-known *Wednesbury* test: that the court would not intervene in an administrative decision if the right matters had been taken into account in making it and it was not so unreasonable that no reasonable authority could ever come to it.[70]

8.66 The evolution of judicial review is particularly evident in the reasonableness test or—as it is perhaps better framed—the test for rational, evidence-based

---

66 The phrase is from Sunstein (1989) at 522.

67 Dyson (2015) gives the quote at 3, summarizing the purposes of judicial review as the avoidance of illegality, irrationality, and procedural impropriety.

68 Cf. Sunstein (1989) at 523, but note that once an odious outcome involves a grave interference with fundamental rights, as in *Smith and Grady v. UK* (1999) 29 EHRR 493, even a procedurally well-founded and legal administrative decision may be overturned.

69 Dyson (2015) at 4.

70 The *Wednesbury* case, *Associated Provincial Picture Houses Limited v. Wednesbury Corporation [1948] 1 KB 223*, which gave birth to this criteria related to the granting of a licence under the

decision making.[71] This ground for review have become more expansive, and the relatively high bar of demonstrating an absence of Wednesbury reasonableness has been lowered. This is partly in recognition of the need to protect the rights of individuals affected by administrative decisions, and partly in response to the evolving global administrative law notion of reasonableness discussed in the previous section.

8.67 Four classes of ground for review, each familiar from global administrative law, can be discerned in modern cases:

- *Permissible goal.* Is there a clear goal which the action is intended to achieve and which is within their competence?[72]
- *Evidential fairness.* Were the right things considered, and did the decision maker take reasonable steps to gather relevant evidence?[73]

Sunday Entertainments Act 1932 to show films on a Sunday. The question was whether the original decision to grant the license was reasonable. Lord Greene's formulation at 410 was that:

The court is entitled to investigate the action of the local authority with a view to seeing whether they have taken into account matters which they ought not to take into account, or conversely, have refused to take into account or neglected to take into account matters which they ought to take into account. Once that question is answered in favour of the local authority, it may still be possible to say that, although the local authority have kept within the four corners of the matters which they ought to consider, they have nevertheless come to a conclusion so unreasonable that no reasonable authority could ever have come to it.

This two-part test clearly gives three routes to review; that a decision was taken based partly on matters which should not have been considered; that it taken without consideration of matters which should have been considered; or that it was unreasonable in the sense given.

71 Rawlings (2008) describes the changes here as 'interesting shifts' in the nature of judicial review, while cautioning that the transplants into English administrative law from the EU largely responsible for it may call for some 'mental gymnastics' given that 'major, overlapping jurisdictional sources are more or less closely linked together'. These shifts are not over. In particular, in July 2020 the government launched an independent review of administrative law which will 'examine the need for potential reforms of judicial review': see https://www.gov.uk/government/news/government-launches-independent-panel-to-look-at-judicial-review.

72 As Lord Bingham made clear in *R (Corner House Research) v. Director of the Serious Fraud Office* [2009] AC 756, an application for judicial review of the decision by the directors of the Serious Fraud Office not to pursue a criminal investigation into alleged bribery in relation to an arms supply contract, the issue is not 'whether his decision was right or wrong' but 'whether it was a decision which the Director was lawfully entitled to make'.

73 In situations like financial regulation where the decision maker has discretion over what to consider, the standard for review based on the selection of evidence is, broadly, (Wednesbury) unreasonableness, so the bar is quite high. See *R v. Secretary of State for Transport Ex p. Richmond LBC* at 95. However, the court will act where the decision maker had failed to take into account 'matters so obviously material to a decision on a particular project that anything short of direct consideration of them' would not be in accordance with the intention of the statutory power conveyed. See *CREEDNZ Inc. v. Governor-General* [1981] 1 NZLR 172 at p. 183.

- *Procedural fairness.* Were affected parties aware that a decision was contemplated and given a fair hearing? Was the evidence that the decision maker intended to rely upon disclosed before the hearing and the reason for the decision given after it?[74]

- *Rational action to meet the goal.* Have the authorities rationally concluded that the proposed action does indeed meet the goal, given the evidence?[75]

Judicial review of financial regulation

8.68 There is a significant history of judicial review of *bank supervisory decisions,*[76] but little action relating to financial *rule making* in English Courts.[77] Since the type of UK financial regulation discussed here was, until very recently, implemented in EU law, for instance through the Capital Requirements Directives and Regulations, review by the European Court of Justice would also be possible via article 263 of the Treaty of the Functioning of the European Union ('TFEU').

8.69 The encounter with European law has influenced English judicial review. In particular, in the EU context, grounds for review include failure to consult on the legislation or to hear an addressee of the proposed rule, failure to indicate the legal basis of rule making, failure to respect self-imposed internal procedure requirements and, most pertinently, failure to provide a statement of reasons showing that the rule is a proportional response to the issue, in accordance with article 296 of the TFEU. This article (reiterating article 1) states in part:

---

74 For instance, in *R (Buckinghamshire County Council and Others) v. Secretary of State for Transport* [2013] EWHC 481, the court found that the consultation process for a proposed compensation scheme related to properties blighted by a high-speed railway line was so unfair as to be unlawful. The government had failed to provide adequate information to consultees on the implications of the scheme and had failed to properly consider the claimants' consultation response.

75 In *Office of Fair Trading v. IBA Health Ltd* [2004] EWCA Civ 142, the Court, in rejecting an appeal against the Competition Appeal Tribunal's quashing of a decision by the Office of Fair Trading ('OFT'), held that the failure of the OFT 'adequately to justify the belief they formed' was a factor. This suggests that authorities' beliefs about the efficacy of a proposed rule should be 'reasonably and objectively justified by the relevant facts'. The failure to provide reasoning is not necessarily a defence: as Lord Upjohn said in *Padfield* [1968] AC 997, if the decision maker 'does not give any reason for his decision it may be ... that a court may be at liberty to come to the conclusion that he had no good reason for reaching that conclusion and order a prerogative writ to issue accordingly'.

76 For instance, regarding the decision not to pay compensation to the shareholders of Northern Rock when it failed in 2008 (in *SRM Global Master Fund LP v. The Commissioners of HM Treasury* [2009] EWCA Civ 788) or the Bank of England's supervision of BCCI (in *Three Rivers District Council v. Governor and Company of the Bank Of England (No. 3)* [2000] 2 WLR 12).

77 For a discussion of the wider issue of judicial review of central bank action, see Goodhart & Lastra (2018).

Where the Treaties do not specify the type of act to be adopted, the institutions shall select it on a case-by-case basis, in compliance with the applicable procedures and with the principle of proportionality.

8.70 If this European interpretation of proportionality holds, there would seem to be a route for judicial review where no justification has been given that a proposed financial regulation is necessary to achieve a desired goal, albeit that this approach has not yet been taken by a claimant.

Regulatory discourse and judicial review

8.71 The rule making process used by the Basel Committee may not meet the standard that the court would use to review administrative actions for similar reasons to those discussed earlier in the chapter for its questionable legitimacy under global administrative law:[78]

- The goal of rule making is often unstated, so—while it might be easy to state and clearly permissible if stated—the permissible goal test is not automatically passed.
- Evidential fairness is difficult to demonstrate as it is not clear what the decision making body considered.
- Procedural fairness is questionable given the lack of truly public hearings and the inability to evidence consideration of comments.
- The failure to disclose the purported mechanism by which a rule works means that it is hard to establish that it is a rational means of meeting the goal.

8.72 Consider the 2013 consultative paper on the leverage ratio. As discussed in Chapter 4, many of the responses to this consultation discussed issues with the leverage ratio treatment of derivatives and recommended changes to it.[79] There was no response to these comments from the Committee and they were not acted upon. No evidence supporting the Committee's decision and no mechanism supporting the necessity of it were disclosed. This fact pattern supports questions of evidential fairness, procedural fairness, and rational means.

[78] There is an arbitrage of administrative law in the use of the Basel Committee. Many of the countries who are active members of the Committee have substantial bodies of administrative law and freedom of information provisions. Due to its international status and Swiss domicile, the Basel Committee is not bound by these provisions. So British, American, EU, and other regulators can go to Basel and conduct proceedings unhampered by their home country requirements. Once an Accord has been reached in Basel, this can then be used to justify its imposition locally.

[79] Also mentioned widely were problems with the treatment of repo: an issue that eventually led to the changes discussed in footnote 45 in Chapter 4. The comment letters from the 2013 consultation are available at https://www.bis.org/publ/bcbs251/comments.htm.

8.73 The broader picture is that the vast majority of the evidence for the Basel 3 leverage ratio relates to a rule which is substantially different from and less onerous than the one implemented; many other steps were simultaneously being taken in furtherance of the same goal of financial stability;[80] there were objections from stakeholders to details of the proposal which were dismissed without explanation; and no mechanism was proposed to explain why the proposed rule meets the desired goal.[81] These are not insubstantial grounds for a challenge.

8.74 In summary, judicial review of rules implementing financial regulation is not impossible, and the principles under which it would take place are at least broadly clear. In some cases, there are potential grounds. However, there is little case law to suggest how the courts would view the questions of whether the regulators had articulated their goal, whether they had justified that their proposed rule was a proportional response to it, and whether their proceedings had been conducted fairly. It is also unclear how transnational bodies would react to such a challenge.

Position limits

8.75 One of the few cases of court review of derivatives regulation is in the United States. It relates to position limits for commodity derivatives. These have a long history:[82] as long ago as 1936, Congress gave authority for position limits to be imposed on commodity derivatives, acknowledged the potential for market disruptions resulting from excessive speculative trading. The Dodd-Frank Act updated this, requiring[83] that the CFTC establish a framework of commodity position limits. The rationale here is that overly large position in derivatives can disrupt the market in the underlying commodity, causing 'sudden or unreasonable price fluctuations' which can create 'an undue and unnecessary burden on interstate commerce'. In imposing position limits, the CFTC therefore seemed to be on relatively firm ground: Congress had set out the goal, and the means to achieve it. The CFTC simply had to write rules to implement Congress' intent.

8.76 The Commission issued a final rule in 2011, but it was quickly challenged. The plaintiffs argued,[84] in summary, that the CFTC misinterpreted its statutory

80 These include changes to the definition of capital, to required capital ratios, to the calculation of RWAs, the imposition of liquidity regulation, and the introduction of the G-SIB framework, among others. See https://www.bis.org/basel_framework/.

81 It is an interesting exercise to consider what would constitute sufficient evidence that the 165 articles, let alone all the regulatory technical standards, of the EU directive implementing Basel 3.1, CRD IV, are the least onerous means necessary to achieve the authorities' objectives.

82 See the CFTC's original rule making, R. CFTC (2011) and Helleiner et al. (2018) at 199.

83 R. US Congress (2010) at §§737. See also 57 FR 1276 for the CFTC's 1992 position limit revisions.

84 See *International Swaps & Derivatives Association et al. v. US Commodity Futures Trading Commission*, 887 F. Supp. 2d 259 (DDC 2012) for the case and *International Swaps & Derivatives*

authority 'in imposing position limits without making a determination that such limits are necessary and effective in relation to the identifiable burdens of excessive speculation on interstate commerce'. In other words, while the Commission had statutory authority to impose limits, it first had to demonstrate that the particular limits it was proposing actually achieved the goal of relieving the burden of sudden or unreasonable price fluctuations on interstate commerce.

8.77 In a complex decision, the court agreed, and vacated the rule, saying that the Commission had 'failed to bring its expertise and experience to bear when interpreting the statute and offered no explanation for how its interpretation comported with the policy objectives of the Act'. This was an encouraging decision for advocates of the benefits of judicial scrutiny: a clear goal and authority to use a particular means to achieve it was not enough: a rational connection was also needed between the proposed policy and the achievement of the goal.

8.78 The revised version of the Commission's rules, R. CFTC (2020), addresses the problem, setting out how the Commission balanced the need to curb excessive speculation with the cost of liquidity for hedgers, and setting limits only for the most economically significant physically settled contracts where derivatives positions could be expected to have the most economically substantial effects. Reflecting the balance involved, the limit for the front month is set at or below 25% of estimated total deliverable supply for the referenced commodity, and there is a regime of exemptions for hedging.

Legitimacy and regulatory review

8.79 The bar for judicial review is high, so it is troubling that some aspects of post-crisis financial rule making may not clear it. This is not to say that judicial review is the perfect tool for analysing regulation: even if the expertise of the courts in these matters is not considered to be an issue,[85] there is no mandate to review regulation for optimality, and even decisions with large costs and nugatory benefits, such as mandatory clearing for most end-users, may not meet the criteria of unreasonableness. Rather, there is a need for a mechanism which provides robust, independent analysis of the effectiveness and efficiency of regulators' actions. This should look beyond the fig leaf of 'because Basel said so', and analyse how optimal regulatory action really was. Chapter 12 returns to this issue.

Association et al. v. US Commodity Futures Trading Commission, No. 1:2011cv02146 – Document 69 (DDC 2012) for the argument.

85 More is made of this point than it may deserve. The courts have ruled sensibly on highly technical derivatives issues, as Braithwaite (2020) describes—see for instance *ANZ v. Société Générale* [2000] CLC 833 or *Lehman Brothers International (Europe) v. Lehman Brothers Finance* [2012] EWHC 1072 (Ch)—so there is no evident problem here.

9

The Quantitative Analysis of Financial Regulation

Analysis in General

9.1 The effects of regulation can be analysed, either in the rule writing phase or after it has been finalized. This process can provide information on the potential costs, benefits, and risks of the rules. It can also reveal features which where not evident to the rule writers. However, it is a contestable process: different stakeholders can reasonably differ on what constitutes a 'good' analysis, and what conclusions can be drawn from it.

9.2 This chapter addresses these issues. It begins with a discussion of the need for analysis, the tools used to conduct it, and the parties involved. Given that financial regulation is often quantitative, particular insights are available from conducting a cost-benefit analysis, so this approach is discussed in some detail. A framework for comparing costs and benefits is introduced, based on potential harm in futures states of the world with and without regulation.

9.3 Cost-benefit analysis can be used in pursuit of a range of objectives from the optimization of regulation to the justification of prior policy, whatever its merits.

9.4 The authorities published an impact assessment of the post-crisis OTC derivatives regulatory reforms in 2013. This report, from the Macroeconomic Assessment Group for Derivatives, or 'MAGD', asserts that the benefits of the reforms exceed their costs: a quantitative analysis supporting this claim is provided.

9.5 Two case studies are used to demonstrate some of the issues that arise in the analysis of prudential regulation, and to demonstrate the pursuit of different objectives. The first is the MAGD report, which will be found to comprise a policy justification and a defence of regulatory authority. In contrast, a cost-benefit analysis of the anti-procyclicality tools discussed in Chapter 7 will show how a review can uncover some of the features of a policy and improve them.

Why analyse regulation?

9.6 It is clear from Chapters 4 to 7 that writing derivatives regulation is a difficult and error-prone activity. Analysis of proposed regulations can reduce errors, identify inconsistencies and inefficiencies, and highlight potential vulnerabilities. A good analysis can help to elucidate the mechanism by which a rule achieves its goal under certain circumstances, or the processes which can thwart its ability to achieve it in others. Analysis therefore serves both to identify the preconditions of success and failure of a rule, and as a potential justification for the decisions taken in its construction. This, in turn, can provide legitimacy—something that would be absent from an unexplained edict.

9.7 The financial system evolves in response to many factors, including regulation. Another reason to analyse regulation is to consider its continuing appropriateness in the face of change.

9.8 Calibration is an important issue in many rules. The general argument that capital requirements are required for certain risks does not inform the question of how high they should be. That requires a detailed analysis of the frequency and severity of the risk, the impact it has on the institutions bearing it, regulators' desired safety standard for those institutions, and the effects of policy choices on third parties. Connecting causes to effects in turn requires a model of the mechanisms involved. Such a model could give insight into how costs and benefits vary with the calibration of regulation.

What is involved in this analysis?

9.9 The analysis of financial regulation[1] is a complex area, and an entire book could be devoted to it. The principal elements which should be considered are, understandably, closely related to the criteria for legitimacy in global administrative law discussed in the last chapter. They are:

- *Justification.* A justification of rule making requires a statement of the problem being addressed, an analysis of why regulation is required to solve it, and evidence that it lies within the authority of the regulator who is proposing to act. The mechanism by which the rule works should be described. If there are uncertainties or risks in the connection from problem through ameliorating mechanism to desired outcome, they should be set out. Analysis can then consider this justification. If it has not been given, the first step in analysis will often be to reconstruct it.

[1] The analysis of regulation is meta-regulatory, in the sense of being about 'the oversight or governance of regulation' and the 'performance monitoring of regulatory institutions': see Grabosky (2017) for a longer discussion of this.

- *Effectiveness and proportionality*. The method of achieving the desired regulatory goal should at least be effective, if not optimal.[2] The burdens should not significantly outweigh the benefits: a regulation can be effective, but involve a disproportionate imposition on rights.
- *Least onerous means*. Other means of achieving the same objective should be considered in any analysis. For instance, if the chosen regulatory approach is to ban something, would disincentives, charges, disclosure, and/or rationing be better?[3]
- *Process*. The issues here involve whether due process in rule making was followed by the regulator. It is helpful for analysts if the grounds for regulatory decisions are available to them, including both the evidence used by the regulator and any that it discarded. Another relevant concern following implementation is the tracking of the effects of the regulation and the validation (or not) of the purported regulatory mechanism.
- *Interactions and indirect effects*. Regulations can have indirect effects and unintended consequences. Analysis should capture the costs and benefits which result from these. The factors which should be considered include: interactions with other regulations or laws, adaptations of the regulated, and redistributive or competitive effects. When these broader impacts are taken into account, it may reveal that the scope of the goal considered in the original justification of the policy was too narrow.

Approaching the analysis of regulation

9.10 The methods available to the regulatory analyst depend on the stage at which analysis is conducted. If it is being done as part of the regulatory development process, perhaps in support or criticism of a particular proposal, then much is necessarily conjectural. Some form of cost-benefit analysis will almost certainly be possible, if not comparing precise costs with benefits, at least setting out what is known about them. This would involve quantifying them where possible, and recording uncertainty otherwise.[4]

---

2 There are multiple competing notions of optimality of regulation. Train (1991) defines it as producing prices which perfectly capture externalities, but this simply means that risks are properly priced, not necessarily that they are reduced. Moreover, there may be situations when suboptimal prices in Train (1991)'s sense are justified by their distributional effects. For an example of this, see Bento et al. (2013), and for a discussion of moral considerations, Hausman et al. (2017).

3 For more on regulatory methods, see, for instance, Baron (1989), Cole & Grossman (2003), Fong et al. (2000), Gunningham & Sinclair (2017).

4 As Posner (2000) puts it at 138, 'It is not the equality or inequality sign that marks analysis as cost-benefit but the collection and display of costs and benefits.'

9.11 It should be possible to analyse the purported mechanism by which the rule works. For instance, if the goal is the reduction of acid rain below a certain level, the mechanism by which certain pollutants give rise to it should be identified, the various sources of those pollutants quantified, and a model produced demonstrating that the proposed regulatory mechanism will reduce those pollutants sufficiently to meet the goal.[5]

9.12 Post implementation review will usually have more evidence available to guide it. Costs and benefits will be clearer. Side effects, unintended consequences, and redistributional effects may have revealed themselves. The adaptation of the regulated to regulation may be evident. There may also have been challenges to the regulation, and these may reveal issues of, for instance, drafting, authority, or scope which were not evident before implementation.[6]

Quantitative Models of Regulation

9.13 Costs and benefits are core measures of regulatory effectiveness, so it is natural that cost-benefit analysis, or 'CBA', is a common form of quantitative analysis of regulation.[7] This section uses CBA as a frame to uncover some of the issues in the quantitative analysis of regulation. It is somewhat quantitative, so illustrations of the ideas are also provided: paragraphs which can be omitted by the less mathematical reader are marked with a $\ast$.

9.14 Financial regulation is often so complicated in its design and uncertain in its effects that complete, reliable quantification of it is impossible. This does not mean that analysis is pointless. Incomplete models of complex phenomena can reveal unexpected behaviour and can act as a succinct statement of what is known and what is not. Sometimes, attempting to quantify uncertainty is itself useful. Moreover, models can often be refined over time as their predictions are compared with outcomes and uncertainty reduces.

---

5 Acid rain is caused by sulphur dioxide and nitrogen oxides. These are produced by various activities including burning fossil fuels and metal ore smelting. In the United States, the Acid Rain Program and the Cross-State Air Pollution Rule, established under the 1990 Amendments to the Clean Air Act, implemented cap and trade programmes designed to reduce emissions of these pollutants from power plants. Thus, there is a clear link between the regulation, which prices acid-rain-producing emissions, and the goal, reducing acid rain.

6 For post-implementation analysis of the Acid Rain Program, see https://www.epa.gov/acidrain/acid-rain-program.

7 A related term is 'regulatory impact analysis', a systematic appraisal of how proposed rulemaking 'will affect certain categories of stakeholders, economic sectors, and the environment', as Radaelli and de Francesco (2010) puts it at 2: see also Shapiro (2013). Regulatory impact analysis is used for a study, often mandatory, which precedes or justifies rule making, while CBA can take place at any point in the life cycle of a policy.

9.15 One starting point for quantitative analysis is a method introduced by Shavell (1993) for determining the optimal structure of law enforcement. This has subsequently been used extensively in regulatory theory. It proceeds by comparing *ex ante* regulation, which imposes fixed regulatory costs with the intention of preventing bad outcomes, with *ex post* liability should a bad outcome materialize.

9.16 In the simplest setting, the probability, p, of the bad outcome is known and fixed. The total harm to all stakeholders should the bad outcome materialize is H. Suppose that the bad outcome is always detected if it occurs, and the fine imposed is this harm. Then, the expected fine to the actor with *ex post* liability is pH. *Ex ante* regulation with cost c is preferred if $c < pH$. Essentially, prevention is better if its cost is not higher than the expected—which is to say probability-weighted—harm. This framework therefore encapsulates a simple form of CBA.

9.17 One important modification to the framework is to consider a setting where *ex ante* regulation does not with certainty eliminate the bad outcome, but rather changes its probability from p to q, and where it changes the harm if it occurs from H to G. Clearly regulation is only effective if it lowers expected harm, i.e. $qG < pH$. The obvious generalization of Shavell's thinking is that *ex ante* regulation with cost c is preferred if $c < pH - qG$. Note that when regulation is advantageous, we do not know either that $q < p$ or that $G < H$.

Visualizing regulatory outcomes

9.18 A tool for visualizing the impact of regulation is helpful here. Suppose we know all possible future states of the world. In some of these states, there are bad outcomes. Each state has a probability. We will write s for a typical state and S for the set of all such states, and assume that exactly one thing happens. The unit interval is exactly tiled by the probabilities of future states. This is easiest to see with two possible states of the world, s and t. We must have $p(s) = 1 - p(t)$, because the two probabilities must add up to 1. This means that we can associate the interval $[0, p(s))$ with s and the interval $[p(s), 1]$—which is of length $p(t)$—with t. The length of the interval associated with each state equals its probability.

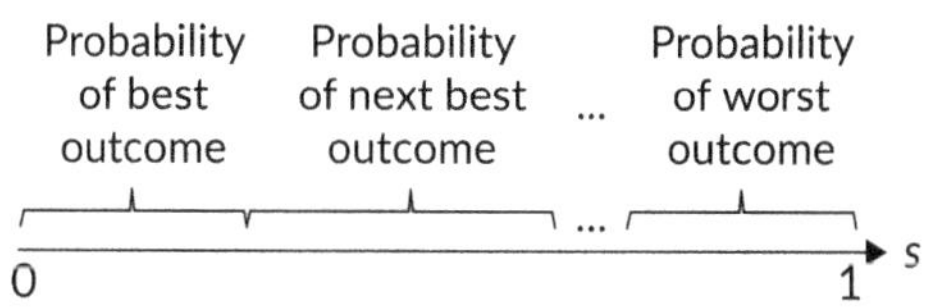

Figure 9.1– An illustration of various outcomes ordered by severity and their probabilities tiling the unit interval

9.19 We will use the convention that states of the world are ordered by the severity of the harm associated with them: Figure 9.1 depicts the idea. This convention means that for any x between 0 and 1, there is a unique outcome associated with it. If x is close to zero, this will be a low harm state; if it is close to one, the harm is higher. We will write $H(s)$ of the harm associated with the state s. Ordering states of the world by harm means that if $H(s) < H(t)$ then s is closer to 0 than t.

9.20 To make this concrete, imagine that a bad state of the world that happens a fifth of the time, with harm of ten. The rest of the time, a good thing happens, with no harm, so we have $S = \{\text{good}, \text{bad}\}$, $p(\text{good}) = \frac{4}{5}$, $p(\text{bad}) = \frac{1}{5}$, $H(\text{good}) = 0$, and $H(\text{bad}) = 10$. The probability-weighted cost of harm in this case is two.

9.21* If there is one bad outcome with probability p and harm N, and otherwise a good outcome, with zero harm, we would have $H(\text{good}) = 0$, and $H(\text{bad}) = N$. This example is illustrated in Figure 9.2. Here, states of the world occupy intervals of the x axis with length equal to their probability of occurrence, while harm is on the y axis. Plots like this allow us to visualize the harm of the situation that is being regulated for: common but relatively low harm situations lie long and low on the x-axis, while uncommon but high harm ones spike near to one.

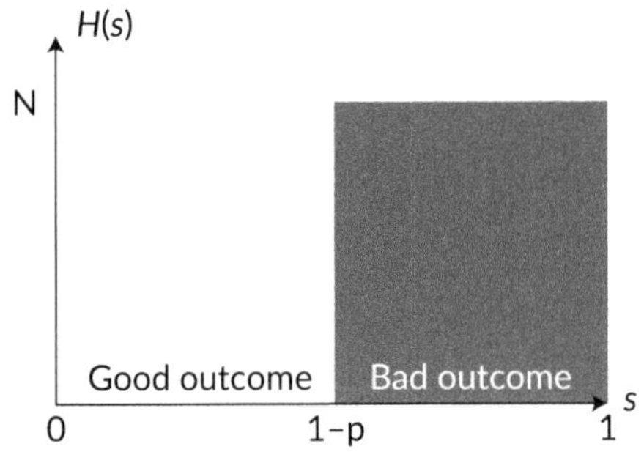

Figure 9.2– An illustration of a single bad outcome

9.22* To see this, consider a slightly more complicated situation with a good outcome, a bad one, and a worse one, as illustrated in the left panel of Figure 9.3.

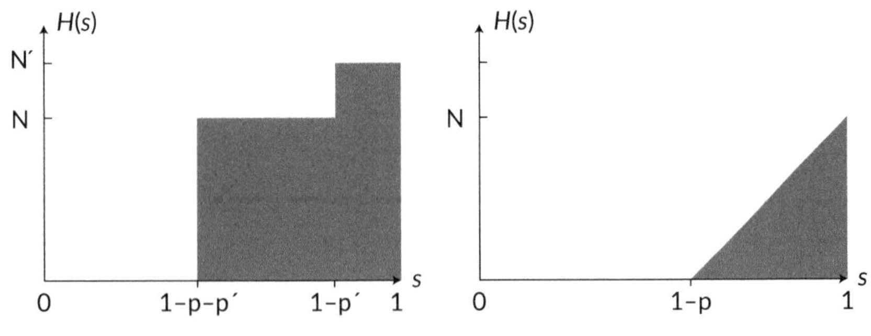

Figure 9.3– An illustration of two distributions of harm

9.23* Here, the good outcome has zero harm as before, the bad outcome has severity of harm N, and the worse one, N'. The probabilities of the bad and worse outcome are p and p', respectively, and our convention puts the states along the x axis in order good; bad; worse, so we would have: $H(\text{good}) = 0$, $H(\text{bad}) = N$, $H(\text{worse}) = N'$. The right panel of the Figure, in contrast, shows a situation with one good outcome and where the harm in bad outcomes is uniformly distributed between 0 and N.

Expected harms and the analysis of regulation

9.24* The expected harm in this framework is obtained by probability-weighting across all states of the world. Before regulation, it is:[8]

$$\sum_s p(s)H(s)$$

9.25 The impact of regulation can be visualized by how it changes the shape of the severity plot. For instance, if regulation reduces both the impact from $H(s)$ to $G(s)$ and probability of a bad outcome s from $p(s)$ to $q(s)$, it would reduce the probability-weighted harm from the area of the darker grey box to the area of the lighter grey box in Figure 9.4.

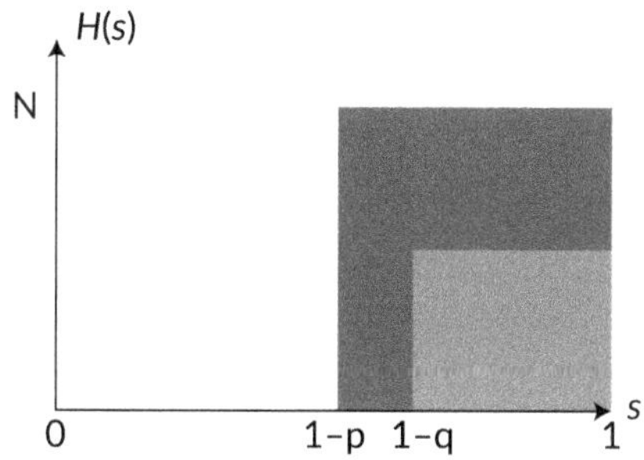

Figure 9.4– An illustration of the impact of effective regulation on a single bad outcome in reducing both its probability and severity

9.26* The costs of regulation can depend on the state of the world, so for generality we would replace fixed costs c with state dependent ones $c(s)$. Shavell's condition that the costs of *ex ante* regulation are justified if the difference between the expected harm of bad outcomes without regulation and the expected harm with regulation are bigger than the cost of regulating is then

$$\sum_s q(s)c(s) \le \sum_s p(s)H(s) - \sum_s q(s)G(s)$$

8 An economist might recognize this as a von Neumann-Morgenstern utility: see, for instance, Schoemaker (1982). Note that economic benefits as well as harms could be included by allowing $H(s)$ to be negative for some s. If S is continuous, integrals replace the sums.

9.27 It can be seen that Shavell's condition can be satisfied in three ways: regulation can reduce the probability of a bad outcome but not its severity; it can reduce its severity but not its probability; or it can reduce both. It can even *increase* either probability or severity and still be worth doing if the reduction in the other variable is large enough.

9.28 In the visual language of Figure 9.4, the area of the pale grey (after regulation) rectangle must be smaller than that of the dark grey (before regulation) rectangle, and Shavell's criteria is that difference in areas must be bigger than the costs of regulating.

9.29 The full set of possible regulatory outcomes are shown in Figure 9.5: on the vertical axis, regulation changes the severity of the outcome, while on the horizontal axis, it changes its probability. Regulations which improve matters in either severity or probability appear in the bottom right, while self-defeating regulations—ones which make matters unambiguously worse—are on the top left.[9] In the other corners, top left and bottom right, are situations where regulation makes either harm or probability worse but the other better.

9.30 Bad outcomes are less likely in the top left, but more severe if they happen; here regulation is storing up more trouble for later. In contrast, in the bottom left of the diagram are situations where bad things happen more often under regulation, but they are less severe when they do. This can be an improvement, in that more probable, less severe events can often be easier to manage. A good example of this situation is the use of flood plains and run-off channels in the management of river flooding. By accepting that some land will be flooded more of the time, the impact of very severe floods can be reduced.[10]

9.31 This discussion illustrates the diverse ways in which regulation can change the probability and/or severity of future states of the world, and hence potentially achieve its goal. However, it also emphasizes the importance of being alert to the possibility that regulation may introduce new, unwelcome possibilities as well as ameliorating old risks.[11]

---

[9] See Sunstein (1990) for a discussion of self-defeating or iatrogenic regulatory strategies.

[10] This is the idea behind the 'Room for the River' programme in the Netherlands. Before this project, an important technique in flood management was to build dykes. This had the effect of decreasing the probability of flooding but increasing its severity when the dykes were breached. The new programme instead 'restores the river's natural flood plain in places where it is least harmful in order to protect those areas that need to be defended'. It creates 'marshy riverine landscapes to serve once again as natural 'water storage' sponges and provide biodiversity and aesthetic and recreational values.' See *Dutch Water Program Room for the River*, available at https://dredging.org/media/ceda/org/documents/events/ceda/room%20for%20the%20river.pdf.

[11] The role of the leverage ratio in disincentivizing repo market intermediation and the provision of client clearing, as discussed in Chapter 4, is an example of this.

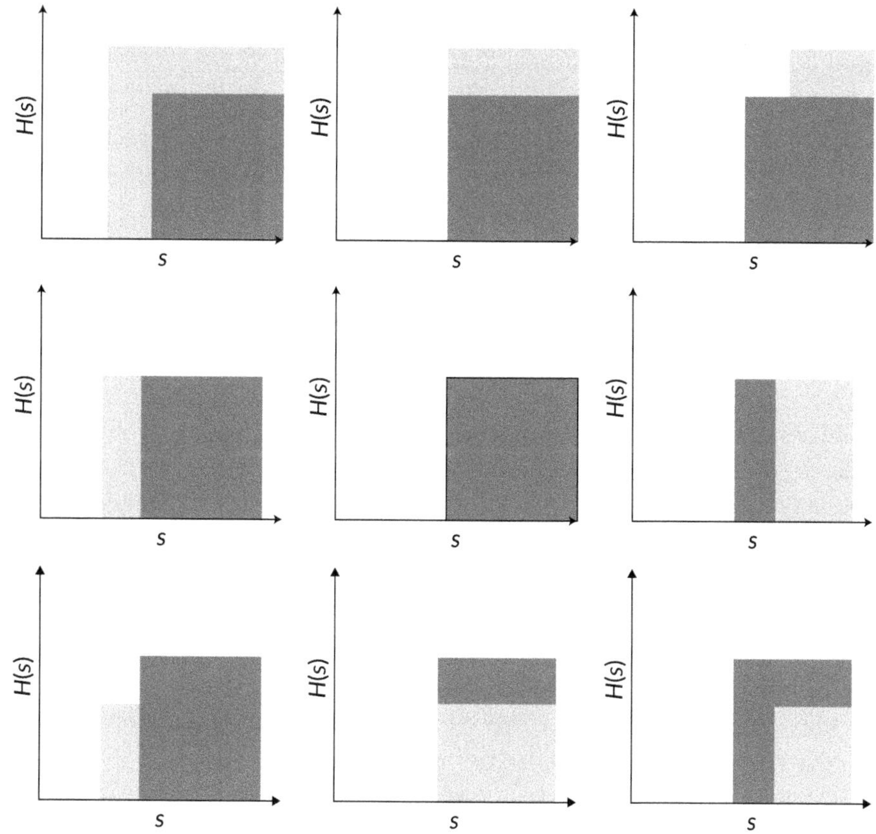

Figure 9.5– An illustration of the potential effects of regulation. The situation without regulation is shown in the centre. The columns represent regulation increasing, not affecting, or decreasing the probability of the bad outcome. The rows represent regulation increasing, not affecting, or decreasing its severity

Cost-benefit analysis of regulation

9.32 The discussion above suggests a definition of cost-benefit analysis as:

- The specification of a set of all relevant possible futures;
- For each possible future, a statement of the probability of its occurrence without regulation and a harm were it to occur;
- For each possible future, a cost of regulation, a statement of its probability of occurrence with regulation, and a harm were it to happen with regulation; and
- A comparison of the probability-weighted cost of regulation with the benefit in probability-weighted harm reduction.

9.33* In our prior notation, this would involving for each state $s \in S$, estimating the harms $G(s)$ and $H(s)$ with and without regulation, the cost of regulating $c(s)$, and the probabilities $p(s)$ and $q(s)$. The cost-benefit comparison is of[12]

$$\sum_s q(s)c(s) \qquad \text{with} \qquad \sum_s (p(s)H(s) - q(s)G(s))$$

How cost-benefit analysis can go wrong

9.34 Now that the framework is clear, it is important to analyse how it can fail. The first class of issues arises in the concept of CBA. Here harm is measured in monetary units: the implicit assumption is that harms can be quantified and that bigger harms are always worse. This is a strong and questionable form of utilitarianism. For instance, Rawls (1972) points out that it matters who the harm falls on, while Sen (1987) and Posner & Sunstein (2017) emphasizes the missing morality—the 'issue of rights and freedom'—in this analysis. CBA would suggest that a policy that takes £20 from everyone in the UK and gives £2 billion of benefit to one person who was already a billionaire would be justified, as the net benefit is positive[13] even though its redistributional consequences are odious.[14]

9.35 Any CBA involves the definition of costs and benefits. But costs and benefits to whom? The exercise inevitably involves a normative choice, 'with regard to whose interests are to count'. Perspective matters. Consider a proposed new property development on the edge of a town: does this impose costs on government, in providing services, or does the lack of services impose costs on the developer?[15] Who has the right to what? The choice cannot be made without revealing a ranking of some rights over others.[16]

9.36 Another set of problems arises when the set of all relevant futures is not known or the probabilities of them cannot be estimated.[17] This is the issue of

[12] In the continuous version, this is a comparison of $\int q(s)c(s)\,ds$ with $\int (p(s)H(s) - q(s)G(s))\,ds$. The integrals must exist and should be finite: for this it suffices that $c(s)$, $H(s)$ and $G(s)$ are piecewise continuous and bounded, given that p and q obey $\int p(s)\,ds = \int q(s)\,ds = 1$.

[13] The current population of the UK is about 70 million, so the cost would be around £1.4 billion.

[14] For a further discussion and examples, see Ackerman & Heinzerling (2002).

[15] The quote and example are from Samuels (1978) at 101 where the assumption is that these costs fall on the town or municipality, as they would in the United States, rather than on national utilities, as they partly would in Europe. This emphasizes the normative nature of the choices made.

[16] See Sen (1987) at 56.

[17] Often probability stands in for incomplete knowledge. Consider the outcome of a spin of the roulette wheel. This is usually thought of as purely probabilistic. However, with sufficient knowledge about the initial throw of the ball and the rotation of the wheel, it is possible to make useful predictions about the outcome: see Small & Tse (2012) for details. Thus, while an uninformed gambler might bet on a 16, an informed one (especially if they have associates who bounce lasers off the ball and the wheel, measure reflections to derive position and velocity information, and

Knightian uncertainty: when the future 'cannot be fully foreseen with probabilistic rules'.[18] Reponses to this include 'minimax', where the probability of the worst possible outcome is minimized, and 'satisficing', where the aim is to ensure that all outcomes have acceptable costs.[19]

9.37 In regulation, Knightian uncertainty leads to the precautionary principle that if p and/or H are not known but there are 'reasonable grounds for concern', meaning roughly that the expected harm $\sum p(s)H(s)$ might well be big enough to worry about, then we should act anyway.[20] As we saw in Chapter 5, the difficulty often lies in justifying the particular level of precautionary intervention chosen.

9.38 The final class of problems have the same effect, in that the analysis is wrong due to failing to model the future correctly, but for different reasons. Here, there are states of the world which can be foreseen, but have never occurred; or states have been assigned the wrong probability and/or the wrong harm. A particular issue here is that we often assume that high regulatory costs $c(s) > H(s)$ are acceptable for 'ordinary' or highly likely states s due to the existence of an improbable but really bad state t with very high harm: i.e. one with $p(t) \ll 1$ but $H(t) \gg c(t)$. This state t would justify the cost of regulation if the harm $H(t)$ is so large that the product $p(t)H(t)$ is material despite $p(t)$ being small. However, if $p(t)$ is not just small but significantly smaller than we think it is, then regulation might not be justified: it might not make sense to regulate to prevent the nearly impossible from occurring. Conversely, if low probability, high severity states are even a little more probable than we think they are, regulation can be justified even in cases where we had previously dismissed regulation as too costly.[21] Particular care, then, is needed in dealing with low probability high severity future states, as they can often make all the difference in the analysis.

---

feed those measurements into a dynamical model of the ball/wheel system) might know that the probability of the ball ending up in that pocket was close to zero.

18 See the discussion in Knight (1921) at 19–20.

19 These tools have been extensively investigated in the planning literature: see, for instance, Trevizan et al. (2007).

20 There is also the related issue of crisis management: if the authorities have effective tools to mitigate some high harm states should they occur, our attitude to precaution might be different.

21 Insurance losses from disasters illustrate the issues here. Between 1970 and 1988, global claims did not exceed \$20B per year. The first higher severity event was Hurricane Andrew in 1992, with an insured loss of \$27B, and by 2005 annual natural disaster losses exceeded \$100B every six years, with major contributions from Hurricanes Katrina, Rita, and Wilma in 2005; earthquakes in Japan and New Zealand and a flood in Thailand in 2011; and Hurricanes Harvey, Irma, and Maria in 2017. The factors responsible include increased coastal house building, higher property values, increased insurance, and warmer seas creating stronger hurricanes. It is clear is that if one had naïvely estimated whether costly protection against hurricanes was justified using data from 1970 to 1988, the estimate of the expected harm $p(\text{big Hurricane})H(\text{big Hurricane})$ would likely have been too low, and hence the wrong conclusion may have been drawn.

9.39 The future might not be like the past, so the estimates of post-regulation probabilities and harms q and G might be wrong. One way that this can happen is risk shifting: reducing risk in one area can mean that it pops up in another. An interesting example here is Australian legislation making the wearing of bicycle helmets compulsory.[22] Some of the issues this regulation raises are:[23]

- There was risk shifting[24] whereby either cyclists wearing helmets took more risks, or drivers treated them with less care, or both. Thus, for future states with an accident, s, it seems likely that $q(s) > p(s)$.
- Cycling reduced after enactment. Since cycling has health and environmental benefits, this suggests that for states s' where the cyclist does not have an accident, both $p(s')H(s')$ and $q(s')G(s')$ are negative, and after regulation, this benefit is smaller, because $p(s') < q(s')$.
- While there is mixed evidence as to whether compulsory helmet legislation reduces the probability and severity of accidental head injuries, this is difficult to interpret as there were simultaneous other improvements in road safety. Given the large costs of compulsory helmets,[25] it is possible—even likely—that the costs do not exceed the benefits.

9.40 This bring out a final key issue with cost-benefit analysis: it might tell us whether a given policy has sufficient benefits to justify its costs, but it does not tell us if there is a different policy with lower costs or higher benefits or both. Bicycle helmets protect to some degree against head injuries while cycling, but most bike accidents involving head injuries are caused by cars. Better bike lanes, lower speed limits in areas with a high density of cyclists, and better driver education of the danger they pose to cyclists, might all be better policies than making the wearing of bicycle helmets compulsory.

Quantitative Review of Financial Regulation

9.41 Cost-benefit analysis, despite its limitations, can offer insights into the attractiveness of a proposed regulation. It has been used extensively in policy

22 The legislation is in 1999 amendments to the Trade Practices Regulations: the most recent version is Trade Practices (Consumer Product Safety Standard) (Bicycle Helmets) Regulations 2001.

23 The facts here are contested. Compare Walter et al. (2011) with Rissel (2012).

24 Peltzman (1975) evocatively describes this behaviour with regard to the mandatory use of seat belts in cars by evoking 'the belted-milquetoast-turned-daredevil'.

25 See Hendrie et al. (1999) for a discussion of costs and benefits, and Robinson (2006) for a review of the evidence from various countries on trends in head injuries to cyclists.

development, and it is mandated in some situations.[26] In the United States, a legal requirement to analyse means that CBA has been often applied to financial regulation. This has generated a substantial debate both about the general merits of the cost-benefit analysis of financial regulation and about particular instances of it.[27]

Issues in the use of CBA for financial regulation

9.42 The financial system is complicated and dynamic, so it is hardly surprising that it is difficult to create good financial regulation, and that analysis can reveal features which were not evident to rule writers. The cost-benefit analysis of financial regulation is, however, not without problems. These follow the concerns around its use more broadly, but some of them become more pointed in this context. Some of the important considerations are:

- *CBA can be used as camouflage for supervisory discretion.* One of the reasons that bureaucracies cleave to complex, jargon-ridden processes replete with arbitrary classifications and recondite mechanisms is because they can provide ready justifications for most actions. A good team of economists can provide an analysis which shows that the benefit of more or less any policy is greater than its cost, just as a good story teller can make a world where the principal means of transport is flying elephants seem plausible. Moreover the analysis can be made opaque enough that the appearance of soaring pachyderms is well disguised.[28]
- *Estimation errors.* It is unclear if it is meaningful to speak of the probability of a financial crisis in the next year. Either there is one, or there isn't. The financial system cannot be rerun from the same initial conditions to explore other alternatives. Some insight can be obtained by looking at outcomes in different countries, but this approach is limited as there are a relatively small number of sophisticated financial systems and they are not independent. This means that in the key area of interest—estimating the impact of a proposed regulation on the probability and severity of a financial crisis—there is substantial uncertainty about estimates of p, q,

[26] Requirements to provide a CBA of regulation have a long history, especially in the United States: see the executive orders on regulatory planning and review 12,291, 12,866, 13,422, 13,535, and 13,563 from the Reagan, Clinton, Bush, Bush, and Obama presidencies, respectively. The version in force at time of writing requires that each regulatory agency must 'propose or adopt a regulation only upon a reasoned determination that its benefits justify its costs (recognizing that some benefits and costs are difficult to quantify)': see R. Obama (2011).

[27] See Awrey (2010b), Coates (2015), Cochrane (2014), Philippon (2015), and Posner & Weyl (2014).

[28] Similarly, as Driesen (2005) points out, the requirement for CBA can be used to weaken regulation if policy makers have to conclusively demonstrate that costs are definitely smaller than benefits.

H and *G*. The uncertainty is often so great as to throw into question any conclusions drawn from a cost-benefit analysis.[29]

- *Reflexivity and unintended consequences.* The financial system reacts to regulation, so regulating can introduce new failure modes or change the dynamics of old ones.[30] This means that the probability of a bad state after regulation can be close to or even bigger than its probability before regulation, and/or that harm may be materially underestimated.[31]
- *Choice of rights.* A major issue in conducting a CBA is the choice of which costs and benefits to count. This is, as discussed above, a normative choice, involving value judgements beyond the mandate of regulators. A common problem in financial regulation is focusing on bank costs and benefits and ignoring the rights of users of the financial system.
- *Improbable states imposing great harms.* The use of reduction in probability-weighted harm as the measure of benefit is contentious when considering states with very large harms, such as those associated with financial crises. If $H(s)$ is, say, 50% of GDP, does it really matter if $p(s)$ is 1% or 0.1%? Is this harm big enough that even quite large costs are tolerable, even absent good estimates of probabilities?
- *Costs v. benefits as determinative.* Given all of the above, CBA puts too much focus on using the relative sizes of (necessarily estimated) costs and benefits as a decision making tool.

Effective CBA for financial regulation

9.43 The issues outlined above highlight the difficulty of performing CBA on financial regulation. They do not invalidate the exercise. CBA is a good discipline, even if the final comparison is clouded by uncertainty in estimation. Its point is

[29] Coates (2015) makes the case that cost-benefit analysis of financial regulation 'should be understood not as science but as number-laden guesswork' which is not 'replicable, reliable or predictive'.

[30] A good example here is the imposition of mandatory derivatives clearing. This reduced the probability that losses caused by a failure of an OTC derivatives counterparty would cause a chain of defaults. The probability of this event was low anyway because the exposures in chains involving systemically important counterparties were small compared to the capital available to absorb the loss. Mandatory clearing did, however, increase the risk that the failure of a central counterparty could endanger the financial system. Since CCPs are relatively much less well capitalized than banks and can fail for reasons other than default loss, it could well be that the probability-weighted harm of financial instability after the imposition of mandatory central clearing was bigger than it was before. In order to address this issue, another regulatory intervention was necessary: the development of CCP recovery and resolution plans.

[31] Gordon (2015) argues that the CBA of financial regulation is, as a result of reflexivity, 'a serious category mistake' and as a result is 'virtually useless in the setting of optimal financial regulation'.

not to always to demonstrate conclusively that costs are lower than benefits, but rather to quantify what can reasonably be quantified, including the uncertainties in estimates, document those things that matter and cannot be quantified, and justify the choices made.

9.44 This stance on the role of CBA raises several questions. Why are *these* costs and benefits the right ones to consider? What is the mechanism by which the benefits will flow from the proposed regulatory intervention, and what might thwart that? How might the system adapt to regulation? What has not been considered? What are the policy alternatives, and what are their costs and benefits? The discipline of mapping the limits to policy makers' ability to answer these questions may be as important as the answers themselves.

9.45 The CBA in the SEC's cross-border swaps rules has received attention in the literature.[32] These rules give the SEC supervisory nexus over cross-border activity in the securities-based swaps market 'in order to promote effective and consistent global regulation'.[33] The rule making contains an extensive economic analysis.

9.46 The SEC's analysis here is notable in several regards. First, it appeared alongside the rule proposal, and clearly informed it, rather than merely forming a *post hoc* justification. Second, it acknowledges the difficulty of quantifying many of the costs and benefits. Third, it accepts that part of this difficulty arises because 'the practices of market participants are expected to evolve'.[34] Finally, it attempts to analyse the impact of different parts of the rules rather than just the overall impact, and in so doing, throws some light on potentially more and less costly, and more and less beneficial areas of policy. While there has been some reasonable criticism of the 'conceptual' nature of the document,[35] the work on these rules demonstrates that authorities can use cost-benefit analysis to improve regulation.

Calibration via CBA

9.47 Financial regulation often involves free parameters, which regulators must calibrate. CBA is a useful tool here. As an example, consider the capital problem: what is the optimal minimum capital ratio?[36] At least for some range, higher ratios of risk-weighted assets to capital increase financial stability, but they impose costs on both banks and—because they are passed on—the broader economy. At some point, there are diminishing returns: banks with a capital ratio of 25% are not

32 See CCMR (2013) and, partly in comment on this, Coates (2015). The proposed rules can be found in 78 Federal Register 30,967.

33 Dodd-Frank Act §§752.

34 78 Federal Register 31,119.

35 Coates (2015) at 982.

36 For more on this issue, see Barrell et al. (2009), Murphy et al. (2021), and Walther (2016).

much safer than those with 20%, but that extra 5% reduces credit provision to, and creates costs for, the economy.[37]

9.48* To make this concrete, suppose that a regulation has a parameter, α, which determines its cost in various states of the world. This cost is

$$\sum_{s} q_{\alpha}(s) c_{\alpha}(s)$$

9.49* Similarly, the benefit of regulation depends on the parameter because it affects the probability and severity of harm:

$$\sum_{s} (p(s)H(s) - q_{\alpha}(s)G_{\alpha}(s))$$

9.50* An evidence-based calibration would examine how the costs and benefits varied with the calibration parameter, α.

Other forms of quantitative review

9.51 The cross-border swaps rule analysis discussed in the last section demonstrates that the quantitative analysis of regulation does not have to be limited to costs and benefits. It can also address issues of market structure, market quality, and redistribution.

9.52 Derivatives regulation often has consequences for market structure, and forming a view on the desirability of these consequences often involves difficult judgements. For instance, as DAT (2018) demonstrated,[38] one of the effects of the post-crisis derivatives reforms has been a concentration in the provision of client clearing.

9.53 The question then arises whether a market structure with a small number of better capitalized, more liquid dealers is better or worse than one with a larger number of less safe dealers. A dealer failure is less likely in the former but more severe if it occurs. It may be difficult to make a robust cost-benefit comparison in this situation as estimates of pH and qG are uncertain. Nevertheless, mapping the change in market structure is important as it reveals the potential need to intervene to reduce concentration, or at least to stop it getting any worse.

9.54 Similar issues arise in market microstructure analysis. Is a market with, on average, tighter bid-offer spreads, but with occasional flash crashes and episodes of illiquidity, better or worse than one with higher average transaction costs but which is more robust in stress?

---

[37] The choice to view this is a benefit—to see credit as a good—is itself of course a normative one.

[38] At 53.

Two Analyses of Derivatives Reforms

9.55 This section compares two analyses of derivatives reforms: the authorities' 2013 macroeconomic impact assessment of OTC derivatives regulatory reforms presented in MAGD (2013), and a quantitative analysis of the anti-procyclicality tools required by EMIR and discussed in Chapter 7.

9.56 The 2013 MAGD report was published after the initial rule making, and thus had no influence over it. Rather it attempted to demonstrate that 'the economic benefits of [the post-crisis derivatives] reforms are likely to exceed their costs'. It was, in short, post hoc justification. In contrast, we will analyse the anti-procyclicality tools through an exploratory exercise capable of uncovering policy options and informing the rule making process.

The approach of the MAGD

9.57 The MAGD was based on a simple model of the core of the OTC derivatives system. It included 41 banks and no clients. This demonstrates a very narrow set of concerns: the analysis completely ignores the essential function of derivatives markets, namely providing risk transfer markets for end-users. It is solely focused on bank stability in a stylized derivatives market: in particular, one where CCPs never fail. Moreover, because the costs borne by clients (including clearing costs, bilateral margin requirements, and the cost of increased earning volatility resulting from less efficient risk transfer) are not included, the estimate of the cost of regulation (c in the notation earlier in the chapter) is likely too low.

9.58 The issues with the MAGD are not confined to what was modelled: how the model is constructed is problematic too. In order to obtain an estimate of the benefit of reform, the report proposes a mechanism whereby increasing CDS spreads on banks lead to CVA losses and increasing leverage. When a sufficient proportion of banks in the network have leverage ratios at or above a threshold, the financial system is assumed to tip into crisis. It is further assumed that the derivatives reforms reduce the probability of this crisis. There are three key problems with this approach:

- *The connection between CVA losses and leverage.* Other post-crisis reforms, notably enhanced capital and liquidity regulation, and resolution policy, have made banks more robust and decreased the loss given default on their senior obligations, such as derivatives. Therefore banks are less sensitive to CVA losses than before and, if they fail, the resulting recoveries are likely to be higher. This means that the MAGD overstates the losses in a crisis, $H(\text{crisis})$ in our notation.
- *No mechanism explaining how harm occurs.* MAGD (2013) assumes that if a state of the world occurs where two or more banks' leverage is above 40,

there is a financial crisis.[39] There is no account of why this would happen: just the statement that 'this leverage level has caused financial stress in individual institutions in the past'.[40]

This assumption is unjustified: the major causes of financial crises are real estate losses after credit booms and/or sovereign stress, not derivatives.[41] The MAGD calibrates the cost of banking crises using historical data from crises. It then assumes that the probability of a crisis is reduced due to the derivatives reforms, despite the fact that they do nothing for real estate lending, sovereign exposures,[42] overvalued currencies, or credit booms. Ignoring the actual causes of crises and blaming them instead on derivatives exaggerates the benefits of derivatives reform: $p(\text{crisis})$ is overstated and both $q(\text{crisis})$ and $G(\text{crisis})$ are dramatically understated.

- *No analysis of alternatives.* The MAGD review does not consider alternatives, such as using incentives to clear instead of (rather than as well as) the clearing mandate, or having a much higher threshold for margin requirements. However, it does give away a key insight: that almost all of the benefit modelled comes from variation margin.[43] Thus, the alternative of simply requiring daily inter-dealer cash variation margin would achieve nearly all of the benefits modelled by the MAGD with much lower costs.

9.59 There is much more that could be criticized in the MAGD,[44] but it is already evident from the foregoing that the mechanism proposed in the MAGD is dubious. The derivatives exposures between today's banks, if they were not subject to

[39] See MAGD (2013) at 28.

[40] The caution from Cochrane (2014) that regulators 'often think they know cause and effect, either wrongly or with far more precision than they actually do, and enact regulation on the basis of unverified cause-and-effect speculation' is relevant here.

[41] The classic analysis of financial liberalization, sovereign/banking system interconnection, overvalued currencies, and credit growth leading to banking crises is in Reinhart & Rogoff (2009).

[42] Reinhart & Rogoff (2009), in their analysis of a wide range of banking crises, identify the two most significant indicators of future trouble as deviations from trend of the real exchange rate—indicative of capital inflows—and changes in real house prices.

[43] The 'reforms vastly lower CVAs held against these [OTC derivatives] exposures' (MAGD (2013) at 9) which means that CVA losses from counterparty credit quality declines are not sufficient to push the banks studied over 'the tipping point'. Almost all of this effect comes from variation margin alone: footnote 5 says that 'capital against potential future OTC derivatives exposures … is relatively inconsequential for the benefits analysis'.

[44] To pick a few examples: the calibration of the exposures is questionable, as it relies on notionals, not risk exposures; the threshold in PDs for institution stress is arbitrary and unsupported by post-reform data; the handling of netting benefits is crude and also unsupported by data from modern cleared markets; and the LGDs are set at a level substantially higher than the average for derivatives receivables.

variation margin, could cause significant losses, but it is not inevitable that these losses can plausibly lead to a crisis. The MAGD does not justify mandatory client clearing at all, as it ignores clients, nor does it suggest that any margin policy at all is necessary beyond the dense core of the OTC derivatives network.

APC tools, their costs, and benefits

9.60 Anti-procyclicality tools for initial margin models were introduced in Chapter 7. The concern driving their adoption was that variation in CCP IM requirements might impose unnecessary and excessive liquidity risk on margin participants, which might, in turn, exacerbate the 'dash for cash' just when market intermediation and funding markets are most challenged.

9.61 The 'pre-regulation' state the policy is concerned with therefore involves a change in the markets leading to a rise in initial margin requirements. To mitigate this, EU regulation requires CCPs to apply one of three 'APC tools' to their margin models. Recall that these tools were a floor on margin, a margin buffer, and the use of observations from a stressed period in the calculation of margin.

9.62 An exploratory analysis of these tools will now be presented. The aim will be to use the ideas of cost, benefit, harm, and so on, to uncover the behaviour of the current regulation, and to discover potentially better alternatives.

9.63 One obvious measure of the cost of APC tools is the extra margin they impose. Therefore a long data series of financial returns (the same returns as were used for the graphs in Chapter 7) will be used to study the average amount of margin imposed per day by a typical CCP margin model[45] both with and without the use of one of the EMIR APC tools.

9.64 The two aspects of CCP initial margin model procyclicality—not going too low in placid periods and not spiking too high in stress—require different measures. Reasonable choices are:

- To use the ratio of (close to) the peak margin over a long period of time to the margin trough in order to measure the variation of margin requirements from placid periods to high stress;[46]
- To use (close to)[47] the largest increase in margin over any thirty calendar day period to measure the increase in margin in high stress.

[45] The model is a filtered historical simulation value at risk model with a two year window.

[46] These two measures were introduced in Murphy et al. (2014). The definition in that paper are modified slightly here: the peak-to-trough ratio is very sensitive to the peaks for some margin models, so instead of the absolute maximum and minimum of margin, we use the 99.7th and 0.3th percentiles of margin for the peak and trough respectively.

[47] For similar reasons to those discussed in the last footnote, instead of picking the largest increase, we pick the 99.7th percentile of increases.

9.65 These two measures will be called the 'peak-to-trough' or 'P/T' ratio and 'large call' measures respectively. A cost-benefit analysis of an APC tool takes a margin model, a portfolio, and a history of market returns and analyses the cost of the tool in extra margin versus its benefit in reducing each of these two measures.

9.66 Figure 9.6 presents such an analysis. The original margin model is shown as a triangle: the arrows show the effect of applying the three EMIR APC tools to it. It can be seen that regulatory intervention comes at a cost: applying any of the tools results in higher average levels of margin. All of the tools reduce procyclicality as measured by the P/T ratio. Of the three tools, the floor does this at the lowest cost, while the buffer is most expensive. The reductions are substantial: the P/T ratio falls from over 9 for the unmitigated model to less than 5 for the model with either the floor or the stressed VAR tool applied.

9.67 The situation is less good with respect to the reduction in the large call measure. All the tools are somewhat effective, but even the best—stressed VAR—only reduces the large call measure from over 3.5% to 2.6%.[48]

An alternative APC approach

9.68 The analysis above shows how cost-benefit analysis can aid the policy design process.[49] It raises several issues. First, if the aim is to reduce one or both measures of procyclicality, this should be explicitly stated as the policy goal. If it is something else, that should be disclosed. The policy goal in EMIR is unclear and the approach of mandating use of one of the tools, rather than the desired outcome, is suboptimal. This consideration, in turn, raises the question of whether there are lower cost means of achieving the same benefit. In terms of the graph, can we go further down without going so far to the right?

9.69 The answer, it turns out, is yes. The final point in Figure 9.6, marked 'Alt. Lambda', is the same margin model, but with an alternative parameterization.[50] This model still accurately estimates margin; it has substantially better LC procyclicality properties than any of the other approaches; its PT procyclicality is better than the buffer; and it has substantially lower costs than any of the EMIR APC tools.

9.70 The concepts of probability and severity are helpful here. Very stressed states, with very high risk measures, are typically quite improbable. In the example illustrated, average margin is roughly 2.5%, but margin over 7% occurs more than 0.5% of the time.

[48] These results depend sensitively on when the buffer is released: see Murphy & Vause (2021) for a further discussion.

[49] See Driesen (2005) for a discussion of the advantages of using CBA as an analysis rather than a justification tool.

[50] This model uses a different decay parameter for volatility estimation.

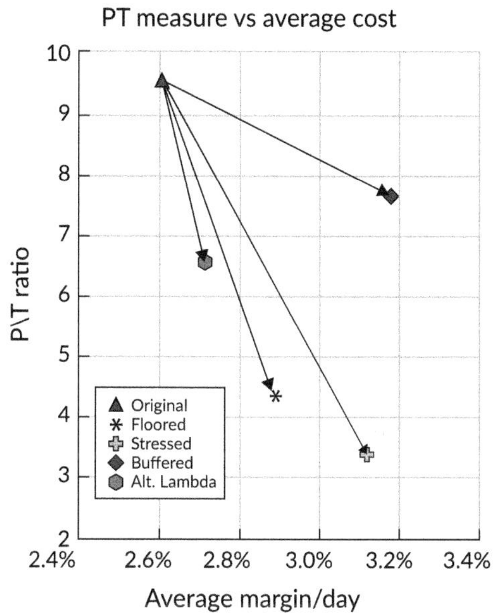

Figure 9.6– The cost-benefit analysis of EMIR's APC tools compared with model recalibration. Above, with benefit given by changes in the P/T ratio; below, using changes in the size of large calls

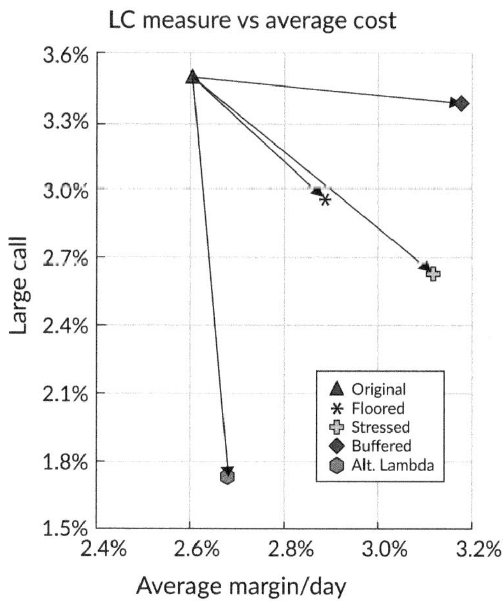

9.71 These improbable states with margin over 7% are responsible for the most significant liquidity stress, so a low-cost approach to procyclicality mitigation would be to focus on margin calls in high stress, adjusting the model so that it is less reactive to it.

9.72 Thus far, the analysis has phrased the benefits of regulation in terms of the two procyclicality measures. However, recall from paragraph 7.108 that margin procyclicality affects different derivatives market participants differently. This means that margin procyclicality in a clearing service primarily serving entities with substantial liquidity buffers can be substantially higher than in one primarily serving end-users, while creating the same risk to the financial system, and thus the same benefit from regulation. Procyclicality policy should be responsive to this, and mindful of the liquidity risk imposed on the real economy of margin arrangements.[51]

CCP initial margin during Covid

9.73 The period of market disruption in March 2020 discussed in Chapter 3 provides an opportunity to perform a post-implementation analysis of margin policy. It was exactly the kind of improbable, high risk period discussed above. One estimate is that the aggregate amount of collateral posted to CCPs rose by nearly 50% during the first quarter of 2020.[52]

9.74 CCPs remained resilient during this period, although no large clearing member defaulted, so their preparations were not severely tested. Increases in margin certainly helped buttress their defences, but they created liquidity stress on market participants and added to the overall demand for cash.[53] In some markets where volatility was particularly high, the effects were unprecedented.[54]

---

[51] For context, the early margin arrangements were requirements for fixed amounts. These were set high enough—and contracts were short enough duration—that there was no need for frequent settlement, i.e. variation margin. The earliest example I am aware of here is in the 1888 *Regulations for Coffee Future Delivery Business* of the London Produce Clearing House, which require a 'deposit, the amount of which shall from time to time be fixed by the Company and duly published, but which shall never be less than £80 per 500 bags'.

[52] FIA (2020) states that the 'aggregate amount of initial margin rose from $563.6 billion at year end [2019] to $833.9 billion at the end of the first quarter [2020].' Perhaps even more telling was their finding that in the United States, 'the total amount of customer collateral in clearing accounts rose by more than $136 billion in the month of March, more than six times larger than any previous single month increase in the history of the industry.'

[53] Variation margin played a major role here. One estimate is that gross variation margin calls on centrally cleared derivatives were over twice their average level on 14 out of 21 business days in March 2020, peaking at over five times the average: see Horrell & Chichkanov (2020).

[54] The front month WTI future, with its swing from $18.27 per barrel to −$37.63 then back to $10.01 was one area where there were substantial variation margin movements. Initial margin on this

It is also important to note that the uncleared derivatives market proved robust, and did not display the same degree of initial margin procyclicality.

9.75 These events demonstrate that post-crisis derivatives policy, with its focus on reducing counterparty credit risk, has created substantial liquidity risk. If the authorities' interventions had not included enormous injections of cheap liquidity, this could have been as dangerous or more dangerous than a solvency-driven stress.[55] Moreover, this liquidity kept banks afloat, but it did not reach non-bank market participants in time to prevent deleveraging, further validating the utility of focusing on improbable, high risk states of the world and considering not just the total size of the margin burden, but also the ways in which different types of firms are subject to different degrees of liquidity stress.[56]

9.76 Anti-procyclicality tools are typically not very effective when confronted with markets which are substantially more stressed than any in their calibration window, so the benefit they can bring is limited here. As an example, consider ten year US Treasury securities. These experienced significantly higher levels of stress in March 2020, at least by some measures, than in any period since the 1970s. APC tools would have been effective at keeping margin from falling too low before this period, but they would have done little to mitigate the impact of the spike in risk measures—and hence margin—which occurred in March.

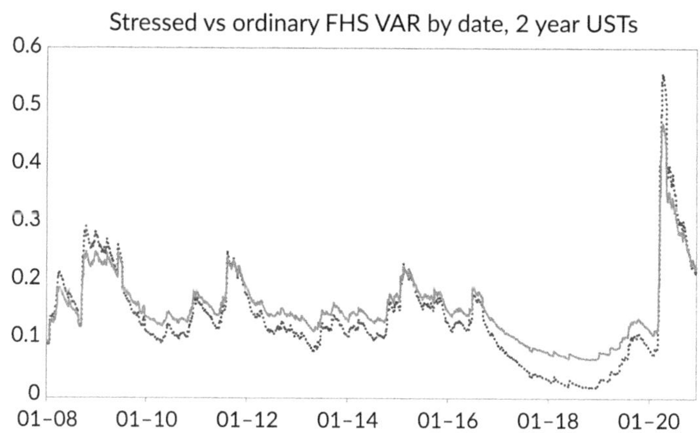

Figure 9.7- Margin for US Treasuries with (darker, dotted line) and without (lighter, solid line) the stressed observations tool

contract at the leading CCPs clearing WTI futures, ICE and CME, jumped by over 60% in less than a month, and continued to increase through April and May 2020.

[55] As FIA (2020) notes, failure to pay at one CCP will likely be an event of default at many other CCPs, so a clearing member has to meet all the liquidity calls on it promptly.

[56] See Barth & Kahn (2020) for a detailed discussion of the part played by margin calls in causing hedge fund deleveraging in the US Treasury market.

9.77 Figure 9.7 illustrates this, showing the level of margin from one model with and without the EMIR stressed observations tool. The peak margin call is only 15% lower with APC. The question arises as to whether this behaviour is societally optimal. If not, then either more effective APC tools are needed, margin model redesign is required, or more risk in high stress should be mutualized.

Concluding Remarks

9.78 The two case studies demonstrate that quantitative analysis of regulation can be informative, and can lead to better policy or 'nudge regulators beyond a baseless enthusiasm for tried but perhaps less helpful models of regulation', as Coates (2015) puts it at 1009. However, it can also act as a purported justification of and camouflage for policies which deserve closer and more disinterested scrutiny that they receive. There is obviously a danger that an analysis performed by the policy writer is not sufficiently objective—but this is not inevitable.[57]

9.79 CBA, then, can encourage consideration of exactly how regulation alters the probability and severity of harmful states, and what that alteration costs. Whether explicitly framed as a comparison of costs vs benefits or in the less constrained form of a regulatory impact analysis, it can inform questions of the proportionality, high severity/low probability failure modes, and regulatory mechanism design. It can be used to improve the design of regulation so as to make it likely that its net benefit is higher.[58] This makes it a useful tool in determining when regulatory intervention is justified. However, it is not a panacea, especially in the presence of Knightian uncertainty and adaption to regulation, and it will not settle all disputes about regulatory design or redistributive effects.

[57] The SEC's cross-border swaps rule referenced in footnote 32 is an example of a diligent authority-conducted analysis which interrogates the rule proposed. Note, however, the analysis of Hertin et al. (2009) based on 22 in-depth policy case studies, which found a 'large variability of process and outcome' in regulatory impact analysis, causing them to conclude that expecting it to provide 'a reliable, objective and comprehensive picture of potential impacts of a planned policy is clearly not realistic'.

[58] See Shapiro (2013) for more on this conclusion.

10

Derivatives Regulation as Modelling

Introduction

10.1 Much of prudential regulation can be thought of as a modelling exercise: it attempts to quantify the risks being run in a portfolio to some level of safety, and then set resources based on this quantification. The first half of this chapter discusses how this framing helps us to evaluate regulation and understand the risks involved in it. In particular, we observe that regulators have standards for banks' use of quantitative models, so we ask what happens if those standards are applied to regulators' own models.

10.2 If many rules rely on models, then we might enquire about the nature of modelling and why some models are preferred to others in particular situations. The second half of the chapter discusses our perspective on regulatory knowledge, considers the types of objects involved in regulation-as-modelling, and suggests how a theoretical stance on them can inform the evaluation of regulation.

Financial Regulation as Modelling

10.3 Regulation is about the future: it attempts to alter the probability of future states of the world, or the severity of harm in them, or both, as we saw in Chapter 9. The modelling exercise implicit in this involves, in sketch, a claim about the dynamics of these measures if unattended; a claim about their altered dynamics when a regulatory constraint is imposed; and a judgement that the latter is 'better'. This is exactly the same kind of object as a pricing model for an OTC derivative or a model for calculating counterparty credit risk. Various regulators have set out rules for good modelling practice:[1] this section describes those standards and applies them to the authorities' models.

[1] See, for instance, R. Fed Board & OCC (2011) or, specifically for models used for capital purposes, R. ECB (2019).

Model risk management

10.4 The official sector perspective on banks' models is illustrated by this quote which introduces one of the pieces of guidance in this area:[2]

> *The expanding use of models in all aspects of banking reflects the extent to which models can improve business decisions, but models also come with costs. There is the direct cost of devoting resources to develop and implement models properly. There are also the potential indirect costs of relying on models, such as the possible adverse consequences (including financial loss) of decisions based on models that are incorrect or misused.*

10.5 The quotation makes it clear that regulators understand the ubiquity and perceived utility of financial modelling. Their concern is the management of model risk—the risk that model outputs will drive bad decisions. Common regulatory standards for model risk management are:

- Models should be introduced with a clear purpose and description of their intended use.
- The choice of what to model, what has not been modelled, why the former is needed and the latter is immaterial, given the use case, should all be documented.
- The data used both to develop the model and as inputs should be considered. Data quality and representativeness must be analysed, and the consequences of this for model reliability appraised.
- The model must be conceptually sound and based on a mechanism or theory that is been demonstrated to hold.
- The model must be both validated for correct implementation of the theory and tested in a wide range of use cases for reliability by a group independent from the model's developers.
- The domain of applicability of the model should be documented, with a clear statement of when it may be less reliable.
- The model's performance in use should be monitored qualitatively and quantitatively.
- Challenges from model users should be sought out and used, together with model performance data, to regularly review whether the model is fit for purpose.

[2] See R. Fed Board & OCC (2011) at 1.

Model risk management of regulators' models

10.6 It is striking how far regulators' practice differs from the behaviour they expect of the regulated. Banks are expected to recognize the partial, situated nature of modelling claims, to attempt to map the boundary of them, and to be alert to changing circumstances which might subvert them. Regulators' own claims—that the client clearing mandate should capture so many firms, for instance—are not subject to the same scrutiny because they not framed similarly. They are instead often portrayed as universal and objective[3] when, in fact, they are just another modelling claim.

10.7 The ragged edge of applicability of regulators' models has already been revealed in earlier chapters. For instance:

- Bank capital regulation uses the category 'residential mortgage'. However, as we saw in Chapter 2, residential mortgages without recourse are much more correlated to a single risk factor—house prices—than those with recourse. A diligent bank regulator would ask questions if a bank tried to use a model developed for floating foreign exchange rates to a managed currency;[4] yet they embrace similar types of error in their own rules.
- In CCP resolution policy, one issue is the category 'CCP', as discussed in Chapter 7. Both the difficulty of resolving a CCP and the systemic importance of so doing vary dramatically across members of this class. It would be more sensible to treat super-systemic CCPs separately. The likely result of this would be to mandate a more powerful—and hence more coercive—approach to resolution for the most systemically risky CCPs.
- Chapter 5 discussed the issues in the calibrations of CVA capital and the SA-CCR. These are, at their heart, modelling errors.

10.8 The account of a modelling practice which is alert to the risks of failures of representation and inference is not confined to finance. The next section explores some of the wider context of this idea.

Situated Knowledge in Financial Regulation

10.9 Financial regulation is a normative system with its own rhetoric: in the terms of Chapter 4, it is autopoietic. It makes its own category definitions, and

[3] Recall the quotation in paragraph 5.100 about the *need* for 'full, timely and consistent implementation of the Basel standards'.

[4] Managed currencies such as the Hong Kong dollar tend to be very stable while the management mechanism holds. However, if it breaks, as it did with Brazilian real in 1999, there can be a sudden, large move. Models of the dynamics of freely floating currencies typically do not take account of these phenomena: a different approach is needed.

translates the regulated system into those categories, often losing important detail in the process. Rules are framed within regulation, but affect much outside. In order to justify this, the claim is made that a particular rule is *necessary* to achieve a desired regulatory outcome.

Foundations of regulatory claims

10.10 It is insightful to interrogate the foundations of these claims.[5] These are usually implicit, and thus will need to be uncovered. As noted above, regulation is usually made to change the distribution of future states of the world, or the severity of harm within them. Therefore a sketch of the knowledge claim underlying rule making might be:

- There are some considered-reliable facts about the financial system, and these are represented within regulation.
- Some feature of this model of the situation has been identified as potentially leading, within the regulators' model, to consequences which are undesirable.
- A proposed rule will change the probability or severity of the undesired consequences in in a way that is at least somewhat predictable.[6]
- The new state of affairs after this change will, in some, perhaps not articulated sense, be better.

10.11 This section outlines some perspectives on this chain of claims.

Regulatory 'facts' and utility

10.12 Financial regulation is a system which determines its own boundaries, definitions and rhetorical rules. Systems like this are a familiar feature of modernity: accounting, psychiatry, and the law are familiar examples.[7] In each of

[5] One obvious question that arises here is why the regulated have not been more forceful in pursuing these questions, concentrating instead on particular rules. Is it perhaps because they have become habituated to regulation—that it now constitutes them? Previously, I have suggested that this is an aspect of regulators' hegemony, whereby the regulated have been conditioned not to question the status of the regulators' truth claims, something I called inverse regulatory capture in Murphy (2020a). The success of this capture is in its ability to make the regulators' framework an assumption of discourse.

[6] The stance should be noted. The regulator situates themselves outside the system with authority over it. They act, and some property measured within regulation, changes: one of the regulator's dials moves.

[7] For accounting, see Morgan (1988); for the law, Hunt (1986) and Tushnet (1991); and more generally O'Neill (1986).

them, we see that knowledge claims are historically contingent, and often best understood in the social context in which they arose.[8]

10.13 If the definitions and logic within a closed bureaucratic system like regulation are internal constructions, this does not mean that any choice is as good as another. All knowledge claims start somewhere,[9] but they are not all equally useful in a particular situation.

10.14 'Useful' is a loaded term, and depends on who has the power to define utility, in service of what aims. But at least this account opens up the possibility of debating criteria for the utility of a regulatory knowledge claim which are rooted in its effects.[10] Utility should mean some measure of explanatory power: if a theory says that one thing, defined within the theory, leads to another, in some situations, then so it should. The definitions and the veracity of the inferences from them should be accepted, in a dialogue of equals, by stake-holders.[11]

Insisting on contingency

10.15 The picture that emerges is one of dialogue, rather than fixedness. As Haraway (1988) puts it:[12] 'rational knowledge does not pretend to disengagement: to be from everywhere and so nowhere, to be free from interpretation, from being represented, to be fully self-contained or fully formalizable. Rational knowledge is a process of ongoing critical interpretation among "fields" of interpreters and decoders ... Decoding and transcoding plus translation and criticism; all are necessary.'

10.16 The responsible model builder, then, should hold themselves accountable for their model's translations, representations, categories, and inferences; be honest about its situated, contingent nature; and be open to challenge.[13] This is a practice of modelling which is likely to be adaptable in the face of change, conscious of its limits and ragged boundaries, and honest about the normative judgements on which it rests.

[8] This is Foucault's archaeology of power, Foucault (1972). It is also an important idea in scholarship on the social construction of technology: see Bijker et al. (1987).

[9] Mignolo (2002), commenting on Dussel, suggests that it is vital to be honest about this, naming 'the absent location of thinking, obscured by the universalizing of modern epistemology'. To put it crudely in the context of financial regulation, the view from the BIS tower should be tagged as such.

[10] As Haraway (1988) nicely puts it (at 579), we simultaneously need 'an account of the historical contingency of all knowledge claims, a critical practice for recognizing our semantic technologies for making meaning, and a no-nonsense commitment to a faithful account of the "real" world.'

[11] This is Habermas' criteria from footnote 73 in Chapter 4.

[12] At 590, discussing the philosophy of science.

[13] See Haraway (1988) at 585, recommending a 'practice of objectivity that privileges contestation, deconstruction, passionate construction'.

Towards assessment

10.17 This chapter and the prior two approached the assessment of financial regulation from different perspectives and using different tools, but the insights they lead to are complementary and coherent. In summary:

- *On the presentation of rule making*, there should be a statement of the problem a given regulation addresses, an analysis of why regulation is required to solve it, a mechanism by which the proposed rule operates, and a description of the benefits of the end state after regulation. Together, this should be seen as documentation of the model regulators are proposing and a necessary part of its justification.
- *On process*, regulation is both more likely to be recognized as legitimate and more amenable to analysis if it is proportionate, made by a predictable process with disclosure of evidence and decision making, and guided by an open dialogue with stakeholders. From the perspective of this chapter, this is the model development process.
- *On risks*, all the perspectives acknowledge the difficulties which can arise in writing effective, proportionate rules in the face of uncertainty and adaptation, and especially when there is incomplete knowledge of the system being steered. There is substantial model risk, which should be disclosed and taken into consideration when evaluating a policy proposal.
- *On review*, it is vital to independently review the proposed model and its justification, and to monitor its performance once in use. Review bodies should be alert to unexpectedly high costs, low benefits, and unintended consequences. Flexibility is needed in the policy revision process to allow these issues to be addressed when they are observed.

10.18 Too often, the existence of a high harm, low probability state has been used to justify precautionary intervention without any consideration of how much intervention costs or how it reduces the probability or severity of harm. Bank regulators are highly sceptical of unverified, model-based claims from regulated entities that there should be a capital benefit for a purported hedge: we should be equally cautious about accepting similar claims about regulatory interventions.

A stance on regulatory knowledge

10.19 The philosophical position on regulatory knowledge taken here is, roughly, that of critical realism.[14] This takes the perspective that objects of study exist

[14] See Archer et al. (2016) and Bhaskar (1979): the former calls critical realism a 'meta-theoretical stance', which nicely expresses its character. There is a large and growing body of scholarship exploring the implications for this stance in the philosophies of science and social science.

independently from knowledge about them.[15] Some empirical observations can be made about these objects, but the real mechanism which determines their behaviour is unknown. Defaults are real, for instance, but we do not know what process creates them.

10.20 Knowledge about these objects is provisional: we can never be sure that our model of the mechanism driving observable phenomena is accurate. Attempting to gather information about the objects of study is not futile—more can often be discovered—but all models are situated and fallible.[16]

10.21 Critical realism accepts that utility is a contested concept, but suggests that there are some criteria which can help us to judge which accounts of the real are 'more useful'.[17] Criteria which are often helpful are:

- *Stability.* Is the explanation stable from day to day, or are different mechanisms, or the same mechanism with a radically different calibration, needed to explain the empirically observed phenomena over time?
- *Predictive accuracy.* Does the account provide predictions about future observable behaviour, and if so, how accurate are they?[18]
- *Plausibility.* Is the account reasonable, on a stand-alone basis and as part of the knowledge framework it is embedded in? Is it more complex than competing explanations?[19]
- *Actionability.* Does the model give some insight into how we can change outcomes?

10.22 Thus the unhappiness of the *Marktgeist* is not a good explanation of the origins of a financial crisis, nor does a stochastic volatility model of a risk factor convince if its calibration is highly unstable.[20] This attitude to modelling is one of realistic paranoia: the question 'does it still work well enough for our purposes?' is continually asked. This stance therefore supports and enriches the perspective on regulatory models and their evaluation discussed earlier in the section.

---

15 Hence the 'realism' in critical realism.

16 This position is sometimes termed 'epistemic relativism'. There is an ethical dimension to this: if it is accepted that models are necessarily incomplete, sometimes inaccurate representations, then the modeller has a duty to communicate uncertainties, shortcomings, and limitations when communicating model predictions.

17 This is termed 'judgemental rationality' in the critical realism literature.

18 Discussing this item and the prior one, Elgin (2017) suggests that in a good model there should be a 'strong and stable' link between the modelled phenomena and the empirically observed ones.

19 Ibid. at 36 suggests that a good account is part of 'a tightly woven tapestry of mutually supportive commitments'.

20 Houllier & Murphy (2017) discusses this situation for GARCH(1,1) models of the S&P 500 index.

Regulatory Rationality: A Summary

10.23 The picture of regulatory knowledge that emerges from this discussion is:

- There are *definitions* of objects within regulation, and a *translation* which determines how financial items—derivatives, securities, balance sheets, and so on—are translated into their regulatory representations.
- There are rules of inference—an internal *rhetoric*—which generate additional regulatory knowledge from existing items. Thus, the minimum size of a CCP's default fund follows from the stressed losses over IM in cleared accounts.
- Regulatory knowledge has *external power* both directly and indirectly. There are consequences of the breach of regulator requirements, so firms' change their behaviour to try to avoid these consequences.
- Translations, regulatory knowledge, and the effect of regulation together comprise a *regulatory rationality*—a system for controlling the behaviour of the regulated based on a particular representation of them and their activities. This system, like any model, is *situated*: it has a particular stance towards the objects it captures and controls, and particular assumptions about them.

10.24 This chapter has been about the quality of the regulatory representation and the accuracy of its conclusions. It has given us some insights into how to think about regulatory knowledge claims, but it explains little about the social process by which they arise. To remedy this, the next chapter turns to some insights from social and political science on regulators and the policy making process.

11

Perspectives from Social and Political Science

Introduction

11.1 Financial regulation is not naturally occurring. It must be created, implemented, and overseen within a regulatory authority. The culture and authority of these organizations, and the incentives of their members, shapes what regulators are inclined—and able—to accomplish. This section, therefore, turns to the sociology and political economy of regulators.

11.2 Our first observation is that financial regulation is a profession. This suggests that the sociology of professions, a substantial area of scholarship in social science, will give insights about the actions, incentives, and ideology of regulators. The next section discusses some of the consequences of this framing.

11.3 If regulation is a profession, then it is one that is embroiled in government, but defended by expertise. Its overarching claim is that a 'rational' application of the appropriate technical means by 'neutral' experts leads to more efficient, effective policy than one 'tainted' by ideology.[1] As the reader will have gathered from the flock of scare quotes in the last sentence, this claim is questionable on a number of grounds. Probing the relationship between independent regulatory agencies and the executive which empowers them reveals common features of this mode of government,[2] or the 'regulatory state', as it is known.

11.4 The regulatory state is pervasive due to the perceived benefits of expert decision making, of pre-committing to a policy approach in the face of complex issues, such as the quest for financial stability, and the challenge of limited political attention. However, this mode of government has been criticized because of the risk of regulatory drift and the difficulty of separating political from technical

[1] See Hindess (1996) at 106.

[2] Or, better, governmentality: see Rose & Miller (1992).

questions, as well as the legitimacy concerns discussed in Chapter 8. Consideration of it reveals that some of the features highlighted in previous chapters, such as the development of financial regulation as a set of interlocking knowledge (and, hence, power) centres, are a result of the broad choice to govern via independent agency regulation, rather than the particularities of bank or market regulatory arrangements.[3]

11.5 However, while some gross features of the regulatory state are an unavoidable consequence of the use of this mode of government, the design of the institutional arrangements for a given regulatory agency can have a substantial effect on its likelihood of benefiting society at an acceptable cost. It is therefore important to attend to the issues of regulatory governance, mandates, and accountability.

11.6 This chapter considers the boundary between politics and regulation. There is clearly an incentive for an independent regulator to characterize policy questions as technical, complicated, risky, and wholly within their expertise. Legislators may prefer this characterization too, as it allows them to dodge difficult issues. We will see that this leads to a kind of punctuated equilibrium, where regulators are permitted to frame and decide policy questions so as to obscure their essential politics for extended periods, but with the executive intervening when political attention rises and neglecting regulation is no longer tenable.[4]

11.7 The chapter ends with a discussion of the community of policy experts, most of whom work for either regulated entities or regulators, and who conduct the vast majority of policy debate. The use of an esoteric regulatory language to propose policy limits the ability to effectively respond to this community, as only they can reply in kind. The result is a closed game of call-and-response. It creates an epistemic community which provides professional status to its members but which discourages any debate that transgresses community norms.

Regulation as a Profession

11.8 In order to understand a body of rules, it is helpful to consider the policy making that gave rise to them as an activity. In this section, some of the insights from the sociology of professions are used to illuminate the behaviour of regulators. The aim is to use a sociological-cum-anthropological question—what kind of work does the policy making tribe do?—to uncover something of the incentive structure and ideological proclivities of regulators.

---

[3] These are essentially principal-agent problems: see Carrigan & Coglianese (2011).

[4] Brassett & Tsingou (2011) rightly exhorts us to remember that 'politics, and the ever-present question of what counts as "political" should be preserved in the discussion of legitimate global governance'.

Features of professions

11.9 There are a number of different approaches to defining a profession in the literature.[5] For our purposes, it suffices to highlight some features of the occupation of financial regulation which suggest that it is a profession.

- Its members have similar social status to those of the classical professions such as medicine and the law.
- It possesses substantial external power.[6]
- It is delimited: to be a financial regulator requires employment by one of a fixed set of regulatory bodies.
- It is socially closed:[7] these employees form a distinct cadre with its own values and myths.
- It has substantial autonomy: regulators both define what counts as regulatory knowledge[8] and what counts as the practice of policy making.
- Professional status in regulation is gained by schooling in this knowledge and adherence to its tenets.
- Internally constructed knowledge is used to defend the boundaries and power of regulation.

Regulation as a transnational profession

11.10 Given the above, financial regulation can reasonably be regarded as a profession, based on its traits, developmental status, and autonomy.[9] Regulation's external power and construction of knowledge have been discussed earlier in the book. Here we turn to the last three professional characteristics: status, social closure, and professional knowledge.

---

[5] The main approaches are based on taxonomy, processes, and/or power. Taxonomic approaches use traits of an occupation to classify it; process-based ones focus on the phases through which an occupation typically transitions to become a profession, and how far a particular occupation has progressed on that journey; while power-based classifications use the extent of the dominance of an occupation over 'the substance of its own work' to determine the boundary of professionalism. The quote is from Freidson (1988) at xvii: see also Saks (2012) for a longer discussion.

[6] As discussed in Chapter 4.

[7] See Saks (2012) at 4, who calls this 'exclusionary closure'.

[8] The right to define what counts as professional knowledge is known as 'epistemic authority:' see Seabrooke (2014) for a discussion.

[9] A major missing item which a taxonomist might note is the lack of a disciplinary body. Financial regulators do not seem to regard formal regulation as so good that they want it for themselves: their regulation is based solely on the codes of the individual institutions they work for.

11.11 Members of this network are typically characterized by relatively high social status, especially the senior members of larger regulators.[10] The social and epistemic characteristics of the network are shaped by the transnational practice of financial policy making.[11] Each country has a small number of financial regulatory agencies, each with distinct mandates. Policy makers in these agencies often spend a lot of their careers dealing with their peers in other countries. This international practice creates an elite transnational professional network. It exerts a normative influence on financial regulators, reinforcing their shared culture, ideology, and rationality.[12]

11.12 Shared myths are a key element in binding members of this elite community together. We turn to them next.

Regulators' myths

11.13 By 'myth', we mean a belonging story. The intent is not pejorative, nor to imply bad faith.[13] Rather, a myth in this context is an active element in the construction of a professional identity.[14] It is necessarily exclusionary: it helps to define the tribe. In the case of financial regulators, the characteristics of those who belong include a public service orientation,[15] independence despite lobbying, and expertise in regulatory knowledge.

11.14 'Public service', is a somewhat nebulous term: it has at its core the idea of working altruistically and with integrity for the public good. Independence is seen as important because, in financial regulation, there is often a framing that the regulator is under siege from a well-funded industry intent on watering down

[10] The line of black Mercedes limousines waiting to ferry Basel Committee members to and from the BIS for their meetings is a stark illustration of this.

[11] See Chapter 8 and Gonzalez-Watty (2016) at 21.

[12] Sociologists from Weber (1978) (at 635–640) have highlighted social closure as a strategy professions adopt to monopolize the rewards of their activity. This is a process by which access to resources and opportunities are limited to a circle of initiates. In regulation, the performance of professional knowledge is an important aspect of initiation, and its elaboration is important for career development. A prominent contribution to the Basel standard setting process—which necessarily involves international cooperation—is almost a *sine qua non* for an ambitious bank regulator, for instance.

[13] There is no suggestion that these myths are 'false', either. It often does not make sense to speak of the truth value of a professional myth.

[14] Fitzpatrick (1992) defines a myth in part as a story 'dealing with origins and identity, and in particular here with the origins and identity of a group or a people'. It often includes a sacred point of origin, quest, or purpose. Myths also serve to locate professional activity, providing members of the group 'with guidance and orientation to a reality which is perceived and lived through myth'. Finally, they set 'the limits of the world, of what can be meant and done'.

[15] See Brereton & Temple (1999).

rules where they can and arbitraging them where they can't.[16] The valour of doing the right thing while under fire is a key part of the myth.

The technocratic myth

11.15 Another important element in the mythology of the regulatory profession is the benefit of technocracy. This is the idea that decisions taken by neutral experts using an evidence-based approach are normatively better than those taken by elected politicians.[17] There are several problems with this claim. First, it is doubly circular: expertise is defined as the possession of technical knowledge,[18] but what counts as technical knowledge, and what qualifies as an evidence-based approach, are both defined by the same experts.[19] Just as significant is the claim that independence is possible,[20] with the accompanying elevation of administrative rationality above what are characterized as ideological motivations. In practice, the claim is procedural: if a decision is taken following an agencies' processes, by that agencies' representatives, then it is certified as evidence-based.

11.16 The technocratic myth is typically unexamined, yet used to justify the current agency position. This allows regulatory bodies to slip from general principles to the specific, situated claims defined within regulation without sign posting. The Fed's description of their functions is a good example.[21] The chapter on prudential supervision begins:

> *The Federal Reserve promotes the safety and soundness of individual financial institutions.*

11.17 So far, so clear. But then, when the safety and soundness of individual financial institutions is described, we find:

> *One major supervisory exercise conducted ... each year is the Comprehensive Capital Analysis and Review (or 'CCAR') of the largest U.S. banking firms. Building on supervisory work coming out of the crisis, CCAR was established*

---

16 Recall the discussion in Chapter 4 and, for the sociology of the situation, see Thiemann & Lepoutre (2017).

17 See Centeno (1993) for a discussion of definitional problems in technocracy and Hilbert (1987) for the case that technocracy is not just a 'a macro/structural organization' but also a 'mentality', a way of formatting the subject to make it governable.

18 See Mügge (2011) at 57, who reminds us that 'expertise is not an objective category'.

19 See Centeno (1993) for a discussion of the definitional issues around technocracy. This author emphasizes that in 'these definitions, the extent of [the technocrat's] power is also critical', with their autonomy within a wide field of action, as well as their claim to the use of methods taken from science or engineering, being a vital characteristic.

20 In a telling critique, Hertin et al. (2009) defines experts as 'agents who try to enforce their discursive version of the truth on the public sphere'.

21 See R. Fed Board (2016).

> *to ensure that each of the largest U.S. BHCs [Bank Holding Companies] maintains (1) rigorous, forward-looking capital planning processes that effectively account for the unique risks of the firm and (2) sufficient capital to continue operations throughout times of economic and financial stress.*

11.18 In other words, there has been a passage from the general—one of the things the Fed should do is promote the safety and soundness of individual financial institutions—to a specific claim within the language of regulation—that a key way to promote safety and soundness is to conduct a particular kind of stress test and to ensure that institutions have enough capital to pass it.

11.19 The point is not that this claim is wrong or incomplete, but that a particular method is framed as an inevitable, scientific response to the mandate. However, this is not a claim like 'if I throw the ball up right now, it will come down'. It is closer to an engineering claim like 'for a bridge across the river in this location, I recommend a steel wire rope suspension bridge compliant with British Standard 19427:2019'. There are other ways to ensure the robustness of individual financial institutions under stress: the Fed has made one (albeit reasonable) choice among them without discussing, or even admitting the existence of, the alternatives.[22]

Advocating for myths as career management

11.20 Knowledge of and adherence to the claims of regulatory knowledge are ways of demonstrating professional status within regulation. Another important myth in the profession is the importance of prudence: regulators display their credentials by evidencing their belief in the need for financial institutions to have more resources. In this sense, 'toughness' on the regulated is a way for individual regulators to demonstrate fitness and perform belonging.[23]

11.21 Thus, the global norms created by transnational regulatory bodies are disseminated through emulation.[24] Moreover, international discussions create

[22] With the bridge, there might be a design competition; for any substantial structure, there would be a planning process, often with public hearings. It is possible to investigate the alternatives and learn why *this* design of bridge was thought best. Moreover, even if the claim that a given technocratically constructed process maximizes welfare is accepted, the questions of whose welfare and how it is measured remain—the best bridge *for whom?*

[23] One way of displaying status is by policing the boundaries of the window of acceptable regulatory discourse. Statements like 'the benefits to global financial stability of Basel III can *only* be fully realized if these global minimum standards are implemented across jurisdictions' (de Cos (2020), emphasis mine) serve not just to make a claim about Basel 3, but also to emphasize the speaker's adherence to one of the key myths of bank regulation. Thus, the repetition of community norms is a key part of the performance of being a regulator.

[24] Brummer (2011) at 285 discusses the reputational pressure for regulators to adhere to agreements their employers have been party to, but the effect is broader. If you want to be considered cool, you have to show that you dig what the cool kids dig, at least in financial regulation.

'shared understandings'[25] which not only largely determine national regulation, but also become incorporated into the corpus of regulatory knowledge. There are 'powerful socialization effects at work within peer networks'[26] and these act to discourage heterodoxy.[27] This incentivizes widespread implementation of international standards, even in developing countries with banking systems where they are manifestly unnecessary. A potential explanation for this is that Basel standard implementation is status-enhancing for the local regulator.[28]

11.22 Regulators' behavioural norms are implicated in the conditions which make regulation possible: a body of people acting together as if bank capital regulation is the only answer to financial stability, with the declarative authority and external power of a regulatory agency, will, absent a crisis, largely achieve their desire of ever-larger capital ratios. Another consequence of behavioural norms is petrification, as the impetus towards regulatory reform is seldom able to overcome the incentives against challenging the current orthodoxy.[29]

Bureaucratic technologies

11.23 A key aspect of regulation-as-profession is its bureaucratic nature. Bureaucracies are rule-based. Experts construct these rules, relying upon recondite, in-group knowledge to do so. The construction and use of rules is core to the professional identity of financial regulators. The ideological perspective on this process within regulation is of a highly rational and effective method of efficient government, similar to Weber's classic theory of bureaucracy.[30]

11.24 Scholars speak variously of an 'administrative rationality' or 'bureaucratic technology' to describe an institutional means of control through a system like this which constructs knowledge, applies rules, and regenerates itself.[31] The inexorable rise of these systems is one of the features of modernity.

---

[25] Or, 'epistemic communities': see Brassett & Tsingou (2011) at 8 and Seabrooke (2014) at 50.

[26] See Jones (2020) at 81.

[27] See Romano (2014a) at 26.

[28] Jones (2020) discusses this phenomenon in detail: see also Beck & Rojas-Suarez (2019) and Gurrea-Martínez & Remolina (2019).

[29] See Romano (2014b) at 56 for a further discussion. The long tenure of senior financial regulators is a factor here: often, it is only possible to question the rules that a senior person was instrumental in forming once they are no longer in post.

[30] See his account of 'domination through knowledge' in Weber (1978) at 225: this is discussed further in Hilbert (1987), who also considers, as we do below, the gap between Weber's idealization and bureaucracy in practice.

[31] Cf. the discussion of autopoiesis in Chapter 4. This renewal is necessary to stop the gap between the rules and the world opening up so far as to threaten the bureaucratic enterprise. There is, to paraphrase Hilbert (1987) at 81, a continual repair whenever it is sensed that the principals are likely to discover the inevitable failure of bureaucratic routines to conform to their expectations of rationality.

11.25 A Weberian bureaucracy is akin[32] to a profession which applies rule-based decision making in pursuit of an external mandate. Application of this approach, rather than institutional form,[33] is a defining characteristic of bureaucracies, and belief in it is important in shaping regulators' professional identities.

11.26 Institutions are seldom microcosms of the societies in which they are embedded and affect.[34] Some views are excluded or marginalized; others become consensus, and (the appearance of) agreement with them is favoured,[35] due to the career incentives for administrators discussed above. The effect of a shared common cognitive framework among bureaucrats—and, in particular, in the 'belief in the ability to arrive at the optimal answer to any discussion through the application of particular [certified objective and scientific] practices'[36]—is to produce a relatively homogeneous and unrepresentative cadre.

11.27 Another key feature here is that significant differences are erased by translation into the internal system of knowledge, with sometimes problematic results. In a successful bureaucracy, most situations are handled acceptably—given the systems' norms—most of the time. But there is always a bleeding edge of applicability.[37] This generates a rarely-visible internal conflict. The bureaucracy resolves the issue through the application of a rule or process: the exception is handled somehow. After the fact, there is a rational reconstruction of the action taken, even if the path taken to it is far from mechanical. Management of the resulting tension between the ideology of bureaucratic method and a messy reality where the world is violently crammed into idealized categories, rules are incomplete, in conflict with each other, and/or lead to highly questionable results, is a key feature of regulators' working lives.[38]

---

[32] Similar in that a bureaucracy is instantiated in a hierarchical organization with a chain of command; it has a delimited area of activity with an associated body of internally constructed; status within the organization is largely dependent on expertise in that knowledge; and the organization has a formalized decision making process which aims to ensure the continuous execution of a mandate, which has powerful effects beyond the bureaucracy itself: see Hilbert (1987).

[33] It is also important to focus on the economic in the characterization of bureaucratic technology: O'Neill (1986) calls it 'a strategy for the reproduction of the state's relation to the economy'.

[34] See Prendergast (2007) and Carrigan & Coglianese (2011) at 122.

[35] As Brassett & Tsingou (2011) discuss, the question with expert consensus is whether it arises because all the experts with the power to speak are members of the same 'epistemic community' who, because they share an affiliation with a particular policy paradigm and are embedded in the same transnational network, are limited in the solutions they will consider.

[36] The quote is from Centeno (1993) at 312: see also Habermas (1996) at 364.

[37] This is the boundary of model applicability, in the terms of Chapter 10. Heyman (2004) makes this point in the following way: 'bureaucratic rationality is "bounded," limited and flawed in its information, facing considerable unpredictability, and guided by past trial and error'.

[38] Successful bureaucrats are often those who manage this tension by performing their duties within the bureaucratic rule system disassociated from the rest of their life: see Kallinikos (2004) at 21.

Financial regulation as technology

11.28 The 'technology' in bureaucratic technology suggest exploring the methods of modern financial regulation. These are increasingly based on information technology. The rule book is too large and it is changed too often for a printed copy to be available. The reporting demanded by regulators from financial institutions is only practical electronically, and this is even more true of derivatives transaction reporting.[39] Supervisors often use tools to explore this data, rather than interacting with it directly, and the formalized rules of the bureaucracy are directly implemented in software.

11.29 A *compositional* rationality is in use here: financial regulation relies on the idea that the behaviour of a whole can be understood by piecing together an enormous number of discrete parts.[40] This offers the potential of truly evidence-based decision making, but it also poses a substantial challenge, in that even relatively minor data quality or representational issues can challenge the ability to conclude anything meaningful.[41] In short, regulators, having chosen to measure the financial system in particular, complex ways, are constrained in how they can think about new policies by the difficulty of accurately translating finance into those formats.[42] The overhead of this choice of representation, and the problems of translating the evolving financial system into it, are considerable.

Performing authority through continuous rule making

11.30 Having the authority to make a rule is not like having a hat: rather, it is constructed with every use. When a regulator proclaims that 'this is the rule', they not only seek to make it so,[43] they buttress their authority—their right to make rules—by evidencing it.[44]

---

39 Lelyveld (2017) quotes the EMIR trade reporting data as coming in 'at roughly 900Mb/day'. This is not what a big data specialist would call massive—there were roughly 500 million tweets a day in 2020, so Twitter is much bigger than derivatives in this sense—but it is far beyond any regulator's team of analysts' ability to process without twenty-first-century technology.

40 This was noted below in paragraph 5.35 in the context of the SA-CCR, but the point is much wider: the methodology of many standardized rules in prudential regulation is to add up contributions to a resources requirement from every element of a bank's business. It therefore depends on accurately estimating the incremental contribution to the requirement of each of many millions of positions. In contrast, a standard like cover 2 bases its requirements on the risk of a whole portfolio: the object addressed is the portfolio, not the position.

41 A consistent refrain in Basel Committee quantitative impact studies is of data quality challenges; BCBS (2020a) states that 'banks are included in the various analyses below only to the extent that they were able to provide data of sufficient quality to complete the analyses'.

42 This is akin to the question 'where does the longan fit in the classification of fruit for my salad?'.

43 And thus make a performative utterance, as we discussed in Chapter 4.

44 See Bourgoin et al. (2002) for more on the performance of authority and how it assigns external objects their allocated place within the rationality of the speaker.

11.31 This means that, absent supervening external events, there will be a steady stream of new rules written within the dominant regulatory ideology. Regulatory agencies may drift in different areas, towards industry preferences,[45] or to 'exercise more authority than was consciously granted',[46] but the chief difficulties for the regulator are managing complexity as the rule set inexorably grows. Political attention is mostly absent. Thus a key challenge in designing the institutional arrangements for an independent regulator is obliging and/or incentivizing them to continue to act as their principals wish. With this in mind, we turn to the relationship between regulators and politicians.

The Regulatory State

11.32 'Regulation as a mode of governance'[47] has become increasingly prevalent globally since the 1980s.[48] It had been a feature of the American administrative state since the New Deal reforms,[49] and it acquired a new vigour as one of the principal bureaucratic technologies used to construct EU institutions and governance.[50] As a result, state power deployed through a regulatory framework is now a key feature of global governance.[51]

11.33 The form of bureaucratic technology used to regulate differs across countries and areas of application, but it is representative of two general trends. One is the growth of a conception of government as facilitating activity within limits, rather than directing it.[52] Simultaneously and congruently, power has moved from directly accountable actors to agencies with greater insulation from political pressure. These agencies govern under a mandate, through the promulgation and policing of rules, under the banner of technocracy, as we saw above.

11.34 Different ideologies of government suggest different kinds of regulatory state.[53] A narrow government version would focus on infrastructure, support for

---

45 This may be an instance of regulatory capture, as highlighted by Stigler (1971).

46 The quote is from Mügge (2011) at 58.

47 The phrase is from Jordana & Levi-Faur (2005), who discuss the phenomenon: see also Centeno (1993) and Moran (2002).

48 Hindess (1996) at 147 says evocatively that it 'spread like a plague', 'killing off ... other world views in the process'.

49 The cornerstone of US administrative law, the Administrative Procedure Act, 5 USC §§551ff., dates from 1946.

50 See Majone (1994) for an account of this.

51 See Levi-Faur (2017) for a discussion of the place of regulation in neoliberal capitalism.

52 Moran (2002) calls this a 'movement from hierarchy; command; interventionism; and ambitious social engineering' and notes that this implies a 'notion of state withdrawal'.

53 See Rose & Miller (1992) who, at 287, discuss how a regulatory state operationalizes a programme of government.

contracting, and the enforcement of bargains.[54] A wider vision of government might promote a regulatory state which acknowledges and attempts to correct market failures such as externalities, monopoly power, and information asymmetries,[55] while an even more expansive framing would include the provision of collective goods by regulated actors, and the use of regulation to enact explicitly redistributive policies.[56]

11.35 Within a given notion of the provision of regulated services, there are a variety of styles. Regulators can be tightly bound to the regulated,[57] narrowly constraining their path, or more distant, setting broad limits but making little or no intervention within them. The heavier the touch, the more mutually constitutive regulation and the regulated are.

11.36 The sundering of many of the functions of the intervening state into regulators and regulated allows the former to inherit a measure of legitimacy, not least because a regulator can—in extremis—often call upon the state for additional powers.[58] The delegation of power to regulators is contingent on the continuing political acceptability of the arrangement but, subject to this, the tendency is towards expansion of the territory of 'apolitical' policy making and the contraction of the realm of politics.[59]

The attraction of regulation as a mode of government

11.37 The growth of the regulatory state reflects its attractiveness to elected politicians and regulators. The advantages for them are said to include:[60]

- *Increasing the cost of policy inconsistency.* By empowering a (quasi-) independent agency to regulate under delegated authority, the state signals its

[54] In derivatives, this entails a legal system which underpins contracting under a master agreement, enforces collateral and close-out netting provisions, and which has notions of good faith, reasonableness, and negligent misrepresentation. Deakin et al. (2017) describes this as law 'constituting the economic institutions of capitalism'.

[55] In derivatives regulation, this might include the idea that the negative externality of potential contagion created by uncontrolled counterparty credit risk taking should be corrected, for instance by capital or margin requirements.

[56] Requirements for the provision of services of general economic interest, as discussed in paragraph 6.86, would fall within this broader notion of the role of the state.

[57] This 'structural coupling' is more likely to lead to capture of one party by the other: see, for instance, the discussion of nuclear regulation in the United States in Baumgartner & Jones (1993).

[58] Sometimes the state even asks if the regulator needs help: one of the questions PRA (2020) was required by statute to answer, for instance, was whether the regulator's powers 'are, and might be expected to continue to be, sufficient to enable it to advance its objectives in relation to relevant authorized persons who engage in proprietary trading'.

[59] Levi-Faur (2013a) puts it like this at 12: 'Regulatory agencies have become the citadels that fortify the autonomous and influential role of the regulocrats in the policy process.'

[60] See Jordana & Levi-Faur (2005), Majone (1994), and Moran (2002) for a further discussion.

commitment to a consistent policy stance. It could (and sometimes does) change tack, but the cost of this are sufficiently high that it will only do so when the current regulatory approach is viewed as substantially flawed or there is powerful external pressure. It often requires a crisis to generate this pressure.

- *Decision and blame avoidance.*[61] If an agency is responsible for a sector capable of generating highly negative societal outcomes, such as finance, air travel, or power generation, then regulation gives politicians an ablative shield: in the event of disaster, they can burn the regulator,[62] and meanwhile they can avoid having to make difficult decisions.[63]
- *Nurturing expertise and keeping attention.* An independent[64] regulatory agency facilitates the separation of financial regulation as a career, with its own (self-created) knowledge, career structure, and culture, as discussed in the first section of this chapter. It ensures that there is a body of people who are always focused on regulatory issues, but also that new rules will always be under construction.
- *Dealing with complexity.* The increasingly recondite nature of social, financial and administrative structures require new forms of knowledge to render them governable. Outsourcing the development of that framework to experts mitigates the risks of the principals being overwhelmed by the complexity of the problem.[65]
- *Faster, better decision making.* Delegation to agencies can reduce the cost of decision making, as agency staff have the expertise necessary to identify candidate solutions and choose one more efficiently than legislators. The claim is that the resulting decisions are less contentious as they are based on evidence rather than ideology.[66]

Successes of the regulatory state

11.38 The regulatory state has delivered societal improvements: Sunstein (1990) cites pollution control and road safety improvements, among others. Its very

[61] See Majone (1998) for a discussion of blame avoidance in the regulatory state.

[62] Black (2012) points out that this was the fate of the UK FSA after 2008, despite the fact that there was widespread politician support for its strategy pre-crisis.

[63] Levitin (2014) calls the luxury of using regulatory agencies to avoid making contentious moral judgements about policy trade-offs, 'moral avoidance'.

[64] The issue of the pros and cons of integrated vs ramified regulatory models is not considered here: see Awrey (2010a) for a discussion in the context of derivatives regulation.

[65] Centeno (1993) evokes the issue nicely in a discussion of the Mexican Finance Ministry, suggesting that the problems it manages were perceived to be 'full of esoteric complications'.

[66] See Majone (1998) for more on this point.

pervasion evidences its acceptability to a wide range of political ideologies.[67] However, this mode is no panacea, as pre-crisis financial regulation evidences.

Evolving regulatory approaches

11.39 One theme in the evolution of the diverse modes of the regulatory state is that of reformation followed by counter-reformation. Command and control regulation was an important regulatory technique at first. The potential for more efficient allocation via incentive-based regulation, self-regulation, and other 'new governance'[68] techniques then led to a broadening of regulatory style as political confidence in markets and 'scepticism over the capacities of political authorities to govern everything for the best' grew.[69] A 'new spirit of adversarialism' then became more prevalent.[70] This tendency towards a heavier regulatory touch was bolstered by the 2008 crisis[71] and further intensified as the broadly neoliberal consensus of the 1990s and 2000s was challenged, first by rising nationalism, then by the management of the Covid pandemic.[72]

Critiques of the regulatory mode of governance

11.40 One set of issues with the regulatory state follow from the disintermediated nature of agency regulation: as soon as you have someone do something for you, you have to specify what it is, motivate the actor, and monitor their performance. Thus questions of mandate, agency costs, and oversight arise.[73]

11.41 The regulatory theory literature was particularly concerned with the problem of regulatory capture in this context: this is a bigger risk in areas where a concentrated, well-resourced interest group—such as banks—is pitted against a much larger, more diffuse one—such as their customers.[74] The perceived danger

[67] As Centeno (1993) notes at 328, a bureaucratic technology 'cannot sustain prolonged crises of confidence in its abilities'.

[68] The term is from Black (2012): see also Moran (2002).

[69] This is the ideology of pre-crisis regulation: see paragraph 2.46. The quote is from Rose & Miller (1992) at 296.

[70] The term is due to Froud et al. (2012).

[71] This is not to say that the post-2008 state returned to public mechanisms. Rather, as we saw in Chapter 7, private means—market-based tools, as Duff & Zaring (2013) call them—were mandated in the furtherance of public policy objectives.

[72] This turn away from the 'new governance' techniques discussed in Black (2012) and Carrigan & Coglianese (2011) was more related to their inability to inspire confidence in this new political climate than their ineffectiveness.

[73] See Majone (1998) and Moran (2002) for more extended discussions.

[74] Kastnera (2014) suggests that the situation is not utterly bleak, in that a 'growing number of civil society organizations have developed capacities to engage in the debate on reforming global finance'. See also Helleiner et al. (2018) at 143 for a discussion of the diverse and varying interest groups in the regulatory reform debate.

of regulatory capture is one factor in the counter-reformation in financial regulatory style discussed earlier.[75]

11.42 More recently, attention has focused on the democratic gap created by the use of certified–technocratic regulatory modes of government. If regulation reduces the cost of decision making because 'of the greater difficulty of reaching agreement when the costs and benefits of the proposed measures are spelled out in detail',[76] does that simply mean that *necessarily* political decisions are being taken by technocrats with unexamined priors?

11.43 Another strand of critique examines the role of regulation in supporting the diffusion of neoliberal capitalism,[77] highlighting the unconsidered premises that cross-border flows should be encouraged, that barriers to them should be removed, that common standards facilitating global trade are always good, and that regulation can reduce the risk of the interconnections created by these choices to an acceptable level, while preserving democratic legitimacy. In this reading, the regulatory state is not *always* neoliberal,[78] but, in practice, it is often deployed to shield market-centred policies from criticism.[79] This strand of criticism suggests that a regulatory state is more honest when it is transparent about the normative assumptions on which it founded.

11.44 Scholars rightly note here the diversity of arrangements in the regulatory state.[80] The scope of the power delegated; the mechanisms for monitoring agency performance; governance arrangements; the style of rule making; and enforcement powers all vary from regulator to regulator. There is a developing body of work in regulatory theory which analyses the consequences of particular arrangements for the behaviour, performance, and legitimacy of regulation.[81] This and related[82] scholarship highlights the importance of institutional design

[75] Young (2012) examines potential regulatory capture of the Basel Committee at the time of Basel 2, and concludes that while the Committee 'during this period was non-transparent and unaccountable' there was 'more resistance to private sector pressures than is commonly appreciated', so this danger is perhaps overstated.

[76] The quote is from Majone (1998) at 3.

[77] See, for instance, Levi-Faur (2017) who coins the evocative term 'regulatory capitalism'.

[78] See Levi-Faur (2013a) and Rose & Miller (1992) for a discussion of these issues. The case against the essential neoliberalism of the regulatory state is perhaps harder to make for transnational regulatory arrangements which assert the right to override national democratic processes.

[79] This was particularly noticeable in the privatization of formerly state-owned utilities, where the presence of a regulator was used to mollify concerns over the monopoly power of the privatized entities: see, for instance, Littlechild (1983) at 4.6.

[80] See Levi-Faur (2013b) and Rose (2014).

[81] See, for instance, Drahos (2017), Jordana & Levi-Faur (2005), and Levitin (2013).

[82] There is also a growing political economy literature on the control of administrative agencies: see, for instance, McCubbins et al. (1989) and Rodriguez & Weingast (2015).

in extracting the benefits of delegation to experts while preserving transparency and accountability. Majone puts it well:[83]

> *It is up to the political principals to structure relationships with their agents so that the outcomes produced through the agents' efforts are compatible with basic requirements of democratic accountability, given the choice to delegate in the first place.*

Financial Regulation in the Regulatory State

11.45 The record of independent financial regulatory agencies since the crisis is mixed.[84] Regulators would tout the lack of bank failures during the early Covid period as evidence of the success of their endeavours,[85] but, as the idiom has it, one swallow does not make a summer. Moreover, the costs of financial regulation are enormous, and we have not attempted to make policies which have as their central aim supporting financial system functioning, rather than just preventing disorderly bank failures.[86]

11.46 If financial regulation has not worked as well as we might have hoped, how much of this is due to the nature of the institutional arrangements it operates under? The discussion in the previous section suggests that three questions might be helpful in uncovering aspects of this question:

- What are the effects of choosing agency regulation to govern finance, rather than more politically responsive arrangements?
- What is the consequences for the legitimacy of financial regulation of its technocratic norm?
- What criteria should we use to design institutional arrangements for financial regulation which would assist in making it more effective, legitimate, and accountable?

---

83 See Majone (1998) at 13 and compare with Rose (2014) at 12.

84 See, for instance, Giordana & Schumacher (2013) on the robustness associated with compliance with Basel 3 liquidity regulation, and Doumpos et al. (2015) on the benefits of central bank independence, but note the results of Ayadi et al. (2016) that overall Basel core principles compliance, or indeed compliance with any of its individual pieces, has no association with bank efficiency, and of Delis & Staikouras (2011), who find that Basel capital requirements 'prove to be rather futile in controlling bank risk'.

85 See de Cos (2021), but note that 'success' is defined within the language of regulation: he says that banks 'risk-weighted CET1 capital ratio now stands at around 13%, compared with 7% in 2011'; that their 'Tier 1 leverage ratios rose from 3.5% to over 6%;' and their liquidity ratios rose too. Bank robustness is being *identified with* high scores on the metrics regulators introduced.

86 Recall the discussion in paragraph 3.2 on the functions of the financial system: alternative choices of mandate for regulators are possible. We return to this point in Chapter 12.

Choosing independent regulation for finance

11.47 By choosing agency regulation, the principal accepts a degree of loss of control. Their agent, the regulator, is given some freedom to act, and this allows them to stake out some territory. As Rose & Miller (1992) notes, experts have the capacity to generate 'relatively bounded locales or types of judgement within which their power and authority is concentrated, intensified and defended.' This power base allows regulators to frame policy questions using their normative assumptions, conception of the nature of the subject of regulation, and rationality.[87] Agency regulation is not a restaurant that allows you to order off-menu: having chosen to go there, your options are constrained.

11.48 The choice of agency regulation allows expertise to be nurtured and deployed, but it results in a regulatory hegemony whereby some solutions are promulgated and others are obscured.[88] Some questions become difficult to ask because they conflict too severely with the regulator's assumptions. One example, as Levitin (2014) points out,[89] is:

> *Are implicit guarantees and ex post bailouts really less socially efficient than higher ex ante capital requirements?*

The answer may well be no, but because it highlights the hidden normative assumptions of bank capital regulation, the question is deeply uncongenial to regulators. In derivatives regulation:

> *Is the clearing mandate necessary and justifiable?*

has the same character. Thus, agency regulation, with its internal language, is exclusionary: policy issues are framed as questions within the language of regulation, and are only addressable by those that speak that language and are willing to operate within the regulators' frame.[90] This can mean that debate is replaced by an appeal to authority rooted in expertise.[91] Even where this is not the case, it

---

87 In other words, following the discussion in Chapter 10, the seemingly dull acts of constructing definitions, translations, and rules of inference, together with the external power of regulation, render finance governable.

88 As Seabrooke & Tsingou (2014) highlight, professional ideology can constrain what ideas and policy options members can or wish to be associated with.

89 At 2034, in a discussion of the call for much higher bank capital.

90 It requires a substantial effort to learn the language of regulation, so it often 'strongly informs' the professional identity of its speakers, as Seabrooke & Tsingou (2014) suggests.

91 The use of discursive authority to settle policy questions creates a revelatory conflict when different authorities come into conflict, as we saw with CCP resolution in Chapter 7. The flip side of this authority is belief in it by the listener: as Weber (1978) suggests at 263, 'the basis of every authority, and correspondingly of every kind of willingness to obey, is a belief, a belief by virtue of which persons exercising authority are lent prestige.'

constrains both who are seen as having standing to participate in the debate and the range of conceivable policy adjustments.

11.49 For another example, consider CCP margin policy. The debate here assumes substantial technical knowledge of PFE calculation, margin periods of risk, methods for calculating haircuts on securities collateral, and so on. There is a fundamental tension between CCPs and clearing members on one side, who prefer higher margin levels, as this makes their contributions to the default waterfall—skin in the game and the default fund, respectively—safer; and clients, who pay the costs of higher margin. But few clients are fluent enough in the language of this debate to make impactful contributions.[92] Thus, the narrative 'higher margin makes CCPs safer' dominates.[93]

Obscuring the politics of financial regulation

11.50 Sunstein[94] states another important problem with the regulatory mode:

> *The argument for the independent agency stems largely from a belief in the need for expert, apolitical, and technically sophisticated administration of the laws. Even if independent agencies achieved this end, one might question the goal itself. Independent agencies often must make important judgements of policy and principle, and on those judgements expertise is never decisive ... [Polices are not based] solely on technocratic judgements, and so may properly belong in the political rather than the regulatory sphere.*

11.51 Financial regulation is particularly susceptible to this problem because it necessarily affects the relative and absolute costs of different financial services. As a result, areas of political sensitivity—such as access to and the cost of residential mortgages[95] are contested between politicians and regulators; on the other, areas (perhaps temporarily) without political protection—such as OTC derivatives after the 2008 crisis—become scapegoats.[96]

11.52 The framing of a policy issue in the language of regulation can obscure the political issues in play. Consider, for instance, this statement about the problem of CVA risk:

> *Bank losses due to CVA risk were substantial during the crisis, so it is important that this risk is properly captured in the bank capital framework.*

---

92 The counterexample to this are the large asset managers, but their needs are rather different from those of non-financial end-users.

93 In this case, the narrative is true, but it is partial: higher margin do not make *clients* safer.

94 Sunstein (1990) at 426.

95 Calomiris & Haber (2015) discusses this case in detail.

96 This discussion is continued in the next chapter: see Bell & Hindmoor (2017) for a related discussion of the decline in political influence of banks on regulatory reform in the UK after 2008.

Contrast this with:

What is the socially optimal approach to facilitating risk transfer for small to medium-sized non-financial end-users?

11.53 The choice to use a regulatory agency focused on bank stability means that policy issues will be framed in the former way: the latter reveals the underlying, unavoidably political, trade-off between a minuscule increase in bank stability and a large impact on end-users' risk transfer costs.

11.54 The political salience of financial regulation varies depending on the rule in question—but it is often low.[97] It is usually in regulators' interest to de-emphasize political factors, as this protects their authority; politicians collude with this as it allows them to avoid difficult decisions.[98]

The punctuated equilibrium in regulatory ideology

11.55 The 2008 crisis did not change legislators' attitude to the use of agency regulation for finance, nor the constitutive role of transnational cooperation.[99] The G-20 intervened in the short term, as we saw in Chapter 2, but their attention soon turned elsewhere. Rather, the crisis created a brief period in which financial regulation was in the spotlight, and during which big changes in the ideology of and institutional arrangements for regulation were possible. During this period, politicians and regulators[100] rushed to defend and extend their territory; to provide plans; and to build support for their preferred approach. Narratives were promoted and criticized. Competition to tell the dominant story happened at national, bloc and transnational levels[101] in a complex interplay of interests and authority claims.[102] This contest was soon over, and political attention faded.

97 See chapter 8 of James & Quaglia (2020) for a further discussion.

98 As Tsingou (2015) points out, even in the case of clearing and settlement, the technical can become inherently political. A good example is the fair, reasonable, and non-discriminatory access requirement to clearing discussed in Braithwaite & Murphy (2021): this requires that criteria which restrict access to clearing shall be permitted only to the extent that their objective is to control risk. The club cannot blackball aspiring members arbitrarily. On the one hand, this requirement might, at the margin, increase access to clearing: but on the other, it serves to direct attention away from the question of whether clearing was the right answer in the first place.

99 Tsingou (2015) suggests that the 'implicit contract between public and private, between finance and the state, as to what happens when things go wrong, remain[ed] unchallenged.'

100 Romano (2014b) evocatively calls these people 'policy entrepreneurs'.

101 Barnett & Finnemore (1999) accurately describe the situation in ascribing distinct and conflicting views to staff in various agencies. During the most contested periods, it can make little sense to ask, for instance, what 'the UK' wants or proposes, given the diversity of views of policy-focused individuals in institutions such as the Bank of England, Her Majesty's Treasury, and Parliament.

102 See Benjamin (2010) and Froud et al. (2012) for discussions of contested narratives in the crisis and its aftermath: this contest is typical of the short phase after the loss of policy concord and before its return.

11.56 The result was a rapid shift in policy from a stable pre-crisis consensus to a different, and similarly stable, post-crisis one. It could be described as a 'punctuated equilibrium'[103] in regulatory ideology: relative stability was interrupted by a hurried and heated argument over what should change once the crisis hit,[104] with different stories being advertised on the basis of the toughness of their narratives on the regulated.[105] Speed was necessary because there was enormous political pressure to be able to respond to the popular cry of 'something must be done' with 'something is being done'. As a result, the new (elite) consensus incorporated a bricolage of borrowed and sometimes redundant elements.[106] Once the new dominant narrative emerged—a revised regulatory ideology—rule making proceeded within its frame. Whether what was done was optimal, and if the story told was an accurate account,[107] are not questions that politicians have been eager to return to.[108]

11.57 The transient nature of concentrated political attention on financial policy making intensified the legitimacy problems discussed in Chapter 8: leaving the formulation of most of the rules and their implementation to regulators without an effective review mechanism risks overreach,[109] mis-calibration,[110] failure to achieve the desired benefits,[111] and unintended consequences.[112] After the crisis, legislators abandoned the financial system to the consequences of the new regulatory ideology.

---

103 The term in the policy context is originally due to Baumgartner & Jones (1993), but their usage is slightly different: they refer to an equilibrium of policy, where rules are stable for long periods. Our use is one of ideology, where the rules can change, but the authorities' norms, apportionment of responsibilities and regulatory strategy remain fixed.

104 See the account in Froud et al. (2012) of the crisis as an 'evolving series of elite narratives' and (at 24) the sometimes bizarre positions taken in this struggle for discursive authority. Echoing this, Kentikelenis & Seabrooke (2017) describes how actors interact and compete globally to construct dominant policy scripts consisting of 'a diagnosis of problems followed by a set of prescriptions'.

105 James & Quaglia (2020) states, for instance, that UK regulators' advocacy for tough OTCD regulation in transnational fora after the crisis was because they 'had a powerful incentive to pursue harmonized standards in order to manage the significant cross-border externalities generated by derivatives'. This may be true, but it was also a strong signal at a decisive moment for regulators' careers of their fitness to lead the tribe.

106 Hence, central clearing for OTC derivatives because it had worked well for exchange-traded derivatives, but more capital and more margin too.

107 'Accurate' in the sense of Chapter 10's judgemental rationality.

108 We tend to share the pessimistic perspective of Shapiro & Borie-Holtz (2015) that regulatory reform is often better explained as the service of self-interests than as a rational improvement in the Weberian mode.

109 As with the bilateral margin rules and clearing mandate.

110 As with the CVA rules and the SA-CCR.

111 As with trade reporting.

112 As with the leverage ratio.

Situating derivatives regulation within the regulatory state

11.58 Derivatives regulation is a classic example of the regulatory state. It is a complex area, where expertise is valuable; political attention is rarely present; there is substantial value in commitment to policy consistency; and politicians are happy to defer difficult, value-laden decisions to technocrats. It could therefore be expected to demonstrate many of the advantages and drawbacks of the regulatory mode of governance, and it does. However, the regulatory regime that governs derivatives is also shaped by the ideological positions held and the institutional arrangements chosen, so we now consider the way in which these contingencies have shaped its results.

11.59 There has been an equilibrium of policy ideology since the crisis, with the rules being set by the same bodies, using the same regulatory mode, and with broadly the same framing of the issues and menu of solutions. The body of regulation—and hence regulatory knowledge—produced has been enormous, so expert attention has certainly been lavished on finance.[113] However, given that some of these measures will not be fully implemented until 2027,[114] almost 20 years after the crisis, the claim that independent regulation leads to faster, more efficient decision making is difficult to fully substantiate in this area.

11.60 Financial institutions have a strong preference for cross-border trading, as this allows them to access the deepest pools of liquidity. Policy makers chose not to question this. As a result, to discourage regime arbitrage, they had to agree global standards in many areas.[115] The resulting cooperative policy making increased the expertise available, but limited the potential solutions[116] to those agreeable to all members.[117] Complex diplomacy, involving the negotiation of thousands of pages of rules, meant that the rule making process was slow and full of compromise.

113 A partial list just at the transnational level and just focusing on rules relevant to derivatives discussed in prior chapters is: R. BCBS (2009), R. BCBS (2010), R. BCBS (2011a), R. BCBS (2011b), R. BCBS (2013b), R. BCBS (2013b), R. BCBS (2013d), R. BCBS (2014a), R. BCBS (2014b), R. BCBS (2014c), R. BCBS (2015), R. BCBS (2017), R. BCBS (2019a), R. BCBS (2019b), R. BCBS (2020c), R. BCBS & IOSCO (2013), R. BCBS & IOSCO (2020), R. CPMI & IOSCO (2012), R. CPMI & IOSCO (2014), R. CPMI & IOSCO (2015), R. CPMI & IOSCO (2017), R. CPMI & IOSCO (2020), R. FSB (2010), R. FSB (2017a) and R. FSB (2020b).

114 This is the Basel Committee's current intended date for the output floor to come fully into effect.

115 There are some national barriers: see, for instance, the discussion of location policy starting at paragraph 7.140.

116 Brassett & Tsingou (2011) at 7 discuss how transnational policy making 'reduces significantly the opportunities for raising important political issues such as the desired choice of systemic risk/regulatory cost trade-off, the distribution of risks and post-crisis costs, and the feasibility of certain policies'.

117 Or, at least, all veto-holding members: see Tsingou (2015).

11.61 The transnational nature of rule making also creates petrification, as so many professionals are involved in it. Each of these rule writers has a stake in the continuity of 'their' policies. This, together with the high evidential bar for policy reform, means that rules are very difficult to change once enacted.[118]

11.62 Another feature of the post-crisis ideology of regulation is its focus on the correction of perceived market failures. As with the choice not to intervene in cross-border flows, this political choice has meant that regulators have used a limited menu of capital-friendly solutions: no serious consideration was given to nationalizing CCPs, for instance.[119]

11.63 The mandate handed down to the regulators of financial institutions, which focuses principally on the robustness of individual institutions, and on financial stability,[120] is another feature of the particular kind of regulation chosen which has negative consequences. It has led to an unduly but variably cautious regulatory approach which pays little heed to the constraints it places on the ability of the financial system to fulfil its functions, especially in stress.[121]

11.64 In other areas, regulatory norms have led to redistributive outcomes being portrayed as an inevitable and necessary result of the quest for financial stability. The additional cost of risk transfer for non-financial end-users created by CVA capital rules, bilateral margin rules, and the clearing mandate discussed above are one good example; the growth of fragile, non-bank market intermediation is another. This use of a narrowly technocrat gloss to hide essentially political decisions again serves to hide these choices from appropriately political scrutiny.

Designing institutional arrangements

11.65 In the broad, there are three parts to institutional design: structure, delegation, and monitoring. Institutional structure refers to the features of the regulatory agency:[122] their governance; the appointment process, tenure, and grounds for dismissal of executives; and how they are funded.

---

118 See Romano (2014b) at 28.

119 As Bernstein (2011) and Eisner (2013) discuss, if we assume that policy makers must have a clear market failure to justify intervening, we are simultaneously assuming that market outcomes should be accepted as given if there is no market failure. Thus, for instance, Shiller (2012)'s call to consider better contractual structures with payment insurance in the housing market has been ignored.

120 See R. Fed Board (2016) for these and other aspects of the FED's mandate, as an example.

121 Interestingly, there is a hint of an efficiency objective in the FED's macro-prudential mandate. This describes a 'healthy and stable financial system' as one that 'links, *at the lowest possible cost*, savers and investors seeking to grow their money with borrowers and businesses in need of funds' (emphasis mine). However, it does not require the FED to seek financial system health in this sense: see R. Fed Board (2016) at 56.

122 See Hogue et al. (2017) for a longer discussion of the dimensions of agency structure.

11.66 CFTC commissioners and senior staff serve at the pleasure of the President, but a substantial change in Presidential preferences from Obama to Trump to Biden produced remarkably little change in the ideology of derivatives regulation, matching the policy consistency of agencies whose management were not politically appointed. This suggests that institutional structure has not been determinative, at least in national derivatives regulation. So what about delegation and monitoring?

11.67 The key questions in delegating authority relate to the mandate of the agency and the powers available to it. Mandates change infrequently and shape the whole character of the agency's action, so it is vital that they fully express the delegator's wishes. A prominent regulator, Lord Hill, described the issue with a narrow stability mandate like this:[123]

> *While we want stability, we don't want the stability of the graveyard. Without risk there is no growth ...*
>
> *It is natural that when a micro-prudential regulator or supervisor has to assess risk, they take a highly cautious approach ... While that is perfectly understandable—and may indeed be what they are required to do under their terms of reference—the problem comes if a number of different regulators or supervisors are all taking an equally risk-averse approach. Then the cumulative impact of a series of micro-prudential judgements can itself become a source of macro-prudential risk. In short, I concluded that whereas after 2008 the greatest threat to financial stability had been the financial crisis, over time the greater threat had become the lack of growth itself.*

11.68 A similar issue arises with the total cost of regulation. If this is unconstrained by the agency's mandate, it is likely to keep rising. There is no reporting of this, so it is difficult to assess. We do not know the total cost of derivatives regulation, let alone which rules create which contribution to the total.[124] Given the incentives and opacity in this area, one can sympathize with the suggestion in Majone (1997)[125] that the delegation of authority should be accompanied by a constraint on the total costs of regulation.

11.69 Effective monitoring requires both transparency and accountability. Their presence—or absence—is constrained by the nature and form of the dialogues between regulators and politicians and between regulators and stakeholders. The next section discuss each of these dialogues.

---

[123] The quote is from Hill (2016).

[124] The cost of regulation includes not just the cost of the regulator and of compliance with the rules—the extra capital, margin, and so on that are required—but also the cost of the inefficiency created as the financial system adapts to regulation.

[125] At 150.

Regulators Talking, Listening, and Ignoring

11.70 It is impossible to draw a line between technocratic questions and political ones in financial regulation that will attract general agreement.[126] The characterization of a decision as 'technical' or 'political' may, as Centeno (1993) puts it at 318, 'have less to do with the inherent complexity of the issue and more to do with the interests of those who benefit from the exclusion of those no longer able to participate' in one or other choice.

11.71 This gives rise to a problematic incentive where regulators encourage and facilitate politicians' moral avoidance in order to extend their territory, and because they genuinely believe that their expertise is relevant. This results in a narrowing of the range of policies considered to those within the currently dominant regulatory ideology. In finance, the result tends to be a relatively sparse dialogue between regulators and politicians, with conflict confined to relatively small set of policy questions.[127] The distributional effects of regulation are seldom discussed. It might therefore be helpful to broaden and legitimize the policy debate by enhancing the monitoring of financial regulators and requiring that their interactions with stakeholders constitute more of a debate.

Accountability and monitoring

11.72 One of the roots of the concept of accountability is stewardship. Here, a defined right of use is granted in exchange for an obligation to use the right in pursuit of a delegated objective, and the steward is held accountable for the discharge of their obligation.[128] Thus, accountability is an obligation for an actor, in which they are required to justify their conduct with respect to previously delegated authority within a mandate, their actions can be questioned, and there are consequences if they are found to be wanting.

11.73 Accountability is a discipline to improve regulatory outcomes and to check policy drift.[129] In the modern regulatory state, there are multiple accountors including the judiciary, the executive, legislators, the regulated, and wider stakeholders.[130] The character of regulatory accountability to each of these accountors

---

126 See Mügge (2011) at 68 for a further discussion of the argument that questions of money are always political.

127 For instance, in derivatives regulation, the desirability of position limits is relatively controversial: the clearing mandate is not.

128 See Bovens (2007), Hüpkes et al. (2006), and Scott (2014) for further discussions.

129 As Scott (2014) says, we 'tolerate the detachment of regulation from the normal mechanisms of control and accountability associated with the public service only because of an expectation that regulation will be apolitical and expert'—so it is necessary to regularly check if it is.

130 See Hogue et al. (2017) at 20.

varies from the grounds for judicial review discussed in Chapter 8,[131] through scrutiny by legislative committees[132] and the processes for hiring and firing senior regulators, to transparency requirements.

11.74 There are multiple potential dimensions of accountability,[133] including financial, procedural, and personal aspects. For a financial regulator, there might be requirements to justify rule making before action, for instance by publishing a regulatory impact analysis, as discussed in Chapter 9, after action,[134] or on demand. The requirement may relate to each piece of policy, or only to the overall impact, and it may—but often does not—include considerations of efficiency.

11.75 Transparency obligations,[135] such as mandatory cost-benefit analysis, support accountability, in that they allow stakeholders to monitor policies that affect them, and suggest questions to formal accountors which might otherwise escape their limited attention.[136]

11.76 A well-designed accountability framework[137] would facilitate both the investigation of individual policies and their effects, and scrutiny of the agency's norms, ideology, and overall performance. This is particularly important in financial regulation where evidence on its effectiveness at meeting the goal of preventing a banking crisis is only available once every ten or twenty years. There should be mechanisms for monitoring costs[138] and benefits which do not rely solely on the non-occurrence of rare events.[139]

11.77 As we discussed in Chapter 8, a particular confounding factor for financial regulation is the lack of accountability of transnational policy making bodies.[140]

---

131 There is also the interesting question of the civil liability of regulators: see Cherednychenko & Andenas (2020).

132 The hearings of the Treasury Select Committee in the UK, or the House Banking and Agriculture Committees would fall into this category. (The House Agriculture Committee oversees the CFTC.)

133 See Hogue et al. (2017) at 6.

134 There a good case for reviewing regulation once the system has adapted to it. As Sunstein (1990) says, the system is not 'constant after regulations have been issued. Strategic responses, the creation of perverse incentives for administrators and regulated entities, unanticipated changes in product mix and private choice—these are the hallmarks of the paradoxes of the regulatory state.'

135 See Lodge (2005) for a further discussion of regulatory transparency.

136 Thus, transparency is a mitigant to, as Scott (2014) puts it at 4, 'the limited technical capacity of elected government'.

137 See Jordana et al. (2015) and Lodge (2005) for further discussions of regulatory accountability frameworks.

138 It is particularly striking that we do not know which policies contribute which costs and which benefits to the overall framework of financial regulation.

139 Scott (2014) discusses this 'performance evaluation' as a mechanism to addresses claims to technical expertise of regulators and thus 'to evaluate regulators on their own terms': see also the discussion in Mügge (2011) at 68 of the 'output legitimacy' of regulation.

140 See also Gonzalez-Watty (2016).

These bodies are purposive actors rather than mere coordination mechanisms,[141] but existing, primarily state-based, accountability mechanisms do not reach them. Thus, while there is 'a growing normative consensus on the need for greater democracy in global governance',[142] this need is poorly met in most transnational financial regulation.

The regulated talking back

11.78 The process of producing financial regulation is often extended. Even if a rule is only developed by a single regulator, it can take a year or more from idea to final text; for rules which originate in transnational cooperation, the process is substantially longer. This means that there are many potential points of influence for external actors on policy development. Against this, their knowledge of the policy process is incomplete, and their ability to evaluate the salience of a particular proposal to their interests is limited. Lobby late, and many of the features of a rule will already be fixed; try to lobby early, and you will chase a lot of shadows.[143]

11.79 Compounding the complexity here is the fact that private sector actors are far from unified. Informal coalitions develop on particular issues as the balance of interests becomes clear,[144] but the compositions of these coalitions varies substantially from issue to issue.[145] The game is repeated, because the high level of expertise in regulatory knowledge required to be effective creates a cadre of regulatory policy specialists on both sides.[146]

11.80 These specialists are situated in national and transnational authorities, regulated firms, trade associations, and advisors. They form a 'linked ecology'[147] with significant population mobility, sometimes called the 'revolving door'. One might also think of members of this epistemic community as wandering bards,

[141] Barnett & Finnemore (1999) discuss this point in more detail.

[142] See Bernstein (2011) at 42.

[143] See Lall (2011) for a further discussion of the role of time in lobbying financial regulators. The other aspect, which I am not aware of being treated in the literature, is who to lobby, at which level. The choices include national rule writers, transnational organizations, politicians, and civil servants. The convention is to match seniority, so only the most senior bank executives would reach out to senior regulators, or vice versa.

[144] See, for instance, Pagliari & Young (2016)'s description of the coalitions which developed on exemptions to the clearing mandate.

[145] For the authorities, policy views can differ between CCP regulators, bank regulators, macroprudential authorities, and resolution authorities. For the affected, interest groups include broker-dealers, CCPs, client clearing service providers, investment managers, principal trading firms, pension funds, and non-financial end-users. Coalitions of any of these parties can form on a particular issue.

[146] This cadre is highly dependent on the favour of the regulator, and thus particularly prone to inverse regulatory capture.

[147] The term is from Seabrooke & Tsingou (2014).

telling broadly the same story in different locales, with modifications for local preferences. Their goal, on a given issue, is dominance of a complex, technical narrative, and their ability to achieve this forms a large part of their attractiveness to employers.

11.81 The punctuated equilibrium in regulatory ideology means that members of this linked ecology are usually operating within a settled framework. The 'window' of acceptable discourse is relatively narrow, due in part to the hegemonic practices of authorities and the low political salience of most financial policy questions.[148] The situation was very different in the immediate post-crisis phase when there was an intense struggle for domination of the narrative. Here the effectiveness of policy specialists depended on their ability to quickly adjust to emerging narratives[149] and their rapidly altering instrumental power.[150]

11.82 The new spirit of adversarialism in regulation has changed the character of the policy debate. Before 2008, technical expertise largely determined the perceived salience of a commenter: now, their location is significant too. The myth of regulators under siege means that even highly expert, evidence-based comments are sometimes dismissed as mere self-interest. What has been lost is the possibility that a comment can be both accurate and self-interested.

Some insights from sociology and political economy

11.83 The reality of financial regulation, when illuminated by some insights from sociology and political economy, is revealed as far-from-neutral technocracy. It is competitive, status-imbued, framed by myths, and ridden with principal-agent problems. The epistemic community of financial policy experts[151] structures and dominates debate in the long lulls between the short episodes of political attention. Regulatory ideology, and the largely hidden normative assumptions which define 'acceptable' policy debate, are relatively constant during these equilibrium periods. Regulators' mandates, transparency, and institutional arrangements, and the processes for monitoring their actions and conducting debate, could all be better designed to achieve more efficient and legitimate outcomes for society.

---

148 See Seabrooke & Tsingou (2014) for a further discussion of who determines which policy ideas are debatable.

149 See Froud et al. (2012) and Pagliari & Young (2016) for a further discussion of this point.

150 One hypothesis that might be ventured is that the large banks had negative instrumental power with most authorities in the immediate post-crisis period: if they suggested a particular policy, it made it less attractive to the policy maker.

151 This book is partly an attempt to grapple with my complicity in the actions of this community.

12

Improving the Rules and Institutional Arrangements of Derivatives Regulation

The Approach Taken

12.1 One of the central suggestions in this book has been that it is naïve to either take or oppose the position that more derivatives regulation is good. The details of individual rules matter, so generalizations are impossible.[1] A particular policy might or might not be an appropriate response at a particular time, given the goal, the balance of stakeholders' rights, the rule's cost, the available alternatives, the anticipated side effects, the redistributional consequences, and the rule's interaction with the rest of the policy framework.

12.2 This means that each rule requires detailed examination. Regulations can be effective, as with compulsory inter-dealer variation margin on bilateral derivatives. They can be based on an effective mechanism, but mis-calibrated, as with the thresholds for bilateral margin posting for non-financial entities. Or they can be largely ill-conceived, as with mandatory client clearing. Sometimes the initial regulatory impulse was right, and changes to it can reflect watering down or the opening of barn door exemptions; but in other cases, the policy might have been misguided, and in need of refinement or abandonment. The policy on execution requirements immediately after the crisis is a good example here: many derivatives are not suitable for execution on a central limit order book, and (albeit belated) recognition of that fact by the authorities has improved regulation.

12.3 Another of our motivating ideas has been that various areas of scholarship yield different, valuable insights into derivatives regulation. Legal scholarship, regulatory theory, the economics of regulation, the philosophy of modelling, the sociology of professions, and research from the political economy community

[1] Consider the example of the threshold for mandatory clearing, discussed in Chapter 6. Whether it is set at €3 billion or €100 billion has a huge impact on who is affected by this rule, even though it makes little difference to systemic risk.

have been used as searchlights to pick out different features of our object of study. The suggestion has been that prior to asking a question such as

Is the clearing mandate a good idea?

It is useful to ask the question

What kind of claim is 'the clearing mandate is necessary to achieve financial stability', and what motivates and purports to justify this claim?

12.4 Without the insights that come from a wider perspective, post-crisis derivatives regulation is a puzzle, as we noted in the Introduction. There are discernible threads from some causes of financial stress to some of the policies which were enacted, but the whole quilt is threadbare in some places and patched over again and again in others. There is no single safety standard being targeted, no criteria for how big precautionary measures should be, and no unified account of why the permitted exemptions are justified. This chapter begins by reviewing the key insights about derivatives regulation set out in earlier chapters, mapping these connections, holes, and overlapping interventions.

12.5 The next three sections then make some suggestions concerning areas of regulatory reform. The first discusses improvements in the rules: these could mostly be pursued within the current structure of derivatives regulation. The next two are more foundational, addressing the rule making process and the institutional arrangements for financial regulation.

12.6 The penultimate section considers the implications of our approach for scholarly enquiry into financial regulation. Inspired, like much of this book, by scepticism towards claims that particular courses of action can be unequivocally decided by experts based on an institutionally constructed body of knowledge, we advance the idea that it would be fruitful to explore some of the avenues that *critical* regulatory studies might explore. The final section summarizes our position and the suggestions for regulatory reform which derive from it.

Context and motivations

12.7 Chapter 1 explained what derivatives are and how they give rise to risks. It described the mitigation of these risks and introduced the models developed to measure and manage them. We saw how counterparty credit risk created a network of exposures between derivatives market participants, how collateral could be used to reduce these exposures, but also how the requirement to post margin can create funding liquidity risk.

12.8 Before the 2008 crisis, regulators were junior members of the epistemic community of finance, and somewhat in thrall of more senior members. They adhered to a market-centred ideology. The crisis punctuated that equilibrium, and both politicians and regulators rushed to formulate stories about what went wrong and to advocate for them in a struggle to control the narrative.

12.9 The crisis, as discussed in Chapter 2, was primarily caused by vulnerabilities in the US residential mortgage market. It was then spread by a financial system that had too little capital and too much short-term funding, so even relatively small losses could create a contagious loss of confidence. In response, given the urgent need to demonstrate action, the political weakness of the banks after the crisis, and the lack of will to intervene in the politically sensitive housing market, the authorities quickly settled on a narrative which demonized derivatives.

12.10 'The important role that derivatives play in the economy',[2] as a former CFTC chair Heath Tarbert put it, was ignored.[3] He was making the point that risk transfer makes the real economy more efficient and reduces firms' risk.[4] This fact did not sway the post-crisis debate which led to a new regulatory ideology. Instead, in their scrabble to forge a new international regulatory consensus, the authorities made choices in derivatives regulation that reduced economic efficiency while creating meagre benefits for financial stability or bank safety.

12.11 The financial system was stable during the Covid market stress of early 2020, as Chapter 3 sets out. This provides some evidence of the effectiveness of post-crisis regulation: some of the choices made in it resulted in a more robust financial system. However, it does not demonstrate that all of the policies created in the enormous burst of post-crisis rule writing were necessary. Nor does it demonstrate that every regulation's benefits justifies its costs to the real economy. Indeed, the official sector justification of post-crisis derivatives policy discussed in Chapter 9 suggests that inter-dealer variation margin would have sufficed to mitigate counterparty credit risk: the clearing mandate was not necessary.

12.12 Post-crisis regulatory reform was not sufficient, either. It did not comprehensively address regulation of the mortgage market; of the GSEs which played such a large role in it; or of credit protection written by insurers, the most problematic class of derivatives in the crisis.

2 Thus, we agree with the perspective of Shiller (2012) that 'a good deal of the economic inequality in the modern world is due to the persistence of unmanaged risks, and financial technology is ideally suited to deal with these risks'. This is not to advocate always and everywhere for market-based solutions, but simply to suggest that punishing a technology is not likely to be an effective policy stance.

3 See Tarbert (2020) at 162, from whom the 'demonization' in the last paragraph is taken.

4 One does not have to believe that market prices are always right, or that markets always produce the right allocation of resources, or that there are no dangers in financialization, to believe that the ability for non-financial end-users to transfer risk is a good: see Awrey (2010b) at 170 for a discussion of the benefits of derivatives, and Arrow (1971) for the classical theory of the economic benefits of risk transfer.

Regulations

12.13 Part II showed how the post-crisis reforms increased the cost of risk transfer, but unevenly so. The types of non-financial end-user that the financial system should serve have been worst affected, while financial entities with ready access to collateral have seen substantially smaller impacts. Some systemically important markets are now more fragile, and the lack of robust policing of arbitrages makes hedging more difficult and creates real costs. The primary driver of this has been regulatory reforms, such as the leverage ratio, which discourage banks from providing market intermediation, as discussed in Chapter 4. These rules were developed using a post-crisis regulatory rationality based on translations into idealized schemata defined in the language of regulation, the use of rule-based inferences, and the application of external power. They demonstrate the shortcomings inherent to the regulators' approach. One of the most prominent of these is an inattentiveness to side effects and unintended consequences.

12.14 Chapter 5 examined regulators' models for market and counterparty credit risk. The market risk reforms in Basel 2.5 were seen to improve the quality of estimates of potential market risk losses. Matters took a different turn with Basel 3 due to the challenge of attempting to satisfy conflicting policy objectives. The desires for prudence; for capital ratios of different banks to be comparable; for capital requirements to be risk-sensitive; and for stakeholders to have confidence in the prudential framework, are in tension. The attempt to simultaneously satisfy these preferences created an unnecessarily complex framework with many interacting constraints. Derivatives were held to a much higher standard than many other forms of risk taking, and the quality of regulatory models declined.

12.15 Transnational agreements are policed by regulators' professional identity, hegemonic narratives, and formal disciplinary mechanisms such as regulatory consistency assessment programmes. The overzealous capital regulation of derivatives is evident from the fact that, despite these powerful mechanisms, both the US and the EU have decided to deviate from transnational standards for counterparty credit risk, in favour of somewhat more proportionate approaches.

12.16 Consideration of the development of derivatives markets reveals a gradual evolution to meet specific business needs within a particular legal, social, and epistemic context. For OTC derivatives markets in particular, the result by 2008 was an opaque network of contracts which created concerns about the size of the exposures between some participants. Post-crisis regulation reduced these exposures by mandating clearing and bilateral margin, as discussed in Chapter 6. These requirements use the regular exchange of margin as a key risk reduction technology, something that must, to be effective, be conducted properly on every occasion, and which relies on the availability of collateral assets and a robust repo market. The scope of the standards was seen to be so broad as to go well beyond the goal of reducing systemic risk. The chapter suggested that many clients experience little benefit from either mandatory clearing or the obligation to post margin on bilateral derivatives portfolios. Since the reforms, most clients have suffered from higher cost, less convenient risk transfer.

12.17 Chapter 7 showed how clearing houses also developed incrementally in response to the needs of their users. CCPs were then repurposed in post-crisis regulation to meet public policy objectives. The principles-based approach to their regulation in the PFMI was found to be largely successful. It reduced counterparty credit risk in the interconnected heart of the derivatives system through multilateral netting and the presence of substantial resources in CCP default waterfalls. However, clearing houses remain susceptible to failure from a variety of risks, with non-allocatable non-default losses posing a significant threat due to the relative paucity of the mitigations available for them. Liquidity needs in default management were also identified as an issue for CCPs without access to a central bank liquidity backstop.

12.18 We saw how the super-systemic nature of some CCPs in global markets motivates recovery and resolution policy, and raises questions of supervisory nexus. Regulators are understandably keen to have knowledge of and influence over these entities, but this desire is in tension with supervision based on domicile. Cooperative supervisory arrangements and location policies have emerged in a partially successful response to this conflict.

12.19 In short, the urgent need to make policy after the 2008 crisis led to a lot of rule making, of variable quality.[5] Bank and CCP resilience has increased. Risk transfer and funding markets have been fundamentally re-engineered, but their efficiency and ability to serve society's needs were not prioritized in this process. Certain forms of contracting, including many unmargined and some uncleared derivatives, were banned. As a result of these changes, liquidity risk has been substituted for counterparty credit risk. Another result is that largely private entities—the globally systemic CCPs—have been put at the centre of derivatives markets. The question of whether their private nature was optimal for the public policy purpose they were required to serve was not addressed. Thus, while the details of the rules are important, this overall picture of overreaction and poorly justified, inefficient derivatives reform should not be lost.

[5] Even where there is a clear connection between a legitimate goal and the regulation meeting it, a failure to implement effective rules has often resulted in substantial costs without delivery of all of the potential benefits. OTC derivatives trade reporting is a good example here: legal restrictions mean that no authority has a complete view of the network, as noted in Chapter 2, so market participants pay the cost of reporting, but the information is less useful than it would be if it could be used to create a comprehensive map of exposures.

12.20 It is difficult to write good financial regulation. There was so much new policy after the crisis that it is was inevitable that there would be suboptimal choices. However, a comparison of the Basel Committee's approach with that of CPMI and IOSCO reveals that agreeing principles-based standards which are alert to the need to adapt to local specificities and respect jurisdictional prerogatives is more efficient and effective than attempting to write detailed, now-and-forever global rules. Many of the shortcomings of post-crisis regulation stem from the transnational negotiation of standards which are then very difficult to change.

Perspectives on rules and rule making

12.21 Chapter 8 turned to the transnational policy making process. Regulatory cooperation is understandable, given the complexity of the issues, the global nature of the financial system, and the benefits of sharing the costs of regulatory development. However, transnational rule making suffers from a legitimacy gap due to its opacity, lack of detailed policy justification, failure to demonstrate proportionality, and the absence of an independent review mechanism. These issues are less serious for principles-based regulation which can be implemented with sensitivity to local particularities,[6] and where there is more scope for national administrative law requirements to improve regulatory outcomes.

12.22 Cost-benefit analysis was discussed in Chapter 9 and found to be a useful tool in the design and review of regulation. It raises the question of how a rule transforms the probability and severity of harm in future states of the world: this is fundamental to assessing regulatory effectiveness.

12.23 Chapter 10 developed the framing of regulation-as-model, noting that models are always incomplete and situated, and even plausible ones which give stable, accurate, actionable predictions in one area can become distorted over time or applied outside their domain of applicability.[7] It is good practice, therefore, to document models and their drawbacks; supply them with relevant, good quality data; and carefully monitor their performance. It is also important to be clear about—and debate—the criteria for a model to be considered acceptable, so that this monitoring can be grounded in empirical evidence. Regulators' models score badly on these criteria.

12.24 Insights from social science and political economy were discussed Chapter 11. Regulation, like most successful professions, was seen to operate by social closure and the creation of belonging stories or myths. We traced how, within the

[6] See Riles (2013a) for a discussion of this in a private law context which nicely illustrates the tensions and accommodations which can arise between global schema and the situation in a locale far from the standard setter.

[7] The corollary of this is that we should beware models that are used without an understanding of their limits or framed by (perhaps implicit) claims of universal applicability.

community of regulators, a spirit of adversarialism has coloured dialogue since the crisis, and how the assumption of the efficacy of technocratic prescriptions makes measures badged as such difficult to challenge.

12.25 Regulation was considered as a bureaucratic technology which proceeds by constructing its own categories, defining translations and rules of inference, and applying power as a result of this knowledge. The rationality in use is compositional: it builds up a complex internal representation of regulated entities piece by piece, with (often unacknowledged) model risk at every stage.

12.26 The regulatory state was introduced as a family of methods of governing based on an assumption of the value of independent expertise, a commitment to policy consistency, and a technocratic approach. These methods are strategies for the reproduction of particular types of socio-economic relations. Their common tactic is the construction of knowledge and its use to steer, limit, and discipline the regulated. They raise questions of legitimacy and independence, with the inherent politics of policy questions sometimes hidden by a regulatory veil. It is often convenient for politicians to ignore this.

12.27 Financial regulation, politics, and the financial system are mutually constitutive and locked in a three-way struggle both for power and of mutual dependency. After 2008, there was a brief period of transnational debate in which a new regulatory ideology was formed. This debate offered an opportunity for financial regulators to acquire power and epistemic territory in this struggle: the current corpus of regulation is an embodiment of their success. The discursive authority of the transnational regulatory community, and their resulting ability to limit debate to a window of acceptable topics discussed in the language of regulation, has severely limited the opportunities to review the performance of regulators' models and their underlying assumptions since then.

Towards a New Regulation: Rules

12.28 This section is the first of three on derivatives regulatory reform. It treats the rules themselves, setting out some areas where policy revision should be considered. The intent is not to suggest what ought to change, as each policy proposal would require much more substantial documentation, consideration of evidence, and analysis of alternatives than we have room for. The objective, instead, is to suggest some review projects that should be undertaken. Our plan here follows earlier chapters, with the bank capital rules considered first; then the clearing mandate and bilateral margin rules; then CCP regulation. Regulatory reforms which are outside the current window of policy making are discussed in the final subsection.

Projects in bank capital reform

12.29 The leverage ratio is implicated in the declines in market quality seen since 2008, and especially in the fragility of the systemically important repo market in stress.[8] The justification for *a* leverage ratio is regulators' inability to write good risk-weighted capital rules, while the justification for the particular leverage ratio regulators implemented is scant. The Basel 3.1 leverage ratio adds enormous complexity to regulation,[9] and it herds banks into largely the same business model, making the financial system more fragile. The necessity for the leverage ratio should be reviewed, and exemptions for low risk assets like high quality government bonds should be considered if a leverage ratio is still deemed necessary.[10]

12.30 For similar reasons, other precautionary measures that have not been well justified should be reviewed. These include backstops in capital requirements such as the output floor.

The prudential regulation of market and counterparty credit risk

12.31 The risk-weighted capital rules in the trading book are hugely complicated and incoherent. The FRTB will make this worse. Implementation of this set of rules should be halted, and a project undertaken to simplify the whole trading book framework. The first step would be to clearly articulate the regulatory goal, including a statement of the intended safety standard.[11]

12.32 The current risk-based capital rules demonstrate the tension between having risk-sensitive models-based approaches and the desire for different banks' capital requirements to be comparable and reliable. In the trading book, this could be managed by integrating market, CVA, and counterparty credit risk into a single framework based on a pure stressed VAR or expected shortfall, plus an incremental risk charge, with conservatism provided by a multiplier at the highest level of the framework alone.[12]

---

[8] In particular, derivatives policy relies on well-functioning repo markets for collateral provision and investment, as discussed in Chapter 7.

[9] In the UK, there are six capital stacks: three each in CET1, T1 and total capital for both RWAs and leverage. Removing the leverage ratio would halve that.

[10] One reasonable possibility would be to exempt from the leverage ratio central bank reserves and any asset that a government money fund in the United States or its cognate in other developed economies could buy. This would allow banks to provide liquidity to systemically important government bond repo markets—perhaps subject to minimum haircuts—without a leverage ratio penalty.

[11] A useful first step would be producing a conceptual framework for bank prudential regulation analogous to R. IASB (2018) for IFRS.

[12] If necessary, comparability could be enhanced by providing guidance on the selection of stressed periods.

12.33 At the same time, the standard rules for market risk and SA-CCR should be recalibrated using realistic portfolios to match the models-based approaches as well as possible. There would be no need for CVA rules at all, as CVA and its hedges would be included in the trading book and treated by the revised market risk framework.

The prudential regulation of credit risk

12.34 The banking book is a bigger problem, given the paucity of reform of the models-based rules for credit risk in the bank capital framework since 2006. As with the trading book, the first step should be the articulation of a credible safety standard, followed by the development of a methodology for accurate risk estimation in high stress. A central concern should be the modelling of losses on real estate lending portfolios after large falls in prices, as this type of stress is an important driver of financial instability.

12.35 At the same time, mortgage risk taking by non-banks should be considered on a consistent basis. In the United States, the prudential framework for the GSEs is an issue: perhaps these entities could be included in the FED's stress testing programme so that their capital resources are assessed under the same standards as the largest US banks.[13]

12.36 Currently, bank regulation shows a marked preference for credit risk over market risk, and for certain ways of taking risk over others. Disincentives for many types of derivative abound. Bank regulators should be more alert to the inefficiencies and incentives their rules create, and should secure a clear political mandate for any selection of winners and losers in different markets and in different forms of risk transfer.

The clearing mandate

12.37 The most obvious candidate in derivatives regulation for review is the clearing mandate. For the interconnected core of the derivatives system—the biggest dealers—it is unnecessary, as there are substantial incentives for these parties to clear anyway. For clients, the mandatory clearing threshold is almost certainly set too low. Moreover, several areas of policy, including CCP governance arrangements, the size of CCP skin in the game, the need for APC tools, and the vexing question of who should pay in a CCP recovery or resolution, are made more challenging by mandatory clearing. If using CCPs was not required by bright line rules, these issues would become less urgent.

12.38 For similar reasons, the threshold for posting bilateral margin should be revisited, with a focus on capturing systemic risk, the avoidance of barn door

[13] If the state wishes to hold its own enterprises to a lower standard than private sector firms carrying out the same activity, it should at least articulate why.

exclusions like the hedging exemption, and properly treating FX risk. Requirements for a concentration margin add-on for bilateral derivatives should also be examined, as concentrated positions are at the root of some of the most prominent episodes of derivatives-related stress.

Central counterparties

12.39 The transnational CCP regulatory framework works reasonably well.[14] The key issues are with the small number of globally systemic CCPs, where a higher standard of safety is necessary, given the consequences of their failure. Consideration should be given to creating a new class comprising the most systemic clearing houses, probably numbering fewer than ten globally.[15] For these CCPs, the policy questions concern financial resources for absorbing non-allocatable non-default losses, access to central bank lending in stress, and barriers to resolvability.

12.40 Concentration risk is also an issue for CCPs, so consideration should be given to better supervision of this element of CCP margin models, especially for exchange-traded derivatives, where a one day margin period of risk gives very little time to manage a large position.

Wider horizons

12.41 The last few subsections all contained ideas that could be implemented within the current regulatory ideology. While some of them are controversial, they do not fundamentally challenge the post-2008 consensus. This subsection considers several matters that require political debate and, if change is decided upon, intervention. They relate to the nature of the entities conducting key roles in the financial system and the bargain struck with them. Historical contingencies, as we have seen, shaped the financial system. This inheritance does not necessarily represent the optimal arrangement for current needs. The underlying question in each case is whether the nature, rights, and obligations of the entities remain appropriate.

12.42 The first issue concerns the providers of market intermediation. Banks' share of market making grew in the 1980s as non-bank players were unable to provide sufficient credit, capital, and ancillary functions to compete.[16] It then

[14] The same cannot be said of all national or bloc implementations of the PFMI, as we saw with the cost-benefit analysis of EMIR's APC tools in Chapter 9.

[15] Exposures of major intermediaries to the largest CCPs are now much larger than their exposures to each other. If we have put all our eggs in the CCP basket, as Dudley (2017) puts it, 'it is particularly important now to closely watch that basket'.

[16] The liberalization of the London Stock Exchange culminating in the 'big bang' reforms of 1986 are a good example: see Section I of Oren & Blyth (2018). Less well known is the move from specialist non-banks intermediating the European base metals derivatives market prior to the second EU

fell as credit intermediation by dealers became less important and hedge funds and principal trading firms exploited their advantages in high volume electronic markets.[17] Today, banks are constrained by the leverage ratio, risk-weighted capital rules, and liquidity regulation, among others. This stops them from providing consistent, deep intermediation capacity to many financial markets. Most non-bank market makers have insufficient stable funding to be able to maintain market quality in episodes like the March 2020 'dash for cash': their reliance on the leverage provided by repo makes their market liquidity provision fragile. This can mean that, in stress, no one wants to meet the market's need for intermediation.

12.43 A debate is therefore needed about the role of private actors in market making which includes both their rights and their responsibilities.[18] If the result of a mass withdrawal of intermediation providers in stress is societally damaging, should we disincentive this withdrawal, prohibit it via the rules for accessing markets, or mitigate it by authority action? If the last route is taken, can the resulting moral hazard be justified?[19] How should central banks be compensated for the backstop they provide in acting as market makers of last resort? Perhaps there is a role for a fee on all market transactions in exchange for this guarantee of market liquidity?[20] If, instead, it is decided that banks should be the swing providers of additional intermediation capacity in stress, how should regulation change to (perhaps strongly) encourage it? The underlying question here is, for a given market structure, how much intermediation is needed to support the market quality that is socially desirable, especially in stress, and what kind of entity should provide it.

12.44 Relatedly, it is important to note that more market liquidity is not always better. Sometimes it can make markets more fragile and less able to serve the real economy. Several questions arise from this observation. One concerns the role of financial transaction taxes, or 'FTT's. These have a larger impact on short-term

---

Capital Adequacy Directive to bank intermediation after it. This second example is interesting as it was caused by regulation despite the fact there was no perceived market failure to correct: the metals futures brokers were simply a casualty of the definition of 'investment firm' in CAD II.

17 For a further discussion of the role of these non-bank intermediation providers, see Box 3 in the Bank of England July 2019 *Financial Stability Report*, available at https://www.bankofengland.co.uk/financial-stability-report/2019/july-2019.

18 The idea of minimum obligations of market makers has a long history: see for instance the summary in Weaver (2012). These could be combined with incentives such as a favourable tax treatment for market making inventory and access to the central bank window.

19 One of the problems with the claim that post-crisis regulation has been an unequivocal success is that it leads to the moral hazard of the authorities feeling obliged to intervene when systemically important markets fail.

20 This is an extension of the idea proposed in Winters (2012) at §§275 of charging banks for their access to central bank liquidity.

trading strategies than long-term ones, so it seems likely that they would damp down behaviours that depend on short-term interactions, such as flash crashes.[21] In contrast, real economy risk transfer transactions would be relatively unaffected by an FTT set at a low level. FTTs therefore have an appeal as a tool for managing excessive short-term trading in markets for risky assets.[22]

12.45 The need for better market quality in government bond and government bond repo markets requires a different solution. One suggestion here has been that more clearing and all-to-all trading would help.[23] This may well be true, but it brings its own problems, not least the need for the relevant CCP to have certain access to very large amounts of funding in default management. Clearing is also unlikely to solve the problem that market intermediation capacity is inadequate in stress: it will probably be necessary to address this problem head on, as discussed in paragraph 12.43. Without such action, the assumption that margin will mitigate the systemic risk of derivatives may not to be true, as market participants, in stress, might not turn out to be able to source or invest cash via repo.

12.46 Turning to securities-based derivatives, another intervention to improve market robustness which deserves consideration is an extension of transparency obligations and position limits. There have been numerous examples of market disruption in securities and security-based derivatives markets due to outsized positions taken via derivatives.[24] There is a good case for imposing transparency obligations on positions taken via derivatives to those that apply on the underlying securities. The benefit to market integrity of extending the commodity derivatives position limits regime discussed in Chapter 8 to security-based derivatives should also be considered. Securities prices too can be subject to violent fluctuations if positions in derivatives based on them are large compared to the amount of the underlying asset available for delivery.[25]

12.47 The final issue relates to clearing houses. Private ownership of super-systemic CCPs creates challenges for resolution. The conflict between their role as for-profit institutions and as systemic risk managers is difficult to navigate. This

---

[21] See Kirilenko et al. (2017).

[22] For more details, see Burman et al. (2016) who discuss the design issues in the implementation of FTTs and their helpful distributional impacts.

[23] See Duffie (2020).

[24] In equity derivatives, these include the 2021 default of Archegos capital after losses on positions taken via total return swaps and Porsche's 2008 short squeeze on Volkswagen via equity options. In credit derivatives, the 2019 Sears and 2005 Delphi Corp. defaults are examples: the former is discussed in Cahill et al. (2019).

[25] This would not address all forms of 'engineered' CDS, but it would mitigate the risk of short squeezes in CDS auctions and reduce the risk of equity price disruptions caused by derivatives positions.

form of CCP arose when exchanges demutualized,[26] but their nature now means that central clearing is a partial solution to the problem of a large default in the derivatives market. CCPs can reduce risk for cleared trades, but if they themselves can fail, a new, low probability but very high severity risk has been introduced.

12.48 The question arises whether resolution policy is enough here, both as a matter of risk and of fairness. If the taxpayer is going to pay to recapitalize a failing CCP anyway, perhaps they should have the revenues from clearing in good times too? Moreover, all of the functions which are carried out in CCPs do not have to occur in the same entity: it would be perfectly possible to separate out the systemically important roles of being the counterparty to cleared trades and holding margin from the other functions of CCPs.[27]

Towards a New Regulation: The Rule Making Process

12.49 We have seen how some of the post-crisis regulations for derivatives are well-motivated, safety-enhancing, and proportional, while others are not. This variability arises largely because regulation has been constructed by negotiation from a base of situated and historically contingent knowledge which, in turn, has been shaped by the interests of regulators, legislators, and financial institutions, among others. These interests, and their interplay, have not been fully interrogated.[28]

12.50 There are two inter-linked goals to reforming the rule making process: improving the legitimacy of financial regulation; and improving the quality of the rules made. These are mutually supportive.[29] They suggest that an important element in the reform of rule making is improving the dialogue with stakeholders. This would enhance legitimacy and it would increase the intellectual resources,

[26] See Cox & Steigerwald (2016) for an account of this 'incomplete demutualization'.

[27] This is a partial answer to the problem that nationalized or utility CCPs are less innovative than privately held ones: the innovation in e.g. margin model design, ancillary services such as compression, and product design can occur in a private sector entity who—much like a train operator using a nationalized track network—would operate under the rules of the entity who owns the systemically important object, the netting set. See Cerezetti et al. (2019) for a further discussion.

[28] The inspiration here is the call in Derrida (1992) for 'a de-sedimentation of the superstructures of law that both hide and reflect the economic and political interests of the dominant forces of society'.

[29] The requirements from article 21 of the Legislative and Regulatory Reform Act (2006) that 'regulatory activities should be carried out in a way which is transparent, accountable, proportionate and consistent' and that 'regulatory activities should be targeted only at cases in which action is needed' do not apply to most regulatory rule making, but form a good benchmark.

evidence, and analytical capability available to improve proposed regulation and to monitor its performance.[30] Regulatory practice should therefore be re-framed around a more self-critical,[31] adaptable,[32] power-equalizing dialogue. It is only by regulators giving reasons for their suggestions, listening to others' views, and incorporating them into a jointly constructed model that aesthetic motivations—essentially, 'we are doing this because we like it'—can be distinguished from the search for an efficient, effective model.[33] The characteristics of this new settlement should be modesty, dynamism, and an openness to the possibilities of error, of being out of date, and of creating as well as mitigating instability.

12.51 There are two obvious classes of remedy here. The first is to open up the rule making process. This would entail imposing administrative law obligations on both national *and transnational* rule making where they do not already exist. These would entail for every new rule:

- Requiring that every proposal includes a clear statement of the goal—what harm is being mitigated and to what degree of confidence?
- Mandating a regulatory mechanism analysis which sets out what processes are thought to lead to undesirable states of the world, how it is proposed to intervene in them, and how the success of that intervention could be judged. In particular, for any proposal, performance indicators should be clearly set out.[34] Evidence on the size of the risk and the circumstances under which it might crystallize should be gathered and presented.[35]
- Making all consultative meetings on rule making public and freely available online.

---

[30] Thus we agree with Elgin (2017)'s suggestion that there is a propensity for uncoerced conversations to uncover and correct modelling errors. Financial regulation should not be exempted from the requirement to justify its models. Indeed, the offensiveness of imposing models which are substantially less well scrutinized than they should be is a major motivation for increasing transparency in and accountability for rule making.

[31] Regulatory agencies can be self-critical after firms fail: see, for instance, the SEC's report into its supervision of Bear, Stearns, SEC (2008). But regulation can malfunction less dramatically too, slowly strangling firms through excessive prudence.

[32] For a discussion of how the supervision of large banks became more reliant on international standards and less tailored to individual institutions, see Menand (2018). Reversing this trend would improve bank regulation.

[33] In this sense, the output floor is the regulators' version of the flying buttress in neo-gothic architecture: an unnecessary ornament.

[34] A derivatives pricing model is monitored by examining whether it really does explain changes in the value of a derivative and its hedges from day to day: see R. Fed Board & OCC (2011) at 14. For a model which estimates a resources requirement, a cognate test would entail a comparison of the realized requirements with the estimated ones, given the safety standard targeted.

[35] Bull & Ellig (2017) suggest a 'best available evidence' standard here.

- Directing the provision of a proportionality analysis that considers alternative means, shows that there is no less onerous approach which would achieve the goal, and explains why the interference with rights proposed is proportionate to the goal.[36]
- Establishing an independent dispute resolution mechanism where one is not currently available.
- Applying freedom of information provisions to financial regulation. Information on the intent to make rules and the rationale for these plans; evidence on the size of the problem being discussed; the minutes of policy making meetings, including at the working group level; the data used to understand impacts and calibrate rules (anonymized if necessary); regulators' analysis of it; and their judgement of comments,[37] should be made freely available. Provisions like these have been in place for some national regulators for many years without adverse effect:[38] it is now time to require them for all national and transnational financial regulatory bodies.

12.52 Even better, rather than concocting regulations in secret and then asserting their optimality, regulators could instead issue calls for policy proposals, setting out their goal and safety standard, and inviting interested parties to propose rules which meet their objectives. These 'open source' proposals should be considered in a transparent process, with full disclosure of (if necessary, anonymized) evidence, comments, and analysis.

12.53 Given the advantages to regulators of the current opaque transnational rule making process, it is unlikely that they would accede to these suggestions.[39] The

[36] Stephenson (2006) makes the good point that the willingness to shoulder this burden would represent signalling from the authorities that they considered the benefits of their proposed policy to be high.

[37] The tendency for regulators to dismiss observations from the regulated without consideration of their merits would be reduced if their analysis of comments had to be published. The new adversarialism in financial regulation should not mean that regulators can dismiss comments based solely on who is making them.

[38] In the UK, see Chapter 3B of R. FSMA (2000) or the Regulator's Code enabled by §§21–23 of R. LRRA (2006). In the US, the CFTC makes public 'substantive ex parte communications, both written and oral, that provide significant, material information addressed to the merits of a proposed rule. It is also the Commission's practice to make public on its website all ex parte meetings held on proposed rules, including the names and affiliations of attendees': see https://www.cftc.gov/LawRegulation/CommissionRulemakingExplained/index.htm.

[39] Urueña (2012) says that we 'lack a criteria for deciding when a regulatory network is useful'. One might suggest that they are often useful to their members: what we need is a criteria for deciding when the standards they produce are useful for all the jurisdictions they are imposed upon, and to restructure their practice where this is not the case.

alternative is to limit the amount of detail decided at the transnational level,[40] allowing space for local administrative law to provide legitimacy. This would permit the principles of financial regulation to be agreed internationally, but would defer the details to local regulators, who could then tailor them to the needs of their particular financial systems and be held accountable for their success or failure in so-doing.

12.54 Regulators might object, saying that these obligations are burdensome. The response is that the complex and inefficient body of post-crisis regulation suggests that a higher bar for rule making would be a good thing.[41] Put other way, if regulators cannot justify the initial and ongoing efficacy not just of doing *something*, but of doing *exactly what they suggest*, why should we let them act?

Towards a New Regulation: Institutional Arrangements

12.55 Financial regulation is a historically contingent bureaucratic technology that produces knowledge, possesses external power, and continually seeks to legitimate itself as *the* rationality for understanding financial stability.[42] It thus ensures the docility of stakeholders,[43] despite its costs, side effects, and distributional consequences. Regulators' totalizing claims prompt the questions: 'Who is speaking? Who, among the totality of speaking individuals, is accorded the right to use this sort of language? Who is qualified to do so? Who derives from it his own special quality, his prestige, and from whom, in return, does he receive if not the assurance, at least the presumption that what he says is true?'[44]

12.56 This structure has not arisen by conscious design. Rather, it is the outcome of incentives playing out in the political economy of regulation. Fortunately, there are tools for understanding these situations and methods of ameliorating their

40 See Romano (2014a) for a similar call for a 'non-harmonized' approach to transnational bank capital regulation.

41 Imagine the most efficient regulation for a given safety standard. This would impose the minimum cost on society to achieve the socially desired behaviour of the financial system. Now consider that regulation plus a requirement that each bank employ 1,000 people to submit random numbers to the regulator monthly. Without justification, transparency, and monitoring, how would we know that we had the former rather than the latter?

42 See Derrida (2003) at 105: 'The dominant power is the one that manages to impose and, thus, to legitimate, indeed to legalize (for it is always a question of law) on a national or world stage, the terminology and thus the interpretation that best suits it in a given situation'.

43 Disciplinary projects like financial regulation are, in this conception, not just rules and enforcement but conceptual frameworks. Success for the system is making this framework an assumption of all discourse so that the possibility of non-compliance seems impossible to imagine.

44 The quote is from Foucault (1972) at 50.

deleterious effects. The first step is to uncover the structures of power by which financial regulation's claims are promulgated, justified, and sustained. Simply abolishing a rule like the leverage ratio might correct an unnecessary and inefficient distortion, but it does nothing to explain the kind of knowledge that has been created nor to make it less likely that such a complex object ridden with undesirable side effects will appear again: structural change in how policy is made is needed for that.

12.57 We suggest that this perspective is important for improving the institutional arrangements of financial regulation. It would be unhelpful to replace one totalizing framework and one dominant narrative with another, slightly different but equally well-defended one.[45] Instead, we should consider the processes which create dialogues between financial regulation and its stakeholders, including mandates, accountability mechanisms, requirements to consult, and review structures. Transnational regulatory cooperation has too often sidestepped domestic requirements for enhancing legitimacy and transparency, as we saw in the previous section, and this has consequences for institutional arrangements too. Based on this, some areas where change should be considered are proposed.

Mandates

12.58 If you don't ask for something, it is often harder to get it. Moreover, improving regulation after the fact via review is more difficult than developing it properly in the first place. Regulatory mandates act as the frame for policy development, so they play a key role in guiding the rule making process and ensuring that regulators deliver a rule set that steers the financial system towards meeting societal needs.

12.59 At the moment, mandates for bank (and broker/dealer) regulators are often too focused on preventing the collapse of regulated firms. For instance, R. FSMA (2000) defines the UK Prudential Regulatory Authority's general objective as 'promoting the safety and soundness' of PRA-authorized entities.[46] This choice of mandate was likely motivated by the assumption that markets could be relied upon to deliver financial services, leading to the belief that the regulation should address disorderly firm failure and its consequences for financial stability.

[45] See Fischl (1992) for a discussion of this problem.

[46] This objective is 'advanced primarily by' 'seeking to ensure that the business' of these entities—"persons" in the language of the statute—'is carried on in a way which avoids any adverse effect on the stability of the UK financial system' and 'seeking to minimize the adverse effect that the failure of a PRA-authorized person could be expected to have on the stability of the UK financial system'. There is a requirement to avoid adverse effects resulting 'from the disruption of the continuity of financial services' and a secondary objective to facilitate 'effective competition in the markets for services provided by PRA-authorized persons in carrying on regulated activities'.

It simply was not envisaged that regulation might constrain market participants so much that they would stop intermediating repos or offering client clearing, for example. Now we know better. If we press too hard, some functions leave the regulated system—and the consequences of that might be worse than keeping them inside the regulatory perimeter.[47]

12.60 The mandate of prudential regulators should be rewritten to focus on the *efficient* provision of core financial services in all conditions by regulated entities. Micro-prudential robustness and financial stability follow from this, but do not—even together—imply it. An efficient provision mandate would facilitate a much-needed debate about what 'efficient' and 'core' should mean, and would focus attention on the effects of regulation on the cost of various financial services for the real economy.[48]

Accountability and politics in financial policy

12.61 The features of a good accountability framework for financial regulation are well-understood: as discussed in Chapter 11, an accountor should have the right information, technical expertise, legitimacy, and sufficient resources. It should respond dynamically to evidence about the performance of regulation and to new proposals.

12.62 Of these, acquiring sufficient information is one of the hardest. The accountor needs to be able to draw a detailed map of which rules impose which costs and which benefits, and how different rules interact to constrain the financial system.[49] The transparency advocated in paragraph 12.51 is required for this, and it could be supplemented by the requirement for rule writers to produce an assessment, perhaps annually, of the costs, benefits, and performance of the whole regulatory framework they are responsible for.[50]

47 As an example of key functions leaving the regulatory perimeter, see Darst et al. (2020). These authors report that, in the United States, private credit from non-bank financial institutions, 'to high risk, middle market firms had been the fastest growing portion of the loan market … as of 2018. Market participants have pointed to higher costs from stricter "prudential regulation" as one of the reasons why banks no longer serve this market.'

48 As Majone (1994) at 87 insightfully points out, a key feature which distinguishes regulation from policies involving the direct expenditure of public funds is that 'the real costs of most regulatory programmes are borne directly by the firms and individuals who have to comply with them.' If regulators had to make their case for these costs to legislators alongside the purported benefits, they might be less free in imposing them: requiring efficiency coequally with micro- and macro-prudential objectives would at least force regulators to consider the balance here.

49 Philippon (2015) suggests an attempt to measure the net cost per unit of risk transfer: this would be an interesting—albeit difficult—measure to produce, and would either validate or refute the suggestion that regulators are implicitly picking winners and losers in risk transfer markets.

50 The fact that this would be an enormous task for contemporary bank prudential regulation is another indication that the framework is too complicated.

12.63 The accountor for financial regulation should be truly independent from the rule makers: it should not import their ideology by employing current or ex-regulators, and it should design its own set of key performance indicators for regulatory agencies, rather than allowing them to develop the marking scheme for their own homework. These indicators should be used to prioritize the areas of the rules subject to detailed review. In order to carry out these functions, the accountor will require substantial analytical and data support.

12.64 If information and expertise are required, so is authority. The accountor must have the power to require that rules it considers suboptimal are altered. For controversial areas of rule making, the executive might wish to impose sunset clauses, so that rules only persist if they receive affirmative sign-off by the accountor.[51]

12.65 It would be natural for the accountor to review the policy making process and the evidence produced during it. This would include:

- consideration of whether each policy has a clearly articulated goal and whether regulation is necessary to meet the goal;
- exploration of whether each regulation reliably assures that the goal is met in a proportional manner using an appropriate form;
- scrutiny of whether due process was followed in making each rule, and, in particular, whether comments on the rule were properly considered;
- evaluation of the consequences of each policy, whether intended or unintended, how the regulated adapt to it, and whether this change in behaviour materially affects the optimality of the chosen approach;
- review of the distributional consequences of regulation and their fairness;
- consideration of potential alternative policies which might also meet the goal either with more certainty, or with lower cost, or fewer side effects; and
- analysis of regulatory calibration.

12.66 The accountor could also hold hearings with stakeholders to hear their concerns. The aim would be to foster an open dialogue while remaining outside the system. In other words, the accountor should not be a regulators' regulator, but rather a facilitator who assists in revealing and questioning the hidden normative premises and unexamined choices made in the regulatory process.

12.67 We have seen that political judgements are constitutive of regulatory practice, but that regulators often hide this essential politicization with claims of

[51] See Romano (2014b) for a further discussion of the role of sunset clauses in financial regulation.

technocratic objectivity. One way to address the trespassing of regulators on political decisions would be to create boundary-crossing obligations.

12.68 First, when making policy, regulators should be mandated to consider the impact of their proposals on the ability of the financial system to robustly provide key functions to the real economy.[52] Redistributional effects and relative costs should also be considered: too often, rules suit financial institutions rather than real economy end-users.

12.69 Regulatory agencies should be instructed to refer policies which had significant effects on financial system functioning to legislative committees.[53] In addition, the executive should have the right to call back regulatory rules for political scrutiny if they deem it necessary.[54] This right could be exercisable during the comment period on rules, and would delay their implementation, allowing time for appropriate democratic investigation of regulatory proposals. If the proposed rules could not be justified during this process, they would be vacated.

Transnational policy making and consistency

12.70 Some regulatory consistency assessment programmes are based on the assumption that unelected bureaucrats know better than elected politicians what the right regulatory framework for a country is. This is odious. If transnational standard setters who set detailed rules do not reform themselves, national governments should consider explicitly repudiating their jurisdiction.[55] In the UK

---

[52] As Philippon (2015) points out, the SEC already has an efficiency mandate: other financial regulators should be given one too. The problem is that such a mandate is antithetical to the current bank regulatory ideology that puts bank robustness above any other consideration.

[53] Mügge (2011) suggests that the problem is best addressed by first considering the 'distribution of the benefits and costs of [an] alternative financial system', then 'what kinds of rules would be necessary' to achieve it, before choosing how and with what institutions to regulate. I am sympathetic to this suggestion, but it suffers from a 'how to get there from here' problem: we already have a substantial architecture of financial regulation, and there is no obvious force which could disrupt the current elite consensus on regulatory ideology. Somewhat more modest institutional design interventions may therefore stand more chance of success than a call to rebuild from the ground up, with the corresponding risk of rebuilding a totalizing structure.

[54] The European Parliament advocated for a call-back right with regard to delegated legislative measures: see Visscher et al. (2008) at 25. Sadly, they were not successful in achieving their wish here, but the general idea is a good one, albeit that its implementation would depend on the local administrative law context.

[55] The problem is well illustrated by Edey (2015). In this speech, talking about post-crisis derivatives reforms in general and the clearing mandate in particular, the speaker says that the initial response from the Australian authorities was 'to intervene only where necessary, so as to preserve appropriate incentives and avoid imposing unnecessary costs on industry participants'. No clearing mandate would have been imposed. The authorities then changed their mind, 'driven importantly by considerations of international consistency'. In reversing their decision, the 'regulators took into

context, a helpful additional step would be to remove the requirement in statute for the regulatory authorities to 'have regard to relevant standards recommended by the Basel Committee'.[56]

12.71 Simultaneously, as discussed above, countries should demand that transnational cooperation is conducted as a purely principles-based activity. An assessment of the result of the Basel 3 project does not suggest that constructing a subsequent accord on the same basis is a good idea. There is no need for a Basel 4 until transnational bank standards setting has been reformed.

A Stance in Scholarship: Critical Regulatory Studies

12.72 Critical legal studies is a project which, among other things, is sceptical of claims that legal questions can be decided entirely within the law.[57] Broadly, it is sensitive to the implications of the observation that when 'one understands the moral, epistemological, and empirical assumptions embedded in any particular legal claim, one will see that those assumptions operate in the particular setting in which the legal claim is made to advance the interests of some identifiable political grouping'.[58]

12.73 Thus, doubt about the existence of deductive methods capable of giving determinate solutions to particular problems of legal choice, and a critical attitude towards a willingness to work entirely within a framework created by a given institutional tradition,[59] are important features of the stance often taken in critical legal studies.

12.74 This echoes our suspicion of regulatory claims for the necessity of particular policy responses, and prompts the question of what analogous *critical regulatory studies* might consist of. Such studies could use tools from regulatory theory, critical legal studies, economics, and political economy[60] to open up

account the benefits that could arise in such cases from favourable comparability assessments of the Australian regime'. In other words, fear of a negative consistency assessment was a factor in the Australian authorities imposing a policy that they did not initially view as optimal for Australia.

56 See Part 9D of R. FSA (2021). In practice, 'have regard to' is a high standard: it is typically interpreted as meaning 'obey unless there is a very good reason not to'.

57 Hunt (1986) cites this opposition to legal positivism as a defining characteristic.

58 The quote is from Hunt (1986) at 1517. In contrast, Tushnet (1991) suggests that critical legal studies is better thought of as a political location rather than a body of theory

59 See Unger (1983) at 564–565.

60 It would therefore offer an opportunity to enact the suggestion in Coutinho (2016) for a dialogue which would connect regulatory theory with the economic development literature, and thus probe 'the argument that regulatory regimes ... are contingent, disputable, adaptable up to certain constraining limits, and are also part of democracy as a long-term institutional effort'. (The first part of this conjunction may turn out to be more robust than the second.)

regulatory power structures, reveal obscured knowledge practices, and challenge both the purported optimality of regulation and whose interests claims of regulatory efficacy really serve. They would operate from plural perspectives and at multiple, interacting levels including those of the rule text and the central banker's speech; the political economy of IOSCO and the sociology of the Basel tower; the politics of comment letters; and the analysis of the costs and benefits of a rule or rule set. These practices should facilitate a loosely-bound collection of critical dialogues on regulation rather than attempting to form a singular theory.

12.75 Critical regulatory studies, then, if aptly named, would continually seek to examine the effects of regulation in practice[61] and demand justifications for them.[62] Such studies would remain alert to the operation of regulatory power[63] and maintain an interrogation of the origin, construction, and limits of regulation's conceptual, theoretical, and normative apparatus. A core motivation for this stance would be the belief that a constant dialogue with and questioning of regulation is an important tool in uncovering alternative policies and regulatory practices which might serve society better and with greater legitimacy. This, for me, is an effective catalyst to the study of regulation.

In The End

12.76 The success of the financial system depends on and supports systems of regulation, legal enforceability, and political consent.[64] Modern finance without property rights, mechanisms for enforcing contracts, or robust markets would be impossible. There is ample evidence that the externalities created by finance, if unaddressed, create instability. Such a dangerous system will only be tolerated if its benefits are not evidently lower than its costs. Moreover, to flourish, finance needs political legitimacy. Governments have largely sub-contracted the provision of financial stability to regulators, so regulation is a critical ingredient in the contract between the financial system and society.

[61] Carrigan & Coglianese (2011) suggests that 'understanding how regulation gets made and implemented—and who influences regulatory decisions in order to get what, when, and how—has been a long-standing, persistent research challenge for political scientists, economists, and legal scholars'. I agree that this is an important problem, and suggest that the framing question of what the costs, benefits, and risks of the resulting regulation are is salient too.

[62] As Scott (2014) puts it at 7, regulatory accountability requires us to ask 'difficult questions about how effective the regulator is and how they can *demonstrate* the quality and effects of what they do' (emphasis mine).

[63] If the construction and use of a model within regulation renders the financial system manageable by regulators, whose interest is that management in the service of?

[64] See Deakin et al. (2017) for a longer account of this position.

12.77 There are benefits from the relationships created by this. The financial system coordinates the actions of economic actors. Financial institutions gain from regulation as it provides an independent and freely available assessment of safety: a counterparty can usually see if they are dealing with a regulated entity, and they often have more confidence when they are.[65] Regulators have higher status and more resources when they have an important and vibrant system to regulate. Thus, these three parties—government, financial regulators, and the financial system—are mutually constitutive. They shape each other, nurture each other, and are beholden to each other.

12.78 The consequences of this arrangement have not always served society well. In the years leading up to 2008, for instance, an elite-endorsed market-friendly ideology allowed an unsustainable bubble in real estate to develop, inflated by ultimately unaffordable lending. After the tumult caused by the bursting of that bubble, the prior 'light touch' regulatory consensus crumbled and there was a short, intense period of debate about what should replace it. During that period, many questions about what happened and what should be done about it were open, and there was a scrabble to articulate and defend competing answers. Evidence was scant and played a relatively small role in the discussion.

12.79 During this period, derivatives were vulnerable, while more important causes of the crisis—prominently, lax residential mortgage lending—were better defended. The understandable public outrage at the damage caused by the crisis meant that there was a strong incentive to say that something had been done. This resulted in an enormous wave of derivatives regulation. Once regulatory ideology solidified, potent hegemonic mechanisms closed down debate and promulgated the winning narrative.

12.80 The resulting regulatory framework is inefficient, partially ineffective, and sometimes counterproductive. Inefficient because it imposes costs which are not justified by the risks; ineffective because it does not address important issues which could threaten financial stability; and counterproductive because it creates unnecessary obstacles to the financial system's ability to deliver critical economic functions.

12.81 One key problem is that the global post-crisis settlement between governments and financial policy makers has allowed essentially political questions to be disguised as technocratic ones and answered by regulators rather than politicians.[66] In order to open these questions, we advocate for a wide, free debate about how the financial system can serve society best, then an evidence-based

---

[65] There is also the economically important bargain whereby regulation is the price of deposit insurance and access to the central bank widow.

[66] See Tucker (2019) for one ex-central banker's perspective on this.

exploration of how to reform regulation to encourage that. The analytical tools that we have discussed could help with this. Some of the changes which emerged after 2008, such as mandatory inter-dealer variation margin, incentives to clear, and higher amounts of bank capital,[67] will likely survive a genuinely independent evidence-based review—but many may not.

12.82 The role of regulatory knowledge has been central in our account. Regulators' modelling involves violent abstraction: it requires cramming reality, with all its complexity, into idealized schemata.[68] Inferences are made using these categories, not the original, messier objects. A responsible use of this form of rationality involves being honest about its situated, contingent nature. An eagerness for challenge is important, too: dialogue improves models. Instead, often, financial regulation has used its discursive authority to propagate and defend its constructions, hide the normative claims on which they are founded, and discourage consideration of alternatives. This process has been supported and defended by regulatory authority and prestige, professional incentives created by the sociology of the international club of regulators, and formal disciplinary mechanisms such as the RCAP.

12.83 Society deserves better than the resulting rules, especially as the rule making process leads to petrification, so we are increasingly stuck with them. Even where a regulatory model was a good approximation at first, it will become worse over time—but it will be very hard to update, as the bar for changing an international standard is too high. We suggest that a more local, modest, dynamic, and open regulatory process is needed. Financial regulators have formidable defences which are deployed when change they find uncongenial is suggested: these must not be a bar to fundamental reform.

12.84 Derivatives regulation is a fascinating and insightful case study in the strategies and knowledge practices of the regulatory state. Our analysis validates the importance of being attentive to the conditions and processes through which these bureaucratic technologies operate, and of modifying them where necessary to better serve the common good. The payoff of this modification for derivatives regulation would be simpler, more effective and efficient rules, less interference with rights, and a more useful financial system. Better regulation is possible if we dare to demand it.

---

[67] More capital is useful for absorbing losses providing that the regulatory minimum is not too high. At the moment, it probably is, giving banks too much unusable capital and too slim a buffer of genuinely loss-absorbing capital. That, however, is another story.

[68] As we have argued, there is a case that one of the most significant errors made in pre-crisis regulation was putting recourse and non-recourse mortgages in the same category, and treating the former as no riskier than the latter.

Bibliography

Abdel-Raheem (2013) Abdel-Raheem, A., *Metaphor of the global financial crisis after 2008: reconstructing confidence by Arab and Western financial medias*, Sciences de la société, Vol. 88, pp. 160-182, 2013, available at https://doi.org/10.4000/sds.446

Acharya (2012) Acharya, V., *The Dodd-Frank Act and Basel III: Intentions, unintended consequences, and lessons for emerging markets*, Asian Development Bank Institute Working Paper No. 392, 2012, available at https://www.econstor.eu/bitstream/10419/101252/1/728682958.pdf

Ackerer (2017) Ackerer, D., *Dependent defaults and losses with factor copula models*, Dependence Modeling, Vol. 5, No. 1, 2017, available at https://doi.org/10.1515/demo-2017-0022

Ackerman & Hassler (1981) Akerman, B., and Hassler, W., *Clean Coal/Dirty Air: Or How the Clean Air Act Became a Multibillion-Dollar Bail-Out for High-Sulfur coal Procedures and What Should be Done About It*, Yale University Press, 1981

Ackerman & Heinzerling (2002) Ackerman, F., and Heinzerling, L., *Pricing the Priceless: Cost-Benefit Analysis of Environmental Protection*, University of Pennsylvania Law Review, Vol. 150, No. 5, pp. 1553-1584, 2002, available at http://www.jstor.com/stable/3312947

Acosta-Smith et al. (2018) Acosta-Smith, J., Grill, M., and Lang, J., *The leverage ratio, risk-taking and bank stability*, Bank of England working paper No. 766, Bank of England, 2018, available at https://www.bankofengland.co.uk/working-paper/2018/the-leverage-ratio-risk-taking-and-bank-stability

Ahnert et al. (2018) Ahnert, T., Chapman, J., and Wilkins, C., *Should Bank Capital Regulation Be Risk Sensitive?*, Bank of Canada Staff Working Paper 2018-48, 2018, available at https://www.bankofcanada.ca/wp-content/uploads/2018/09/swp2018-48.pdf

Aldasoro et al. (2020) Aldasoro, I., Fender, I., Hardy, B., and Tarashev, N., *Effects of Covid-19 on the banking sector: the market's assessment*, BIS Bulletin No. 12, 2020, available at https://www.bis.org/publ/bisbull12.pdf

Alshorbagy (2012) Alshorbagy, A., *On the Failure of a Legal Transplant: The Case of Egyptian Takeover Law*, Indiana International & Comparative Law Review, Vol. 22, No. 237, 2012, available at https://ssrn.com/abstract=1956579

Amato & Remolona (2003) Amato, J., and Remolona, E., *The credit spread puzzle*, BIS Quarterly Review, December 2003, available at www.bis.org/press/p031208.htm

Anbil et al. (2020) Anbil, S., Anderson, A., and Senyuz, Z., *What Happened in Money Markets in September 2019?*, FEDS Notes, 2020, available at https://www.federalreserve.gov/econres/notes/feds-notes/what-happened-in-money-markets-in-september-2019-20200227.htm

Andersen et al. (2017) Andersen, L., Pykhtin, M., and Sokol, A., *Rethinking the margin period of risk*, Journal of Credit Risk, Vol. 13, No. 1, 2017, pp. 1-45

Andersen et al. (2018) Andersen, L., Duffie, D., and Song, Y., *Funding value adjustments*, NBER Working Paper No. 23680, 2018, available at http://www.nber.org/papers/w23680

Anderson et al. (2019) Anderson, E., Cerezetti, F., and Manning, M., *Supervisory stress testing for central counterparties: A macro-prudential, two-tier approach*, Journal of Financial Market Infrastructures, Vol. 8, No. 1, 2019, available at https://doi.org/10.21314/JFMI.2019.115

Archer et al. (2016) Archer, M., Decoteau, C., Gorski, P., Little, D., Porpora, D., Rutzou, T., Smith, C., Steinmetz, G., and Vandenberghe, F., *What is Critical Realism?*, Perspectives of the American Sociological Association, Vol. 38, No. 2, 2016, available at http://www.asatheory.org/current-newsletter-online/what-is-critical-realism

Arias-Barrera (2018) Arias-Barrera, L., *Regulation and Supervision of the OTC Derivatives Market*, Routledge, 2018

Arrow (1971) Arrow, K., *Insurance, Risk, and Resource Allocation*, in Essays in the Theory of Risk-Bearing, North Holland, 1971

Ascolese et al. (2017) Ascolese, M., Molino, A., Skrzypczynski, G., Cerniauskas, J., and Pérez-Duarte, S., *Euro-area derivatives markets: structure, dynamics and challenges*, Paper at the IFC-National Bank of Belgium Workshop on Data needs and Statistics compilation for macroprudential analysis, 2017, available at https://www.bis.org/ifc/publ/ifcb46y.pdf

Ashcraft et al. (2011) Ashcraft, A., Goldsmith-Pinkham, P., Hull, P., and Vickery, J., *Credit Ratings and Security Prices in the Subprime MBS Market*, The American Economic Review, Vol. 101, No. 3, pp. 115-119, 2011, available at http://www.jstor.com/stable/29783725

Atkinson & Tietenberg (1991) Atkinson, S., and Tietenberg, T., *Market Failure in Incentive Based Regulation: The Case of Emissions Trading*, Journal of Environmental Economics and Management, Vol. 21, pp. 17-31, 1991, available at https://doi.org/10.1016 /0095-0696(91)90002-Z

Avalos et al. (2019) Avalos, F., Ehlers, T., and Eren, E., *September stress in dollar repo markets: passing or structural?*, BIS Quarterly Review, December 2019, available at https://www.bis.org/publ/qtrpdf/r_qt1912v.htm

Avdjiev et al. (2020) Avdjiev, S., Eren, E., and McGuire, P., *Dollar funding costs during the Covid-19 crisis through the lens of the FX swap market*, BIS Bulletin No. 1, 2020, available at https://www.bis.org/publ/bisbull01.pdf

Awrey (2010a) Awrey, D., *The FSA, Integrated Regulation, and the Curious Case of OTC Derivatives*, University of Pennsylvania Journal of Business Law, Vol. 13, 2010, available at https://scholarship.law.cornell.edu/cgi/viewcontent.cgi?article=2779&context=facpub

Awrey (2010b) Awrey, D., *The Dynamics of OTC Derivatives Regulation: Bridging the Public-Private Divide*, European Business Organization Law Review, Vol. 11, pp. 155-193, 2010, available at https://doi.org/10.1017/S1566752910200010

Ayadi et al. (2016) Ayadi, R., Naceur, S., Casu, B., and Quinn, B., *Does Basel compliance matter for bank performance?*, Journal of Financial Stability, Vol. 23, pp. 15-32, 2016, available at http://dx.doi.org/10.1016/j.jfs.2015.12.007

Bailey (2017) Bailey, A., *The future of LIBOR*, Speech, 27 July 2017, available at https://www.fca.org.uk/print/news/speeches/the-future-of-libor

Bair (2006a) Bair, S., *Statement On Interagency Proposals Regarding The Basel Capital Accord And Commercial Real Estate Lending Concentrations*, before the Subcommittee on Financial Institutions And Consumer Credit of the Committee on Financial Services, US House of Representatives, 2006, available at https://www.fdic.gov/news/speeches/archives/2006/chairman/spsep1406.html.

Bair (2006b) Bair, S., *Testimony before the US Senate Committee on Banking, Housing and Urban Affairs*, 2006, available at https://www.banking.senate.gov/imo/media/doc/ACF4A61.pdf

Bajaj et al. (2018) Bajaj, R., Binmore, A., and Dasgupta, R., *Banks internal capital markets: how do banks allocate capital internally?* Bank of England Quarterly Bulletin Q2 2018, available at https://www.bankofengland.co.uk/quarterly-bulletin/2018/2018-q2/banks-internal-capital-markets-how-do-banks-allocate-capital-internally

Baker (2016) Baker, C., *When Regulators Collide: Financial Market Stability, Systemic Risk, Clearinghouses and CDS*, Virginia Law and Business Review, Vol. 10, No. 3, pp. 343-394, 2016, available at https://ssrn.com/abstract=2796830

Baker (2019) Baker, C., *Incomplete Clearinghouse Mandates*, American Business Law Journal, Vol. 56, No. 3, pp. 507-581, 2019, available at https://doi.org/10.1111/ablj.12149

Ball (2016) Ball, L., *The Fed and Lehman Brothers*, Cambridge University Press, 2016

Bamford & Mackenzie (2018) Bamford, A., and Mackenzie, D., *Counterperformativity*, New Left Review, Vol. 113, 2018

Bank of England (2019) Bank of England, *Financial Stability Report*, July 2019, available at https://www.bankofengland.co.uk/-/media/boe/files/financial-stability-report/2019/july-2019.pdf

Bardoscia et al. (2018) Bardoscia, M., Bianconi, G., and Ferrara, G., *Multiplex network analysis of the UK OTC derivatives market*, Staff Working Paper No. 726, Bank of England, 2018, available at https://www.bankofengland.co.uk/working-paper/2018/multiplex-network-analysis-of-the-uk-otc-derivatives-market

Barnett & Finnemore (1999) Barnett, M., and Finnemore, M., *The Politics, Power, and Pathologies of International Organizations*, International Organization Vol. 53, No. 4, pp. 699-732, 1999, available at https://doi.org/10.1162/002081899551048

Baron (1989) Baron, D., *Design of regulatory mechanisms and institutions* in Vol. II of Schmalensee & Willig (1989), pp. 1347-1447, 1989

Barr & Miller (2006) Barr, M., and Miller, G., *Global Administrative Law: The View from Basel*, The European Journal of International Law, Vol. 17, No. 1, 2006, available at https://repository.law.umich.edu/articles/1000/

Barrell et al. (2009) Barrell, R., Davis, E., Fic, T., Holland, D., Kirby, S., and Liadze, I., *Optimal regulation of bank capital and liquidity: how to calibrate new international standards*, FSA Occasional Paper No. 38, 2009, available at http://www.ephilipdavis.com/op38.pdf

Barth & Kahn (2020) Barth, D., and Kahn, J., *Basis Trades and Treasury Market Illiquidity*, Brief Series 20-01, Office of Financial Research, 2020, available at https://www.financialresearch.gov/briefs/2020/07/16/basis-trades-and-treasury-market-illiquidity/

Bartolini (2005) Bartolini, S., *Restructuring Europe: Centre formation, system building and political structuring between the nation-state and the European Union*, Oxford University Press, 2005

Bassnett (1998) Bassnett, S., *The Translation Turn in Cultural Studies*, in Bassnett, S., and Lefevere, A., (eds.), *Constructing Cultures, Essays on Literary Translation*, Clevedon: Multilingual Matters, 1998

Baudrillard (1987) Baudrillard, J., *Modernity*, Canadian Journal of Political and Social Theory/Revue canadienne de théorie politique et sociale, Vol. XI, No. 3, pp. 63-72, 1987

Baudrillard (1988) Baudrillard, J., *Selected Writings*, Poster, M., (ed.), Stanford University Press, 1988

Baumgartner & Jones (1993) Baumgartner, F., and Jones, B., *Agendas and Instability in American Politics*, Chicago University Press, 1993

BCBS (2003) Basel Committee on Banking Supervision, *Quantitative Impact Study 3—Overview of Global Results*, 2003, available at https://www.bis.org/bcbs/qis/qis3results.pdf

BCBS (2005a) Basel Committee on Banking Supervision, *Studies on the Validation of Internal Ratings Systems*, Working Paper No. 14, 2005, available at www.bis.org/publ/bcbs_wp14.pdf

BCBS (2005b) Basel Committee on Banking Supervision, *An Explanatory Note on the Basel II IRB Risk Weight Functions*, 2005, available at https://www.bis.org/bcbs/irbriskweight.pdf

BCBS (2013a) Basel Committee on Banking Supervision, *The regulatory framework: balancing risk sensitivity, simplicity and comparability*, Discussion paper, 2013, available at https://www.bis.org/publ/bcbs258.htm

BCBS (2013b) Basel Committee on Banking Supervision, *Regulatory Consistency Assessment Programme: Analysis of risk-weighted assets for credit risk in the banking book*, 2013, available at https://www.bis.org/publ/bcbs256.htm

BCBS (2014) Basel Committee on Banking Supervision, *Foundations of the standardised approach for measuring counterparty credit risk exposures*, Working Paper No. 26, 2014, available at https://www.bis.org/publ/bcbs_wp26.htm

BCBS (2015a) Basel Committee on Banking Supervision, *The interplay of accounting and regulation and its impact on bank behaviour: Literature review*, Working Paper 28, 2015, available at https://www.bis.org/bcbs/publ/wp28.htm

BCBS (2015b) Basel Committee on Banking Supervision, *Fundamental review of the trading book – interim impact analysis*, 2015, available at https://www.bis.org/bcbs/publ/d346.pdf

BCBS (2020a) Basel Committee on Banking Supervision, *Basel III Monitoring Report*, 2020, available at https://www.bis.org/bcbs/publ/d500.pdf

BCBS (2020b) Basel Committee on Banking Supervision, *Eighteenth progress report on adoption of the Basel regulatory framework*, 2020, available at https://www.bis.org/bcbs/publ/d506.pdf

Beck & Rojas-Suarez (2019) Beck, T., and Rojas-Suarez, L., *Making Basel III Work for Emerging Markets and Developing Economies*, Centre for Global Development Task Force Report, 2019, available at https://www.cgdev.org/sites/default/files/making-basel-iii-work-emerging-markets-developing-economies.pdf

Behn et al. (2016) Behn, M., Haselmann, R., and Vig, V., *The limits of model-based regulation*, European Central Bank Working Paper No. 1928, 2016, available at https://ssrn.com/abstract=2804598

Bell & Hindmoor (2017) Bell, S., and Hindmoor, A., *Structural Power and the Politics of Bank Capital Regulation in the United Kingdom*, Political Studies, Vol. 65, No. 1, pp. 103-121, 2017, available at https://doi.org/10.1177/0032321716629479

Benjamin (2010) Benjamin, J., *The Narratives of Financial Law*, Oxford Journal of Legal Studies, Vol. 30, No. 4, pp. 787-814, 2010, available at https://doi.org/10.1093/ojls/gqq030

Benmelech & Dlugosz (2010) Benmelech, E., and Dlugosz, J., *The Credit Rating Crisis*, in Acemoglu, D., Rogoff, K., and Woodford, M., (eds.), *NBER Macroeconomics Annual 2009*, Vol. 24, 2010, available at https://www.nber.org/papers/w15045

Bento et al. (2013) Bento, A., Freedman, M., and Lang, C., *Redistribution, Delegation, and Regulators' Incentives: Evidence from the Clean Air Act*, SSRN Electronic Journal, February 2013 available at https://ssrn.com/abstract=2219523

Berger & Bouwman (2013) Berger, A., and Bouwman, C., *How does capital affect bank performance during financial crises?*, Journal of Financial Economics Vol. 109, 2013, available at https://doi.org/10.1016/j.jfineco.2013.02.008

Berkowitz (2010) Berkowitz, J., *Testing Density Forecasts with Applications to Risk Management*, Journal of Business and Economics Statistics, Vol. 19, 2001, available at https://www.jstor.org/stable/1392281

Bernstein (2011) Bernstein, S., *Legitimacy in intergovernmental and non-state global governance*, Review of International Political Economy, Vol. 18, No. 1, pp. 17-51, 2011, available at https://doi.org/10.1080/09692290903173087

Berrahoui et al. (2019) Berrahoui, M., Islah, O., and Kenyon, C., *Revisiting SA-CCR*, Risk, 2019, available at https://www.risk.net/cutting-edge/banking/6597386/revisiting-sa-ccr

Betz et al. (2014) Betz, F., Oprica, S., Peltonen, T., and Sarlin, P., *Predicting Distress in European Banks*, Journal of Banking and Finance, Vol. 45, Issue C, 2014, available at https://doi.org/10.1016/j.jbankfin.2013.11.041

Beylin (2015) Beylin, I., *A Reassessment of the Clearing Mandate: How the clearing mandate affects swap trading behaviour and the consequences for systemic risk*, Columbia Law and Economics Working Paper, 2015, available at https://ssrn.com/abstract=2612755

Bhaskar (1979) Bhaskar, R., *The possibilities of naturalism: A philosophical critique of the contemporary human sciences*, Harvester Press, 1979

Bijker et al. (1987) Bijker, B., Hughes, T., and Pinch, T., (eds.), *The Social Construction of Technological Systems*, MIT Press, 1987

Binder (2021) Binder, J.-H., *Central Counterparties' Insolvency and Resolution—The New EU Regulation on CCP Recovery and Resolution*, European Banking Institute Working Paper Series, No. 82, 2021, available at https://ssrn.com/abstract=3778649

Black (1995) Black, J., *Which Arrow? Rule Type and Regulatory Policy*, Public Law, Vol. 9, pp. 94-117, 1995

Black (2001) Black, J., *Decentering Regulation: Understanding the role of regulation and self-regulation in a 'post-regulatory' world*, Current Legal Problems, Vol. 54, No. 1, 2001, available at https://doi.org/10.1093/clp/54.1.103

Black (2008) Black, J., *Constructing and contesting legitimacy and accountability in polycentric regulatory regimes*, Regulation & Governance, Vol. 2, pp. 137-164, 2008, available at https://doi:10.1111/j.1748-5991.2008.00034.x

Black (2012) Black, J., *Paradoxes and Failures: 'New Governance' Techniques and the Financial Crisis*, The Modern Law Review , Vol. 75, No. 6, pp. 1037-1063, 2012, available at https://doi.org/10.1111/j.1468-2230.2012.00936.x

Black et al. (2007) Black, J., Hopper, M., and Band, C., *Making a success of Principles-based regulation*, Law and Financial Markets Review, 2007, available at https://doi.org/10.1080/17521440.2007.11427879

Bordo et al. (1993) Bordo, M., Rockoff, H., and Redish, A., *A Comparison of the United States and Canadian Banking Systems in the Twentieth Century: Stability vs. Efficiency?*, NBER Working Paper No. 4546, 1993, available at https://www.nber.org/papers/w4546

Borio & Toniolo (2006) Borio, C., and Toniolo, G., *One hundred and thirty years of central bank cooperation: a BIS perspective*, BIS Working Papers, No. 197, 2006, available at https://www.bis.org/publ/work197.pdf

Borio et al. (2016) Borio, C., McCauley, R., McGuire, P., and Sushko, V., *Covered interest parity lost: understanding the cross-currency basis*, BIS Quarterly Review, September 2016, available at https://www.bis.org/publ/qtrpdf/r_qt1609e.pdf

Bourgoin et al. (2002) Bourgoin, A., Bencherki, N., and Faraj, S., *"And Who Are You?": A Performative Perspective on Authority in Organizations*, Academy of Management Journal, Vol. 63, No. 4, 2020, available at https://doi.org/10.5465/amj.2017.1335

Bovens (2007) Bovens, M., *Analysing and Assessing Accountability: A Conceptual Framework*, European Law Journal, Vol. 13, No. 4, pp. 447-468, 2007, available at https://doi.org/10.1111/j.1468-0386.2007.00378.x

Brainard (2021) Brainard, L., *Some Preliminary Financial Stability Lessons from the COVID-19 Shock*, Remarks at the 2021 Annual Washington Conference Institute of International Bankers, 2021, available at https://www.bis.org/review/r210303b.htm

Braithwaite (2016) Braithwaite, J., *The Dilemma of Client Clearing in the OTC Derivatives Markets*, European Business Organization Law Review, Vol. 17, pp. 355–378, 2016, available at https://doi.org/10.1007/s40804-016-0044-0

Braithwaite (2020) Braithwaite, J., *The Financial Courts*, Cambridge University Press, 2020

Braithwaite & Murphy (2017a) Braithwaite, J., and Murphy, D., *Central counterparties and the law of default management*, Journal of Corporate Law Studies, Vol. 17, No. 2, 2017, available at https://doi.org/10.1080/14735970.2016.1254448

Braithwaite & Murphy (2017b) Braithwaite, J., and Murphy, D., *Get the balance right: private rights and public policy in the post-crisis regime for OTC derivatives*, Capital Markets Law Journal, Vol. 12, No. 4, pp. 480–509, 2017, available at https://doi.org/10.1093/cmlj/kmx033

Braithwaite & Murphy (2019) Braithwaite, J., and Murphy, D., *Improving resolvability: partial property transfers and central counterparties*, Capital Markets Law Journal, Vol. 14, No. 4, pp. 431–450, 2019

Braithwaite & Murphy (2021) Braithwaite, J., and Murphy, D., *Take On Me: OTC Derivatives Client Clearing in the European Union*, in Saguato, P., and Binder, J.-H., (eds.), Financial Market Infrastructure: Law and Regulation, Oxford University Press, 2021

Brassett & Tsingou (2011) Brassett, J., and Tsingou, E., *The politics of legitimate global governance*, Review of International Political Economy, Vol. 18, No. 1, pp. 1-16, 2011, available at https://doi.org/10.1080/09692290.2010.495297

Brereton & Temple (1999) Brereton, M., and Temple, M, *The New Public Service Ethos: An Ethical Environment for Governance*, Public Administration, Vol. 77, No. 3, pp. 455-474, 1999, available at https://doi.org/10.1111/1467-9299.00163

Brigo et al. (2013) Brigo, D., Morini, M., and Pallavicini, A., *Counterparty Credit Risk, Collateral and Funding: With Pricing Cases For All Asset Classes*, John Wiley & Sons, 2013

Brummer (2010) Brummer, C., *Territoriality as a Regulatory Technique: Notes from the Financial Crisis*, University of Cincinnati Law Review, Vol. 79, No. 2, pp. 499-526, 2010, available at https://ssrn.com/abstract=1616341

Brummer (2011) Brummer, C., *How International Financial Law Works (and How it Doesn't)*, Georgetown Law Journal, Vol. 99, 2011, available at https://ssrn.com/abstract=1542829

Bruner (1986) Bruner, J., *Actual Minds, Possible Worlds*, Harvard University Press, 1986

Buckmann et al. (2021) Buckmann, M., Gallego Marquez, P., Gimpelewicz, M., Kapadia, S., and Rismanchi, K., *The more the merrier? Evidence from the global financial crisis on the value of multiple requirements in bank regulation*, Bank of England Staff Working Paper No. 905, 2021, available at https://ssrn.com/abstract=3778190

Budding & Murphy (2014) Budding, E., and Murphy, D., *Design Choices in Central Clearing: Issues Facing Small Advanced Economies*, Reserve Bank of New Zealand Analytical Note 2014/08, 2014, available at https://ssrn.com/abstract=3599897

Buiter & Sibert (2007) Buiter, W., and Sibert, A., *The Central Bank as the Market Maker of last Resort: From lender of last resort to market maker of last resort*, VoxEU, 2007, available at https://voxeu.org/article/subprime-crisis-what-central-bankers-should-do-and-why

Bull & Ellig (2017) Bull, R., and Ellig, J., *Judicial Review of Regulatory Impact Analysis: Why not the best?*, Administrative Law Review, Vol. 69, No. 4, pp. 725-840, 2017, available at https://ssrn.com/abstract=2953014

Bulwer-Lytton (1834) Bulwer-Lytton, E., *Address to the House of Commons on Stamps on Newspapers*, 22 May 1834, available in Hansard at https://hansard.parliament.uk/Commons/1834-05-22/debates/e0ce906c-f589-475a-8438-4088e5dafb90/StampsOnNewspapers

Burman et al. (2016) Burman, L., Gale, W., Gault, S., Kim, B., Nunns, J., and Rosenthal, S., *Financial Transaction Taxes in Theory and Practice*, National Tax Journal, Vol. 69, No. 1, pp. 171–216, 2016, available at https://ssrn.com/abstract=3385503

Caballero et al. (2017) Caballero, R., Farhi, E., and Gourinchas, P-O., *The Safe Assets Shortage Conundrum*, Journal of Economic Perspectives, Vol. 31, No. 3, 2017, available at https://www.aeaweb.org/articles?id=10.1257/jep.31.3.29

Cafaggi & Pistor (2013) Cafaggi, F., and Pistor, K., *Regulatory Capabilities: A Normative Framework for Assessing the Distributional Effects of Regulation*, Columbia Public Law Research Paper No. 13-354, 2013, available at https://doi.org/10.1111/rego.12065

Cahill et al. (2019) Cahill, G., McMurray, L., and Tambe, J., *Short-Squeeze Risks Loom Again In CDS Markets*, Note, Jones Day, 2019

Calomiris (1989) Calomiris, C., *Deposit insurance: Lessons from the record*, Chicago FED Economic Perspectives, Vol. 13, No. 3, 1989, https://www.chicagofed.org/publications/economic-perspectives/1989/06mayjune1989-part2-calomiris

Calomiris (2010) Calomiris, C., *Banking crises yesterday and today*, Financial History Review, Vol. 17, No. 1, pp. 3-12, 2010, available at https://www.researchgate.net/publication/227391896_Banking_Crises_Yesterday_and_Today_Banking_Crises_Yesterday_and_Today_1

Calomiris & Haber (2015) Calomiris, C., and Haber, S., *Fragile by Design: The Political Origins of Banking Crises and Scarce Credit*, Princeton University Press, 2015

Calomiris & Khan (2015) Calomiris, C., and Khan, U., *An Assessment of TARP Assistance to Financial Institutions*, Journal of Economic Perspectives, Vol. 29, No. 2, pp. 53-80, 2015, available at https://doi.org/10.1257/jep.29.2.53

Canabarro et al. (2003) Canabarro, E., Picault, E., and Wilde, T., *Analysing Counterparty Credit Risk*, Risk magazine, Vol. 16, No. 9, 2003

Cannadine (1983) Cannadine, D., *The Context, Performance and Meaning of Ritual: The British Monarchy and the 'Invention of Tradition', c. 1820–1977*, in E. Hobsbawm and T. Ranger (eds.), *The invention of tradition*, Cambridge University Press, 1983

Carney (2017) Carney, M., *Ten years on: fixing the fault lines of the global financial crisis*, Banque de France Financial Stability Review No. 21, 2017, available at https://www.fsb.org/wp-content/uploads/BdF-Financial-Stability-Review.pdf

Carney (2018) Carney, M., *True Finance—Ten years after the financial crisis*, Speech to the Economic Club of New York, 2018, available at https://www.bis.org/review/r181025b.pdf

Carrigan & Coglianese (2011) Carrigan, C., and Coglianese, C., *The Politics of Regulation: From New Institutionalism to New Governance*, The Annual Review of Political

Science, Vol. 14, pp. 107-129, 2011, available at https://www.annualreviews.org/doi/abs/10.1146/annurev.polisci.032408.171344

Carter & Cole (2017) Carter, L., and Cole, D., *Central Counterparty Margin Frameworks*, Reserve Bank of Australia Bulletin December 2017, available at https://www.rba.gov.au/publications/bulletin/2017/dec/pdf/bu-1217-10-central-counterparty-margin-frameworks.pdf

Cassese (2005) Cassese, S., *Administrative Law without the State? The Challenge of Global Regulation*, New York University Journal of International Law and Politics, Vol. 37, pp. 663-694, 2005

CCMR (2013) Committee on Capital Markets Regulation, *A Balanced Approach to Cost-Benefit Analysis Reform*, 2013, available at https://www.capmktsreg.org/2013/10/01/a-balanced-approach-to-cost-benefit-analysis-reform

Centeno (1993) Centeno, M., *The New Leviathan: The Dynamics and Limits of Technocracy*, Theory and Society, Vol. 22, No. 3, pp. 307-335, 1993, available at https://www.jstor.org/stable/657736

Cerezetti et al. (2019) Cerezetti, F., Cruz Lopez, J., Manning, M., and Murphy, D., *Who pays? Who gains? Central counterparty resource provision in the post-Pittsburgh world*, Journal of Financial Market Infrastructures, Vol. 7, No. 3, pp. 21-44, 2019, available at https://doi.org/10.21314/JFMI.2018.108

CFTC (2020) Commodity Futures Trading Commission, *Interim Staff Report on Trading in NYMEX WTI Crude Oil Futures Contract Leading up to, on, and around April 20, 2020*, November 2020, available at https://www.cftc.gov/MarketReports/StaffReports/index.htm

CGFS (2014) Committee on the Global Financial System, *Market-making and proprietary trading: industry trends, drivers and policy implications*, CGFS Papers No. 52, 2014 available at https://www.bis.org/publ/cgfs52.pdf

Chamorro-Courtland (2016) Chamorro-Courtland, C., *Collateral Damage: The Legal and Regulatory Protections for Customer Margin in the U.S. Derivatives Markets*, William and Mary Business Law Review, Vol. 7, No. 3, pp. 609-682, 2016, available at https://scholarship.law.wm.edu/wmblr/vol7/iss3/2

Cherednychenko & Andenas (2020) Cherednychenko, O., and Andenas, M., (eds.) *Financial Regulation and Civil Liability in European Law*, Edward Elgar, 2020

Clearing House (2013) Clearing House, *Re: Revised Basel III Leverage Ratio Framework and Disclosure Requirements*, Comment Letter, 2013, available at https://www.bis.org/publ/bcbs251/theclearinghous.pdf

Clemens (2015) Clemens, J., *Redistribution in the Market for Health Insurance*, American Economic Journal: Applied Economics, Vol. 7, No. 2, pp. 109-134, 2015, available at http://dx.doi.org/10.1257/app.20130169109

Coase (1939) Coase, R., *Rowland Hill and the Penny Post*, Economica, Vol. 6, No. 24, pp. 423-435, 1939

Coates (2015) Coates, J., *Cost-Benefit Analysis of Financial Regulation*, The Yale Law Journal, Vol. 124, No. 4, pp. 882-1011, 2015, available at http://www.jstor.com/stable/43617045

Cochrane (2014) Cochrane, J., *Challenges for Cost-Benefit Analysis of Financial Regulation*, in Sloan (2014)

Cœuré (2012) Cœuré, B., *Panel intervention at the ILF Conference on Resolution in Europe: the unresolved questions*, 2018, available at https://www.bis.org/review/r180504a.htm

Coffee (2012) Coffee, J., *The Political Economy of Dodd-Frank: Why Financial Reform Tends to be Frustrated and Systemic Risk Perpetuated*, Columbia Law School Working Paper No. 414, 2012, available at https://scholarship.law.columbia.edu/faculty_scholarship/517

Coffee (2014) Coffee, J., *Extraterritorial Financial Regulation: Why E.T. Can't Come Home*, Cornell Law Review, Vol. 99, No. 6, pp. 1259-1302, 2014, available at https://scholarship.law.cornell.edu/clr/vol99/iss6/1

Cohen & Edwards (2017) Cohen, B., and Edwards, G., *The new era of expected credit loss provisioning*, BIS Quarterly Review, pp. 39-56, 2017, available at https://www.bis.org/publ/qtrpdf/r_qt1703f.pdf

Cole & Grossman (2003) Cole, D., and Grossman, P., *When Is Command-and-Control Efficient? Institutions, Technology, and the Comparative Efficiency of Alternative Regulatory Regimes for Environmental Protection*, in Helfand & Berck (2013)

Colliard & Georg (2020) Colliard, J.-E., and Georg, C-P., *Measuring Regulatory Complexity*, Centre for Economic Policy Research Discussion Paper DP 14377, 2020, available at https://repec.cepr.org/repec/cpr/ceprdp/DP14377.pdf

Condat et al. (2018) Condat, A-L., Puce, A., and Nommels, C., *EMIR data and derivatives market policies—How EMIR data help regulators better understand the impact of policies*, Financial Conduct Authority Research Note, 2018, available at https://www.fca.org.uk/publication/research/research-note-emir-data-derivatives-market-policies.pdf

Correa et al. (2020) Correa, R., Du, W., and Liao, G., *U.S. Banks and Global Liquidity*, Board of Governors of the Federal Reserve System, International Finance Discussion Papers, No. 1289, 2020, available at https://www.federalreserve.gov/econres/ifdp/files/ifdp1289.pdf

Cotterrell (2009) Cotterrell, R., *Spectres of Transnationalism: Changing Terrains of Sociology of Law*, Queen Mary School of Law Legal Studies Research Paper No. 32/2009, available at https://ssrn.com/abstract=1476954

Coutinho (2016) Coutinho, D., *Regulation and its crisis*, in Lodge, M., (ed.), Regulation scholarship in crisis?, Discussion Paper No. 84, Carr centre for the analysis of risk and regulation, London School of Economics, 2016, available at https://www.lse.ac.uk/accounting/Assets/CARR/documents/D-P/Disspaper84.pdf

Cox (2008) Cox, C., *Sound Practices for Managing Liquidity in Banking Organizations*, Letter to Nout Wellink, Chairman, Basel Committee on Banking Supervision, 2008, available at https://www.sec.gov/news/press/2008/2008-48.htm

Cox (2015) Cox, R., *Central counterparties in crisis: the Hong Kong Futures Exchange in the crash of 1987*, Journal of Financial Market Infrastructures, Vol. 4, No. 2, pp. 73-98, 2015, available at https://doi.org/10.21314/JFMI.2015.049

Cox & Steigerwald (2016) Cox, R., and Steigerwald, R., *'Incomplete demutualization' and financial market infrastructure: central counterparty ownership and governance after the crisis of 2008–9*, Journal of Financial Market Infrastructures, Vol. 4, No. 3, pp. 25-38, 2016, available at https://doi.org/10.21314/JFMI.2016.057

Cox & Steigerwald (2017) Cox, R., and Steigerwald, R., *A CCP is a CCP is a CCP*, Federal Reserve Bank of Chicago, Policy Discussion Paper No. 2017-01, 2017, available at https://www.chicagofed.org/publications/policy-discussion-papers/2017/pdp-1

Cox et al. (2016) Cox, R., Murphy, D., and Budding, E., *Central counterparties in crisis: the International Commodities Clearing House, the New Zealand Futures and Options Exchange and the Stephen Francis Affair*, Journal of Financial Market Infrastructure, Vol. 4, No. 3, 2016, available at https://doi.org/10.21314/JFMI.2016.054

CPMI (1997) Committee on Payments and Market Infrastructures, *Clearing Arrangements for Exchange-Traded Derivatives*, BIS, 1997, available at https://www.bis.org/cpmi/publ/d23a.pdf

Cranston (2007) Cranston, R., *Law in practice: London and Liverpool Commodity Markets c.1820–1975*, LSE Law, Society and Economy Working Papers 14/2007, available at https://ssrn.com/abstract=1021952

Cranston (2021) Cranston, R., *Making Commercial Law through Practice 1830–1970*, Cambridge University Press, 2021

Crawford et al. (2009) Crawford, A., Graham, C., and Bordeleau, É., *Regulatory Constraints on Leverage: The Canadian Experience*, Bank of Canada Financial System Review, June 2009, available at https://www.bankofcanada.ca/wp-content/uploads/2012/01/fsr-0609-crawford.pdf

Crew & Kleindorfer (2002) Crew, M., and Kleindorfer, P., *Regulatory Economics: Twenty years of progress?*, Journal of Regulatory Economics, Vol. 21, No. 1, 2002

Cross (2000) Cross, F., *Pragmatic Pathologies of Judicial Review of Administrative Rulemaking*, North Carolina Law Review, Vol. 78, No. 4, pp. 1013-1070, 2000, available at http://scholarship.law.unc.edu/nclr/vol78/iss4/3

Crump & Santos (2018) Crump, R., and Santos, J., *Review of New York Fed Studies on the Effects of Post-Crisis Banking Reforms*, Federal Reserve Bank of New York Economic Policy Review Vol. 24, No. 2, 2018, available at https://www.newyorkfed.org/research/epr/2018/epr_2018_banking-reform-studies_crump.html

Cruz Lopez et al. (2017) Cruz Lopez, J., Harris, J., Hurlin, C., and Pérignon, C., *CoMargin*, Journal of Financial and Quantitative Analysis, Vol. 52, No. 5, 2017, available at https://ssrn.com/abstract=1943562

Csatlós (2019) Csatlós, E., *Public Administrative Law in a Globalized Concept: Legal Nature of the Collaboration of the EU and the Basel Committee*, Journal of International Economic Law, Vol. 22, pp. 229-245, 2019, available at https://doi.org/10.1093/jiel/jgz015

Cunliffe (2020) Cunliffe, J., *Financial System Resilience: Lessons from a real stress*, Speech, 2020, available at https://www.bankofengland.co.uk/speech/2020/jon-cunliffe-speech-at-investment-association

Daly (2017) Daly, P., *Administrative Law: Characteristics, Legitimacy, Unity*, University of Cambridge Legal Studies Research Paper No. 2, 2017, available at https://ssrn.com/abstract=2833338

Danielsson et al. (2016) Danielsson, J., James, K., Valenzuela, M., and Zer, I., *The Model Risk of Risk Models*, Journal of Financial Stability, Vol. 23, pp. 79-91, 2016, available at https://doi.org/10.1016/j.jfs.2016.02.002

Darst et al. (2020) Darst, R., Refayet, E., and Vardoulakis, A., *Banks, Non Banks, and Lending Standards*, Staff Working Paper No. 2020-086, Federal Reserve Board, 2020, available at https://www.federalreserve.gov/econres/feds/files/2020086pap.pdf

DAT (2018) Derivatives Assessment Team, *Incentives to centrally clear over-the-counter (OTC) derivatives*, Report, Financial Stability Board, 2018, available at https://www.fsb.org/2018/11/fsb-and-standard-setting-bodies-publish-final-report-on-effects-of-reforms-on-incentives-to-centrally-clear-over-the-counter-derivatives/

de Cos (2019) de Cos, P., *Post-Basel III: time for evaluation*, Keynote address at the 14th ASBA-BCBS-FSI High-level Meeting on Global and Regional Supervisory Priorities, 2019, available at https://www.bis.org/speeches/sp191024.htm

de Cos (2020) de Cos, P., *Basel III: the implementation imperative*, Keynote address at the 15th BCBS-FSI High-level Meeting for Africa on Strengthening financial sector supervision and current regulatory priorities, 2020, available at https://www.bis.org/speeches/sp200130.pdf

de Cos (2021) de Cos, P., *Evaluating the effectiveness of Basel III during Covid-19 and beyond*, Keynote address at the BCBS-Bundesbank-CEPR workshop on evaluating financial regulation, 2021, available at https://www.bis.org/speeches/sp210420.pdf

Deakin et al. (2017) Deakin, S., Gindis, D., Hodgson, G., Kainan, H., and Pistor, K., *Legal institutionalism: Capitalism and the constitutive role of law*, Journal of Comparative Economics, Vol. 45, No. 1, pp. 188-200, 2017, available at https://doi.org/10.1016/j.jce.2016.04.005

Delis & Staikouras (2011) Delis, M., and Staikouras, P., *Supervisory Effectiveness and Bank Risk*, Review Of Finance, Vol. 15, pp. 511-543, 2011, available at https://doi.org/10.1093/rof/rfq035

Derham (1985) Derham, S., *Set-off and Agency*, Cambridge Law Journal Vol. 44, No. 3, 1985, available at https://doi.org/10.1017/S0008197300114916

Derham (2010) Derham, R., *The Law of Set-Off*, Oxford University Press, 2010

Derrida (1992) Derrida, J., *Force of Law: The 'Mystical Foundation of Authority'*, in Cornell, D., Rosenfeld, M., and Carlson, D., (eds.), *Deconstruction and the Possibility of Justice*, Routledge, 1992

Derrida (2003) J. Derrida, *Autoimmunity: Real and Symbolic Suicides* in G. Borradori (ed.), *Philosophy in a Time of Terror: Dialogues with Jurgen Habermas and Jacques Derrida*, University of Chicago Press, , pp. 87-136, 2003

Devlin (1979) Devlin, P., *The Judge*, Oxford University Press, 1979

Diamond & Dybvig (1983) Diamond, D., and Dybvig, P., *Bank Runs, Deposit Insurance, and Liquidity*, The Journal of Political Economy, Vol. 91, No. 3, pp. 401-419, 1983, available at https://www.jstor.org/stable/1837095

Doumpos et al. (2015) Doumpos, M., Gaganis, C., and Pasiouras, F., *Central bank independence, financial supervision structure and bank soundness: an empirical analysis around the crisis*, Journal of Banking & Finance, Vol. 61, pp. S69–S83, 2015, available at https://doi.org/10.1016/j.jbankfin.2015.04.017

Drahos (2017) Drahos, P., (ed.), *Regulatory Theory: Foundations and applications*, ANU Press, 2017

Drake & Neale (2011) Drake, P., and Neale, F., *Financial Guarantee Insurance and Failures in Risk Management*, Journal of Insurance Regulation, Vol. 30, pp. 29-76, 2011, available at https://ssrn.com/abstract=1703602

Driesen (2005) Driesen, D., *Is cost-benefit analysis neutral?*, 2005, available at https://ssrn.com/abstract=708402

Dudley (2009) Dudley, W., *More Lessons from the Crisis*, Speech, 2009, available at https://www.newyorkfed.org/newsevents/speeches/2009/dud091113.html

Dudley (2017) Dudley, W., *Lessons from the Crisis*, Speech, 2017, available at https://www.bis.org/review/r171107b.pdf

Duff & Zaring (2013) Duff, A., and Zaring, D., *New paradigms and familiar tools in the new derivatives regulation*, The George Washington law review, Vol. 81, No. 3, pp. 677-706, 2013, available at http://www.gwlr.org/wp-content/uploads/2013/04/Zaring.pdf

Duffie (2016) Duffie, D., *Financial regulatory reform after the crisis: an assessment*, European Central Bank Forum on Central Banking, 2016, available at https://www.ecb.europa.eu/pub/conferences/ecbforum/shared/pdf/2016/duffie_paper.pdf

Duffie (2020) Duffie, D., *Still the World's Safe Haven? Redesigning the U.S. Treasury Market After the COVID-19 Crisis*, Hutchins Center Working Paper No. 62, 2020, available at https://www.brookings.edu/wp-content/uploads/2020/05/WP62_Duffie_v2.pdf

Duffie & Zhu (2011) Duffie, D., and Haoxiang Zhu, *Does a Central Clearing Counterparty Reduce Counterparty Risk*, The Review of Asset Pricing Studies, Vol. 1, No. 1, 2011, available at https://doi.org/10.2139/ssrn.1348343

Durnil (1999) Durnil, G., *How much information do before exercising precaution?*, in Raffensberger, C., and Tickner, J., (eds.), *Protecting Public Health and the Environment: Implementing the Precautionary Principle*, Island Press, 1999

Dyson (2015) Dyson, J., *Is judicial review a threat to democracy?*, The Sultan Azlan Shah Lecture, 2015, available at https://www.judiciary.uk/wp-content/uploads/2015/12/is-judicial-review-a-threat-to-democracy-mr.pdf

EBA (2017) European Banking Authority, *Basel III Monitoring Exercise—Results based on data as of 31 December 2017*, available at https://eba.europa.eu/risk-analysis-and-data/quantitative-impact-study/basel-iii-monitoring-exercise/archived-reports

Edey (2015) Edey, M., *The transition to central clearing of OTC derivatives in Australia*, Speech at the International Swaps and Derivatives Association's 2015 Annual Australia Conference, 2015, available at https://www.bis.org/review/r151023a.pdf

Eisner (2013) Eisner, M., *Beyond the Logic of the Market: Toward an Institutional Analysis of Regulatory Reforms*, in Levi-Faur (2013b)

Elgin (2017) Elgin, C., *True Enough*, MIT Press, 2017

Ellis (2008) Ellis, L., *The housing meltdown: Why did it happen in the United States?*, BIS Working Papers No. 259, 2008, available at https://www.bis.org/publ/work259.pdf

ESMA (2020) European Securities and Markets Authority, *Report on Trends, Risks and Vulnerabilities*, No. 2, 2020, available at https://www.esma.europa.eu/sites/default/files/library/esma_50-165-1287_report_on_trends_risks_and_vulnerabilities_no.2_2020.pdf

Estrella et al. (2000) Estrella, A., Park, S., and Peristiani, S., *Capital Ratios as Predictors of Bank Failure*, Federal Reserve Bank of New York Economic Policy Review, 2000, available at https://www.newyorkfed.org/medialibrary/media/research/epr/00v06n2/0007estr.pdf.

European Commission (2013) European Commission, *Guide to the application of the European Union rules on state aid, public procurement and the internal market to services of general economic interest, and in particular to social services of general interest*, Commission Staff Working Document, 2013, available at https://ec.europa.eu/competition/state_aid/overview/new_guide_eu_rules_procurement_en.pdf

Farag (2018) Farag, H., *A Review of the Fundamentals of the Fundamental Review of the Trading Book II: Asymmetries, Anomalies, and Simple Remedies*, Journal of Risk, Vol. 20, No. 6, 2018, available at https://doi.org/10.21314/JOR.2018.412

FCIC (2011) Financial Crisis Inquiry Commission, *Final Report of the National Commission on the Causes of the Financial and Economic Crisis in the United States*, 2011, available at https://www.govinfo.gov/content/pkg/GPO-FCIC/pdf/GPO-FCIC.pdf

Fender & Lewrick (2015) Fender, I., and Lewrick, U., *Calibrating the leverage ratio*, BIS Quarterly Review, December 2015, available at https://www.bis.org/publ/qtrpdf/r_qt1512f.htm

Fender & Scheicher (2009) Fender, I., and Scheicher, M., *The pricing of subprime mortgage risk in good times and bad—evidence from the ABX.HE indices*, ECB Working Paper No. 1056, 2009, available at https://www.ecb.europa.eu/pub/pdf/scpwps/ecbwp1056.pdf

Ferran (2017) Ferran, E., *Recognition of third country equivalence in EU financial law—an obstacle or a way forward for future EU-UK bilateral arrangements?*, Proceedings of the 2017 ECB Legal Conference, 2017, available at https://www.ecb.europa.eu/pub/pdf/other/ecblegalconferenceproceedings201712.en.pdf

FIA (2020) Futures Industry Association, *Revisiting Procyclicality: The Impact of the COVID Crisis on CCP Margin Requirements*, Working Paper, 2020, available at https://www.fia.org/resources/fia-issues-white-paper-impact-pandemic-volatility-ccp-margin-requirements

FIA & ISDA (2020) Futures Industry Association and International Swaps and Derivatives Association, *CCP Non‐Default Losses*, Report, 2020, available at https://www.isda.org/a/dM9TE/FIA-ISDA-CCP-Non-Default-Losses-final.pdf

Fischer (2015) Fischer, M., *Copula-Specific Credit Portfolio Modeling—How the Sector Copula Affects the Tail of the Portfolio Loss Distribution*, In Innovations in Quantitative Risk Management, Springer Proceedings in Mathematics & Statistics, Vol. 99, 2015

Fischl (1992) Fischl, M., *The Question that Killed Critical Legal Studies*, Law & Social Inquiry, Vol. 17, No. 4, pp. 779-820, 1992, available at https://doi.org/10.1111/j.1747-4469.1992.tb00640.x

Fišera et al. (2019) Fišera, B., Horváth, R., and Melecký, M., *Basel III Implementation and SME Financing Evidence for Emerging Markets and Developing Economies*, World Bank Policy Research Working Paper No. 9069, 2019, available at https://documents.worldbank.org/en/publication/documents-reports/documentdetail/441951575300867782/basel-iii-implementation-and-sme-financing-evidence-for-emerging-markets-and-developing-economies

Fisher (2000) Fisher, E., *Drowning by Numbers: Standard Setting in Risk Regulation and the Pursuit of Accountability in Public Administration*, Oxford Journal of Legal Studies, Vol. 20, No. 1, pp. 109-130, 2000, available at https://doi.org/10.1093/ojls/20.1.109

Fitzpatrick (1992) Fitzpatrick, P., *The Mythology of Modern Law*, Routledge, 1992

Fleming & Ruela (2020) Fleming, M., and Ruela, F., *Treasury Market Liquidity during the COVID-19 Crisis*, Liberty Street Economics, Federal Reserve Bank of New York, 2020, available at https://libertystreeteconomics.newyorkfed.org/2020/04/treasury-market-liquidity-during-the-covid-19-crisis.html

Fleming & Sarkar (2014) Fleming, M., and Sarkar, A., *The Failure Resolution of Lehman Brothers*, Federal Reserve Bank of New York Economic Policy Review, 2014, available at https://www.newyorkfed.org/medialibrary/media/research/epr/2014/1412flem.pdf

Fletcher (2019) Fletcher, G., *Engineered Credit Default Swaps: Innovative or Manipulative?*, New York University Law Review Vol. 94, pp. 1073-1145, 2019, available at https://www.repository.law.indiana.edu/facpub/2863

Fligstein & Roehrkasse (2015) Fligstein, N., and Roehrkasse, A., *The Causes of Fraud in Financial Crises: Evidence from the Mortgage-Backed Securities Industry*, IRLE Working Paper No. 122-15, 2015, available at http://irle.berkeley.edu/workingpapers/122-15.pdf

Fong et al. (2000) Fong, A., Weil, D., Graham, M., and Fagotto, E., *The Political Economy of Transparency: What makes disclosure policies effective?*, Oxford Journal of Legal Studies, Vol. 20, No. 1, pp. 109-130, 2000, available at https://doi.org/10.1093/ojls/20.1.109

Foucault (1972) Foucault, M., *The Archaeology of Knowledge*, Sheridan Smith, A., (trans.), Pantheon, 1972

Foucault (1982) Foucault, M., *Subject and Power*, Critical Inquiry, Vol. 8, No. 4, pp. 777-795, 1982

Foucault (2003) Foucault, M., *'Society Must be Defended': Lectures at the Collège de France, 1975-1976*, M. Bertani and A. Fontana (eds.), D. Macey (trans.), Picador, 2003

Frait & Tomšík (2014) Frait, J., and Tomšík, V., *Impact and Implementation Challenges of the Basel Framework for Emerging, Developing and Small Economies*, Comparative Economic Studies, Vol. 56, pp. 493-516, 2014, available at https://doi.org/10.1007/978-1-137-56905-9_13

Frame et al. (2015) Frame, W., Fuster, A., Tracy, J., and Vickery, J., *The Rescue of Fannie Mae and Freddie Mac*, Federal Reserve Bank of New York Staff Report No. 719, 2015, available at https://www.newyorkfed.org/research/staff_reports/sr719.html

Freidson (1988) Freidson, E., *Profession of Medicine: A Study of the Sociology of Applied Knowledge*, University of Chicago Press, 1988

Friedman (1975) Friedman, L., *The Legal System*, Russell Sage Foundation, 1975

Froud et al. (2012) Froud, J., Nilsson, A., Moran, M., and Williams, K., *Stories and Interests in Finance: Agendas of Governance before and after the Financial Crisis*, Governance Vol. 25, No. 1, pp. 35-59, 2012, available at https://doi.org/10.1111/j.1468-0491.2011.01561.x

FSA (2010) Financial Services Authority, *The prudential regime for trading activities: A fundamental review*, DP10/4, 2010, available at https://www.fca.org.uk/publication/discussion/dp10_04.pdf

FSB (2015) Financial Stability Board, *Historical losses and recapitalisation needs*, Findings Report, 2015, available at https://www.fsb.org/wp-content/uploads/Historical-Losses-and-Recapitalisation-Needs-findings-report.pdf

FSB (2020) Financial Stability Board, *OTC Derivatives Market Reforms: 2020 Note on Implementation Progress*, 2020, available at https://www.fsb.org/2020/11/otc-derivatives-market-reforms-2020-note-on-implementation-progress/

Fullerton (2011) Fullerton, D., *Six Distributional Effects of Environmental Policy*, NBER Working Paper 16703, 2011, available at http://www.nber.org/papers/w16703

Fung et al. (2004) Fung, A., Graham, M., Weil, D., and Fagotto, E., *The Political Economy of Transparency: What Makes Disclosure Policies Effective?*, Ash Institute for Democratic Governance and Innovation, Harvard University, 2004, available at https://ash.harvard.edu/publications/political-economy-transparency-what-makes-disclosure-policies-effective

Funk & Hirschman (2014) Funk, R., and Hirschman, D., *Derivatives and Deregulation: Financial Innovation and the Demise of Glass–Steagall*, Administrative Science Quarterly, Vol. 59, No. 4, pp. 669-704, 2014, available at https://doi.org/10.1177/0001839214554830

Gai et al. (2019) Gai, P., Kemp, M., Sánchez Serrano, A., and Schnabel, I., *Regulatory complexity and the quest for robust regulation*, European Systemic Risk Board, Reports of the Advisory Scientific Committee, No. 8, 2019, available at https://www.esrb.europa.eu/pub/pdf/asc/esrb.asc190604_8_regulatorycomplexityquestrobustregulation~e63a7136c7.en.pdf

Gareau (2010) Gareau, B., *A critical review of the successful CFC phase-out versus the delayed methyl bromide phase-out in the Montreal Protocol*, International Environmental Agreements, Vol. 10, No. 3, 2010, available at https://doi.org/10.1007/s10784-010-9120-z

Garland (1985) Garland, M., *Deregulation and Judicial Review*, Harvard Law Review, Vol. 98, No. 3, pp. 505-591, 1985, available at https://www.jstor.org/stable/1340869

Geithner (2009) Geithner, T., *Testimony before the House Financial Services and Agriculture Committees Joint Hearing on Regulation of OTC Derivatives*, 10 July 2009, available at https://www.treasury.gov/press-center/press-releases/Pages/tg204.aspx

Genito (2019) Genito, L., *Mandatory clearing: the infrastructural authority of central counterparty clearing houses in the OTC derivatives market*, Review of International Political Economy, Vol. 26, pp. 938-962, 2019, available at https://doi.org/10.1080/09692290.2019.1616596

Gerding (2016) Gerding, E., *The Dialectics of Bank Capital: Regulation and Regulatory Capital Arbitrage*, Washburn Law Journal, Vol. 55, No. 2, 2016, available at https://www.jstor.org/stable/2889615

Ghent & Kudlyak (2011) Ghent, A., and Kudlyak, M., *Recourse and Residential Mortgage Default: Evidence from US States*, The Review of Financial Studies, Vol. 24, No. 9, pp. 3139-3186, 2011, available at https://doi.org/10.1093/rfs/hhr055

Giddens (2012) (Attorneys for) Giddens, J., *Report of the Trustee's Investigation and Recommendations regarding the SIPA Liquidation of MF Global Inc.*, 2012, available at https://www.cftc.gov/sites/default/files/idc/groups/public/@newsroom/documents/file/mfglobaliinvestreport060412.pdf

Giordana & Schumacher (2013) Giordana, G., and Schumacher, I., *Bank liquidity risk and monetary policy: Empirical evidence on the impact of Basel III liquidity standards*, International Review of Applied Economics, Vol. 27, pp. 633-55, 2013, available at https://doi.org/10.1080/02692171.2013.778821

Giovanoli (1997) Giovanoli, M., *Legal Issues Regarding Payment and Netting Systems* in Effros, R., (ed.), *Current legal issues affecting central banks*, International Monetary Fund, 1997

Goel et al. (2017) Goel, T., Lewrick, U., and Tarashev, N., *Bank Capital Allocation under Multiple Constraints*, Bank for International Settlements Working Papers, No. 666, 2018, available at https://www.bis.org/publ/work666.pdf

Gonzalez-Watty (2016) Gonzalez-Watty, A., *The Quest for Accountability in Transnational Regulatory Networks: The Case of the Basel Committee on Banking Supervision*, D. Phil. thesis, Oxford University, 2016

Goodhart (1975) Goodhart, C., *Problems of Monetary Management: The U.K. Experience*, Papers in Monetary Economics, Reserve Bank of Australia, 1975

Goodhart (2011) Goodhart, C., *The Basel Committee on Banking Supervision: A History of the Early Years, 1974-1997*, Cambridge University Press, 2011

Goodhart & Lastra (2018) Goodhart, C., and Lastra, R., *Central Bank Accountability and Judicial Review*, SUERF Policy Note No. 32, SUERF, 2018, available at https://www.suerf.org/policynotes/2585/central-bank-accountability-and-judicial review

Gordon (2015) Gordon, J., *The Empty Call for Benefit-Cost Analysis in Financial Regulation*, in Sloan (2014)

Gorton (2008) Gorton, G., *The Panic of 2007+*, NBER Working Paper No. 14358, 2008, available at https://www.nber.org/papers/w14358

Grabosky (2017) Grabosky, P., *Meta-regulation*, in Drahos (2017)

Gramsci (1971) Gramsci, A., *Selections from the Prison Notebooks*, Hoare, Q., and Nowell-Smith, G., (ed. and trans.), Lawrence & Wishart, 1971

Graziadei (2009) Graziadei, M., *Legal Transplants and the Frontiers of Legal Knowledge*, Theoretical Inquiries in Law, Vol. 10, 2009, available at https://doi.org/10.2202/1565-3404.1231

Greenlaw et al. (2008) Greenlaw, D., Hatzius, J., Kashyap, A., and Shin, H., *Leveraged Losses: Lessons from the Mortgage Market Meltdown*, Proceedings of the US Monetary Policy Forum, pp. 7–59, 2008

Gregory (2020) Gregory, J., *The xVA Challenge: Counterparty Risk, Funding, Collateral, Capital and Initial Margin*, Wiley, 2020

Griffith (2011) Griffith, S., *Governing Systemic Risk: Towards a Governance Structure for Derivatives Clearinghouses*, Emory Law Journal, Vol. 61, No. 5, 2011, available at https://ssrn.com/abstract=2157693

G-20 (2009) Group of Twenty, *Leaders' Statement—The Pittsburgh Summit*, 2009, available at http://www.g20.utoronto.ca/2009/2009communique0925.html

Grynberg & Silva (2006) Grynberg, R., and Silva, S., *Harmonization without Representation: Small States, the Basel Committee, and the WTO*, World Development Vol. 34, No. 7, pp. 1223-1236, 2006, available at https://doi.org/10.1016/j.worlddev.2005.11.018

Guizzardia & Halpin (2008) Guizzardia, G., and Halpin, T., *Ontological foundations for conceptual modelling*, Applied Ontology, Vol. 3, 2008, pp. 1–12, available at https://doi.org/10.3233/AO-2008-0049

Gullifer (2012) Gullifer, L., *What Should We Do about Financial Collateral?*, Current Legal Problems, Vol. 65, pp. 377-410, , 2012, available at https://doi.org/10.1093/clp/cus001

Gullifer & Payne (2011) Gullifer, L., *Intermediated Securities: Legal Problems and Practical Issues*, Hart Publishing, 2011

Gunningham & Sinclair (2017) Gunningham, N., and Sinclair, D., *Smart regulation*, in Drahos (2017)

Gurrea-Martínez & Remolina (2019) Gurrea-Martínez, A., and Remolina, N., *The Dark Side of Implementing Basel Capital Requirements: Theory, Evidence and Policy*, Journal of International Economic Law, Vol. 22, No. 1pp. 125-152, 2019, available at https://doi.org/10.1093/jiel/jgz002

Gurrola Perez (2018) Gurrola-Perez, P., *The Validation of Filtered Historical VaR Models*, Journal of Risk Model Validation, Vol. 12, No. 1, pp. 85-112, 2018, available at https://ssrn.com/abstract=3037099

Gurrola Perez & Murphy (2015) Gurrola-Perez, P., and Murphy, D., *Filtered Historical Simulation Value-at-Risk Models and Their Competitors*, Bank of England Working Paper No. 525, 2015, available at https://ssrn.com/abstract=2574769

Guseva (2016) Guseva, Y., *Destructive Collectivism: Dodd-Frank Coordination and Clearinghouses*, Cardozo Law Review, Vol. 37, pp. 1639-1772, 2016, available at https://ssrn.com/abstract=2710945

Guzman & Meyer (2010) Guzman, A., and Meyer, T., *International Soft Law*, Journal of Legal Analysis, Vol. 2, No. 1, 2010, available at https://ssrn.com/abstract=1353444

Habermas (1996) Habermas, J., *Between Facts and Norms: Contributions to a Discourse Theory of Law and Democracy*, MIT Press, 1996

Hahn et al. (2003) Hahn, R., Olmstead, S., Stavins, R., *Environmental Regulation during the 1990s: a retrospective analysis*, in Harvard Environmental Law Review, Vol. 27, No. 2, 2003, available at https://scholar.harvard.edu/stavins/publications/environmental-regulation-1990s-retrospective-analysis

Hale et al. (2013) Hale, T., Held, D., and Young, K., *Gridlock: Why Global Cooperation Is Failing When We Need It Most*, Polity Press, 2013

Hall (2000) Hall, N., *The Liverpool Cotton Market: Britain's First Futures Market*, Transactions of the Historical Society of Lancashire and Cheshire, Vol. 149, 2000, pp. 99-118, available at https://www.hslc.org.uk/wp-content/uploads/2017/05/149-6-Hall.pdf

Haraway (1988) Haraway, D., *Situated Knowledges: The Science Question in Feminism and the Privilege of Partial Perspective*, Feminist Studies, Vol. 14, No. 3, pp. 575-599, 1988, available at https://www.jstor.org/stable/3178066

Haraway (1991) Haraway, D., *Simians, Cyborgs and Women: The Reinvention of Nature*, Routledge, 1991

Harding (2002) Harding, P., *Mastering the ISDA Master Agreement: A Practical Guide for Negotiation*, Financial Times Prentice Hall, 2002

Harrington (2009) Harrington, S., *The Financial Crisis, Systemic Risk, and the Future of Insurance Regulation*, NAIC Public Policy, 2009, available at http://namic.org/pdf/090908SystemicRiskAndTheFuture.pdf

Haubrich (2020) Haubrich, J., *A Brief History of Bank Capital Requirements in the United States*, Federal Reserve Bank of Cleveland Economic Commentary No. 2020-05, 2020, available at https://www.clevelandfed.org/newsroom-and-events/publications/economic-commentary/2020-economic-commentaries/ec-202005-evolution-bank-capital-requirements.aspx

Hauser (2020) Hauser, A., *Seven Moments in Spring: Covid-19, financial markets and the Bank of England's balance sheet operations*, Speech, 2020, available at https://www.bankofengland.co.uk/speech/2020/andrew-hauser-speech-hosted-by-bloomberg-via-webinar

Hausman et al. (2017) Hausman, D., McPherson, M., and Satz, D., *Economic Analysis, Moral Philosophy, and Public Policy*, Cambridge University Press, 3rd Edition, 2017

Haynes et al. (2018) Haynes, R., McPhail, L., and Haoxiang Zhu, *Assessing the Impact of the Basel III Leverage Ratio on the Competitive Landscape of US Derivatives Markets: Evidence from Options*, CFTC Policy Brief, 2018, available at https://www.cftc.gov/sites/default/files/About/Economic\%20Analysis/oce_leverage_and_options.pdf

He et al. (2020) He, Z., Nagel, S., and Song, Z., *Treasury Inconvenience Yields during the COVID-19 Crisis*, Working Paper, 2020, available at https://cpb-us-w2.wpmucdn.com/voices.uchicago.edu/dist/6/2325/files/2020/06/writeup06122020.pdf

Helfand & Berck (2013) Helfand, G., and Berck, P., (eds.), *The Theory and Practice of Command and Control in Environmental Policy*, Routledge, 2013

Helleiner et al. (2018) Helleiner, E., Pagliari, S., and Spagna, I., *Governing the World's Biggest Market: The Politics of Derivatives Regulation After the 2008 Crisis*, Oxford University Press, 2018

Hendrie et al. (1999) Hendrie, D., Legge, M., Rosman, D., Kirov, C., and Ryan, T., *An economic evaluation of the mandatory bicycle helmet legislation in Western Australia*, Proceedings of the 1999 Insurance Commission of Western Australia Conference on Road Safety

Hermans et al. (2013) Hermans, L., McGoldrick, P., and Schmiedel, H., *Central counterparties and systemic risk*, European Systemic Risk Board Macro-prudential Commentaries, No. 6, 2013, available at https://www.esrb.europa.eu/pub/pdf/commentaries/ESRB_commentary_1311.pdf

Hertin et al. (2009) Hertin, J., Jacob, K., Pesch, U., and Pacchi, C., *The Production and Use of Knowledge in Regulatory Impact Assessment - An empirical analysis*, Environmental Policy Research Centre, Freie Universität Berlin, Report 01, 2009, available at https://refubium.fu-berlin.de/bitstream/handle/fub188/19576/FFU_rep_01_2009.pdf

Heyman (2004) Heyman, J., *The Anthropology of Power-Wielding Bureaucracies*, Human Organization, Vol. 63, No. 4, pp. 487-500, 2004, available at https://www.jstor.org/stable/44127393

Hilbert (1987) Hilbert, R., *Bureaucracy as Belief, Rationalization as Repair: Max Weber in a Post-Functionalist Age*, Sociological Theory, Vol. 5, No. 1, pp. 70-86, 1987, available at https://www.jstor.org/stable/201996

Hill (2016) Hill, J., *Keynote speech at Bruegel on the Call for Evidence: The impact of the EU regulatory framework for financial services*, 2016, available at https://ec.europa.eu/commission/presscorner/detail/en/SPEECH_16_2503.

Hindess (1996) Hindess, B., *Discourses of Power: From Hobbes to Foucault*, Oxford University Press, 1996

Hogue et al. (2017) Hogue, H., Labonte, M., and Webel, B., *Independence of Federal Financial Regulators: Structure, Funding, and Other Issues*, Congressional Research Service Report No. 43391, 2017, available at https://fas.org/sgp/crs/misc/R43391.pdf

Holden et al. (2016) Holden, H., Houllier, M., and Murphy, D., *I want security: stylized facts about central counterparty collateral and its systemic context*, Journal of Financial Market Infrastructures, Vol. 5, No. 2, pp. 53-75, 2016, available at https://doi.org/10.21314/JFMI.2016.070

Horrell & Chichkanov (2020) Horrell, R., and Chichkanov, P., *What role did margin play during the Covid-19 shock?*, Bank Overground blog, Bank of England, 2020, available at https://www.bankofengland.co.uk/bank-overground/2020/what-role-did-margin-play-during-the-covid-19-shock

Hou & Skeie (2014) Hou, D., and Skeie, D., *LIBOR: Origins, Economics, Crisis, Scandal, and Reform*, Federal Reserve Bank of New York Staff Reports No. 667, 2014, available at https://www.newyorkfed.org/medialibrary/media/research/staff_reports/sr667.pdf

Houllier & Murphy (2017) Houllier, M., and Murphy, D., *Borderline: Judging the Adequacy of Return Distribution Estimation Techniques in Initial Margin Models*, Bank of England Working Paper No. 673, available at https://ssrn.com/abstract=3031790

Hughes & Manning (2015) Hughes, D., and Manning, M., *CCPs and Banks: Different Risks, Different Regulations*, Reserve Bank of Australia, Quarterly Bulletin, December 2015, available at https://www.rba.gov.au/publications/bulletin/2015/dec/pdf/bu-1215-8.pdf

Hunt (1986) Hunt, A., *The Theory of Critical Legal Studies*, Oxford Journal of Legal Studies, Vol. 6, No. 1, pp. 1-45, 1986, available at https://www.jstor.org/stable/764467

Hüpkes et al. (2006) Hüpkes, E., Quintyn, M., and Taylor, M., *Accountability Arrangements for Financial Sector Regulators*, International Monetary Fund Economic Issues No. 39, 2006, available at https://www.imf.org/external/pubs/ft/issues/issues39/ei39.pdf

Husa (2018) Husa, J., *Developing Legal System, Legal Transplants, and Path Dependence: Reflections on the Rule of Law*, Chinese Journal of Comparative Law, Vol. 6, No. 2, 2018, available at https://doi.org/10.1093/cjcl/cxy008

Husserl (1913) Husserl, E., *Logische Untersuchungen*, 2nd Ed., 1913, available as *Logical Investigations*, Findlay, J., (trans.), Routledge, 1970

IMF (2009) International Monetary Fund, *Global Financial Stability Report*, April 2009, available at https://www.imf.org/en/Publications/GFSR/Issues/2016/12/31/Global-Financial-Stability-Report-April-2009-Responding-to-the-Financial-Crisis-and-22583

IMF (2018) International Monetary Fund, *Euro Area Policies: Financial System Stability Assessment*, Country Report No. 18/226, 2018, available at https://www.imf.org/en/Publications/CR/Issues/2018/07/19/Euro-Area-Policies-Financial-System-Stability-Assessment-46100

ISDA (2019) International Swaps and Derivatives Association, *SIMM: Methodology*, Version 2.2, 2019, available at https://www.isda.org/a/osMTE/ISDA-SIMM-v2.2-PUBLIC.pdf

ISDA et al. (2018) International Swaps and Derivatives Association, Global Financial Markets Association and the Institute of International Finance, *The Industry Response to the BCBS Consultation Paper Revisions to the minimum capital requirements for market risk*, 2018, available at https://www.isda.org/a/W7rEE/ISDA-GFMA-IIF-FRTB-Consultation-Response-June-2018.pdf

IFC (2018) Irving Fisher Committee on Central Bank Statistics, *Central banks and trade repositories derivatives data—2018 survey conducted by the Irving Fisher Committee on Central Bank Statistics*, 2018, available at https://www.bis.org/ifc/publ/ifc_report_cb_trade_rep_deriv_data.pdf

ISSA (2017) International Securities Services Association, *Inherent Risks within the Global Custody Chain*, Report, 2017, available at https://www.issanet.org/e/pdf/ISSA_Report_Inherent_Risk_February_2017.pdf

ISDA (2011) International Swaps and Derivatives Association, *Counterparty Credit Risk Management in the US Over-the-Counter (OTC) Derivatives Markets, Part II—A Review of Monoline Exposures*, Report, 2011

Jaffee (1994) Jaffee, D., *The Swedish Real Estate Crisis*, Fisher Centre for Real Estate and Urban Economics, University of California at Berkeley, Working Paper No. 94-224, 1994, available at https://escholarship.org/uc/item/1rh7720t

James & Quaglia (2020) James, S., and Quaglia, L., *The UK and Multi-Level Financial Regulation: From Post-Crisis Reform to Brexit*, Oxford University Press, 2020

Jones (2000) Jones, D., *Emerging problems with the Basel Capital Accord: Regulatory capital arbitrage and related issues*, Journal of Banking & Finance, Vol. 24, pp. 35-58, 2000, available at https://doi.org/10.1016/S0378-4266(99)00052-7

Jones (2020) Jones, E., (ed.), *The Political Economy of Bank Regulation in Developing Countries*, Oxford University Press, 2020

Jones & Baumgartner (2005) Jones, B., and Baumgartner, F., *The Politics of Attention—How Government Prioritizes Problems*, University of Chicago Press, 2005

Jordana & Levi-Faur (2005) Jordana, J., and Levi-Faur, D., *The Politics of Regulation in the Age of Governance*, in Jordana, J., and Levi-Faur, D., (eds.), *The Politics of Regulation*, Elgar, 2005

Jordana et al. (2015) Jordana, J., Bianculli, A., and Fernández-i-Marín, X., *When Accountability Meets Regulation*, in Bianculli, A., Fernández-i-Marín, X., and Jordana, J., (eds.), Accountability and Regulatory Governance, Palgrave Macmillan, 2015

Jouini (2001) Jouini, E., *Arbitrage and control problems in finance: A presentation*, Journal of Mathematical Economics, Vol. 35, pp. 167-183, 2001, available at https://doi.org/10.1016/S0304-4068(00)00063-X

Kallinikos (2004) Kallinikos, J., *The Social Foundations of the Bureaucratic Order*, Organisation, Vol. 11, No. 1, pp. 13-36, 2004, available at https://doi.org/10.1177/1350508404039657

Kargar et al. (2020) Kargar, M., Lester, B., Lindsay, D., Liu, S., Weill, P-O., and Zúñiga, D., *Corporate Bond Liquidity During the COVID-19 Crisis*, NBER Working Paper No. 27355, 2020, available at https://www.nber.org/papers/w27355

Kastnera (2014) Kastnera, L., *'Much ado about nothing?' Transnational civil society, consumer protection and financial regulatory reform*, Review of International Political Economy, Vol. 21, No. 6, pp. 1313-1345, 2014, available at http://dx.doi.org/10.1080/09692290.2013.870084

Kentikelenis & Seabrooke (2017) Kentikelenis, A., and Seabrooke, L., *The Politics of World Polity: Script-writing in International Organizations*, American Sociological Review, Vol. 82, No. 5, pp. 1065-1092, 2017, available at https://doi.org/10.1177/0003122417728241

Keohane et al. (1998) Keohane, N., Revesz, R., and Stavins, R., *The Choice of Regulatory Instruments in Environmental Policy*, Harvard Environmental Law Review, Vol. 22, 1998, available at https://scholar.harvard.edu/stavins/publications/choice-regulatory-instruments-environmental-policy

Keynes (1936) Keynes, J., *The general theory of employment, interest, and money*, Harcourt Brace, 1936

King et al. (2020) King, T., Nesmith, T., Paulson, A., and Prono, T., *Central Clearing and Systemic Liquidity Risk*, Finance and Economics Discussion Series No. 2020-009, Board of Governors of the Federal Reserve System, 2020, available at https://www.federalreserve.gov/econres/feds/files/2020009pap.pdf

Kingsbury et al. (2005) Kingsbury, B., Krisch, N., and Stewart, R., *The Emergence of Global Administrative Law*, Law and Contemporary Problems, Vol. 68, pp. 15-61, 2005, available at https://scholarship.law.duke.edu/lcp/vol68/iss3/2

Kingsbury (2009) Kingsbury, B., *The Concept of 'Law' in Global Administrative Law*, The European Journal of International Law, Vol. 20, No. 1, pp. 23-57, 2009, available at https://doi.org/10.1093/ejil/chp005

Kirilenko et al. (2017) Kirilenko, A., Kyle, A., Samadi, M., and Tuzun, T., *The Flash Crash: High-Frequency Trading in an Electronic Market*, The Journal of Finance, Vol. 72, No. 3, 2017, available at https://doi.org/10.1111/jofi.12498

Knaack (2015) Knaack, P., *Innovation and deadlock in global financial governance: transatlantic coordination failure in OTC derivatives regulation*, Review of International Political Economy, Vol. 22, No. 6, pp. 1217-1248, 2015, available at 10.1080/09692290.2015.1099555

Knight (1921) Knight, F., *Risk, Uncertainty and Profit*, Harper, 1921

Kotidis & van Horen (2018) Kotidis, A., and van Horen, N., *Repo market functioning: the role of capital regulation*, Bank of England Staff Working Paper No. 746, 2018, available at https://www.bankofengland.co.uk/working-paper/2018/repo-market-functioning-the-role-of-capital-regulation

Krahnen & Pelizzon (2016) Krahnen, J., and Pelizzon, L., *"Predatory" margins and the regulation and supervision of central counterparty clearing houses (CCPs)*, SAFE White Paper, No. 41, Goethe University Frankfurt, 2016, available at http://nbn-resolving.de/urn:nbn:de:hebis:30:3-416899

Kratochwil (2020) Kratochwil, M., *Credit exposure under the new standardised approach for counterparty credit risk: fixing the treatment of equity options*, Journal of Credit Risk, Vol. 16, No. 4, pp. 1-30, 2020, available at https://doi.org/10.21314/JCR.2020.265

Kriebel et al. (2001) Kriebel, D., Tickner, J., Epstein, P., Lemons, J., Levins, R., Loechler, E., Quinn, M., Rudel, R., Schettler, T., and Stoto, M., *The precautionary principle in environmental science*, Environmental Health Perspectives, Vol. 109, No. 9, 2001, available at https://www.ncbi.nlm.nih.gov/pmc/articles/PMC1240435/

Kroszner (2000) Kroszner, R., *Lessons from Financial Crises: The Role of Clearinghouses*, Journal of Financial Services Research, Vol. 18, No. 2/3, pp. 157-171, 2000, available at https://doi.org/10.1023/A:1026534619637

Lall (2011) Lall, R., *From failure to failure: The politics of international banking regulation*, Review of International Political Economy, Vol. 19, No. 4, pp. 609-638, 2011, available at http://dx.doi.org/10.1080/09692290.2011.603669

Laurent et al. (2016) Laurent, J.-P., Sestier, M., and Thomas, S., *Trading book and credit risk: How fundamental is the Basel review?*, Journal of Banking & Finance, Vol. 73, pp. 211-223, 2016, available at https://doi.org/10.1016/j.jbankfin.2016.07.002

Lears (1985) Lears, T., *The Concept of Cultural Hegemony: Problems and Possibilities*, The American Historical Review, Vol. 90, No. 3, pp. 567-593, 1985, available at http://www.jstor.org/stable/1860957

Lelyveld (2017) Lelyveld, I., *The use of derivatives trade repository data: possibilities and challenges*, presented at the Irving Fisher Committee and National Bank of Belgium

Workshop on Data needs and Statistics compilation for macroprudential analysis, 2017, available at https://www.bis.org/ifc/publ/ifcb46z.pdf

Levi-Faur (2013a) Levi-Faur, D., *The Odyssey of the Regulatory State: From a "Thin" Monomorphic Concept to a "Thick" and Polymorphic Concept*, Law & Policy, Vol. 35, Nos. 1-2, 2013, available at https://doi.org/10.1111/lapo.12000

Levi-Faur (2013b) Levi-Faur, D., (ed.), *Handbook on the Politics of Regulation*, Edward Elgar, 2013

Levi-Faur (2017) Levi-Faur, D., *Regulatory capitalism*, in Drahos (2017)

Levine (2006) Levine, M., *Why Weren't the Airlines Reregulated?*, Yale Journal on Regulation, Vol. 23, No. 2, 2006, available at https://digitalcommons.law.yale.edu/yjreg/vol23/iss2/5

Levitin (2013) Levitin, A., *Skin-in-the-Game: Risk Retention Lessons from Credit Card Securitization*, The George Washington Law Review, Vol. 81, pp. 813-855, 2013, available at https://ssrn.com/abstract=1898763

Levitin (2014) Levitin, A., *The Politics of Financial Regulation and the Regulation of Financial Politics: A Review Essay*, Harvard Law Review, Vol. 127, pp. 1991-2068, 2014, available at https://cdn.harvardlawreview.org/wp-content/uploads/2014/05/vol127_-levitin.pdf

Lewis & McPartland (2017) Lewis, R., and McPartland, J., *Nondefault loss allocation at central counterparties*, Journal of Financial Market Infrastructures, Vol. 6, No. 1, pp. 29-44, 2017, available at https://doi.org/10.21314/JFMI.2017.082

Lewis & McPartland (2018) Lewis, R., and McPartland, J., *One for my baby (and one more for the road): incentives, default waterfalls and central counterparty skin-in-the-game*, Journal of Financial Market Infrastructures, Vol. 6, No. 4, pp. 55-70, 2018, available at https://doi.org10.21314/JFMI.2018.096

Li (2009) Wenli Li, *Residential Housing And Personal Bankruptcy*, Federal Reserve Bank of Philadelphia, Business Review, Issue Q2, pp. 19-29, 2009, available at https://www.philadelphiafed.org/-/media/res earch-and-data/publications/business-review/2009/q2/brq209_housing-and-bankruptcy.pdf

Lin & Surti (2014) Lin, L., and Surti, J., *Capital requirements for over-the-counter derivatives central counterparties*, Journal of Banking and Finance, Vol. 52, pp. 140-155, 2014, available at https://doi.org/10.1016/j.jbankfin.2014.08.015

Litowitz (2000) Litowitz, D., *Gramsci, Hegemony, and the Law*, Brigham Young University Law Review, Vol. 2000, No. 2, available at https://digitalcommons.law.byu.edu/lawreview/vol2000/iss2/1

Littlechild (1983) Littlechild, S., *Regulation of British Telecommunications' Profitability*, Report to the Secretary of State, Department of Industry, 1983, available at https://www.eprg.group.cam.ac.uk/s-littlechild-report-regulation-of-british-telecommunications-profitability-1983/

Lockwood (2020) Lockwood, E., *From bombs to boons: changing views of risk and regulation in the pre-crisis OTC derivatives market*, Theory and Society, Vol. 49, pp. 215–244, 2020, available at https://doi.org/10.1007/s11186-020-09386-1

Lodge (2005) Lodge, D., *Accountability and Transparency in Regulation: Critiques, Doctrines and Instruments*, in Jordana, J., and Levi-Faur, D., (eds.), *The Politics of Regulation*, Elgar, 2005

Logan (2020) Logan, L., *Treasury Market Liquidity and Early Lessons from the Pandemic Shock*, Remarks at Brookings-Chicago Booth Task Force on Financial Stability meeting, October 2020, available at https://www.newyorkfed.org/newsevents/speeches/2020/log201023

Longstaff (2010) Longstaff, F., *The subprime credit crisis and contagion in financial markets*, Journal of Financial Economics, Vol. 97, pp. 436-450, 2010, available at https://doi.org/10.1016/j.jfineco.2010.01.002

Lubben (2017) Lubben, S., *Always Crashing in the Same Car—Clearinghouse Rescue in the United States under Dodd-Frank*, Journal of Financial Regulation, Vol. 3, No. 2, pp. 133-158, 2017, available at https://doi.org/10.1093/jfr/fjx007

Luhmann (1984) Luhmann, N., *The Self-Reproduction of Law and Its Limits*, in Teubner, G., (ed.), Dilemmas of Law in the Welfare State, Walter de Gruyter, 1984

McCaffrey (2006) McCaffrey, D., *The Transformation of the Over the Counter Derivatives Market 1984-2016*, Working Paper, 2016, available at https://ssrn.com/abstract=2642216

McCubbins et al. (1989) McCubbins, D., Noll, R., and Weingast, B., *Structure and Process; Politics and Policy: Administrative Arrangements and the Political Control of Agencies*, Virginia Law Review, Vol. 75, pp. 431-82, 1989, available at https://www.jstor.org/stable/1073179

McDonald & Paulson (2015) McDonald, R., and Paulson, A., *AIG in Hindsight*, Journal of Economic Perspectives, Vol. 29, No. 2, pp. 81-106, 2015, available at https://doi.org/10.1257/jep.29.2.81

McHenry (2017) McHenry, P., *Letter to Janet Yellen, 31 January 2017*, available at https://ftalphaville-cdn.ft.com/wp-content/uploads/2017/02/02155349/McHenry-letter-letter-to-Yellen1.pdf

McNamara (2014) McNamara, S., *Financial Markets Uncertainty and the Rawlsian Argument for Central Counterparty Clearing of OTC Derivatives*, Notre Dame Journal of Law, Ethics & Public Policy, Vol. 28, No. 1, 2014, available at https://scholarship.law.nd.edu/ndjlepp/vol28/iss1/6

McPartland & Lewis (2017) McPartland, J., and Lewis, R., *The Goldilocks problem: How to get incentives and default waterfalls "just right"*, Federal Reserve Bank of Chicago Economic Perspectives No. 1, 2017, available at https://www.chicagofed.org/publications/economic-perspectives/2017/1-mcpartland-lewis

MacKenzie & Millo (2002) MacKenzie, D., and Millo, Y., *Constructing a Market, Performing Theory: The Historical Sociology of a Financial Derivatives Exchange*, American Journal of Sociology, Vol. 109, No. 1, pp. 107–145, 2003, available at https://www.jstor.org/stable/10.1086/374404

MAGD (2013) Macroeconomic Assessment Group on Derivatives, *Macroeconomic impact assessment of OTC derivatives regulatory reforms*, Bank of International Settlements, 2013, available at https://www.bis.org/publ/othp20.pdf

Majone (1994) Majone, G., *The rise of the regulatory state in Europe*, West European Politics, Vol. 17, No. 3, pp. 77-101, 1994, available at http://dx.doi.org/10.1080/01402389408425031

Majone (1997) Majone, G., *Regulatory State: Causes and Consequences of Changes in the Mode of Governance*, Journal of Public Policy, Vol. 17, No. 2, pp. 139-167, 1997, available at https://doi.org/10.1017/S0143814X00003524

Majone (1998) Majone, G., *The Regulatory State and its Legitimacy Problems*, Institute for Advanced Studies, Vienna, Research Report, Political Science Series No. 56, 1998, available at https://www.ssoar.info/ssoar/handle/document/24670

Mariathasana & Merrouche (2014) Mariathasana, M., and Merrouche, O., *The manipulation of Basel risk-weights*, Journal of Financial Intermediation, Vol. 23, No. 3, pp. 300-321, 2014, available at https://doi.org/10.1016/j.jfi.2014.04.004

Mayes & Stremmel (2014) Mayes, D., and Stremmel, H., *The Effectiveness of Capital Adequacy Measures in Predicting Bank Distress*, SUERF Studies, No. 2014/1, SUERF, 2014, available at https://www.suerf.org/studies/3991/the-effectiveness-of-capital-adequacy-measures-in-predicting-bank-distress

Meissner (2009) Meissner, G., *Credit Derivatives: Application, Pricing, and Risk Management*, John Wiley & Sons, 2009

Menand (2018) Menand, L., *Too Big to Supervise: The Rise of Financial Conglomerates and the Decline of Discretionary Oversight in Banking*, Cornell Law Review, Vol. 103, No. 6, pp. 1527-1588, available at https://scholarship.law.cornell.edu/clr/vol103/iss6/8

Menkveld (2017) Menkveld, A., *Crowded Positions: An Overlooked Systemic Risk for Central Clearing Parties*, The Review of Asset Pricing Studies, Vol. 7, No. 2, pp. 209-242, 2017, available at https://doi.org/10.1093/rapstu/rax016

Merton & Bodie (1995) Merton, R., and Bodie, Z., *A conceptual framework for analyzing the financial system*, in The Global Financial System: A Functional Perspective, Harvard Business School Press, 1995

Meyer et al. (2008) Mayer, C., Pence, K., and Sherlund, S., *The Rise in Mortgage Defaults*, Finance and Economics Discussion Series No. 2008-59, Board of Governors of the Federal Reserve System, 2008, available at https://www.federalreserve.gov/pubs/feds/2008/200859/200859pap.pdf

Mignolo (2002) Mignolo, W., *The Geopolitics of Knowledge and the Colonial Difference*, South Atlantic Quarterly, Vol. 101, No. 1, pp. 57-96, 2002, available at http://dx.doi.org/10.1215/00382876-101-1-57

Mishkin (2011) Mishkin, F., *Over the Cliff: From the Subprime to the Global Financial Crisis*, Journal of Economic Perspectives, Vol. 25, No. 1, pp. 49-70, 2011, available at https://doi.org/10.1257/jep.25.1.49

Mitchell (1989) Mitchell, T., *The World as Exhibition*, Comparative Studies in Society and History, Vol. 31, No. 2, pp. 217-236, 1989, available at https://www.jstor.org/stable/178807

Möller (2012) Möller, K., *Proportionality: Challenging the critics*, International Journal of Constitutional Law, Vol. 10, pp. 709-731, 2012, available at https://doi.org/10.1093/icon/mos024

Moloney (2020) Moloney, N., *Reflections on the EU third country regime for capital markets in the shadow of Brexit*, European Company and Financial Law Review, Vol. 17, No. 1, pp. 35-71, 2020, available at https://doi.org/10.1515/ecfr-2020-0002

Moran (2002) Moran, M., *Understanding the Regulatory State*, British Journal of Political Science, Vol. 32, No. 2, 2002, available at https://www.jstor.org/stable/4092224

Morgan (1988) Morgan, G., *Accounting as reality construction: Towards a new epistemology for accounting practice*, Accounting Organizations and Society, Vol. 13, No. 5, pp. 477-485, 1988, available at https://doi.org/10.1016/0361-3682(88)90018-9

Moser (1994) Moser, J., *Origins of the Modern Exchange Clearinghouse: A History of Early Clearing*, Federal Reserve Bank of Chicago Working Paper WP-94-3, 1994, available at https://fraser.stlouisfed.org/files/docs/historical/frbchi/workingpapers/frbchi_workingpaper_1994-03.pdf

Mügge (2011) Mügge, D., *Limits of legitimacy and the primacy of politics in financial governance*, Review of International Political Economy, Vol. 18, No. 1, pp. 52-74, 2011, available at https://www.jstor.org/stable/41061585

Muller & Mendelsohn (2009) Muller, N., and Mendelsohn, R., *Efficient Pollution Regulation: Getting the Prices Right*, American Economic Review, Vol. 99, No. 5, 2009, available at https://www.aeaweb.org/articles?id=10.1257/aer.99.5.1714

Murphy (2009) Murphy, D., *Unravelling the Credit Crunch*, Chapman and Hall/ CRC, 2009

Murphy (2012) Murphy, D., *Maintaining Confidence*, LSE Financial Markets Group Special Paper 216, 2012, available at http://www.lse.ac.uk/fmg/assets/documents/papers/special-papers/SP216.pdf

Murphy (2013) Murphy, D., *OTC Derivatives: Bilateral Trading and Central Clearing: An Introduction to Regulatory Policy, Market Impact and Systemic Risk*, Palgrave, 2013

Murphy (2017) Murphy, D., *I've got you under my skin: large central counterparty financial resources and the incentives they create*, Journal of Financial Market Infrastructures, Vol. 5, No. 3, pp. 1-18, 2017, available at https://doi.org/10.21314/JFMI.2017.073

Murphy (2020a) Murphy, D., *Our Lessons Have Returned: Insights into Post-crisis Financial Regulation from Mandatory OTC Derivatives Clearing Policy*, LSE Law, Society and Economy Working Papers 6/2020, available at https://ssrn.com/abstract=3561599

Murphy (2020b) Murphy, D., *Too much, too young—improving the client clearing mandate*, Journal of Financial Market Infrastructures, Vol. 8, No. 3, 2020, available at https://ssrn.com/abstract=3768398

Murphy & Macdonald (2016) Murphy, D., and Macdonald, D., *Identifying historical episodes for central counterparty stress testing*, Journal of Financial Market Infrastructures, Vol. 4, No. 3, pp. 93-115, 2016, https://doi.org/10.21314/JFMI.2016.053

Murphy & Nahai-Williamson (2014) Murphy, D., and Nahai-Williamson, P., *Dear Prudence, won't you come out to play? Approaches to the analysis of central counterparty default fund adequacy*, Bank of England Financial Stability Paper No. 30, 2014, available at https://ssrn.com/abstract=3700306

Murphy & Vause (2021) Murphy, D., and Vause, N., *A CBA of APC—Analysing approaches to procyclicality reduction in CCP initial margin models*, Bank of England Staff Working Paper No. 950, 2021

Murphy et al. (2014) Murphy, D., Vasios, M., and Vause, N., *An Investigation into the Procyclicality of Risk-Based Initial Margin Models*, Bank of England Financial Stability Paper No. 29, 2014, available at https://ssrn.com/abstract=2437916

Murphy et al. (2016) Murphy, D., Vasios, M., and Vause, N., *A comparative analysis of tools to limit the procyclicality of initial margin requirements*, Bank of England Staff Working Paper No. 597, 2016, available at https://ssrn.com/abstract=2772569

Murphy et al. (2021) Murphy, D., Coughlan, J., and Roberson, M., *Optimising Risk-based Regulation Using Realistic Portfolios: The Example of the Standardised Approach to Counterparty Credit Risk*, Manuscript, 2021

Nadauld & Sherlund (2009) Nadauld, T., and Sherlund, S., *The Role of the Securitization Process in the Expansion of Subprime Credit*, Finance and Economics Discussion Series No. 2009-28, Board of Governors of the Federal Reserve System, 2009, available at https://www.federalreserve.gov/pubs/feds/2009/200928/200928pap.pdf

NAO (2009) National Audit Office, *The nationalisation of Northern Rock*, 2009, available at http://media.nao.org.uk/uploads/2009/03/0809298.pdf

Nobes & Stadler (1989) Nobes, C., and Stadler, C., *How arbitrary are international accounting classifications? Lessons from centuries of classifying in many disciplines, and experiments with IFRS data*, Accounting, Organizations and Society, Vol. 38, pp. 573-595, 2013, available at https://doi.org/10.1016/j.aos.2013.10.001

Okina et al. (2000) Okina, K., Shirakawa, M., and Shiratsuka, S., *The Asset Price Bubble and Monetary Policy: Japan's Experience in the Late 1980s and the Lessons*, Institute for Monetary and Economic Studies Discussion Paper No. 2000-E-12, 2000, available at https://www.imes.boj.or.jp/research/papers/english/00-E-12.pdf

O'Neill (1986) O'Neill, J., *The Disciplinary Society: From Weber to Foucault*, The British Journal of Sociology, Vol. 37, No. 1, pp. 42-60, 1986, available at https://www.jstor.org/stable/591050

Oren & Blyth (2018) Oren, T., and Blyth, M., *From Big Bang to Big Crash: The Early Origins of the UK's Finance-led Growth Model and the Persistence of Bad Policy Ideas*, New Political Economy, Vol. 24, No. 5, 2018, available at https://doi.org/10.1080/13563467.2018.1473355

Ozdagli & Peek (2013) Ozdagli, A., and Peek, J., *Cliff Notes: The Effects of the 2013 Debt-Ceiling Crisis*, Public Policy Brief No. 13-9, Federal Reserve Bank of Boston, 2013, available at https://www.bostonfed.org/-/media/Documents/Workingpapers/PDF/economic/ppb/2013/ppb139.pdf

Pagliari & Young (2016) Pagliari, S., and Young, K., *The interest ecology of financial regulation: interest group plurality in the design of financial regulatory policies*, Socio-Economic Review, Vol. 14, No. 2, pp. 309-337, 2016, available at https://doi.org/10.1093/ser/mwv024

Patrick (2015) Patrick, S., *The New 'New Multilateralism': Minilateral Cooperation, but at What Cost?*, Global Summitry, Vol. 1, No. 2, pp. 115-134, 2015, available at https://academic.oup.com/globalsummitry/article/1/2/115/2362958

Paulson (2008) Paulson, H., *Statement by Secretary Henry M. , Jr. on Treasury and Federal Housing Finance Agency Action to Protect Financial Markets and Taxpayers*, 2008, available at https://www.treasury.gov/press-center/press-releases/Pages/hp1129.aspx.

Peltzman (1975) Peltzman, S., *The Effects of Automobile Safety Regulation*, Journal Political Economy, Vol. 83, 1975, available at https://www.journals.uchicago.edu/doi/abs/10.1086/260352

Perdue (1987) Perdue, W., *Manipulation of Futures Markets: Redefining the Offense*, Fordham Law Review Vol. 56, No. 3, pp. 345-402, 1987, available at https://ir.lawnet.fordham.edu/flr/vol56/iss3/3

Philippon (2015) Philippon, T., *Efficiency and Benefit-Cost Analysis of the Financial System*, in Sloan (2014)

Plosser & Santos (2014) Plosser, M., and Santos, J., *Banks' incentives and the quality of internal risk models*, Federal Reserve Bank of New York Staff Report No. 704, 2014, available at https://www.newyorkfed.org/medialibrary/media/research/staff_reports/sr704.pdf

Posner (2000) Posner, R., *Frontiers of Legal Theory*, Harvard University Press, 2004

Posner & Sunstein (2017) Posner, E., and Sunstein, C., *Moral Commitments in Cost-Benefit Analysis*, Virginia Law Review , Vol. 103, No. 8, pp. 1809-1859, 2017, available at https://chicagounbound.uchicago.edu/cgi/viewcontent.cgi?article=13508&context=journal_articles

Posner & Weyl (2014) Posner, E., and Weyl, E., *Benefit-Cost Paradigms in Financial Regulation*, in Sloan (2014).

Power (1989) Power, M., *Reconnecting Accounting to the Problem of Freedom*, in Barker, E., (ed.), *LSE on Freedom: A Centenary Anthology*, Routledge, 1989

PRA (2020) Prudential Regulatory Authority, *Proprietary Trading Review*, 2020, available at https://www.bankofengland.co.uk/-/media/boe/files/prudential-regulation/report/proprietary-trading-review-2020.pdf

PRC (2007) Payments Risk Committee, *Financial Market Infrastructure Risk*, Current Report of the Financial Market Infrastructure Risk Task Force, Federal Reserve Bank of New York, 2007, available at https://www.newyorkfed.org/medialibrary/microsites/prc/files/FMIMay07.pdf

Prendergast (2007) Prendergast, C., *The Motivation and Bias of Bureaucrats*, The American Economic Review, Vol. 97, No. 1, pp. 180-196, 2007, available at https://www.jstor.org/stable/30034390

Quarles (2020) Quarles, R., *What Happened? What Have We Learned From It? Lessons from COVID-19 Stress on the Financial System*, Speech, 2020, available at https://www.bis.org/review/r201019d.htm

Radaelli and de Francesco (2010) Radaelli, C., and de Francesco, F., *Regulatory Impact Assessment* in Baldwin, R., Cave, M., and Lodge, M., (eds.), *The Oxford Handbook of Regulation*, Oxford University Press, 2010

Raeburn (2014) Raeburn, R., *Re: CVA risk capital charge exemption for non-financial counterparties*, Letter to Andrea Enria, 17 November 2014, available at https://www.treasurerst.org/ACTmedia/EACT_Letter_on_CRD_IV_CVA_exemption.pdf.

Rancière (2010) Rancière, J., *Dissensus—On Politics and Aesthetics*, S. Corcoran (trans.), Continuum, 2010

Rawlings (2008) Rawlings, R., *Modelling Judicial Review*, Current Legal Problems, Vol. 61, No. 1, pp. 95-123, 2008, available at https://doi.org/10.1093/clp/61.1.95

Rawls (1972) Rawls, J., *A Theory of Justice*, Harvard University Press, 1987

Raykov (2018a) Raykov, R., *Reducing margin procyclicality at central counterparties*, Journal of Financial Market Infrastructures, Vol. 7, No. 2, pp. 43-59, 2018, available at https://doi.org/10.21314/JFMI.2018.106

Raykov (2018b) Raykov, R., *Risk mutualization and financial stability: recovering and resolving a central counterparty*, Journal of Financial Market Infrastructures, Vol. 6, No. 2/3, pp. 163-185, 2018, available at https://doi.org/10.21314/JFMI.2018.093

Reinhart & Rogoff (2009) Reinhart, C., and Rogoff, K., *This Time It's Different: Eight Centuries of Financial Folly*, Princeton University Press, 2009

Riggs et al. (2020) Riggs, L., Onur, E., Reiffen, D., and Haioxang Zhu, *Swap trading after Dodd-Frank: Evidence from index CDS*, Journal of Financial Economics, Vol. 137, No. 3, pp. 857-886, 2020, available at https://doi.org/10.1016/j.jfineco.2020.03.008

Riles (2013a) Riles, A., *Collateral Expertise: Legal Knowledge in the Global Financial Markets*, Current Anthropology, Vol. 51, No. 6, pp. 795-818, 2010, available at https://doi.org/10.1086/657627

Riles (2013b) Riles, A., *Managing Regulatory Arbitrage: A Conflict of Laws Approach*, Cornell International Law Journal, Vol. 47, No. 1, 2014, available at https://doi.org/10.2139/ssrn.2335338

Rissel (2012) Rissel, C., *The Impact of Compulsory Cycle Helmet Legislation on Cyclist Head Injuries in New South Wales, Australia: A Rejoinder*, Accident Analysis & Prevention, Vol. 45, pp. 107-109, 2012, available at http://doi.org/10.1016/j.aap.2011.11.017

Robinson (2006) Robinson, D., *No clear evidence from countries that have enforced the wearing of helmets*, BMJ, Vol. 332, No. 7543, pp. 722–725, 2006, available at http://doi.org/10.1136/bmj.332.7543.722-a

Rodriguez & Weingast (2015) Rodriguez, D., and Weingast, B., *The "Reformation of Administrative Law" Revisited*, The Journal of Law, Economics, and Organization, Vol. 31, No. 4, pp. 782–807, 2015, available at https://doi.org/10.1093/jleo/ewv018

Roe (2011) Roe, M., *The Derivatives Market's Payment Priorities as Financial Crisis Accelerator*, Stanford Law Review, Vol. 63, 2011, available at https://www.jstor.org/stable/41105408

Roe (2013) Roe, M., *Clearinghouse Overconfidence*, California Law Review, Vol. 101, pp. 1641-1703, 2013, available at https://ssrn.com/abstract=2224305

Rogowski (2015) Rogowski, R., *Autopoiesis in Law*, in International Encyclopedia of the Social & Behavioral Sciences, 2nd edition, 2015

Romano (2014a) Romano, R., *For diversity in the international regulation of financial institutions: Critiquing and recalibrating the Basel architecture*, Yale Journal on Regulation, Vol. 31, 2014, available at https://ssrn.com/abstract=2127749

Romano (2014b) Romano, R., *Regulating in the Dark and a Postscript Assessment of the Iron Law of Financial Regulation*, Hofstra Law Review, Vol. 43, No. 1, 2014, available at http://scholarlycommons.law.hofstra.edu/hlr/vol43/iss1/2

Rosati & Vacirca (2019) Rosati, S., and Vacirca, F., *Interdependencies in the euro area derivatives clearing network: a multi-layer network approach*, European Central Bank Working Paper No. 2342, 2019, available at https://www.ecb.europa.eu/pub/pdf/scpwps/ecb.wp2342~ab1a8078c3.en.pdf

Rose (2014) Rose, N., (ed.), *Economic Regulation and its Reform*, University of Chicago Press, 2014

Rose & Miller (1992) Rose, N., and Miller, P., *Political Power beyond the State: Problematics of Government*, The British Journal of Sociology, Vol. 43, No. 2, pp. 173-205, 1992, available at https://www.jstor.org/stable/591464

Ruffini & Steigerwald (2014) Ruffini, I., and Steigerwald, R., *OTC derivatives—A primer on market infrastructure and regulatory policy*, Federal Reserve Bank of Chicago Economic Perspectives, Vol. 38, No. 3, 2014, available at https://www.chicagofed.org/publications/economic-perspectives/2014/3q-ruffini-steigerwald

Russo et al. (2002) Russo, D., Hart, T., and Schönenberger, A., *The evolution of clearing and central counterparty services for exchange-traded derivatives in the United States and Europe—a comparison*, ECB Occasional Paper No. 5, European Central Bank (ECB), 2002, available at https://ssrn.com/abstract=748968

Saguato (2017) Saguato, P., *The Ownership of Clearinghouses: When 'Skin in the Game' Is Not Enough, the Remutualization of Clearinghouses*, Yale Journal on Regulation, Vol. 34, No. 2, pp. 601-666, 2017, available at https://digitalcommons.law.yale.edu/yjreg/vol34/iss2/5

Saguato (2020) Saguato, P., *The unfinished business of regulating clearinghouses*, Columbia Business Law Review, Vol. 2020, No. 2, 2020, available at https://doi.org/10.52214/cblr.v2020i2.7219

Saks (2012) Saks, M., *Defining a Profession: The Role of Knowledge and Expertise*, Professions and Professionalism, Vol. 2, No. 1, pp. 1-10, 2012, available at https://doi.org/10.7577/pp.v2i1.151

Samuels (1978) Samuels, W., *Normative Premises in Regulatory Theory*, Journal of Post Keynesian Economics, Vol. 1, No. 1, 1978, available at https://doi.org/10.1007/978-94-009-8766-1_6

Samuels (2013) Samuels, S., *Why markets do not trust Basel II internal ratings-based approach: what can be done about it?*, Journal of Risk Management in Financial Institutions, Vol. 6, No. 1, 2013

Schenk (2011) Schenk, C., *Summer in The City: The 1974 international banking crisis in London and its implications for regulatory reform*, The English Historical Review, Vol. 129, No. 540, 2014, available at https://doi.org/10.1093/ehr/ceu261

Schmalensee & Willig (1989) Schmalensee, R., and Willig, R., (eds.), *Handbook of Industrial Organisation*, North Holland, 1989

Schoemaker (1982) Schoemaker, P., *The Expected Utility Model: Its Variants, Purposes, Evidence and Limitations*, Journal of Economic Literature, Vol. 20, 1982, available at https://www.jstor.org/stable/2724488

Scott (2014) Scott, C., *Evaluating the Performance and Accountability of Regulators*, Seattle University Law Review, Vol. 37, No. 2, pp. 353-374, 2014, available at http://digitalcommons.law.seattleu.edu/sulr/vol37/iss2/3/

Schrimpf et al. (2020) Schrimpf, A., Shin, H., and Sushko, V., *Leverage and Margin Spirals in Fixed Income Markets During the Covid-19 Crisis*, Bank of International Settlements Bulletin No. 2, 2020, available at https://www.bis.org/publ/bisbull02.pdf

Schwarcz (2015) Schwarcz, S., *Derivatives and Collateral: Balancing Remedies and Systemic Risk*, University of Illinois Law Review, pp. 699-720, 2015, available at https://scholarship.law.duke.edu/faculty_scholarship/3253

Schwarcz & Sharon (2015) Schwarcz, S., and Sharon, O., *The Bankruptcy-Law Safe Harbor for Derivatives: A Path-Dependence Analysis*, Washington and Lee law review, Vol. 71, No. 3, 2014, available at https://scholarship.law.duke.edu/faculty_scholarship/3151

Seabrooke (2014) Seabrooke, L., *Epistemic arbitrage: Transnational professional knowledge in action*, Journal of Professions and Organization, Vol. 1, pp. 49-64, 2014, available at https://doi.org/10.1093/jpo/jot005

Seabrooke & Tsingou (2014) Seabrooke, L., and Tsingou, E., *Distinctions, affiliations, and professional knowledge in financial reform expert groups*, Journal of European Public Policy, Vol. 21, No. 3, 2014, available at https://doi.org/10.1080/13501763.2014.882967

SEC (2008) Securities and Exchange Commission, Office of the Inspector General, *SEC's Oversight of Bear Stearns and Related Entities: the Consolidated Supervised Entity Program*, Report, 2008, available at https://www.sec.gov/files/446-a.pdf

Sen (1987) Sen, A., *On Ethics and Economics*, Blackwell, Oxford, 1987

Shapiro (2013) Shapiro, S., *The evolution of cost–benefit analysis in US regulatory decision making*, in Levi-Faur (2013b)

Shapiro & Borie-Holtz (2015) Shapiro, S., and Borie-Holtz, D., *The Politics of Regulatory Reform*, Routledge, 2015

Shavell (1993) Shavell, S., *The Optimal Structure of Law Enforcement*, The Journal of Law & Economics, Vol. 36, No. 1, pp. 255-287, 1993, available at https://doi.org/10.1086/467275

Sherrill (2015) Sherrill, M., *In Defense of the Bankruptcy Code's Safe Harbors*, The Business Lawyer, Vol. 70, 2015, available at https://www.americanbar.org/content/dam/aba/publications/business_lawyer/2015/70_4/article-safe-harbors-201510.pdf

Shiller (2012) Shiller, R., *The Subprime Solution: How Today's Global Financial Crisis Happened, and what to Do about it*, Princeton University Press, 2012

Simpson (1991) Simpson, A., *The Origins of Futures Trading in the Liverpool Cotton Market*, in Cane, P., and Stapleton, J., (eds.) *Essays for Patrick Atiyah*, Oxford University Press, 1991

Sinclair (2002) Sinclair, D., *Self-Regulation Versus Command and Control? Beyond False Dichotomies*, Law & Policy, Vol. 19, No. 4, 2002, available at https://doi.org/10.1111/1467-9930.00037

Singh & Turing (2018) Singh, M., and Turing, D., *Central counterparty resolution: an unresolved problem*, Journal of Financial Market Infrastructures, Vol. 6, No. 2/3, pp. 187-206, 2018, available at https://doi.org/10.21314/JFMI.2018.094

Sirri (2010) Sirri, E., *Regulation of Investment Banks*, Testimony before the Financial Crisis Inquiry Commission May 5, 2010, available at https://fraser.stlouisfed.org/files/docs/historical/fct/fcic/fcic_testimony_sirri_20100505.pdf

Sjostrom (2009) Sjostrom, W., *The AIG Bailout*, Washington and Lee Law Review, Vol. 66, 2009, available at https://ssrn.com/abstract=1346552

Sloan (2014) Sloan Foundation, (spon.), *Special Edition of the Proceedings of a Conference on the Benefit-Cost Analysis of Financial Regulation*, Journal of Legal Studies, Vol. 43, 2014, available at https://www.jstor.org/stable/10.1086/678351.pdf

Small & Tse (2012) Small, M., and Chi Kong Tse, *Predicting the outcome of roulette*, Chaos, Vol. 22, 2012, available at https://doi.org/10.1063/1.4753920

Somek (2010) Somek, A., *The Concept of 'Law' in Global Administrative Law: A Reply to Benedict Kingsbury*, The European Journal of International Law, Vol. 20, No. 4, 2010, available at https://doi.org/10.1093/ejil/chp091

State Street (2020) State Street Global Advisors, *SPDR ETFs Throughout the COVID-19 Crisis*, White Paper, 2020, available at https://www.ssga.com/library-content/pdfs/etf/spdr-amid-the-covid19-crisis.pdf

Stephenson (2006) Stephenson, M., *A costly signaling theory of hard look review*, John M. Olin Discussion Paper Series, Harvard University, 2006, available at http://www.law.harvard.edu/programs/olin_center/papers/pdf/Stephenson_539.pdf

Stigler (1971) Stigler, G., *The theory of economic regulation*, The Bell Journal of Economics and Management Science, Vol. 2, No. 1, pp. 3-21, 1971, available at https://www.jstor.org/stable/3003160

Stulz (2014) Stulz, R., *Should We Fear Derivatives?*, Journal of Economic Perspectives, Vol. 18, No. 3, pp. 173–192, 2004, available at https://doi.org/10.1257/0895330042162359

Sunstein (1989) Sunstein, C., *On the Costs and Benefits of Aggressive Judicial Review of Agency Action*, Duke Law Journal, Vol. 522, 1989, available at https://chicagounbound.uchicago.edu/cgi/viewcontent.cgi?article=12390&context=journal_articles

Sunstein (1990) Sunstein, C., *Paradoxes of the Regulatory State*, The University of Chicago Law Review , Vol. 57, No. 2, pp. 407-441, 1990, available at https://chicagounbound.uchicago.edu/cgi/viewcontent.cgi?article=12399&context=journal_articles

Swerts & Van Cauwenberg (2016) Swerts, Q., Van Cauwenberg, S., *CCP resilience and recovery—impact for the CCP users*, National Bank of Belgium Financial Stability Report, 2016, available at https://www.nbb.be/doc/ts/enterprise/activities/oversight/articles/2016-2-ccp-resilience-and-recovery.pdf

Tarbert (2001) Tarbert, H., *Rethinking Capital Adequacy: The Basle Accord and the New Framework*, The Business Lawyer, Vol. 56, No. 2, pp. 767-836, 2001, available at https://www.jstor.org/stable/40687994

Tarbert (2020) Tarbert, H., *The Enduring Legacy of the Dodd-Frank Act's Derivatives Reforms*, Journal of Financial Regulation, Vol. 6, pp. 159-171, 2020, available at https://doi.org/10.1093/jfr/fjaa011

Teubner (1982) Teubner, G., *Substantive and Reflexive Elements in Modern Law*, Law & Society Review, Vol. 17, 1982, available at https://www.jstor.org/stable/3053348

Teubner (1984) Teubner, G., *Autopoiesis in Law and Society: A Rejoinder to Blankenburg*, Law & Society Review, Vol. 18, No. 2, 1984, available at https://doi.org/10.2307/3053406

Thiemann & Lepoutre (2017) Thiemann, M., and Lepoutre, J., *Stitched on the Edge: Rule Evasion, Embedded Regulators, and the Evolution of Markets*, American Journal of Sociology, Vol. 122, No. 6, pp. 1775-1821, 2017, available at https://www.journals.uchicago.edu/doi/abs/10.1086/691348

Train (1991) Train, K., *Optimal Regulation: The Economic Theory of Natural Monopoly*, The MIT Press, 1991

Trebilcock et al. (2013) Trebilcock, M., Howse, R., and Eliason, A., *The Regulation of International Trade*, Routledge, 2013

Trevizan et al. (2007) Trevizan, F., Cozman, F., and de Barros, L., *Planning under Risk and Knightian Uncertainty*, Proceedings of the 20th International Joint Conference on Artificial Intelligence (IJCAI), 2007, available at https://www.aaai.org/Papers/IJCAI/2007/IJCAI07-326.pdf

Tsingou (2015) Tsingou, E., *Club governance and the making of global financial rules*, Review of International Political Economy, Vol. 22, No. 2, pp. 225-256, 2015, available at https://doi.org/10.1080/09692290.2014.890952

Tucker (2013) Tucker, P., *Central Counterparties in Evolving Capital Markets: Safety, Recovery and Resolution*, Banque de France Review No. 17, pp. 179 -184, 2013, available at https://www.bankofengland.co.uk/paper/2013/central-counterparties-in-evolving-capital-markets-safety-recovery-and-resolution

Tucker (2019) Tucker, P., *Unelected Power: The Quest for Legitimacy in Central Banking and the Regulatory State*, Princeton University Press, 2019

Turing (2019) Turing, D., *Central counterparties: magic relighting candles?*, Journal of Financial Market Infrastructures, Vol. 8, No. 1, pp. 27-49, 2019, available at https://doi.org/10.21314/JFMI.2019.114

Turing (2021) Turing, D., *Clearing and settlement*, 3rd Edition, Bloomsbury Professional, 2021

Turk-Ariss (2017) Turk-Ariss, R., *Heterogeneity of bank risk weights in the EU: Evidence by asset class and country of counterparty exposure*, IMF Working Paper Series, No. 17/137, 2017, available at https://www.imf.org/en/Publications/WP/Issues/2017/06/09 /Heterogeneity-of-Bank-Risk-Weights-in-the-EU-Evidence-by-Asset-Class-and-Country-of-44965

Tushnet (1991) Tushnet, M., *Critical Legal Studies: A Political History*, Yale Law Journal, Vol. 100, No. 5, pp. 1515-1544, 1991, available at https://digitalcommons.law.yale.edu/ylj/vol100/iss5/10

Unger (1983) Unger, R., *The Critical Legal Studies Movement*, Harvard Law Review, Vol. 96, No. 3, pp. 561-675, 1983, available at https://www.jstor.org/stable/1341032

Urueña (2012) Urueña, R., *No Citizens Here: Global Subjects and Participation in International Law*, The Erik Castrén Institute Monographs on International Law and Human Rights, Vol. 15, 2012

USGAO (2013) United States Government Accountability Office, *Financial Crisis Losses and Potential Impacts of the Dodd-Frank Act*, Report to Congressional Requesters, GAO-13-180, 2013, available at https://www.gao.gov/products/gao-13-180

USPSC (2011) United States Senate Permanent Subcommittee on Investigations, Committee on Homeland Security and Governmental Affairs, *Wall Street and the Financial Crisis:Anatomy of a Financial Collapse*, Report, 2011, available at https://www.hsgac.senate.gov/imo/media/doc/Financial_Crisis/FinancialCrisisReport.pdf

Valiante (2012) Valiante, D., *Setting the Institutional and Regulatory Framework for Trading Platforms: Does the MiFID definition of OTF make sense?*, ECMI Research Report No. 8, 2012, available at http://aei.pitt.edu/34483/1/ECMI_RR8_DV_MiFID_OTF.pdf

Valukas (2010) Valukas, A., *Lehman Brothers Holdings Inc. Chapter 11 Proceedings Examiner Report*, 2010, available at https://jenner.com/lehman

Varela et al. (1974) Varela, F., Maturana, H., and Uribe, R., *Autopoiesis: The Organization of Living Systems*, Biosystems, Vol. 5, No. 4, 1974, available at https://doi.org/10.1016/0303-2647(74)90031-8

Vazquez & Federico (2015) Vazquez, F., and Federico, P., *Bank funding structures and risk: Evidence from the global financial crisis*, Journal of Banking and Finance, Vol. 61, 2015, available at https://doi.org/10.1016/j.jbankfin.2015.08.023

Vázquez (2011) Vázquez, R., *Translation as Erasure: Thoughts on Modernity's Epistemic Violence*, Journal of Historical Sociology, Vol. 24, No. 1, 2011, available at https://doi.org/10.1111/j.1467-6443.2011.01387.x

Visscher et al. (2008) Visscher, C., Maiscocq, O., Varone, F., *The Lamfalussy Reform in the EU Securities Markets: Fiduciary Relationships, Policy Effectiveness and Balance of Power*, Journal of Public Policy, Vol. 28, No. 1, pp. 19-47, available at https://doi.org/10.1017/S0143814X08000767

Walter et al. (2011) Walter, S., Olivier, J., Churches, T., and Grzebieta, R., *The Impact of Compulsory Cycle Helmet Legislation on Cyclist Head Injuries in New South Wales, Australia*, Accident Analysis & Prevention, Vol. 43, No. 6, pp. 2064-2071, 2011, available at https://doi.org/10.1016/j.aap.2011.11.017

Walther (2016) Walther, A., *Jointly Optimal Regulation of Bank Capital and Liquidity*, Journal of Money, Credit and Banking, Vol. 48, No. 2-3, 2016, available at https://www.bis.org/bcbs/events/bartnf/walther.pdf

Watson (1993) Watson, A., *Legal Transplants: an approach to comparative law*, University of Georgia Press, 2nd Edition, 1993

Weaver (2012) Weaver, D., *Minimum obligations of market makers*, Foresight Project Report, Government Office for Science, 2012, available at https://assets.publishing.service.gov.uk/government/uploads/system/uploads/attachment_data/file/289034/12-1069-eia8-minimum-obligations-of-market-makers.pdf

Weber (1978) Weber, M., *Economy and Society*, Roth, G., and Wittich, C., (ed.), University of California Press, 1978

Weinberg (2013) Weinberg, J., *Support for Specific Institutions 2007-2008*, Federal Reserve History Essay, 2013, available at https://www.federalreservehistory.org/essays/support_for_specific_institutions

Wellink (2008) Wellink, N., *Remarks at the International Conference of Banking Supervisors*, 2008, available at https://www.bis.org/review/r080925b.pdf

Wendt (2015) Wendt, F., *Central Counterparties: Addressing their too-important-to-fail nature*, Journal of Financial Market Infrastructures, Vol. 4, No. 1, pp. 59-84, 2015, available at https://doi.org/10.21314/JFMI.2015.046

Whittington (2015) Whittington, V., *The role of the common law jury as direct deliberative mechanism for the democratic self-legitimation of law*, Studies in Social and Political Thought, Vol. 24, 2015, available at https://sro.sussex.ac.uk/id/eprint/63167/

Winters (2012) Winters, B., *Review of the Bank of England's Framework for Providing Liquidity to the Banking System*, 2012, available at https://www.bankofengland.co.uk/-/media/boe/files/news/2012/november/the-banks-framework-for-providing-liquidity-to-the-banking

Woods (2020) Woods, S., *Strong and simple*, Mansion House Speech, 2020, available at https://www.bankofengland.co.uk/speech/2020/sam-woods-city-banquet

Yadav & Turing (2016) Yadav, Y., and Turing, D., *The Extraterritorial Regulation of Clearinghouses*, Journal of Financial Regulation, Vol. 2, pp. 21-55, 2016, available at https://doi.org/10.1093/jfr/fjw001

Yamai & Yoshiba (2005) Yamai, Y., and Yoshiba, T., *Value-at-risk versus expected shortfall: A practical perspective*, Journal of Banking & Finance, Vol. 29, No. 4, pp. 997-1015, 2005

Young (2012) Young, K., *Transnational regulatory capture? An empirical examination of the transnational lobbying of the Basel Committee on Banking Supervision*, Review of International Political Economy, Vol. 19, No. 4, pp. 663-688, 2012, available at https://doi.org/10.1080/09692290.2011.624976

Young (2016) Young, K., *Tying hands and cutting ties: Explaining the divergence between the EU and the US in global banking reform since the crisis*, Journal of Banking Regulation, Vol. 17, pp. 46-59, 2016, available at https://doi.org/10.1057/jbr.2015.17

Zazzara (2020) Zazzara, C., *The new OTC derivatives landscape: (more) transparency, liquidity, and electronic trading*, Journal of Banking Regulation, Vol. 21, pp. 170–187, 2020, available at https://doi.org/10.1057/s41261-019-00105-0

Zhang & Nadarajah (2018) Zhang, Y., and Nadarajah, S., *A review of backtesting for value at risk*, Communications in Statistics - Theory and Methods, Vol. 47, No. 15, pp. 3616-3639, 2018, available at https://doi.org/10.1080/03610926.2017.1361984

Laws, Rules, and Standards

R. Bank of England (2020) Bank of England, *Sterling Monetary Framework Operating Procedures*, 2020, available at https://www.bankofengland.co.uk/-/media/boe/files/markets/sterling-monetary-framework/operating-procedures.pdf

R. BCBS (1983) Basel Committee on Banking Supervision, *Principles for the Supervision of Banks' Foreign Establishments*, Guidelines, 1983, available at https://www.bis.org/publ/bcbsc312.pdf

R. BCBS (1988) Basel Committee on Banking Supervision, *International convergence of capital measurement and capital standards*, 1988, available at https://www.bis.org/publ/bcbs04a.pdf

R. BCBS (1999) Basel Committee on Banking Supervision, *A New Capital Adequacy Framework*, 1999, available at https://www.bis.org/publ/bcbs50.pdf

R. BCBS (2001) Basel Committee on Banking Supervision, *Overview of The New Basel Capital Accord*, 2001, available at https://www.bis.org/publ/bcbsca03.pdf

R. BCBS (2004) Basel Committee on Banking Supervision, *International Convergence of Capital Measurement and Capital Standards, A Revised Framework*, 2004, available at https://www.bis.org/publ/bcbs107.pdf

R. BCBS (2006) Basel Committee on Banking Supervision, *International Convergence of Capital Measurement and Capital Standards: A Revised Framework - Comprehensive Version*, 2006, available at www.bis.org/publ/bcbs128.htm

R. BCBS (2009) Basel Committee on Banking Supervision, *Revisions to the Basel II market risk framework*, 2009, available at https://www.bis.org/publ/bcbs158.pdf

R. BCBS (2010) Basel Committee on Banking Supervision, *Basel III: A global regulatory framework for more resilient banks and banking systems*, 2010, available at https://www.bis.org/publ/bcbs189_dec2010.pdf

R. BCBS (2011a) Basel Committee on Banking Supervision, *Revisions to the Basel II market risk framework*, 2011, available at https://www.bis.org/publ/bcbs193.pdf

R. BCBS (2011b) Basel Committee on Banking Supervision, *Basel III: A global regulatory framework for more resilient banks and banking systems*, Revised Version, 2011, available at https://www.bis.org/publ/bcbs189.pdf

R. BCBS (2013a) Basel Committee on Banking Supervision, *The liquidity coverage ratio*, 2013, available at https://www.bis.org/publ/bcbs238.pdf

R. BCBS (2013b) Basel Committee on Banking Supervision, *Revised Basel III leverage ratio framework and disclosure requirements*, 2013, available at https://www.bis.org/publ/bcbs251.pdf

R. BCBS (2013c) Basel Committee on Banking Supervision, *The non-internal model method for capitalising counterparty credit risk exposures*, 2013, available at https://www.bis.org/publ/bcbs254.htm

R. BCBS (2013d) Basel Committee on Banking Supervision, *Fundamental review of the trading book: A revised market risk framework*, 2013, available at https://www.bis.org/publ/bcbs265.pdf

R. BCBS (2014a) Basel Committee on Banking Supervision, *Basel III leverage ratio framework and disclosure requirements*, 2014, available at https://www.bis.org/bcbs/publ/d270.pdf

R. BCBS (2014b) Basel Committee on Banking Supervision, *The standardised approach for measuring counterparty credit risk exposures*, 2014, available at https://www.bis.org/publ/bcbs279.pdf

R. BCBS (2014c) Basel Committee on Banking Supervision, *Capital requirements for bank exposures to central counterparties*, 2014, available at https://www.bis.org/publ/bcbs282.pdf

R. BCBS (2014d) Basel Committee on Banking Supervision, *Basel III: the net stable funding ratio*, 2014, available at https://www.bis.org/publ/bcbs295.pdf

R. BCBS (2014e) Basel Committee on Banking Supervision, *The G-SIB assessment methodology - score calculation*, 2014, available at https://www.bis.org/bcbs/publ/d296.pdf

R. BCBS (2014f) Basel Committee on Banking Supervision, *Regulatory Consistency Assessment Programme (RCAP) Assessment of Basel III regulations – European Union*, 2014, available at https://www.bis.org/bcbs/publ/d300.pdf

R. BCBS (2015) Basel Committee on Banking Supervision, *Consultative Document: Review of the Credit Valuation Adjustment Risk Framework*, 2015, available at https://www.bis.org/bcbs/publ/d325.pdf

R. BCBS (2016) Basel Committee on Banking Supervision, *Frequently asked questions on the Basel III leverage ratio framework*, 2016, available at https://www.bis.org/bcbs/publ/d364.pdf

R. BCBS (2017) Basel Committee on Banking Supervision, *Basel III: Finalising post-crisis reforms*, 2017, available at https://www.bis.org/bcbs/publ/d424.pdf

R. BCBS (2018) Basel Committee on Banking Supervision, *Statement on leverage ratio window-dressing behaviour*, 2018, available at https://www.bis.org/publ/bcbs_nl20.htm.

R. BCBS (2019a) Basel Committee on Banking Supervision, *Minimum capital requirements for market risk*, 2019, available at https://www.bis.org/bcbs/publ/d457.htm

R. BCBS (2019b) Basel Committee on Banking Supervision, *The Basel Framework*, 2019, available at https://www.bis.org/basel_framework/index.htm

R. BCBS (2019c) Basel Committee on Banking Supervision, *Leverage ratio treatment of client cleared derivatives*, 2019 available at https://www.bis.org/bcbs/publ/d467.pdf

R. BCBS (2020a) Basel Committee on Banking Supervision, *Measures to reflect the impact of Covid-19*, 2020, available at https://www.bis.org/bcbs/publ/d498.htm

R. BCBS (2020b) Basel Committee on Banking Supervision, *Basel Framework frequently asked questions*, 2020, available at https://www.bis.org/bcbs/publ/d503.pdf

R. BCBS (2020c) Basel Committee on Banking Supervision, *Targeted revisions to the credit valuation adjustment risk framework*, 2020, available at https://www.bis.org/bcbs/publ/d507.pdf

R. BCBS (2020d) Basel Committee on Banking Supervision, *Global systemically important banks: Assessment methodology and the additional loss absorbency requirement*, 2020, available at https://www.bis.org/bcbs/gsib/

R. BCBS & IOSCO (2013) Basel Committee on Banking Supervision and the International Organization of Securities Commissions, *Margin requirements for non-centrally cleared derivatives*, 2013, available at https://www.bis.org/publ/bcbs261.pdf

R. BCBS & IOSCO (2020) Basel Committee on Banking Supervision and the International Organization of Securities Commissions, *Margin requirements for non-centrally cleared derivatives*, 2020, available at https://www.bis.org/bcbs/publ/d499.pdf

R. CFTC (1998) Commodity Futures Trading Commission, *Concept release*, 1998, available at https://www.cftc.gov/sites/default/files/opa/press98/opamntn.htm

R. CFTC (2011) Commodity Futures Trading Commission, *Position Limits for Derivatives*, Federal Register 4752 Vol. 76 No. 17, 2011, available at https://www.cftc.gov/sites/default/files/idc/groups/public/@lrfederalregister/documents/file/2011-1154a.pdf

R. CFTC (2020) Commodity Futures Trading Commission, *Position Limits for Derivatives*, Federal Register 3236 Vol. 86 No. 9, 2020, available at https://www.cftc.gov/sites/default/files/2021/01/2020-25332a.pdf

R. CME (2017) CME Group, *Amendments to the Light Sweet Crude Oil Futures Contract Specifications Commencing with the January 2019 Contract Month and Beyond*, 2017, available at https://www.cmegroup.com/content/dam/cmegroup/notices/ser/2017/12/SER-8050.pdf

R. CPMI & IOSCO (2012) Committee on Payments and Market Infrastructures and International Organization of Securities Commissions, *Principles for financial market infrastructures*, 2012, available at https://www.bis.org/cpmi/publ/d101a.pdf

R. CPMI & IOSCO (2014) Committee on Payments and Market Infrastructures and International Organization of Securities Commissions, *Recovery of financial market infrastructures*, 2014, available at https://www.bis.org/cpmi/publ/d121.pdf

R. CPMI & IOSCO (2015) Committee on Payments and Market Infrastructures and International Organization of Securities Commissions, *Public quantitative disclosure standards for central counterparties*, 2015, available at https://www.bis.org/cpmi/publ/d125.pdf

R. CPMI & IOSCO (2017) Committee on Payments and Market Infrastructures and International Organization of Securities Commissions, *Resilience of central counterparties (CCPs): Further guidance on the PFMI*, 2017, available at https://www.bis.org/cpmi/publ/d163.pdf

R. CPMI & IOSCO (2018) Committee on Payments and Market Infrastructures and International Organization of Securities Commissions, *Implementation monitoring of PFMI: Fifth update to Level 1 assessment report*, 2018, available at https://www.bis.org/cpmi/publ/d179.pdf

R. CPMI & IOSCO (2020) Committee on Payments and Market Infrastructures and International Organization of Securities Commissions, *Central counterparty default management auctions – Issues for consideration*, 2020, available at https://www.bis.org/cpmi/publ/d192.pdf

R. EC (2012a) European Commission, *Regulation (EU) No. 648/2012 of the European Parliament and of the Council of 4 July 2012 on OTC derivatives, central counterparties and trade repositories*, 2012, available at https://eur-lex.europa. eu/legal-content/EN/TXT/?uri=CELEX:32012R0648

R. EC (2012b) European Commission, *Delegated Regulation (EU) No. 149/2013 of 19 December 2012 supplementing Regulation (EU) No. 648/2012*, 2012, available at https://eur-lex.europa.eu/legal-content/EN/TXT/?uri=CELEX%3A32013R0149

R. EC (2012c) European Commission, *Delegated Regulation (EU) No. 153/2013 of 19 December 2012 supplementing Regulation (EU) No. 648/2012*, 2012, available at https://eur-lex.europa.eu/legal-content/EN/TXT/?uri=celex%3A32013R0153

R. EC (2012d) European Commission, *Delegated Regulation (EU) No. 152/2013 of 19 December 2012 supplementing Regulation (EU) No. 648/2012*, 2012, available at https://eur-lex.europa.eu/legal-content/EN/TXT/?uri=celex%3A32013R0152

R. EC (2013) European Commission, *Regulation (EU) No. 575/2013 of the European Parliament and of the Council of 6 June 2013 on prudential requirements for credit institutions and investment firms and amending Regulation (EU) No. 648/2012*, 2013, available at https://eur-lex.europa.eu/legal-content/EN/TXT/?uri=CELEX%3A32013R0575

R. EC (2014) European Commission, *Directive 2014/65/EU of the European Parliament and of the Council of 15 May 2014 on markets in financial instruments and amending Directive 2002/92/EC and Directive 2011/61/EU*, 2014, available at https://eur-lex.europa.eu/legal-content/EN/TXT/?uri=celex%3A32014L0065

R. EC (2016) European Commission, *Regulation (EU) 2016/2251 of 4 October 2016 supplementing Regulation (EU) No. 648/2012*, 2016, available at https://eur-lex.europa.eu/legal-content/EN/TXT/PDF/?uri=CELEX:32016R2251

R. EC (2019) European Commission, *Regulation (EU) 2019/834 of the European Parliament and of the Council of 20 May 2019 amending Regulation (EU) No 648/2012*, 2019, available at https://eur-lex.europa.eu/legal-content/EN/TXT/?uri=CELEX:32019R0834

R. EC (2021) European Commission, *Regulation (EU) 2021/23 of the European Parliament and of the Council of 16 December 2020 on a framework for the recovery and resolution of central counterparties*, 2021, available at https://eur-lex.europa.eu/legal-content/EN/TXT/?uri=CELEX%3A32021R0023

R. ECB (2019) European Central Bank, *ECB guide to internal models*, October 2019 available at https://www.bankingsupervision.europa.eu/legalframework/publiccons/pdf/internal_models_risk_type_chapters/ssm.guiderisktypesp ecific201907.en.pdf

R. ESMA (2013) European Securities and Markets Authority, *Review of Article 26 of RTS No. 153/2013 with respect to MPOR for client accounts*, 2016, available at https://www.esma.europa.eu/sites/default/files/library/2016-429_final_report_review_of_article_26_of_rts_no_153-2013_with_respect_to_mpor_for_client_accounts.pdf

R. FDIC (2020) Federal Deposit Insurance Corporation, *Resolution Handbook*, 2020, available at https://www.fdic.gov/bank/historical/reshandbook/

R. Fed Board (2009) Board of Governors of the Federal Reserve System, *The Supervisory Capital Assessment Program: Design and Implementation*, 2009, available at https://www.federalreserve.gov/bankinforeg/bcreg20090424a1.pdf

R. Fed Board (2016) Board of Governors of the Federal Reserve System, *The Federal Reserve System Purposes & Functions*, 10th Edition, 2016, available at https://www.federalreserve.gov/aboutthefed/files/pf_complete.pdf

R. Fed Board (2020) Board of Governors of the Federal Reserve System, *Regulatory Capital Rule: Temporary Exclusion of U.S. Treasury Securities and Deposits at Federal Reserve Banks from the Supplementary Leverage Ratio*, 2020, available at https://www.federalreserve.gov/newsevents/pressreleases/files/bcreg20200401a1.pdf

R. Fed Board & OCC (2011) Board of Governors of the Federal Reserve System and Office of the Comptroller of the Currency, *Supervisory Guidance on Model Risk Management*, SR Letter 11-7, 2011, available at https://www.federalreserve.gov/supervisionreg/srletters/sr1107.htm

R. Fed Board & OCC (2020) Board of Governors of the Federal Reserve System and Office of the Comptroller of the Currency, *Joint Response About the Effect of Recent Financial Market Volatility on the Market Risk Capital Rule*, 2020, available at https://www2.occ.gov/topics/supervision-and-examination/capital/market-risk-faq.pdf

R. FSA (2021) UK Public General Acts, *Financial Services Act 2021*, available at https://www.legislation.gov.uk/ukpga/2021/22/contents/

R. FSB (2010) Financial Stability Board, *Implementing OTC Derivatives Market Reforms*, 2010, available at https://www.fsb.org/wp-content/uploads/r_111017.pdf

R. FSB (2011) Financial Stability Board, *A Coordination Framework for Monitoring the Implementation of Agreed G20/FSB Financial Reforms*, 2011, available at https://www.fsb.org/wp-content/uploads/r_111017.pdf

R. FSB (2017a) Financial Stability Board, *Guidance on Central Counterparty Resolution and Resolution Planning*, Report, 2017, available at https://www.fsb.org/2017/07/guidance-on-central-counterparty-resolution-and-resolution-planning-2/

R. FSB (2017b) Financial Stability Board, *Guiding Principles on the Internal Total Loss-absorbing Capacity of G-SIBs ('Internal TLAC')*, Report, 2017, available at https://www.fsb.org/wp-content/uploads/P060717-1.pdf

R. FSB (2019a) Financial Stability Board, *Implementation and Effects of the G20 Financial Regulatory Reforms*, 5th Annual Report, 2019, available at https://www.fsb.org/2019/10/implementation-and-effects-of-the-g20-financial-regulatory-reforms-fifth-annual-report/

R. FSB (2019b) Financial Stability Board, *G-SIBs as of November 2019 allocated to buckets corresponding to required levels of additional capital buffers*, 2019, available at https://www.fsb.org/wp-content/uploads/P221119-1.pdf

R. FSB (2020a) Financial Stability Board, *Reforming Major Interest Rate Benchmarks*, 2020 Progress Report, available at https://www.fsb.org/wp-content/uploads/P191120.pdf

R. FSB (2020b) Financial Stability Board, *Guidance on Financial Resources to Support CCP Resolution and on the Treatment of CCP Equity in Resolution*, 2020, available at https://www.fsb.org/2020/11/guidance-on-financial-resources-to-support-ccp-resolution-and-on-the-treatment-of-ccp-equity-in-resolution/

R. FSMA (2000) UK Public General Acts, *Financial Services and Markets Act 2000*, available at https://www.legislation.gov.uk/ukpga/2000/8

R. IASB (2013) International Accounting Standards Board, *IFRS 13 Fair Value Measurement*, 2011, revised December 2013

R. IASB (2018) International Accounting Standards Board, *Conceptual Framework for Financial Reporting*, 2010, revised March 2018

R. IASB (2020) International Accounting Standards Board, *IFRS 9 Financial Instruments*, 2014, revised August 2020

R. Joint Agencies (2017) Joint Agencies: the Office of the Comptroller of the Currency, the Board of Governors of the Federal Reserve System and the Federal Deposit Insurance Corporation, *Regulatory Capital Treatment of Certain Centrally Cleared Derivative Contracts Under Regulatory Capital Rules*, 2017, available at https://www.occ.treas.gov/news-issuances/bulletins/2017/bulletin-2017-27a.pdf

R. Joint Agencies (2020) Joint Agencies: the Office of the Comptroller of the Currency, the Board of Governors of the Federal Reserve System and the Federal Deposit Insurance Corporation, *Standardized Approach for Calculating the Exposure Amount of Derivative Contracts*, Federal Register Vol. 85, No. 16, pp. 4362, 2020, available at https://www.govinfo.gov/content/pkg/FR-2020-01-24/pdf/2019-27249.pdf

R. London Clearing House (2010) London Clearing House Limited, *Default Rules*, 2010 available at https://www.lch.com/system/files/media_root/210210_Default%20Rules_AIP%20Changes_Clean_0.pdf.

R. LRRA (2006) UK Public General Acts, *Legislative and Regulatory Reform Act 2006*, available at https://www.legislation.gov.uk/ukpga/2006/51/contents

R. New York State Senate (2021) New York State Senate, *The Consolidated Laws of New York, Insurance*, 2021, available at https://www.nysenate.gov/legislation/laws/ISC/

R. Obama (2011) Obama, B., *Executive Order 13563 – Improving Regulation and Regulatory Review*, 2011, available at https://obamawhitehouse.archives.gov/the-press-office/2011/01/18/executive-order-13563-improving-regulation-and-regulatory-review

R. PRA (2020) Prudential Regulatory Authority, *Supervisory Statement SS13/13, Market risk*, 2020, available at https://www.bankofengland.co.uk/-/media/boe/files/prudential-regulation/supervisory-statement/2020/ss1313update.pdf

R. US Congress (2008) US Congress, *Emergency Economic Stabilization Act of 2008*, available at https://www.congress.gov/110/plaws/publ343/PLAW-110publ343.pdf

R. US Congress (2010) US Congress, *H.R. 4173, The Dodd-Frank Wall Street Reform and Consumer Protection Act*, 2010, available at https://www.congress.gov/bill/111th-congress/house-bill/4173/text?overview=closed&r=1

Index